FROM WALL STREET TO BAY STREET

The Origins and Evolution of
American and Canadian Finance

When the 2008 financial crisis triggered a global recession, the American banking system experienced massive losses, takeovers, and taxpayer-funded bailouts. In contrast, the Canadian banking system managed to maintain its liquidity and profitability, ultimately withstanding the crisis relatively well. These divergent outcomes can be traced back to inherent differences between these two banking systems and their institutional and political histories.

From Wall Street to Bay Street is the first book written for a lay audience that tackles the similarities and differences between the financial systems of Canada and the United States. Christopher Kobrak and Joe Martin reveal the distinctive paths the two countries have taken since the early nineteenth century, despite their similar British colonial origins. The authors trace the roots of each country's financial system back to the time of Alexander Hamilton and Andrew Jackson and insightfully argue that while Canada has preserved a Hamiltonian financial tradition, the United States has favoured a populist Jacksonian tradition since the 1830s; as such, the innovative but erratic fashion in which the American system has changed over time is at odds with the more evolutionary and stable course taken by its Canadian counterpart. *From Wall Street to Bay Street* offers a timely and accessible comparison of financial systems that reflects the political and cultural milieus of two of the world's top ten economies.

The late CHRISTOPHER KOBRAK was a professor and the Wilson/Currie Chair of Canadian Business and Financial History at the Rotman School of Management and a professor of finance at ESCP Europe, Paris.

JOE MARTIN is the Director of the Canadian Business and Financial History Initiative at the Rotman School of Management as well as President Emeritus of Canada's History Society.

FROM WALL STREET TO BAY STREET

The Origins and
Evolution of American
and Canadian
Finance

CHRISTOPHER KOBRAK AND **JOE MARTIN**

UNIVERSITY OF TORONTO PRESS
Toronto Buffalo London

© University of Toronto Press 2018
Rotman-UTP Publishing
Toronto Buffalo London
utorontopress.com
Printed in Canada

ISBN 978-1-4426-4821-0 (cloth)
ISBN 978-1-4426-1625-7 (paper)

Printed on acid-free, 100% post-consumer recycled paper
with vegetable-based inks.

Library and Archives Canada Cataloguing in Publication

Kobrak, Christopher, author
From Wall Street to Bay Street : the origins and evolution of American and
Canadian finance / Christopher Kobrak, Joe Martin.

Includes bibliographical references and index.
ISBN 978-1-4426-4821-0 (cloth).--ISBN 978-1-4426-1625-7 (paper)

1. Finance – Canada – History – 2. Finance – United States – History
I. Martin, Joe, 1937–, author II. Title.

HG185.C2K63 2018   332.10971   C2017-908064-4

University of Toronto Press acknowledges the financial assistance to its
publishing program of the Canada Council for the Arts and the Ontario
Arts Council, an agency of the Government of Ontario.

 Canada Council   Conseil des Arts
for the Arts   du Canada

ONTARIO ARTS COUNCIL
CONSEIL DES ARTS DE L'ONTARIO
an Ontario government agency
un organisme du gouvernement de l'Ontario

Funded by the   Financé par le
Government   gouvernement
of Canada   du Canada

Canada

To our students: past, present, and future.

Contents

Preface

I first met Chris Kobrak at the 2009 annual Business History Conference in Milan. As I recorded in my diary at the time, "Met Chris Kobrak – very impressive." In 2012 we invited Chris to become a visiting professor at the Rotman School of Management. He accepted our invitation and made such an impression that he was offered the first chair in Canadian business and financial history – the Wilson/Currie Chair, which he assumed on a part-time basis (he was still teaching at École Commerce Superior de Paris) and then, in 2015, he assumed his Rotman duties full time.

When Chris arrived (first as a visiting professor) the associate dean asked me to organize a seminar on Canadian-American relations. When Chris became chair that seminar blossomed into a full-time course, which we originally team taught (this was in addition to his course on the history of finance). We team taught the course to MBA students three times and in 2015 we offered it to undergraduates, a big breakthrough in getting history into the commerce program. Subsequently Chris struck up an acquaintance with the head of the history department and offered the course to both liberal arts and commerce students in 2016.

At Chris's suggestion we decided to convert the course material into a book, a book that would attract general readers who ordinarily might not be reading financial history, but wanted to understand better one of the most important and controversial economic relationships of our time. We proposed the idea originally in February 2012 and the following spring signed a contract with University of Toronto Press. We were to submit the revised manuscript to the publisher and reviewers two weeks after Chris died so unexpectedly in January 2017.

In addition to a passion for business history, Chris and I had similar political views and more importantly loved the great game of baseball. And while he was a long-time Yankee fan and I have been a Blue Jays fan since they arrived on the scene in 1977, we often enjoyed going to games together.

My wife Sally made the following observations about Chris and his impact: "It quickly became clear that he would become not just my husband's respected and valued professional colleague, but a new family friend. Notwithstanding his impressive intellectual achievements, family and friendships were always of central importance to Chris. His legendary generosity, genuine curiosity, and enthusiastic embrace of the peculiarities of Canadian culture (from hockey games to politics to shopping at IKEA) made an indelible and welcome imprint on our lives. Above all, Chris simply filled up the room with his warmth, expansive personality and good humour."

I would be remiss if I did not mention Chris's inspirational role in creating the Canadian Business History Association / l'association canadienne pour l'histoire des affaires (CBHA/ACHA). The association is now over a year old and has ten charter members, including four of the big five Canadian banks, nearly 100 individual members – historians, archivists, academics, and business people, and a website with over 7,000 unique visitors, an online YouTube channel, and it has provided money for young scholars specifically for business history research, a first in Canada.

We all wanted Chris to be the first CBHA chair but he refused and insisted it had to be a Canadian, though he graciously accepted the position as vice-chair. That was evidence of both his wisdom and selflessness. When the board met in February 2017 after his death, we unanimously passed a resolution naming our recently created research fellowship as the CBHA/ACHA Chris Kobrak Research Fellowship. After that we adjourned to the Duke of York, a pub much favoured by Chris when he was in Toronto, and raised a glass or two in his honour. It was a fitting tribute to a good friend, valued colleague, and greatly missed co-author.

Joe Martin

Acknowledgments

This book could not have proceeded without the help of a large number of individuals. First and foremost are the donors to business history at the Rotman School: Lynton "Red" Wilson, Richard Currie, James Fleck, Anthony Fell, Henry N.R. (Hal) Jackman, and John McArthur. Our schools, the Rotman School of Management and ESCP Europe, have provided many forms of support. Over the years, many colleagues have made very helpful comments. They include H.V. Nelles, the late Ed Safarian, Donald Brean, Mira Wilkins, Geoffrey Jones, Richard Sylla, the late Michael Jalland, Paul Halpern, Robert E. Wright, Mark Bonham, Dimitry Anastaskis, and the late Michael Bliss, a donor by virtue of his generous gift of his business history library to Rotman. Important contributions were also made by our research assistants, including Darren Karn, David Verbeeten, Jonathan McQuarrie, Richard Matern, and Harrison Kennedy, by students from our Rotman courses, and by the editorial and production staff at University of Toronto Press, including Jennifer DiDomenico, Anne Laughlin, Ian MacKenzie, and Ani Deyirmenjian.

FROM WALL STREET TO BAY STREET

Introduction:
The Project and Its Benefactors

> History matters. It matters not just because we can learn from the past, but because the present and the future are connected to the past by the continuity of a society's institutions. Today's and tomorrow's choices are shaped by the past. And the past can only be made intelligible as a story of institutional evolution. Integrating institutions into economic theory and economic history is an essential step in improving that theory and history.
>
> Douglass C. North, *Institutions, Institutional Change and Economic Performance*

Near the peak of the Great Depression, both the United States and Canada organized commissions to investigate aspects of their respective financial systems: the well-known Pecora Investigation, part of ongoing, longer U.S. Congressional banking hearings, and the Royal Commission on Banking and Currency (better known as the Macmillan Commission) in Canada, part of the regular decennial reviews of the Canadian Bank Act.[1]

Both countries' economies had been devastated by the crisis, and politicians searched desperately for causes and cures. From peak to trough, U.S. and Canadian per capita income had fallen by 30.8 and 34.8 per cent in each country, respectively.[2] Their stock markets fell by 89 and 90 per cent.[3] Unemployment reached 25 and 30 per cent, respectively. In the Canadian province of Saskatchewan per capita incomes declined by 72.2 per cent.[4]

Despite their shared misery, the two nations' commissions carried out and concluded their missions very differently. Pecora, named after the committee's lawyer, Ferdinand Pecora, lasted a month and was a media circus. Congressmen and their lawyer harangued bank executives in the hearing room and focused on some shady banking practices, especially tax evasion and conflicts of interest. But they found little that could possibly be construed as a significant cause of the Stock Market Crash or the ensuing banking crisis that plagued the American economy over several years and that was particularly hard on small, rural banks. Nevertheless, within months of the hearings and the swearing in of Franklin Delano Roosevelt as president, the United States enacted several pieces of legislation that reinforced limits on the scope of banking activity and strengthened institutional and organizational protection for individual investors against unscrupulous financial elites.[5]

By contrast, the Canadian Royal Commission, chaired by Lord Hugh Macmillan, a distinguished British jurist, included a former Canadian minister of finance, two bankers – one British and one Canadian – and the premier of a Canadian province. The composition of members of the Macmillan Commission was not exceptional by Canadian standards.[6] Although Americans are probably surprised by the number of non-Canadians on the Macmillan Commission, some Canadians found the absence of an American on their banking commission unusual. While the hearings were public, like Pecora, unlike Pecora they lasted just over a month and proceeded like professional seminars in fourteen cities across the length of Canada. The commission produced a divided recommendation – by a vote of three to two[7] – for Canada's first central bank. Supported by the prime minister, the Bank of Canada Act – based on the royal commission report – was passed by Parliament and received royal assent in July 1934. The Bank of Canada began operations in 1935.[8]

A comparison between the activities of the Pecora and Macmillan Commissions highlights some of the differences between American and Canadian attitudes about capitalism and their financial systems. These commissions are not historical anomalies; they reflect long-standing and continuing attitudinal differences in each country's expectations about finance and politics. Finance has played a more divisive role in politics in the United States than in Canada. In the past decade alone, financial issues have led to mass demonstrations in the United States. Presidential campaigns in the United States still include 100-year-old or longer debates about the structure of American finance.

For many reasons, comparisons of the financial systems of the two countries have attracted recent scholarly attention. Historians today seem more attuned to national comparisons as a means of determining what is commonplace and unique, along with what is malleable and immutable, in the two countries.[9] Some recent studies of financial systems have contrasted the Canadian and American political debates and outcomes.[10] On the other hand, one recent study points out similarities in the respective histories of Canada and America, but hardly mentions banking and finance.[11]

Although Americans and Canadians share many experiences, they see the world very differently. Unfortunately, they are still lumped together in many historical and economic texts. Geography and culture produce both common and unique needs and responses.[12] As a Canadian economist argued nearly 100 years ago, the extraction and supply of staples, such as fur, fish, wood, wheat, minerals, and petroleum, to large portions of the world shaped Canada's economic, cultural, and political development.[13] So too did the configuration of shared or particularly American resources help establish a different set of American capacities. But no list of commodities and competencies explains all institutional and organizational development. At the very least, the lists were not static. Talking about path dependencies is useful, but it is also important to remember that the path is not straight. It rather curves and zigzags to conform to or avoid parts of an evolving social landscape whose origins have at times little or nothing to do with economics. Indeed, some results may be better understood as historical accidents rather than parts of some grand social chain of events.[14]

We hope this book will contribute to a better understanding of ongoing relations between the United States and Canada: how differences and similarities affected their economic successes and failures, and how the interaction of the two countries, especially in the realm of finance, affected their respective development. These comparisons are important because our future economic success depends on an understanding of our trading partners.[15] Despite new research into institutions and culture, economic thinking is still too devoid of values. Values help shape economic decisions, and cultures determine values; they change in an complex interplay that defies precise demarcations. "In any culture, a deep structure of beliefs is the invisible hand that regulates economic activity. These cultural preferences, or values, are the bedrock of national identity and source of economic strengths – and weaknesses."[16] Historical narratives describe in part how attitudes evolve in changing circumstances and events, including movements of capital, people, and other economic inputs. When measured in a value spectrum about community, nature of firm, and importance of profits, American and Canadian cultures overlap, but Canadians are almost always closer to Continental Europe and Japan, especially in areas dealing with missions and strategies that affect their financial systems.[17]

Although many other comparisons between North America and other regions are interesting – between that region and South America or Europe, for example – we propose here to compare and contrast the history of two nations that share many geographic and cultural connections yet have made disparate choices over time about the fundamental issues of finance.[18] Our intention is not only to describe the financial architecture of the two countries but also to highlight the social, economic, and political contexts that shaped the configuration of their respective financial systems, systems which have exhibited various strengths and weaknesses before, during, and after the recent financial crisis. Now, more than ever, after the recent shocks to the financial system, a book comparing the strengths and weaknesses of American and Canadian financiers, how they evolved from "handmaids" of modern capitalism[19] to "Masters of the Universe,"[20] is particularly important.

Although our focus is on two nations, we recognize from the outset that both the United States and Canada were shaped and differentiated not only by their relationship to one another, but also by their relationship to a host of other countries, particularly the United Kingdom. Some countries share a special relationship with another country. In fact, Canada has enjoyed at least three such relationships: with France, with the United Kingdom, and with the United States, and none of the relationships have been static. Going back to the late eighteenth century Canada was a dependent part of a political and economic empire that traversed the globe. Today, not only is it politically and economically independent, it acts as an equal on the world stage at summits, including those of the G7 countries, the NATO alliance, and other international organizations. Within 150 years of America's bitter conflict with that empire, the United Kingdom and Canada had become the closest political allies and the most important economic connections for the United States. The cross-border flow of ideas and money not only between Canada and the United States but also between North America and other regions will play a vital role in this story. Understanding how the two systems evolved is unthinkable without understanding their place in a larger financial and political world.

As reflected in our choice of title, however, through virtually all of this narrative the bulk of the flow of ideas and money has been south to north. Indeed, much of Canadian history is a reaction to events and perceived failings "south of the border." Many of Canada's first English-speaking inhabitants, known in Canada as United Empire Loyalists and in the United States as Tories or traitors, travelled north to escape the American Revolution. The United States, in juxtaposition, can hardly be accused of an obsession with its northern neighbour. Like *Democracy in America* by Alexis de Tocqueville, which is considered by many to be the first great tract on American democracy, Max Lerner's *American Civilization*, written in the heyday of American exceptionalism, hardly mentions Canada. Indeed, both emphasize the ethnic and national diversity in forging American democracy, but neither has much to say about Canadian-American relations.[21] Even today, Canadian news is still rarely reported south of the Canada-U.S. border. We hope that this book will contribute to a greater understanding of not only both countries' mutual dependence and differences, but also how much policymakers and practitioners on both sides of the border can learn from one another. We recognize from the outset that this goal is, for many reasons, ambitious and complicated.

This project requires some definition of terms. The basic problem of finance is the allocation of funds across space and time. In other words, how do those with more cash than they want to use for consumption today get those funds into the hands of those who want to consume now or invest for future consumption in productive assets in such a way so as to have a reasonable chance of making a sufficient return to cover the change in the economic value of the cash and the risk of the enterprise? From ancient times to the present, societies have adopted various methods to engender sufficient trust to deal with this financial challenge.

Those methods include very simple to very complex institutions (rules of the game), organizations (groups of individuals bound by a common purpose), and markets (an organized place or system for making economic exchanges) with varying degrees of success in harmonizing individuals' and social needs.[22] They are collectively the framework in which contracts are made and transactions concluded.

Research – indeed, common sense – implies that financial systems are vital to a society's economic growth and even to social peace. With this in mind, we have not confined ourselves to one segment of finance, such as banking or insurance, but rather to an examination of the system in

its totality. We made this decision for several reasons. The lines dividing these segments are seldom clear, and one of the most important elements of each country's story is how the different elements interact and
how the nation's dependence on financial services shifted over time
from one element to another.

Given the above definition of a financial system, our task is broad.
We will explore both nations' ways of measuring and storing value,
regulating transactions, and innovating over a period of more than
200 years. Under the rubric of financial systems fall many institutions
(regulation and informal norms of behaviour), many organizations (for
example, central banks, commercial and investment banks, insurance
companies, venture capital, hedge and private equity funds), and many
markets (equity and bond markets as well as the market for corporate
control, i.e., mergers and acquisitions).

Both elements of content and form make our undertaking ambitious. As the Harvard Business School historian Geoffrey Jones has
argued, business and financial history narratives should address big
issues or else they risk becoming trivial collections of isolated facts.
Without burdening the text with theoretical discussions, we hope
that this work will make some contribution to two or more intertwined literatures.

Our narrative will require coverage of the general history of both
countries, as well as their interaction with one another and an examination of the national stories of those other countries. Finance is a complicated field, requiring more technical explanation than historians
usually feel comfortable providing and their readers digesting. If we
want this work to be accessible to our intended readers, it is vital that
we strike a balance between complexity and oversimplification. Those
readers include but are not limited to those studying American and
Canadian history, business students, and business people, especially
those trained outside the country where they were born or work. We
hope that specialists in American and Canadian financial history will
find this history interesting, but it is not designed for them. Perhaps
naively we hope to attract those general readers who ordinarily might
not be reading financial history. We hope that all of these readers will
find this book useful. To this end, we have tried to avoid burdening
the text with numbers. But facts are important. We have included a
few comparative appendices and a list of case studies, which might be
used as teaching aids.

This study is imbalanced in some ways. To a large extent, it will rely on numerous secondary sources about American finance and financial actors. For Canada, whose financial literature is much less extensive, the authors will integrate new analyses of primary source documents to develop their case.[23] Moreover, the development of finance, like the political development of each nation, did not unfold simultaneously in parallel time frames. Understandably, 1776 makes a convenient starting point for U.S. financial history. Financial history played an integral part of early American history even before the Revolution, but from colonial times to the antebellum period – during which time Canada had limited self-government – discussions of money, banking, taxation, and insurance were interwoven into nearly every social and political debate in the United States. However, the American Civil War, from 1861 to 1865, represents a watershed for both countries, making their chronological development, if not parallel, more comparable.[24]

The comparative nature of the book and interaction of the two countries add other elements to its complexity. Even before the two countries were created, events and circumstances in their territories influenced the histories of the other. For some periods, the countries' stories will not be of equal weight. During the eighteenth century, for example, the financial issues and events were of more complexity "south of the border" than they were in the area that was to become Canada. As such, the Dominion of Canada, as distinct from the Province of Canada, did not come into existence until nearly 100 years after Lexington and Concord. During some periods, each country's interaction with other nations and financial questions was not in sync with that of the other, making the linking of national histories with the time frames and conceptual framework difficult. During the early stages, for example, we will sometimes refer to geographic areas as Canada even though they were not yet officially called that, to aid the flow of the narrative. In general, too, we will begin sections with the U.S. saga, not just because of its greater importance, but rather because developments there preceded those in Canada.

Our story is both chronological and thematic. Some developments will be discussed retroactively, as their real impact post-dates their origin. For example, mutual funds and housing subsidies will be discussed in our post–Second World War chapter, even though their origins can be traced back decades, even centuries.

The chapters follow the great political and economic turning points that bracketed both countries' histories. Chapter 1 highlights the events,

people, and attitudes that shaped the American financial system before
the Civil War. The latter part of the eighteenth century was a period
of intense conflict including, as it did, the "first truly world war." This
event is commonly known as the French and Indian War in the United
States, while it is called the Seven Years' War in the United Kingdom
and Canada. It concluded in 1763 with Quebec becoming part of the
British Empire. Ironically this outcome contributed to the outbreak of
the American Revolution, a revolution that, while ultimately successful, took a large financial toll.

With American coffers in desperate straits after the Revolution,
it fell to the genius of Alexander Hamilton and the Constitutional
Convention of 1787 to bring financial order out of chaos. Chapter 1
outlines the fundamentally different views held by Alexander
Hamilton and Thomas Jefferson as they struggled to resolve this
crisis and shape a financial system for their new country. Elements
of this struggle, the Hamilton versus Jefferson approach, played
out during much of the first seventy years of America's existence,
including the rise and fall of the central banks of the United States.
This work will also examine how regional differences in attitudes
about banking and credit spawned a fragmented financial system,
one in which state control of banking and unit banking dominated.
This chapter concludes with a comment on the economic significance
of slavery, and its effect on the evolution of American politics and
finance.

Chapter 2 focuses on the crucial decade of the 1860s, when America
experienced the turmoil of the Civil War, and the British North American
colonies joined together into a new self-governing country (in domestic
matters at least), the Dominion of Canada. It traces the evolution of this
new dominion from the mid-eighteenth century, when French Canada
became British Canada, and the arrival of the first waves of English-
speaking settlers – refugees from the American Revolutionary War.
Attention is paid to how Canada, like the United States, chose a federal
system of governing, but one based on monarchical/parliamentary
principles rather than the presidential/republican model favoured
by America. While America adopted the poetic, aspirational motto of
"life, liberty and the pursuit of happiness," Canada chose the more
prosaic "peace, order and good government." In so doing, it is argued,
the Fathers of the Canadian Confederation – Macdonald, Cartier,
Brown, et al. – tended to seek resolution through compromise, whereas

the American Founding Fathers – including Jefferson and Hamilton – were more inclined to highlight differences and risk the consequences of fiercely contested debate. Chapter 2 also explores how the events of the 1860s specifically influenced changes in the two countries' financial systems. The Northern-dominated federal government made limited inroads in state power to govern banking and, thereby, currency. Within Canada, regulations inherited from Great Britain were being replaced with those of a home-grown focus, and these differed again from those in place in the United States. In Canada, banking and currency always fell within the federal domain. Yet while the legislative framework became uniquely Canadian and federal, Canadian banks followed principles that were clearly Hamiltonian in structure, and currency was to be denominated in dollars and cents, not pounds, shillings, or pence.

Chapter 3 examines the four and a half decades from the end of the 1860s to the beginning of the First World War. It is within this period – the Maturing, as we call it – that both countries grew dramatically, not only in population and GDP but also in the admission of new states and provinces. While the late nineteenth and early twentieth centuries were marked by both progressivism and populism in the United States, it was not until the defeat of the Reciprocity Treaty in the 1911 Canadian election that Canada began to follow suit.

Despite frequent and severe crises, and heated criticism of its financial system before 1900, the United States failed to establish comprehensive reform of finance. Even a new or third central bank needed a final push, the Panic of 1907. In Canada, by contrast, the passage of the Bank Act of 1871 reflected a national approach to financial regulation and a desire to adapt calmly rather than react precipitously to crisis. But it is in the structure of American versus Canadian banking systems that differences were most obvious. Thousands of standalone unit banks, forbidden to establish branches outside state boundaries, served most Americans' banking needs, while Canadians were served by a concentrated system of large banks that operated hundreds of branches across the country.

In chapter 3 similarities between the two countries' insurance systems are noted, particularly within the areas of non-life (property-casualty) insurance regulations and practices. Non-life in the United States, as in Canada, featured many foreign players, with American companies becoming particularly successful as American society in general became more litigious. With life insurance Americans were more likely to use the mutual form of organization, while Canadian life insurers tended to operate more globally.

Closing out this period, we look at the impact of the technological revolution and how the growth of mammoth railroads (financed mostly by debt and government guarantees, which led inevitably to taxpayer hardship) and the developing oil, steel, auto, and consumer products sectors contributed to the growth of equity markets. Although they played an important role in the Canadian economy, many of the most important companies were American,[25] and therefore they had less impact on Canadian exchanges.

Chapter 4 deals with the "Great Disorder" of two world wars and the Great Depression, which struck the United States and Canada harder than the rest of the world. Canada in particular suffered, as it was engaged in both wars from their beginnings – a full three years before the United States in each case. During the Depression, Canada was hard hit as the Smoot Hawley Tariff negatively affected the commodity-dominated Canadian economy.

In response to the Great Depression, the governments of each country reacted differently. The American government took a much more activist role, making sweeping reforms in banking, housing, and capital markets. Much of this legislation was in response to the thousands of bank failures. By contrast Canada's response was more laissez-faire in tone. The appointment of an inspector general for banks in 1923 and the creation of a central bank (the Bank of Canada) took place two decades after the United States established its third central bank. In spite of these differences, however, both countries had introduced income taxes and made increasing use of them.

During the interwar period, as the United States became the world leader in nearly all matters, including financial, Canada achieved its independence from Great Britain in foreign policy, forming closer ties to the United States. Within Canada, Toronto had become the centre of debt financing during the First World War and of equity financing during the Great Depression. For both countries the Second World War marked a return to dramatic economic growth, full employment, and, particularly for the United States, strength in the financial sector.

Chapter 5 analyses the many dramatic changes that occurred within the financial systems of both countries between the Second World War and the end of the twentieth century as the importance of finance grew in scope and complexity. Particular attention is paid to banking – the large, staggeringly complex American banking system, and its Canadian counterpart, relatively straightforward by comparison.

The post-war period witnessed the development of supranational finance, resulting in new realities such as offshore eurodollar markets. American banks became large global players, as many of the restrictions on their activities, such as the separation of investment and commercial banking, and the restrictions on interstate banking, gradually dropped away. Many relatively new risks and new products arose – along with new financial theory designed to describe, explain, and manage financial affairs – as did new theories of finance, which changed the nature of banking in much of the world.

Canadian banks were not immune to these worldwide developments. By the end of the 1980s, Canadian finance had changed greatly from the decades before. The recommendations stemming from the 1964 Porter Royal Commission and the less developed country (LDC) crisis were of crucial importance. The negative effects of the latter led to the creation of the Office of Superintendent of Financial Institutions in the late 1980s. By the end of the decade, Canadian banks, like their foreign competitors, could engage in many different financial services. The "Little Bang" made its own "little" impact marking the end of the traditional "four pillars" of the Canadian financial system.

And in both countries technology continued to play its revolutionary role, while institutional innovation was a crucial ingredient. The dynamic growth of pension plans and mutual funds in both countries over this period is examined. Differences in the financing of housing are reviewed, revealing a greater bias toward debtors in the American system and to creditors in the Canadian system. In the discussion of insurance, more attention is paid to non-life within the highly litigious American market and to life insurance within the Canadian market. Finally, this chapter discusses the difference in regulations pertaining to securities. In the United States a system of national regulation has been in place since the Great Depression, while in Canada, individual provinces bear that responsibility. Also noted is that while both countries have witnessed changes in the ownership of investment banks, ownership within Canada is concentrated in the commercial banking industry.

The final chapter deals with continuities and discontinuities circa 2000 of the two systems, which had much more in common at their respective inceptions until the Jacksonian era. During the late twentieth century, they did not follow the path dependencies attributed to them by many experts. Rather, the Canadians seemed to learn from their terrible problems during the 1980s and took corrective action. American financiers, central bankers, and regulators demonstrated too much faith in markets, too little appreciation of the weakness in their old and new regulations, and too little willingness to learn from their northern neighbour. Conversely, Canadians learned from and even took advantage of the strengths and foibles of finance as practised south of the border.

As was the case during the Great Depression, the most recent financial crisis reawakened urgent inquiries into how a society should balance both innovation and stability in its financial system. Our study suggests that Canada's financial system made a more consistent contribution to the nation's successes than did its American counterpart. That said, time and context count. Some very good decisions made early on in the United States, for example, led to many long-term benefits, even after the institutions and organizations created by those decisions disappeared. Moreover, the benefits and liabilities of financial architecture change with changing social and economic circumstances. In addition, American innovative spirit and overall economic potential helped overcome myriad shortcomings, especially the instability and fragmentation of its banking system. Lacking some of the enticing economic advantages of the United States, Canada, to its credit, focused more on creating a system that engendered additional trust and efficiency to more carefully marshal resources. If we might be allowed a tautology, too much of either innovation or stability is not conducive to a vibrant society. American finance has been associated with an abundance of the former and not enough of the latter, with Canada assuming the opposite approach. Although history provides no conclusive answer to the question of balance and to what extent excesses of innovation and stability have helped or hindered economic growth in either country, it suggests some insights about the signs and penalties of excess.

Foreign and Domestic Beginnings: From Colonies to Civil War, Events, Individuals, and Ideologies

The Canada Connection

We need a history that understands national history as itself being made in and by histories that are both larger and smaller than the nation's.

Thomas Bender, *A Nation among Nations: America's Place in World History*

From colonial times to the present, business and financial issues – particularly financial regulation – were at the heart of many of the most divisive political battles in U.S. history. The American colonies began for the most part as chartered businesses, units whose financial independence from the Crown imparted a changing set of advantages and disadvantages for both the public and private sectors. Even after most charters were converted into royal administrations, these colonies maintained much of the political and economic independence of the former businesses or sovereign jurisdictions, such as the power to elect legislatures that could tax and even print money. Moreover, some of those businesses attracted a rather heterogeneous stock of newcomers, people from many nations with little or no loyalty to the British Crown.[1] Many post–Second World War historians tend to focus on later periods as seminal to American development; others trace the aspirations and institutions of the American Revolution and early republic to the colonial period.[2] Although Canadian and American ethnic and political origins were far from identical, both areas shared a similar configuration of important economic inputs: plenty of land (perhaps too much), a paucity of labour, and a shortage of capital.

In Canada, as will be discussed in detail in chapters 2 and 3, financial issues were an important part of its early history and post-Confederation debates, but were not as divisive as in the United States. Canada's leaders learned from the strengths and weaknesses of the system south of the border, derived in large part from America's particular historical experience.

Capital formation and allocation – the complex relationship between banks, money, capital, and debt – played a central role in the histories of the two nations. Most of the great political debates between the American colonies and Great Britain that occurred in the United States centred on or at least touched upon the following issues: who should control banking; the banks' ability to create money, how to protect the value of money, how close the creators should be to the communities where the funds were used, and whether (and for what) purposes those capacities should be used for public or private gain.[3] The Founding Fathers in America and the Fathers of Confederation in Canada understood the power of finance, the ability of banks to create money, how capital would be affected by changes in the value of money, and the power and dangers of unchecked borrowing by both government and the private sector.[4]

The World War That Created the United States[5]

Most scholars agree that two intertwined issues, Canada (New France) and money, lay beneath the American Revolution. Even before France gave up its colony in what became Canada and the American Midwest (mostly the Great Lakes and the St Lawrence and Ohio River Valleys), observers on both sides of the Atlantic realized that Great Britain's acquisition of that territory might radically change its relationship to its other North American possessions, which were, even before U.S. independence, developing an almost religious sense of national destiny.

In many ways, the French and Indian War/Seven Years' War (1756–63) changed the relationship between Great Britain and its colonies. Although British regulars fought in North America, Americans fought alongside them, and the colonies organized themselves in a crusade against the French – outnumbered fifteen to one – and against their allies, the Indigenous peoples, who felt threatened by American settlements. Americans' successes created a stronger sense of unity and confidence than they possessed before the war. The British and Americans were the big winners collectively in the war, but the increased expectations and cohesion of the latter eventually reduced the benefits to the former.[6] According to several pamphlets written during this war, there were many key disputes in North America. One school of thought was that the removal of the French threat to the British colonists might make them less docile and less willing to pay for their own defence.

Even before the war ended, the issue of whether France should be forced to give up New France or its sugar island, Guadeloupe, stimulated debate. In 1757 Benjamin Franklin, then in London and identifying himself as a "Briton," made the case for the United Kingdom to acquire New France. He felt obliged to quell British fears that greater territory in North America would encourage American independence. According to Franklin, Canada in French hands would always pose a threat to the British colonies, blocking legitimate growth and fuelling frictions with Native Americans. He argued that the American colonies would use the new Canadian territory to expand, further increase their populations, and grow into a great economic power, but one that was more agricultural and, therefore, more dependent on British-manufactured products and shipping. Blocked by a French Canada, Franklin reasoned, the British colonial population would continue to grow at a rapid pace and become an economic powerhouse, but with more manufacturing.[7]

Despite Franklin's protestations, many in the United Kingdom feared that an expanded colonial base in North America would threaten Britain's highly successful economic order. For a hundred years before the American Revolution, the so-called Triangular Trade played an integral role in British economic development. Commerce was thriving, with Britain providing ships to take slaves to the New World and sugar from Caribbean Islands to the colonies. The ships also brought foodstuffs from the colonies to the islands and tobacco to both the islands and Great Britain, and manufactured goods from the United Kingdom to both with the aid of British financial services. All of these vessels crisscrossed the Atlantic, allowing all the participants to flourish, but in a highly dependent mercantilist fashion. The system functioned to a large extent under the control of British monopolies and forbade trade and shipping with others, and thus rankled the entrepreneurial Americans.[8] By the time of the Revolution, America and Africa accounted for 37 per cent of British imports and 42 per cent of its exports.[9] The British navigation acts were designed to get maximum benefit for the empire from investing in overseas settlements and transatlantic commerce, in part by excluding foreign competition and maintaining a great deal of the value-added processing at home, but in a system that was open to institutional development and diverse immigration and ideas.

The trade tonnage added to other British maritime strengths, such as banking and insurance, and helped diversify British manufacturing, which was especially welcome as the result of weak Continental European demand, and weak agricultural prices.[10]

The mercantile polices had many benefits for the white colonists. From 1650 to 1770 the North American colonies' population grew from 55,000 to 2.3 million inhabitants, of which 467,000 were black.[11] The forty-two-fold increase amounted to one of the greatest population shifts in history, especially astounding considering the difficult Atlantic crossing. Population and economic statistics for the period are notoriously unreliable. But according to at least one source, at the height of the Revolution, the population of New England alone was roughly a tenfold multiple of that in Quebec and Atlantic Canada.[12] By 1774 aggregate GNP as measured in 1980 dollars reached $1.9 billion, reflecting the recent population growth and a near doubling of per capita income from 1650.[13]

But as predicted by some of the pro-Guadeloupe pamphleteers, the French loss of Canada that accompanied peace radically changed Britain's relationship with its other North American colonies. A British Canada meant that the American colonists felt less threatened and less compelled to pay for their own defence. The New World businesses, mostly agricultural, were created with funds from private investors in the "mother country" who expected an ample return. Independent of the Crown, the colonists had the habit of handling their own financial affairs. Their charters acknowledged British sovereignty but gave the businesses many rights, some that went beyond those granted to citizens on the other side of the Atlantic. Most legislatures raised taxes and created their own money. Some even chose and decided on the salaries of the British representatives who oversaw colonial affairs. The political turbulence of the seventeenth and eighteenth centuries added to the colonists' sense of independence. They expected that their charters gave them at least the same powers to which all British subjects were entitled. The British government, for its part, made little investment in its colonies, expecting them to take care of their own needs.[14]

Finance and the American Revolution

The first seeds of revolt were sown by British attempts to shore up its own deficit-laden financial system with colonial taxes and to restrict the colonies' autonomous commercial development – accompanied by restrictions on the extent to which Americans could exploit advantages in Canadian territory. British expectations that the colonies support themselves lessened colonial dependence on the "mother country." But silver and gold coins, bars, and plate were always in short supply in the colonies, as colonial merchants needed them to pay British suppliers.[15] The colonies' successes, moreover, increased British commercial profits but also undermined the fundamental axiom of colonial rule: or dependence on Great Britain. The colonies gradually began to perceive themselves more and more as a semi-independent part of the British Empire. Demographic shifts contributed to the sense of political maturity. Although estimates vary, by 1770 America's population was doubling every twenty years. Trade, which was growing in absolute terms and as a percentage of overall British commerce, and population growth encouraged America's faith in its future and resistance to Great Britain.[16]

By many measures, Great Britain was a very successful colonial power, an achievement that rested in no small measure on its careful use of limited financial resources. Not only was Great Britain one of the first countries to develop financial exchanges, a central bank, and reserve banking, it intelligently marshalled its military resources. Much of that success lay in avoiding investments in or the distribution of large armies, and by building large naval fleets that bested first the Spanish, then the Dutch, and then the French. The American colonists' ability to field armies in North America, along with the deployment of Prussian and Dutch mercenaries in Europe, played well with Britain's strategy, giving its military a global reach at a substantial but cost-effective basis.[17]

The bulk of conflicts between the mother country and the colonies were economic. The context of these issues was marked by a radical shift in the economic fortunes of the colonists. American prosperity grew during the French and Indian War/Seven Years' War but was followed by a depression, which only exacerbated the American sense that Britain exploited its colonies.[18] The colonists needed to sell their goods to the United Kingdom, but they had little patience for being forced to buy goods from the mother country that they could easily make themselves or buy more cheaply elsewhere. The strength of the British colonial system lay in large part in its creation of extensive, complex economic communities, rather than just extractive outposts. In the case of the American colonies, this strategy was its downfall too. These communities had to be maintained, and they developed ambitions of their own.[19] Dependent as they were on complex trading relationships with other regions, any impediments to the sale of American goods, in locations of their choice or on limits to the products they could produce, threatened the vital interests of the merchants, artisans, plantation owners, and lawyers – groups central to the Revolution. The colonists wanted not only to sell goods but also to accumulate specie that would allow for increases in the money supply vital to colonial debtors.

Combined with these matters was the problem of integrating the vast new Canadian territory and the power vacuum left by the French departure. Hunters, gatherers, and religious missionaries, the French had built relations with various Indigenous peoples and penetrated into the Great Lakes and Ohio Valley to the mouth of the Mississippi long before the English colonists eyed those regions for expansion. This was one of the many sources of conflict.[20] In 1763, at the end of the Seven Years' War, Native Americans launched an uprising – Pontiac's Rebellion – in part in response to English colonial expansion into territories to which the less numerous French had provided a buffer. The response of the British government, which outlawed expansion across the Allegheny Mountains, infuriated colonists, who, now like the Indians and French colonists who remained, required more "supervision" – leading to a tripling of the British military presence in North America, a cost the colonists were expected to bear. Burdened with its own financial problems, the British government was between a rock and a hard place.[21]

The first change in colonial governance came not in the form of new laws or taxation, but merely in the enforcement of old ones (see table 1.1). In 1760, even before the official end of the French and Indian/Seven Years' War, British authorities started enforcing statutes designed to prevent smuggling of imports into the colonies, a practice that reduced royal and monopoly revenues. Despite colonial protest and legal battles, other statutes quickly followed.[22] The new levies threatened not only the financial independence of the colonies, but also trade, or at least the trade of some of the colonists.[23] On the whole, however, American reactions notwithstanding, British rule seemed part of a global plan that had many benefits for all the participants. The colonists, for their part, wanted to pick and choose from the measures Britain established for the empire between those they liked and those they did not. As can be seen in table 1.1,[24] the new British costs led to the imposition of or increase in a long list of duties and measures well known to American school children – the Sugar Act (1764), a new Stamp Act (1765, repealed in 1766), the Townshend Acts (1767 and 1768), Tea Tax [1773], the Coercive Acts (1774). These Acts not only threatened colonial economic well-being but also were perceived to violate a fundamental contract

Table 1.1. Key Steps in the Development of Colonial Policy and Its Impact on the Future United States

Event/Statute	Date(s)	Description	Outcome
Limits on settlement	1763	Blocked expansion across the Allegheny Mountains	Key objective of Americans who fought with British in French and Indian War and owned land there, e.g., George Washington
Navigation acts	1651–1850, amended various times, enforcement tightened at times during the decade before the Revolution	Limited use of non-British shipping, trading with non-empire countries, and use of coin	Arguments about economic impact but fuelled desire for independence among some American merchants
Sugar and Stamp Acts	1764–65, repealed 1766	Taxes on sugar and all printed documents designed to pay for the protection of white colonists against Indian attack, introduced during the downturn following French and Indian War (Seven Years' War)	Considered unnecessary by colonists who could protect themselves; just for U.K. benefit. Stamp Act Congress, Sons of Liberty, taxation without representation, repealed (amended) after much protest.
Townshend Acts	1767–8, named after Charles Townshend, chancellor of the exchequer	Series of five acts designed to raise funds, assert Parliament's authority over the colonies, make governors and judges more loyal to the Crown, and enforce trade and other British laws	After strenuous protest in the colonies, many repealed, but Parliament kept the Tea Tax and in principle the right to tax the colonies.
Tea Tax	1773, repealed in 1778 during Revolutionary War	Tax on tea importation to colonies, but duty free from U.K. by British East India Company; designed to reduce company tea glut and demonstrate right to tax	Led to widespread demonstrations, Boston Tea Party, coercive acts, and smuggling
Coercive Acts, Intolerable Acts (colonialists' name)	1774, direct reaction to Boston Tea Party (1773)	Closed Boston Harbor until damages paid; put under direct control of Crown; trials could be moved to other parts of empire; quartering troops	Washington called it the "Murder Act," last straw for many colonists
Quebec Act	1774	Confirmed Quebec boundary into and beyond the Ohio Valley, extended rights of Catholics in province	Americans resented loss of what many considered their territory; some disliked extension of Catholics' rights
First armed insurrection	1775	Lexington, Concord, sieges of Boston and Quebec	British flee Boston, Americans attack Quebec; signing of Declaration of Independence July 1776

and human right that the colonists perceived as British citizens whose only representation was in colonial legislatures.[25]

Salt, not sugar, was added to the wound when Britain gave Canada autonomy – including areas of the Ohio Valley, which were claimed by Virginia, Connecticut, and Massachusetts – from the land-hungry Americans with the Quebec Act of 1774 (see map 1.1), and showed sensitivity to the defeated Québécois and their desire to keep their language and religion, a move that the English-speaking American colonists abhorred. In addition, the new administration of Quebec would be highly centralized, an affront to the Americans' sensibilities about their rights as Englishmen. French colonists had less interest in self-governance than the English, who saw it as their right as Englishmen. Freed from their seigneurs, most of whom had returned to France by the 1770s, French peasants turned to their priests and were assured that their religious, linguistic, and cultural rights would be respected, in the beginnings of the "French exception" in Canada.[26] Although the imperial measures were probably reasonable in that they covered the costs of maintaining the defence of the colonies, they also threatened the colonists' ability to pursue or maximize their own economic interests. In any case, the measures resulted in a torrent of verbal and violent clashes between the colonists and London, which were exacerbated by Canada under British control and the absence of a negotiated quid pro quo. Americans might have swallowed some of the new taxes and other measures more easily if they had been tied to greater financial independence, such as the right to issue bills and expand credit in the colonies, as Ben Franklin had suggested in 1764.[27]

Actual money, not just taxes, had been the source of a long-standing dispute between the colonies and colonial governments in London. Short of specie (coins), the colonies created various forms of paper currency, supported mostly by tax revenue. These bills of credit (short-dated promises to pay) were the principal form of colonial borrowing but also a practical means of exchange, passing among the colonies but not overseas. Not officially convertible into gold, silver, or other commodities, these bills of credit derived their principal value as redeemable for tax payments.[28] Like most countries at the time, Britain maintained a cautious scepticism about the advantages and disadvantages of paper currency, an attitude not shared by the cash-starved colonies. Americans saw the issuance of paper money as the only way through the economic downturns and out of the debt that they had incurred during the French and Indian War, whose economic effects were spread unevenly

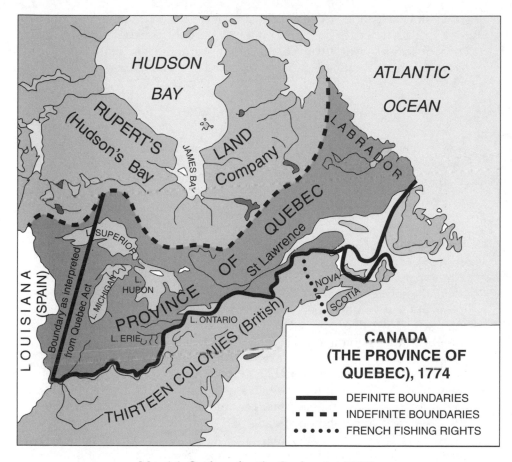

Map 1.1 Quebec after the Quebec Act (1774)

among the colonies. The British authorities encouraged the shipping of British coins back to the United Kingdom and the use of plentiful Spanish ones. In 1751 and then again in 1764, Parliament launched campaigns to suppress colonial currencies, succeeding for the most part in New England and antagonizing the South, by far the richest section of the colonies. British merchants, though, had mixed feelings. Understandably, they feared a reduction in trade by forcing the colonists to use only specie, on the one hand, but also foreign exchange risk by relying on colonial paper currencies for trade, on the other. In 1773 the issue itself was ostensibly settled by legislation that allowed for continuing issuance of paper currency for public, but not private, debt, but the friction had already taken a large toll on colonial relations, and the increase in bills, coupled with the lack of specie, contributed to inflationary pressures.[29]

That Hamilton Touch

The Power of creating new funds upon new objects of taxation, by its own authority would enable the national government to borrow as far as necessities require.

Alexander Hamilton, *Federalist Paper, no. 30*

Detailing the story of the campaigns of the American Revolution (1776–83) is well beyond the scope of this book, but a discussion of the role of Canada and the financial effects of the Revolution are within it. Campaigns connected with the British territory north of the colonies were the subject of some of the greatest successes and greatest frustrations of the revolutionaries. After a 150-day siege, the infamous Benedict Arnold failed to capture Quebec in 1775. Two years later, the defeat of a British expeditionary force from Canada at Saratoga provided the largest military success before the Battle of Yorktown, lifting the rebels' spirits, which had been brought low by the fall of Philadelphia and New York, and encouraged Britain's archenemy, France, to enter the fight. Both battles reminded Americans of the importance of Canada to their security and ambition. The Second Treaty of Paris, which ended the war in 1783, granted to America the Ohio Valley, which had been lost in the conflict, and left many questions about the future of British North America.

The Revolutionary War made finance even more important to the new states and set in motion forces that would shape Canadian and American relations for decades.[30] Between 60,000 and 100,000 people left America right after the Revolution, and thousands more departed in the next few decades for Canada or Great Britain, increasing the English-speaking minority in Canada by 1800 to 40 per cent of the roughly 330,000 residents of European ancestry north of the border.[31] The largest group went to Nova Scotia, where they found the citizens too pro-American. As a consequence they lobbied for and achieved the separation of New Brunswick, henceforth known as the loyalist province, from Nova Scotia. A smaller group went to what was then Quebec, before settling in the Niagara Peninsula and Kingston area, leading eventually to the separation of Ontario from Quebec in 1791.[32] Despite the arrival of these new colonists, the future defence and economic vitality of the former French colony was left unclear. Indeed, during the peace negotiations, there is no record of the French demanding the return of the territory, perhaps because its participation had left France's own finances so shaky, contributing to the downfall of the ancien régime.

The break with Great Britain had profound effects on American finance, stimulating a remarkable political debate and transformation of America's economy. The Revolution left America's fiscal reputation in tatters. There was no effective central government. There was only one bank and no central taxation system. The Articles of Confederation, the law of the land during and just after the Revolution, seemed ill equipped to handle the myriad problems. Following the war, much of the American Confederation suffered from both depression and inflation. U.S. citizens had diverted 15 to 20 per cent of their output to support the war. Although around 10 per cent of the incurred debt came in the form of bonds, for much of the war and after, these financial products were selling at huge discounts on their face values. Congressional currency and short-term loans lost between 80 and 90 per cent of their specie value. Unfortunately for the revolutionaries, they were less adept at financial and logistical management of the war than they were at framing declarations. Their inability to provide money, raise armies, and collect supplies lengthened the war and set the stage for severe economic problems after the peace. Indeed, since taxes had provided the impetus for the American Revolution, raising taxes to fight the war was more ideologically offensive than borrowing or just printing money.[33]

The New Constitution

Economic weakness led to calls for a stronger central government in many quarters, but such sentiments were far from universal. Attitudes about money, reflecting the creditor versus debtor status of opinion makers, played a large role in dividing opinion. Creditors wanted paper money only when based on sound financial principles to ensure the value of future repayment; debtors, mostly agricultural interests, wanted to protect easy credit terms. The dichotomy had some regional and sector breakdowns, but these categories were not watertight. Those who wanted sound money tended to support greater federal power. While money was important, it was not the only factor, and it was tied to other concerns.

By the mid-1780s many Americans shared George Washington's view that the new nation was closer to anarchy than greatness. Although confederation reflected many American ideological preferences for decentralization, the national government also seemed a distant irrelevance to most Americans by proving itself unequal to the task of solving pressing national problems.[34] Under the Articles of Confederation, which was America's first constitution (1777–89), little progress was made in solving the new country's financial problems. Some states were left with heavy debt. States could issue their own paper money. Inflation – at least in terms of what paper money could buy – was rampant, and the country as a whole had a poor credit reputation, especially in Europe. Each state had veto powers over taxation. New state taxes incited revolt, such as Shays' Rebellion in Massachusetts. By the time the Constitutional Congress met in 1787, the central government had not made any payments of principal or interest on its debt for eight years.

Financial issues weighed heavily on those writing and debating the new constitution. Inspired by James Madison, who would become America's fourth president, and crucially backed by Washington, the convention picked up on the work of an earlier attempt to modify the Articles of Confederation. Fifty-five delegates, from twelve of the thirteen states, many of the most brilliant and powerful men in the country – including Benjamin Franklin, Edmund Randolph, and Robert Morris – convened in Philadelphia in May 1787 and debated the principles and details of the new constitution. Many of the thorniest issues revolved around the relative power of the more populated states vis-à-vis the smaller ones. With George Washington presiding and James Madison and Alexander Hamilton leading the debates, the convention resolved to divide congressional power between a Senate, in which each state was represented equally, and a House of Representatives, in which membership was based on population. The convention also resolved that the election of the president be determined by the Electoral College, the membership of which was determined by population (one vote for each representative in the House) and the allocation of two votes to each state.[35] America's second and third presidents, John Adams and Thomas Jefferson, were notably absent, serving respectively as ambassadors to the United Kingdom and France at the time of the convention. As will be discussed, the regulation of finance, however, was left less than clear.

Under the new constitution, despite major political conflicts, America made extraordinary financial progress. Within two decades of the peace treaty, the former colonies witnessed an explosion in home-grown marine insurance, fire insurance, foreign investment, banking, banknotes backed by specie, and the founding of a central bank with branches and exchanges for trading equity and debt.[36]

The Founding Fathers and Conflicts over Finance

The first conflicts about financial and related matters under the constitution, many of which carried on for decades, could be personified by two of America's Founding Fathers, who could not have been more different but whose political destinies were intertwined: Thomas Jefferson and Alexander Hamilton. Both were brilliant politicians and contributed to the Revolution and to solidifying the gains of the new republic. However, they had very different personalities, political orientations, and views about finance. Both were products of their times and their experiences, but they represented different views of and aspirations for the new republic, which led to factions (parties) in which they played leading roles.

Thomas Jefferson, author of the Declaration of Independence and third president of the United States, was born to hold power. Son of a well-heeled Virginia plantation owner who died young, Jefferson was still a teenager when he took the helm of the family business. He also entered politics at an early age. By age twenty-seven, Jefferson was a member of the House of Burgesses (the legislative branch of the colonial Virginia government); by thirty-four, in 1776, he was penning the legendary words, "We hold these truths to be self-evident."[37] An eloquent writer, he was less dynamic as a public speaker. His political instincts, though less than perfect, were better than his business instincts. Perpetually in debt, Jefferson pursued an aristocratic lifestyle in the United States and while serving as America's second ambassador to France after independence. He cultivated a public persona that masked his exuberant support of the French Revolution and his long-standing relationship with, and children by, one of his young slaves. In his youth, Jefferson advocated finding some way to free the slaves. For many personal and political reasons, in later life his opposition to a stronger federal government seemed conditioned in part by his fear that a powerful central state would abolish an institution so crucial to his financial and emotional life. In the 1790s he developed a quasi-paranoid fear of federalist political intentions, one that may have survived for generations.[38] Ironically, despite his bitter conflicts with Hamilton, Jefferson owed a debt to his great rival. His election as president in 1800 was due in part to Hamilton's support in the runoff vote in the House. Moreover, two of Jefferson's greatest triumphs as president, the Louisiana Purchase and the Barbary State Policies, would not have been possible without Hamilton's financial policies.[39] Jefferson's vision for America emphasized the interests of small, independent farmers and businessmen and limited government, but to protect those with little power from those with much. Although he expanded U.S. territory more than any president before or since and supported some of the most revolutionary ideas of his time, his vision of America's future remained oddly patrician and static.

By contrast, Alexander Hamilton was born in the West Indies, outside the thirteen colonies, an impoverished youth with few prospects. At an early age he demonstrated good business skills. Unlike Jefferson, Hamilton distinguished himself in the army, first assisting Washington as a staff officer and then in battle. Regarded as a dashing figure, he owed some of his future career to marrying well but threatened his career and his marriage with at least one extramarital affair. While Jefferson was representing the confederation in France, Hamilton was establishing a successful legal practice in New York City and agitating to amend the Articles of Confederation. Along with James Madison, the fourth president of the United States, and John Jay, the first chief justice of the Supreme Court, Hamilton is considered a primary architect of the Constitution and defender of it in the *Federalist Papers*. Admired for his brilliance rather than his charm, much of his power came from his relationship to the childless George Washington, who treated Hamilton as something of an adopted son – a partnership that had distinct advantages for the two but left Hamilton somewhat isolated after his patron's retirement and even more so following his death. Washington picked his protégé to become the first secretary of the Treasury, a post from which Hamilton could highlight the financial weaknesses of the new country and devise methods to bolster its financial credibility. His competitive zeal and sharp tongue brought him into conflict not only with those who opposed his policies and were jealous of his influence over Washington, such as Jefferson and Madison, but also with leaders of his own faction (Federalists) such as John Adams, America's second president, in whose administration Hamilton pointedly did not serve. In 1804 Hamilton died in a duel with the vice president, in part because Hamilton had denied Aaron Burr the presidency, favouring his long-time adversary Jefferson, whose character he rightly believed far superior to that of the infamous Burr.[40] Hamilton's vision for America was very much for it to be an emulator of and commercial equal to Great Britain, with independent manufacturing, maritime, and financial capacities, supported by a strong government, bolstered by taxing and debt. Like Jefferson's, Hamilton's ideas were adapted by their proponents. Although associated with the protection of creditors and conservative, even monarchist, views, his vision of America's future was commercial, an elitism based on a meritocracy, and an environment of relentless change.

Hamilton's Financial Plan

After ratification of the Constitution in 1789, financial debates centred on Hamilton's analysis and recommendations. Within a few years of Washington's inauguration as the nation's first president, Hamilton produced a lengthy analysis of the country's economic woes and a four-pronged approach for solving them. This approach included giving the federal government taxing authority over imports at a level high enough to raise revenues but not to stifle trade. It also called for a consolidation of state and national debt with new forms of national debt, a clear national definition of the dollar in terms of specie, and most controversial of all, a central bank. His reforms collectively set the stage of America's commercial and capital market development.[41]

In this section, we will focus on the two most controversial aspects of Hamilton's financial plan: consolidation of debt and creation of the central bank. Although he began thinking about the need for a sounder financial system during the Revolutionary War while he was still Washington's adjutant, Hamilton's proposals were predicated on his analysis of America's financial dilemma.[42] His report gave his recommendations a sense of urgency, hard to imagine by modern standards. In 1790, America's federal debt to receipts ratio was a remarkable 457 to 1.[43] Hamilton's analysis also revealed how different each state's situation was. The states that had originally shouldered about 60 per cent of the cost of the war had paid around three-quarters of their debt, but they still owed $18 million collectively by 1790. Armed with taxing powers and profiting from the sale of property once owned by royalists – many of whom had fled to Canada – some of the states, such as Virginia, aggressively paid their liabilities. Others, such as South Carolina and Massachusetts, were more desultory. During the confederation period, seven states started or continued to issue paper currency.

Revolutionary War debt came in basically three forms: foreign, national, and state. Each entailed its own difficulties. Nevertheless, Hamilton argued that all debt should be paid in full, even if it had been bought up from the original creditor at a discount by speculators. He felt that full payment would serve as a welcome assurance to future creditors, but settlement of the foreign portion of the debt at face value was the only option supported by almost everyone. For many years, some people hinted that repudiation of state and national debt would relieve the new nation of its financial burdens. Hamilton led those who opposed this short-term solution on moral and financial grounds, arguing that paying the debt in full would enhance the reputation of the new country and thereby make future borrowing easier.[44]

But Congress repeatedly rejected Hamilton's plan for restructuring and paying off the debt, which included assumption of state debt and paying off "speculators" at face value. The logjam was broken at one of the most famous dinners in American history. At a dinner party with Jefferson, Madison, and Hamilton, in attendance the trio agreed to Hamilton's debt plan as long as the site of the capital was moved to Philadelphia until a new capital could be built on the Potomac River.[45]

Consolidating state debt in new national instruments served as a pillar of Hamilton's plan. Six states of the confederation had virtually all their debts eliminated, leaving most free of long-term debt for many decades. After federal refinancing, the central government had $70 million in debt, including $27 million of domestic principal, $13 million of unpaid interest, $12 million owed to foreigners, and $18 million of assumed state debt. That debt was rescheduled into securities without fixed maturity, similar to British consul bonds, which lowered the government's interest burden from 6 to 4 per cent. By 1791, only the sovereign debt of England and Holland had yields at this level. Some states made out well, receiving even more relief than the total of their debt load. The rescheduling entailed a reduction, however, in the coupon of the domestic portion of the debt. Most controversial, though, was the decision to pay all debt holders, primary or secondary, at face value, a provision that many perceived as a reward to financial speculators who had bought debt at large discounts. To pay the debt Hamilton proposed a tariff on imports, high enough to pay the interest, but low enough for Jeffersonians who disliked high central government taxes and who were dependent on foreign imports.[46]

Other aspects of Hamilton's innovations would rankle the Jeffersonians, requiring compromise. The increase of federal taxing authority bothered some, but its proposed use irked them even more. At the very least, the Jeffersonians wanted the principal of the debt paid down quickly, which would help prevent the development of a new class that could live off its rents. Hamilton in contrast saw a significant national debt market as the anchor of an American financial system. Hamilton's gradual approach to paying the debt appeared paradoxical to many debtors, who feared high taxes, but it appealed to creditors, who liked the regular rents and their effect on banking and capital markets.[47] Both the Jeffersonians and Hamiltonians would make other compromises.

The fourth pillar of Hamilton's program was even more controversial, in part because of its original structure, and in part because of how it evolved. Enactment of the twenty-year charter of America's first central bank, the Bank of the United States, required overcoming Jefferson's constitutional objections and even Washington's misgivings. The Constitution gave to the federal government control of the currency and the power to take steps for the common good. But all powers not explicitly given to the federal government remained with the people or with the states – including, as interpreted by most of the Founding Fathers and as already practised in the United States – the right to create and administer banks, in a division of financial power unknown in most countries. Influenced by both the American experience and that of Britain, Hamilton proposed and succeeded in creating a new form of bank, one that was neither a private commercial bank nor a central bank like those found in the United Kingdom.[48] Following the colonial practice of legislative involvement in banking matters, the bank's ownership, unlike that of the Bank of England, was both private and public. Its primary mission was to create an orderly market for government debt, but it soon was engaging in normal banking business such as issuing notes and making loans to private and public debtors.[49]

The bank, the Bank of the United States (the first BUS), opened for business in 1791 with $3 million in capital from public and private sources, including substantial amounts of foreign investment that equalled the total capital of the five state banks that had been created in Boston, Philadelphia, New York, Baltimore, and Providence. For many years, it was by far the largest business in the republic. Sixty per cent of the investment came in the form of contributions of U.S. government debt. One of its first loans was to the federal government to pay for its capital contribution. Both devices helped achieve the primary goal of helping the federal government order its finances.[50] Moreover, Hamilton quickly approved the creation of branches of the First Bank of the United States, which he at first thought premature, an expansion of power that added to the power of the First Bank. This controversial decision to establish a branch network gave BUS a huge competitive advantage over state chartered banks, including Hamilton's own Bank of New York.[51] The geographic diversity of the BUS, which performed some tasks of completely private commercial banks, gave it a competitive advantage over the smaller, more localized state banks, reinforcing fears of combined private-government power.[52] Although the federal government exercised a good deal of control, the BUS's board had substantial independence. While the federal government had the right to hold 20 per cent of BUS's share capital, it gave up the right to vote for its board members.

However, by the time its charter came up for renewal, the First Bank of the United States had lost its dominant position. The creation of state-chartered private banks was well underway. In 1802 Jefferson decided to sell off the federal government's shareholding to Baring Brothers, the British merchant bank, netting a 45 per cent profit over its par value. By 1812, despite many successes, the BUS accounted for only 15 per cent of the nation's commercial banking capital.[53]

In some ways, the banking system that took shape in the United States during the first twenty years of the Constitution was in the vanguard of progressive financial innovation, and included aspects of banking that are commonplace today. In others, it reflected anti-bank sentiment in the old and new worlds. America was one of the first countries with a central bank, the first with one in which ownership was shared by the private and public sectors. After the debacle of the Banque Royale in the first third of the eighteenth century, France, for example, did not re-establish a central bank until 1800. Although joint-stock corporations with limited liability were known, virtually all banking was limited to partnerships, and most banks had only one office. The United Kingdom did not allow even chartered bank corporations until 1826. Although banks in the British Isles were issuing paper certificates used as money, specie was the rule, not the exception in most of the world. Few countries recognized the joint-stock form as a way of adding to bank security and services. At the end of the eighteenth century Scottish banking was admired by some for its more relaxed rules about the number of partners (unlimited rather than the British restriction of six), which allowed for a broader range of activities, and the degree to which banks could create currency.[54]

In many ways, too, the financial system that developed in the United States was an uncomfortable amalgamation of Jeffersonian and Hamiltonian ambitions and attitudes, reflecting an attitudinal division that goes to the heart of differences between American and Canadian finance. Supporters of Jefferson encouraged two relatively unusual and persistent aspects of American finance. First, they tended to favour financial institutions closely tied to their localities. Second, states retained the power to regulate banking and banks. This principle manifested itself in requirements for local directors and, above all, unit banking, banks with just one office. This structure existed in other countries, but survived longer in the United States, especially as a prohibition against branching across state borders. Some of the Jeffersonians and Jacksonians, including the two presidents themselves, disliked all banks and all paper money.

Hamilton's reforms spearheaded the acceptance of paper money, but with a financial system that insured the value of paper as measured by a fixed amount of specie, thus protecting creditors. Many of his opponents, however, either rejected its use outright, because paper money could be used as a weapon by powerful financial interests, or preferred a system with paper money as long as it was with a "flexible commitment" to its specie value. With paper money's ability to increase loanable funds, albeit with a greater risk of inflation, debtors strongly favoured this form of money, which creditors understandably feared. The Constitution gave the federal government the right to define the value of the dollar, and the financial system developed by Hamilton tied the issuance of paper to amounts of specie. For Hamilton, a national currency was a symbol of the nation. Congress passed acts defining the dollar in terms of gold and silver, making it the government's unit of account, quantifying its relationship to the coins of other countries, and establishing a U.S. Mint, which produced only a trickle of coins.[55] Nevertheless, from colonial times to the present, America's commitment to hard money (backed by specie or another commodity) would often be called into question.[56]

By most accounts, during the first twenty years of the republic, America profited from a well-developed, flexible financial sector, well ahead of that of many other countries. It is a matter of some debate what mixture of prior innovation or Hamiltonian measures created the system. During the first decade of the Hamiltonian financial plans, the federal government paid down little of its debt; nevertheless, the ratio of debt to government revenue fell quickly. Although the Federalists had spent and borrowed more,

the establishment of a national bank and other Hamiltonian measures had clearly contributed to America's capacity to manage its
finances. When Jefferson took office in 1801, the national debt was
actually higher than its 1791 level. But by the time he left office in
1809, it dropped from its peak in 1804 of $86.4 million (just after the
Louisiana Purchase) to $53.2 million. The public Jefferson evidently
had a frugality that the private one lacked.[57] Many aspects of the
Hamiltonian program received bipartisan support. Some Jeffersonians even supported expanding BUS's size. Like many foreign-born
Americans, Albert Gallatin, the fourth secretary of the Treasury, vigorously supported renewing the BUS's charter with a recommendation for increasing its capital in 1811, a vote that was narrowly lost
by a vice-presidential tie-breaking vote in the Senate. Many in Gallatin's own party[58] opposed his recommendations, but not President
Madison.[59]

America and Britain Go to War in Canada – the War of 1812

Resolving many financial issues required political compromises that
only papered over sectional and economic differences. Worse still,
some of the accommodations actually exacerbated future political
problems, many of which were connected to financial issues. Long after
the assumption-of-debt decision, some states continued to resent what
they considered transfers of their money to other states. Some critics
saw Hamilton's reforms as a challenge to private and state financial
initiatives, and a reflection of too great a willingness to placate and
emulate America's former colonial master, at times to the detriment of
the European nation that had come to the colonists' aid.[60] The French
Revolution and ensuing European wars coincided with the first decade
of the new republic, causing bitter political fights as well as financial
problems and opportunities for the new country. Many Americans,
including Jefferson, were very sympathetic to the motives and even
some of the means of the French Revolution. Grateful for France's aid
during the American Revolution, many thought that taking France's
side against the other European powers, led by America's and France's
old enemy, Great Britain, was a question of honour. In contrast, others
such as John Adams thought that France's revolution had little in common with America's and that America's interests could be best served
by closer ties with Great Britain (as argued by Hamilton), or at the very
least that America should strive to stay neutral in the conflicts that lasted

twenty-five years (as argued by Washington). Fearful of foreign manipulation during this period, America passed some of its most illiberal laws[61] and bolstered its military spending to enforce its neutrality.

By the time Napoleon assumed power in 1799, even devoted supporters of the French had lost much of their enthusiasm. Napoleon's continued campaigns led to the greatest single increase in U.S. territory and investment, the Louisiana Purchase of 1803, for $15 million – a sum that would have been impossible to fund without Hamilton's reform – and to greater efforts by the British to cut off France. This eventually led to perceived violations of American neutrality, an embargo on British shipping and products, and the War of 1812.[62] In the face of heavy resistance, especially from New England, President Madison gave way to hawkish, expansionist, pro-French, and anti-British elements in his own party, many of whom believed, like his predecessor Jefferson, in an easy victory over the British forces and colonial militia in Canada. He asked for and received a vote for declaration of war, passed in both houses by less than a two-thirds vote, the lowest approval percentage for any declaration of war in U.S. history. America entered what some called the second revolutionary war, for which in many respects it was less well prepared than the first.

Although the War of 1812 was humiliating for the United States, its long-term effects were mostly positive. Jefferson's prediction that conquering Canada was merely a matter of marching north proved "somewhat optimistic." Despite a thirty-to-one numeric advantage over the Canadians and logistical advantages over the British, there were few victories and many defeats for the Americans. The war had many economic and political costs. The war was so unpopular that much of New England threatened to secede from the Union. In revenge for the burning of York (now Toronto) in Canada, the British attacked Baltimore, one of the most important cities in the republic, and burned much of the new capital of Washington, sending Madison and the government into flight. The only great victory, the Battle of New Orleans, catapulted General Andrew Jackson to the presidency over a decade later, but this battle was fought after the peace had been negotiated. The war changed nothing; no borders were altered in spite of battlefield losses and no reparations demanded. The real issues dividing America and Great Britain had been resolved by Napoleon's defeat and by the return of American property and citizens. The failure of America's Embargo and Non-Importation Acts was perceived and rectified even before the war ended.

There were only two positive outcomes. First, it laid to rest the divisive political issue of America's divided loyalties to France and Britain, two countries that were at war with one another for the better part of 400 years. Second, the war reinforced arguments of those in the United States who wanted a stronger national banking system.

The Bank Wars: Politics and Federal Financial Policy

Andrew Jackson: "The bank, Mr Van Buren, is trying to kill me, but I will kill it!"

Martin Van Buren, *Autobiography*

The story of America's first and second national banks plays an important role in the history of the United States, but also in Canadian finance. Not only was the national bank tainted in the eyes of many rural citizens by its association with powerful urban bankers in the northeast, it also symbolized foreign pressures of various sorts. However, resistance to the idea of central banking or any national banking had many roots, not just agrarian versus urban interests, reflecting the dynamism and complexity of American politics and economics.[63] Access to abundant and cheap money interested many merchants and farmers. Shortages of money played a significant role in the break with the empire and their effects cut across many regions and occupations. Many up-and-coming businessmen felt threatened when their access to funds was controlled by those more loyal to creditors than debtors. Even though government debt had been used as money in the colonies, the role of banks in creating (or misusing) money and credit was not lost on the political classes and reinforced a passion for local control. Even stalwart Federalists, such as the second president, John Adams, railed against banks' feeding the fluctuation of money.[64] With some justification in the eyes of many, Hamiltonian banking was merely an unwelcome import from America's former colonial master and a vehicle to facilitate governments to grow larger through borrowing.

Once again, relations with Canada and the United Kingdom provided a second impetus for American banking reform. Ironically, the Second Bank owed both its birth to the widespread recognition that the absence of a central bank served as a financial impediment to the successful pursuit of the War of 1812 and its demise to that war's greatest American hero, General Andrew Jackson.[65] The War of 1812 forced Republicans to adopt many Federalist measures. The number of banks and notes in circulation increased dramatically, leading to inflation and suspension of conversion of paper into specie. As Beard wrote, "During the war, the management of the treasury had been unhappy to say the least."[66] Canada's first permanent commercial bank, the Bank of Montreal, was established a year after the creation of the second BUS, in accordance with Hamilton's principles, which provided even more international confirmation of the wisdom of having a new central bank.

The financial experience of 1812 was so disastrous that Congress passed the second charter without debate about constitutional principals. Established bankers refused their support for the war, and would-be bankers moved in quickly to fill the vacuum left by the first BUS. Without a central bank, from 1811 to 1816 the number of chartered institutions grew from 88 to 246, doubling the banking notes in circulation, creating inflation, and contributing to defaults and the suspension of specie conversion by all but the New England banks when the American capital fell in 1814. Unable to raise taxes and without a national banking system to manage and distribute its bonds, the federal government still relied on its dubious credit, which increased the discounts offered for cash, tripling the face value of its outstanding bonds to an amount greater than that of the domestic debt during the Revolutionary War. In the face of wildcat paper money and lost government revenues, accepting the legality of a new central bank was considered the lesser of two evils. Given the alternative for the Republicans of making terms with northern bankers – a political transformation that would be repeated nearly 100 years later – tariffs were reinstituted. Even Madison, a leading voice against Hamilton's unconstitutional central bank, surrendered to the "moneyed powers."[67] Like the first Bank of the United States, the Second was endowed with many privileges that irked even conservatives. As a private bank, located in Philadelphia, it served as the repository for public funds (without interest), had extensive powers to issue banknotes (near monopoly), and could not be taxed by the states. While the federal government could appoint five of its twenty-five directors and withdraw public funds, only one-fifth of its capital came from the government, and the task of exercising its control function was cumbersome for the government.[68]

But despite newfound early support among old enemies, the idea of a national bank continued to draw strong opposition in the 1820s, in part because of a new political movement that had evolved out of Jeffersonian principles, Jacksonian democracy. Widespread association of the bank with Hamilton's desire to enhance the powers of the federal government, whose activities were linked to those of well-heeled businessmen, was held in check by former Federalists and Republicans only temporarily. Opposition to the bank had its origins in both powerful economic and ideological inspiration, not all of which sprang from Jeffersonian ideals of an independent, rural America. Westerners in rapidly growing states such as Ohio and Indiana and southerners in rapidly growing states such as Tennessee and Louisiana resented the economic weight and tight money policies of northeastern creditors.

American prosperity in this region came once again partially at a cost for Canadians. The 1803 Purchase of the Louisiana Territory by the United States from France opened vast territories of the Mississippi Valley and the Midwest for American expansion. The new river access circumvented the Canadian monopoly on access to the region, making American expansion easier, a development that was later further exacerbated by the building of the Erie Canal and railroads. But even bankers resented many of the privileges of the Second Bank of the United States that put them at a competitive disadvantage.[69] Some critics clung to specie as the only real measure of value and viewed banks that created paper money as a dangerous contagion to society.[70]

The Second Bank got off to a rocky start. The capital requirements made subscribing more expensive than planned and led to a shortage of specie at the bank. The old charter had allowed branches to be set up; the new one presupposed them. By the end of 1817, eighteen branches had been established. By 1830, there were twenty-five branches, in twenty states. From a governance point of view, this was a hazard, especially given the distance and absence of modern communication and travel. A booming economy provided many temptations for BUS managers to overextend themselves, leading to some problems that were more serious than at some state banks, leading early on to calls for repealing its charter.[71] Some of the weakness in the BUS came from a reduction of its functions. As the country became more self-sufficient, the need to clear foreign transactions was reduced. Even Canadian transactions found their way onto the New York or London markets, circumventing the BUS.[72] The bank's ability to force the state banks to hold more specie, its efficiency at handling transfers that undermined the profits of other state banks, and its monopoly on government transfers, for which there was no charge, robbed the state banks of potential revenues.[73]

The Second died, despite having its charter renewed by Congress. Both the Senate and House passed amended charters in the summer of 1832 – four years before it came to an end – by substantial majorities, but not by enough to override a presidential veto. The new charter even included several provisions designed to address criticisms of the bank. These amendments included limits on the bank's ability to hold real estate, open branches, and issue drafts, as well as shortening the charter's duration to fifteen years. Although supporters of the charter deemed it a precipitous moment, they had not reckoned with the intransigence of "Old Hickory": Andrew Jackson. He vetoed the bill, publishing an effective statement replete with references to defending the poor against the rich and preventing foreign money from controlling America. Famous for his ruthless treatment of Indians and nascent secessionists, Jackson may have kept the Union together (or postponed civil war) by his defiance of Southerners' threat to nullify federal law during his first term and by forging a political alliance of Southerners and newly arrived urban populations in the North, despite his own large slave holding. Not opposed to using patronage to spice up his populist rhetoric, he truly hated banks, paper money, and debt. During his administration, the national debt was actually paid off.[74]

In the face of considerable lobbying by the head of the bank and by some business interests, and buoyed by his re-election in 1832, the election of his friend van Buren in 1836, and other political victories – including withdrawal of public funds from the Bank of the United States – Jackson outmanoeuvred his opponents. His veto was never overturned. Jackson's well-known hostility to banks was due in part to their penchant for insider lending.[75] The Jackson administration also tried to couple the closing of the bank with limits on currency, a return to hard money (specie), but to no avail. After his veto, banks all over the country, including the soon-to-be defunct Second Bank, issued many more notes, feeding an economic boom, driving up prices for labour and commodities, and contributing to one of the worst crashes and series of bank failures in American history, in 1837.[76] In the end, Jackson's veto relied a lot on rhetoric about protecting the common man from the wealthy, but it may also have won substantial popular support due to the bank's close relationship with leading politicians, creating a whiff of scandal not unlike that between the Fannie Mae and politicians in our own day. Many of the functions of the second BUS were assumed by the Treasury and/or distributed among favoured private state banks.

State Banking with and without a Central Bank
before the Civil War (Antebellum Period)

The little slips of green paper pass from hand to hand, emblems of our faith,
trust, and perhaps most important of all, our confidence in both our country
and its currency.

Stephen Mihm, *A Nation of Counterfeiters: Capitalists,*
Con Men, and the Making of the United States

During the antebellum period, banks provided a number of services
essential to the young economy. Studies indicate that states with more
banks in 1830, for example, experienced greater economic growth
between 1830 and 1860, but obviously this correlation begs the causal
question.[77] Although the number of banks in the United States grew
quickly from 1800 to 1860, that growth was plagued by some factors
that were common to many countries and some that were uniquely
American. The issue of bank reliability was of primary concern. Creating banks by legislative act (chartering banks) was a great financial
innovation of the 1780s, in providing a form of government control of
organizations whose activities served both private and public functions and whose failure might have very broad social consequences.
But chartering had many flaws and did not resolve many governance issues, including that of limited liability and the proper balance
of public and private responsibilities. As in Britain, shareholders of
even chartered banks were considered to have limited liability, unless
the charter stated the opposite. The Bank of North America (BNA),
founded by the superintendent of finance of the fledgling United
States, Robert Morris, in 1781, while the Revolution was still going
on, performed private as well as public (government) functions. It
lent money to the Confederation and issued its own notes, the most
reliable paper currency in the 1780s. Morris made it the repository
for central government funds. By 1782, several large states chartered
banks.[78]

After ratification of the new Constitution, states continued to go
through the time-consuming and politically charged process of leg-
islating bank charters, but generally they were for limited durations
of ten or fifteen years. Apart from the BUS's authority to clear transactions and place deposits with reliable banks, since the Constitution
did not mention banking, responsibility for creating and controlling
banks lay with states. As in other matters, any power not given to the

federal government or specifically prohibited by the states remained with the states or the people. But political competition within states and from outside shifted political power. It made limiting the number of chartered banks in a state more difficult and helped reduce direct state control, including the practice of government ownership in banks, and led to the breakdown of unit banking in some states.[79] Moreover, with the shift of the capital from Philadelphia to Washington, the demise of the Second Bank, and the building of the Erie Canal, America's most important banking centre shifted to New York.[80]

In antebellum America, banking was much different from what it is today. The banks had some of the functions that they have today, but they also performed tasks that are no longer needed or that are now done by other organizations. The largest portion of most banks' business came in the form of short-term loans, extending credit against production and shipment of goods. These national and international transactions involved securities hardly seen today. Instead of paying cash, purchasers would issue a form of cheque (clean bill) or a bill of exchange (a promise to pay connected directly to goods). On the basis of the credit risk of the purchaser, or his bank, if the document was confirmed, the seller could discount the bill (collect a portion immediately) with his bank for cash. In large part, the bank performed two services: it provided information about credit risk (overcoming informational asymmetry), and it ultimately cleared the amounts through correspondent relationships.[81] Maturities for this sort of lending varied over time and regions, but the period was usually over 70 and under 120 days.[82] Many banks had been founded by merchants, who in addition to their work as merchants who also issued loans. Many found that collaborating with others with similar interests reduced their own risk, which often morphed into a completely new endeavour for the merchants and led to them to give up their original activities in favour of a new venture.

Banks also issued their own promissory notes, the republic's primary form of money, a practice common in the nineteenth century but rare today. In 1820, at a time when the United States had only $41 million in specie – approximately half in bank reserves, the rest in circulation – 76 per cent of all money available for transaction was in the form of paper currency issued by banks. Clearly, commerce was conducted through the medium of bank-supplied currency.[83] Ostensibly these notes were in return for deposits of specie or state and federal debt, but while in principle redeemable into specie at a rate determined by the federal government, many banks had to suspend convertibility during crises. The value of this paper varied greatly and the opportunities for forgery were plentiful. Maintaining and circulating enough currency that was acceptable in different regions was a major challenge for the new republic. The framers of the Constitution had taken away the rights of states to create currency and given the definition of the dollar to the national government, but, as discussed, the vetting of the organizations that would create money was left largely in state hands. As emphasized in the epigraph that opens this section, creating widespread trust in that paper was no small challenge.[84] With the demise of the second BUS, clearing transactions and trading in banknotes became even more difficult, leading commercial banks to set up interbank operations, a service in which the Boston banks excelled as early as 1810. With the Suffolk system, the first system arrangement for remote banks, Boston banks pooled their resources to form a kind of clearing house for banknotes. As a region, New England excelled in region-wide banknote redemption.[85]

Most towns had banks, but the large ones were in cities, because branching was forbidden in most states. By 1860, New England alone had over 500 banks. Some towns had as many as 40. Most of their activities involved businesses rather than households. The banks also obtained their funds differently. Their liabilities consisted of a few deposits – very few by modern standards – and currency they were then allowed to issue. The vast majority of bank financing, however, came from the capital contributions of their owners, who invested in part to obtain favourable treatment from the bank for discounting for themselves and people close to them, and in part because such investment was the only way of really depositing money with the bank to make a gain, much in the same way a deposit would today. Equity capital accounted for roughly a third of total financing. Management was simpler too. The large banks might have a cashier, several tellers, clerks, and a bookkeeper, all guided by the banks' directors.

American banks had different business models. As Naomi Lamoreaux convincingly argues, many U.S. banks, like those in many other countries, engaged in widespread insider lending.[86] Indeed, in many countries and states, the closeness of the banks to their clients may have contributed to economic growth, as Lamoreaux concludes about many cases in New England. Although most of the bank facilities were short-term, some banks got involved in longer-term regional projects, reinforcing the idea that closeness to their markets was an important economic and social value. Oddly, as insider lending diminished over the years, evaluating bank management became harder and the demands for professionalization and specialization greater. The patterns Lamoreaux identified, however, may have been confined to the states she studied, omitting, for example, New York and Pennsylvania. In those states, banks were more widely owned than those in New England. They were also efficient about gathering credit information and lent to a broad range of the business community, such as artisans and farmers.[87]

With and without a central bank, banking grew quickly in the United States. The end of the second BUS made transfer of the banking authority from the federal government to the states nearly complete. For approximately half a century after the founding of the republic, starting a bank required an expensive outlay to purchase a state charter (by legislative act). In 1790, there were three state chartered banks, in Philadelphia, Boston, and Baltimore. (The Bank of New York was actually opened without a charter in 1784 and chartered in 1791, accounting for its appearance on some lists as a bank at an earlier date.)[88] By the time the second BUS lost its charter, there were 729 state chartered banks. Some large cities had dozens, some small towns two or three; some villages had their own bank.[89]

State requirements varied a great deal, and corruption entered the mix. The Philadelphia Bank had $1 million in paid in capital when it applied for a charter, an amount chosen more to overcome resistance from politically connected competitors than was actually necessary to protect depositors. Sometime sponsors had to offer shares to individuals or to the state itself, or to underwrite state loans. Some banks got charters as alternatives to those established by other political factions, making some banks Republican and others Federalist.[90] Selling shares had many obstacles in addition to capital shortages. Some states limited the amount of capital that could come from individual shareholders, set high par values (maximum exposure of shareholders), and imposed limits on both out-of-state ownership and the voting rights of large shareholders.[91] Finding qualified managers was not easy. Banks often drew on owners, families, and friends, with varying results. Attempts to create boards with members from other states resulted in the problem of getting quorums for meetings, due to the large distances.[92]

The growth in banks was not evenly divided among states and time periods. Apart from the BUS, all banking was state-operated. Despite many state differences, all of the states wrestled with the issues of free banking (allowing banks without state charters), branch banking (determining whether banks would have just one unit or more), and the means to protect bank creditors. At the time of the Revolution, New England was considered the most advanced commercial area, but despite its sophistication and the strong demand for money and banking, the first commercial banks were located in Philadelphia (1782) and New York (1784). Three of the next four were established in New England, but when the Constitution was written, only the Massachusetts bank was in operation. Most banks remained small and were dominated by family ties.[93]

States had different banking regulations. For a variety of reasons and for different aspects of banking, some states served as models. Several states were particularly important to American banking history: Massachusetts, Virginia, Illinois, Louisiana, and New York. With the opening of the Erie Canal in 1825, a great deal of business that had been conducted through Louisiana via the Mississippi and Ohio Rivers now passed through New York.[94] Soon after the demise of the second BUS, New York became the country's largest banking centre. In part this may have been because it was innovative in adapting to the absence of the BUS, and in part because the opening of the Erie Canal turned New York's harbour into the most important outlet to the sea for Upstate New York and the Midwest, circumventing Canada. Many American and foreign banking families opened operations, which we will discuss in chapter 3.

By 1860 the number of banks had grown to 1,562, with $207 million in banknotes in circulation and $254 million in deposits, which doubled and tripled respectively after the demise of the second BUS.[95] The growth reflected the general expansion of the economy, regional patterns, and the need for capital and transactions across space and time. From 1830 to 1860, per capita increases in banknotes in circulation differed greatly by state. In Virginia, the numbers doubled; in a few they decreased or stayed flat; in New York and Louisiana they increased eight- to tenfold. The variations cut across regions, defying generalizations about population increases, economic growth, and commercial diversification.[96]

In the South and West, banks followed a somewhat contradictory trajectory, with near complete freedom from government interference. In some states, the government enjoyed ownership stakes in banks. As late as 1850 the average bank size in Massachusetts, New York, and Pennsylvania was much smaller than that of South Carolina and Kentucky. Banks tended to lend out amounts roughly two times share capital, although in South Carolina and Kentucky the banks appear more conservative.[97] Virginia favoured laws somewhere in between.

It liberalized but kept its state chartering system. During the turbulent generation before the Civil War, Louisiana, the only slave-based economy with important international commercial connections, switched back and forth between a liberalized chartering system and a very strict one, and then to free banking in 1854.[98] Several southern states, such as Virginia, allowed branch banking, but many small agricultural interests, unlike plantation owners, had little interaction with and need for banks.[99] In general, southern banks, while geographically diverse, were less well diversified in business activities than northern ones, especially those northern banks with investments in internal improvements. Only two of Mississippi's twenty-five banks in 1837 survived until 1841. In all regions, banks were founded in response to the need to monetize economies. The increase in bank money was quite startling. In New England, per capita bank money in circulation increased from $7.14 in 1820 to $26.72, by far the most monetized region in 1820. In the Middle Atlantic, the increase was tenfold, but in South Atlantic, Old Northwest, and Old Southwest the increases were more modest, doubling, increasing eightfold, and tripling respectively from much lower bases.[100]

Chartering banks and central bank supervision had served as the principal means of oversight for business forms – including in the banking sector where the risks were perceived to be greater than in other sectors – that allowed for a life independent of a firm's creators and large numbers of shareholders, many of whom were relatively passive and could come and go as they pleased. Although charters lasted for a limited duration, they did not prevent waves of bank failures, which periodically flowed through the American banking system. As discussed, gaining a charter in the state legislature was a cumbersome and very political process, with many problems of patronage and exchange of favours playing a prominent role. While many countries faced these issues, the size of the United States and Canada complicated control matters, making many understandably wary of the corporate form and limited liability.[101]

The demise of the second BUS spawned innovations in how banks could be created and controlled. Without the branches of the BUS, many regions lost liquidity and a means of commercial bank oversight. Demand for bank services increased calls to free bank creation from the cumbersome process of chartering. In the American context, free banking refers to the ability of individuals to open a bank without a legislative act, but these individuals still faced some guidelines for insuring bank safety, such as proscribed levels of liquidity or deposits held with state governments. It was not until the 1830s that states began to allow "free banking," as opposed to chartering. "Free banking," though, required new schemes to protect depositors and to control this important institution with regulation. Unlimited liability and insider trading, for example, created special problems for states and a banking system ingrained with unit banking, which limited diversification. New York passed the first law in 1838 allowing individuals to open a bank when they wanted but requiring registration with the state controller and deposit of state or federal bonds. Despite concerns about too many entries and exits as well as questions about appropriate changes in the money supply, the 1838 law unleashed a twenty-year mad scramble to create state banks in order to spread the economic and political benefits of banking. By 1860, twenty-one states had passed similar versions of the New York law.[102] This approach to bank creation in some sense only expanded with the reintroduction of federal involvement in banking during the Civil War.[103]

Given the limits on geographic and business diversification, American banks were particularly vulnerable to macroeconomic shocks. States experimented with other means of protecting stakeholders in the banking system against the limited liability of shareholders. Some required shareholders to accept double liability over their paid-in capital. In the case of bankruptcy, they would be required to put in an additional amount equal to the first paid-in capital. With its revised Free Banking Act in 1838, New York created the first bank insurance fund in response to criticism of the first Act in 1827, with varying percentages of capital that had to be turned over to the state controller and held for bank creditors in case of failure.[104] Laid low by a series of bank failures shortly after its creation, the fund did not survive even a decade.[105]

But the states undermined financial confidence in other ways during the first half of the nineteenth century. With restrictions on federal government involvement in civic projects and federal debt dwindling, in the 1820s several states began borrowing extensively to build canals and turnpikes, and even to fund banks. By 1830 New York, Pennsylvania, and Ohio had issued $26 million in debt. The 1830s witnessed a binge. By 1843 the aggregate state debt reached $231.6 billion. Cities got into the act. Some borrowed too much, too quickly. In 1841, four states, three in the South and one in the West, defaulted: the next year four more, but only two in the South and West. Four of the nine states repudiated all or part of their debts, while the others managed to refinance them.[106]

The Enduring Financial and Political Legacy of Slavery

A house divided against itself cannot stand. I believe this government cannot endure, permanently, half slave and half free. I do not expect the Union to be dissolved – I do not expect the house to fall — but I do expect it will cease to be divided. It will become all one thing or all the other. Either the opponents of slavery will arrest the further spread of it, and place it where the public mind shall rest in the belief that it is in the course of ultimate extinction; or its advocates will push it forward, till it shall become lawful in all the States, old as well as new – North as well as South.

Lincoln, Acceptance Speech for the Senate Nomination,
16 June 1858

From the early colonial period, slavery has had an indelible effect on American history and finance. Abraham Lincoln's famous phrase "A house divided against itself cannot stand, half slave and half free" not only reflected sound political judgment and the feelings of many contemporaries, but also carried financial implications. Economic historians still debate whether involuntary labour in the United States impeded innovation and growth or, more recently, whether slavery actually contributed to growth and development.[107] Given the many long-term costs of this horrendous institution – economic, social, and reputational to the United States – the idea that slavery's commercial contribution was a net positive to commercial development tests credulity, but such discussion is beyond the scope of this book. However, an understanding of slavery's effect on American financial development requires understanding its political and social impact. Slavery had many financial effects, direct and indirect, but precisely what those effects were is less clear. Despite the importance of slavery, few histories of the institution delve into its impact on banking and insurance.[108] Some books on slavery do not even have the terms *finance, insurance*, or *banking* in their index.[109] More recently, discussions centre on whether slavery was an element of capitalism, with its commodity use of labour, large markets, and complicated financial networks.[110] Before and even after the Civil War, slavery and racial relations have remained a central and cruel part of American history.

Sadly, it might have been otherwise. The new republic might have ended slavery before it became embedded in American politics and economics. Although blacks made up approximately 20 per cent of the colonial population when the Revolution began, like indentured servants, many had achieved their freedom. Except in the South, they were not essential to regional economies. Many of the Founding Fathers, such as Franklin and Hamilton, were opposed to slavery, reflecting an increasing Northern antipathy to the institution. New England freed the slaves before the Constitution was approved; within a decade, most of the other Northern states gradually passed emancipation acts. Even some slave owners were sympathetic to the idea of liberating slaves. During the constitutional debates, the country's foremost slave owner, George Mason, railed against the institution of slavery, especially those clauses of the Constitution that touched on it. Several slave owners freed their slaves in their wills, including George Washington. Jefferson freed only his mistress and the children he had with her, despite his many denunciations of the institution. For nearly one hundred years, the issue was still a political hot potato. Most delegates to the 1787 Constitutional Convention believed that there would be no hope of agreeing on a Constitution if it attacked slavery directly. Indeed, the words *slave* and *slavery* never appear in the document. As Madison said during the convention, "To admit in the Constitution the idea that there could be property in men" would be wrong.[111]

There were four major obstacles to ending the practice. The first was financial. Even ardent abolitionists winced at overturning the property rights of slave owners without compensation. Not only would that compensation be difficult to negotiate, given the financial state of the fledgling government, raising the funds would have been difficult, although conceivable after Hamilton's reforms. Second, America's fourth president, Jefferson's friend James Madison, succeeded in getting into the Constitution the infamous three-fifths clause, which, without mentioning slaves explicitly, based the number of representatives for each state (and thereby electors for president and vice president in the Electoral College) on "the whole Number of free Persons, including those bound to Service for a Term of Years, and excluding Indians not taxed, three fifths of other Persons."[112] The three-fifths clause was a compromise reached over the challenging issue of how to count slaves in the census. Population affected voting rights and thereby government decisions. Slaves were counted as three-fifths of a person in the census of the time. The three-fifths clause was the bulwark of the South's ability to elect presidents and congresses sympathetic to slavery until 1860, despite smaller and smaller proportions of citizens and voters. The clause, combined with the votes for president determined by the Electoral College rather than by popular mandate, skewed the choice of presidents toward Southerners and Southern sympathizers until Lincoln's election. Third, the U.S. Constitution protected the slave trade for twenty years, with a seemingly clear intention to eliminate the practice. To the day of the ban's limit, the U.S. Congress outlawed the slave trade starting in 1808, but, as is often the case, this well-intentioned measure had an unintended consequence. Many planters used the grace period to increase their stock. The limit constrained the supply of African Americans already in bondage, leading to some of the worst aspects of American slavery, including the breeding of new slaves, just as demand skyrocketed. Other nations followed suit. Britain, for example, banned the slave trade a few months after the United States. Even though the practice was still legal in many countries well into the nineteenth century, many countries – including those active in the trade before, such as the United States, France, and Great Britain[113] – agreed to measures that helped enforce the prohibition on trade on the high seas.[114] Fourth, during the first decade of the nineteenth century, cotton cultivation started to benefit from the 1793 invention of the cotton gin. The new machine revolutionized the processing of cotton by providing an efficient way to separate cotton seeds from cotton and making the raising of cotton vastly more profitable.

Indeed, by commerce and by imperial force, cotton was instrumental in transforming political relations over a broad portion of the world. The worldwide cotton empire included plantations in America, Asia, and Africa, and manufacturing in the United States and Europe. The huge investment contributed to the need to establish empires to ensure raw materials and increase markets. All of this contributed to the political impetus to control foreign markets to access raw materials and increase demand, with immense repercussions for finance. Unlike Northern businessmen and farmers, who wanted to finance local business and small-scale agriculture, Southern planters had little need for local banks. The Southerners could rely on distant customer financing, bonds, and insurance, sourced in New York or London, using next year's crop as a guarantee. The more limited need for local financing and community banking, compared with other parts of the country, helps account for the existence of branch banking through much of the South.[115]

It is difficult to overemphasize the importance of cotton to the Southern and for that matter the whole American economy during the first sixty years of the nineteenth century. In the two years after the invention of the cotton gin, American shipments of cotton to the United Kingdom alone soared from 30,000 pounds to 1.5 million.[116] From 1790 to 1860, the volume of U.S. cotton production grew from virtually nothing to 2.2 billion pounds, approximately two-thirds of which was grown on land that had not been part of the United States in 1800. By 1860, too, 70 per cent of all U.K. imports of cotton came from the United States.[117] The value of cotton exports rose from $17.5 million in 1815 to $191.8 million in 1860. As Douglass North has pointed out, cotton accounted for 39 per cent of the value of U.S. exports from 1816 to 1820, rising to 63 per cent in 1836. For a country short of specie, the cotton trade was immensely important. For some parts of the antebellum period, the terms of trade for cotton export were particularly favourable, making imported goods particularly interesting for the Southern states, eager to expand the territory under cultivation, especially as cotton growers did little crop rotation.[118]

For more than forty years, slavery was at the heart of a series of political battles. The South tried to stop any American development that threatened its veto power over abolition. First and foremost, the issue came up when new territories demanded admittance as states in the Union. In 1819, there were twenty-two states, eleven slave and eleven free. In the Senate each state got two votes, and even the number of Southern members of the House of Representatives benefited from the three-fifths clause, although the representation from Northern states by 1819 was already larger. Therefore, the South threw its considerable political muscle into maintaining the free/slave state balance. The matter came to a head as Northerners tried to keep slavery out of the bulk of states created from the Louisiana Purchase (see map 1.2). Out of the ensuing crisis came the Missouri Compromise, which admitted Maine as a free and Missouri as a slave state, but barred slavery from all the territories above 36–30 (the continuation of the Arkansas-Missouri border). This postponed the reckoning by a little over a generation.

Slavery wound its way into other political battles, at times rearing its ugly head in physical confrontations on the congressional floor. By and large, the North supported federal projects, such as railroad construction, using federal land to encourage immigration, and keeping out British manufactured products. Slavery brought the South down on the opposite side of these issues. For the economies dependent on slavery, federal projects seemed only to strengthen the federal government, thereby threatening the rights of states to arrange their labour practices as they saw fit. Homestead Acts would attract more immigrants, which would alter the presidential and congressional balance

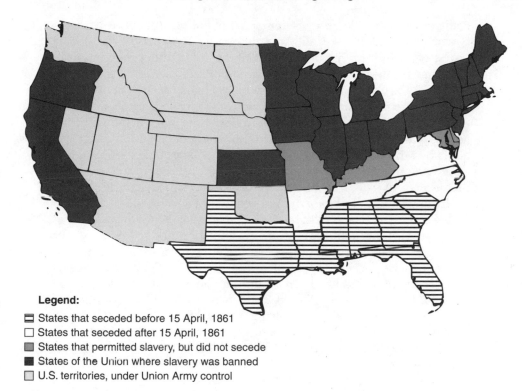

Legend:

⊟ States that seceded before 15 April, 1861
☐ States that seceded after 15 April, 1861
▦ States that permitted slavery, but did not secede
■ States of the Union where slavery was banned
☐ U.S. territories, under Union Army control

Map 1.2 U.S. States and Territories as the Civil War Began:
Status of the States, 1861

of power in favour of the North. Lastly, and perhaps most importantly, even though the North had started its own textile sector, the South's biggest customer for cotton was Great Britain. The idea of selling as much cotton as possible to the British mills and buying British manufactured goods as cheaply as possible lay at the heart of the plantation business model. By and large, even bourgeois Southerners displayed comparatively little enthusiasm for entrepreneurial capitalism and less patience for the North's infant industry arguments, which dated back to Hamilton. Those in the South felt these ideas would only increase their costs.

Given the wide range of issues that emanated from the structural differences between their economies – even leaving aside the increasing moral differences of opinion – slavery put the two regions on a collision course. The South's demand for political equality with the North exploded when California demanded statehood. The debate lasted eight months, involved most of the most important American politicians of the era, and resulted in a complicated series of resolutions, known as the Compromise of 1850, which satisfied neither abolitionists nor slave owners. Among other provisions, it called for California to enter the Union as a free state and the rest of the land "separated from Mexico" to come in as territories without restrictions on slavery. It also abolished the slave trade, not slavery, in the District of Columbia, bolstered the fugitive slave laws, and most importantly proclaimed the illegitimacy of federal authority over the interstate slave trade.[119]

Unsurprisingly, the peace did not last long. The next tick in the bomb arrived four years later with the Kansas-Nebraska Act, which replaced the Missouri and 1850 Compromises with popular sovereignty. For nearly five years the right of those in the territories to choose between becoming a free or slave state unleashed pitched battles of warring factions, many of whom had been brought to the territories to secure that the vote went their way. Added to this slow torture, which inflamed public opinion on both sides of the Mason-Dixon Line that divided North and South, was the Supreme Court's infamous Dred Scott decision, which held that fugitive slaves in free states were still slaves, that the free states were obliged to return the fugitive, and that the Missouri Compromise was unconstitutional.

By 1860, America's population had grown to over 31 million people, of whom 72 per cent were in the North.[120] These Northerners were all free citizens, including nearly half a million African Americans. The South was home to just 5.1 million free whites.[121] Although there is some debate about slavery's contribution to American economic growth, there is much evidence that slavery left the South with a very unbalanced economy, with few cities, immigrants, and new businesses, all of which, had they been encouraged, would have increased demand for financial services in the region. Many of the consequences of the South's reliance on slave labourers – deprived of many opportunities for social advancement – would last well beyond their individual lifespans, had the slaves been freed. Slavery left a vast geographic, social, and even financial scars on the United States that still endure.

The stage had been set for the most cataclysmic war in American history. As evidenced by the Republican convention in 1860, slavery was tied directly and indirectly to many issues. Plank eight of the Republican platform condemned slavery. Calls for high tariffs, free homesteading, public works, and a railroad to the Pacific received louder cheers than the plank adopted for limiting the growth of slavery.[122] Although British attempts to use the liberation of slaves as a weapon in the Revolutionary War and the existence of many freed African Americans in Canada had been sources of tension, the proposed economic measures would have a much greater impact on American-Canadian relations than issues of forced labour.

Oddly, perhaps the conflict that slavery engendered might have had an even greater impact "north of the border." The Civil War for all its costs and economic causation left unresolved many fundamental financial issues that had plagued America since its conception. These unsettled issues include fragmented banking as well as fear of centralized monetary authority and taxation. One but not all of the major economic impediments to a more national banking system had been removed. Whether because of pure economic, ideological, or political interests, many attitudes and institutions remained embedded as an enduring part of America's regulatory architecture.

North of the border the British North American colonies had enjoyed population and economic growth after the colonies had become British, even greater growth than in the United States. But in spite of this growth and the fact that part of America had a slave economy, GDP per capita was only two-thirds that of the United States (see appendix 1). But the colonies were getting ready for change.

CHAPTER TWO

Transitional Decade:
The Birth and Rebirth of Nations

Brother against Brother

One war at a time.

> Abraham Lincoln to advisers who recommended more threats against
> Great Britain

It is hard to overstate the impact of the Civil War on America's social and economic life. But considering the great loss of life and property, the war had limited effect on financial attitudes and institutions. The war and the Thirteenth Amendment theoretically destroyed slavery, the institution that made a mockery of America's pledge of equality, but by making former slaves citizens, it reinforced the expectation that all citizens were equal – not a Canadian delusion in the nineteenth century.

The Civil War's human and economic toll was staggering. In four years of fighting, over 750,000 soldiers died – more than in all other American wars put together, with a loss of roughly 2.4 per cent of the population.[1] Over 400,000 men suffered physical casualties, many of them amputees.[2] Families were divided. Trading relationships were broken, creating fissures that persisted for decades. Many farms and cities, especially in the South, were torched. Many ports and rail lines, again mostly in the South, were left unserviceable. Apart from the human and physical cost, the war was a financial waste. By 1906 government expenditures on the war, including relief for veterans, amounted to $11.3 billion, nearly three times what it would have cost to buy the slaves at $1,000 per person back in 1860.[3] Even more tragically, within a generation, these ostensibly free African Americans laboured under the same or even worse conditions. Slavery and the effects of the war left an indelible stain on American society and economics, helping to create a large underclass. Moreover, the economy of the South was still too dependent on cotton, whose value was falling. That meant that the South remained backward in development of infrastructure, manufacturing, cities, and finance for generations.

Although it came at a much higher price than anyone could have envisioned, the war achieved much. It completely recalibrated American politics. Abraham Lincoln's election, perceived by the thirteen secessionist states as the last straw in Northern domination, actually ended the South's veto power over many measures deemed by Northerners as necessary for economic growth. At first because of secession from the Union and then because of the Thirteenth Amendment to the Constitution, which banned slavery and eliminated the three-fifths clause – the constitutional device that allowed slaves to count for three-fifths of a person, a portion of representation but without the right to vote, as discussed in the last chapter – the power of white Southerners to influence national politics was virtually eliminated for a decade. In one sense James McPherson, one of America's greatest Civil War historians, was right when he wrote that after 1865 the "United States" became a singular noun, by creating a nation, but deep political and social divisions remained.[4]

Since the South's fiscal approaches did not survive the war, we will focus on the North's restructuring of government and finance. During the war, the Republican-dominated Congress passed many pieces of legislation that Northern interests had sought to implement for decades. War expenditures necessitated new sources of revenue and greater ability to raise debt. Between 1860 and 1865, federal government expenditures had increased from 2 per cent to 20 per cent of GDP, approximately what the American national government spends today in peacetime.[5] In addition to raising tariff rates, the Republican majorities created new income and excise taxes, including a stamp tax on real estate transactions, some of which survived the national emergency.[6] Tariff rates as a share of dutiable value, which had been dropping since 1830, increased from 20 to 50 per cent, in 1890, a level attained again only with the introduction of the Smoot-Hawley Tariff in 1930.[7] Several measures were adopted to encourage immigration and infrastructure investment. With slave-state opposition removed, Republicans passed the Pacific Railway Act, which chartered two corporations to build rail lines to the west coast. Despite war expenditures, the companies received direct Treasury subsidies, as well as substantial land.

The Republican-dominated Congress revamped American laws pertaining to banks and currency. They passed the National Currency Act in 1863, National Bank Acts in 1863 and 1864, and a prohibitive tax on state banks that were issuing currency. Over time, this tax motivated those banks either to become national banks or to get out of the business of issuing notes. In effect, the measures gave the New York State free banking law of 1838 national scope by removing the requirement of legislative action to create a national bank. The laws also required the new national banks to back up their notes with government securities, which increased the market for national debt, a welcome source of demand for the Union borrowing for its war effort. The federal government began printing uniform national banknotes, which were distributed to the new national banks in return for federal debt that was then deposited with the comptroller of the currency, located in the Treasury department, the federal agency that was given responsibility for national bank oversight. Although the United States acquired at least one uniform currency – small federal notes – backed up by government debt, banknotes and other aspects of the antebellum financial system did not disappear completely. Perhaps most importantly for the future of American banking, the Office of the Comptroller, in its oversight role, decided that even national banks had to respect the banking laws of the states in which they operated, effectively preventing multi-state and multi-branch banking. Nevertheless, the financial reforms of the Civil War era represented a giant step toward national oversight of banking and a currency issued by the government, rather than a bank.[8]

Although recounting the details of how the war was fought is beyond the scope of this book, describing America's relations with Great Britain is not. At several points during the war, Northern policies toward neutrals almost brought America into military conflict with Britain. But Britain had profoundly mixed feelings about the American Civil War. The practice of slavery was abhorred by large majorities in England. But in 1861 Lincoln declared that the conflict was to preserve the Union, not to end slavery. Moreover, England was highly dependent on trade with the South, especially in raw cotton. With its huge textile manufacturing industry, Britain was particularly vulnerable. In 1860, 530,000 workers were dependent directly on cotton and many relied on it indirectly.

Four-fifths of Britain's cotton came from the United States.[9] Despite the large inventories and high profits of mill owners when the war began, by the winter of 1861–2, in textile production areas, approximately half of the workers had been laid off and were on the public or private dole.[10] Although other factors, such as technological changes, played a role in the decline of textile production, tensions between Britain and the United States peaked when American naval officers boarded the British merchant ship *Trent* and seized two Southern envoys in October 1861. Even after the affair was settled, some British politicians, including a future liberal prime minister, William Ewart Gladstone, wanted to recognize the Southern states, although he later regretted that view. Northerners, for their part, resented the fact that war materiel was being imported from Great Britain; Canadians resented the imposition of passport controls and worried about the threat of American invasion. While passport controls were rescinded, Canadians knew that U.S. Secretary of State William H. Seward believed that all of North America should be American. Luckily, cooler heads prevailed on both sides of the Atlantic.

Great Britain had to be mindful of American ambitions toward the British North American colonies and wary of a long-distance naval and land war. During most of the hostilities, the British government held to a delicate balancing act between Southern demands for recognition and supplies, and Northern threats of retaliation for any real and even perceived foreign intervention, all the while upholding its own economic interests and moral convictions. The American threat was not a delusion. From time to time, Americans talked about annexing territories in the Northwest or even the whole territory north of the border. The question was whether American rivalry would remain friendly or unfriendly in light of British economic and political actions. Before 1860, Britain had little economic interest in the North and was reluctant to lend money for the Northern war effort. But much to its regret, Britain did advance some funds to the South against future cotton deliveries. British willingness to give some support to the South, however, rested on three conditions that the Northern embargo was ineffective, that the South had prospects of winning, and that its winning would not add to the duration of slavery. If these conditions were met, aiding the Southern cause seemed to be in British interests.[11]

By the summer of 1863, none of these conditions were being met. By then, the South was cut off from most of the world, and its defeat at

Gettysburg had quashed its hopes of a positive military outcome. But it was Lincoln's Emancipation Proclamation (announced in September 1862 and implemented in January 1863), freeing the slaves in rebellious states, that settled the issue in Great Britain. So long as the North disavowed any intention that its purpose was to abolish slavery – as it did at the outset of the war – Britain tended to see the conflict as one between two American regions, both of which allowed the existence of slavery. However, in the United Kingdom public opinion would not allow the government to fight a war that would preserve slavery.[12] Moreover, the South's attempts to use Canada as a base of operations for raids against the North led to Canadian legislation to "defend the border against American incursions and to arrest and deport Confederates attacking the North from Canada."[13] But for Britain, the collapse of Southern resistance did not settle the problem completely. The North ended the war with one million men in arms, the largest army in the world, and one of the largest navies. Moving troops north in 1865 by land or up the St Lawrence by water would be a lot easier than it would have been in 1812.[14]

Despite its decided effects, the Civil War left some financial issues unresolved. Even though the South had been conquered and had adopted some Northern policies, regional differences and tensions remained, a situation which Union occupation did little to quell. The Supreme Court struck down the greenback's legal-tender status as unconstitutional in 1870, exacerbating questions about a common currency and whether the dollar would be backed by gold. With national banks receiving heavy criticism for starving agricultural interests of loanable funds, especially in the South, political support for creating truly national banks dwindled.[15] The nation's public and private debt as well as its fragmented financial system understandably continued to frighten foreign investors. In short, the Civil War left America's finances in an ambiguous state. The same could be said for its relationship with its neighbour to the north. With the South's loss of its strong political power, a potential veto of British North America annexation effectively disappeared. The victory of the protectionist Northern states not only raised fears that the United States would annex British North America, but it also increased concerns about the fate of the Reciprocity Treaty in "natural products," a free trade agreement that had been negotiated more than a decade earlier, since the Republican Convention of 1860 had voted for a protective tariff.

The Birth of a Nation

The irritation of the Northern States against Britain during and immediately after the Civil War, and the activities of the Irish Fenians on the Canadian border, had warned Canada that its independence was in danger.

G.M. Trevelyan, *History of England*

The creation of the Canadian Confederation can be better understood against the background of the U.S. Civil War and its aftermath. More than two years after the war's end, but before the United States disarmed, the British North America Act (BNA) created Canada on 1 July 1867. This happened through an Act of the British Parliament, and Canada became the first British colony to become domestically self-governing. The creation of the Canadian federation cannot be traced to one single cause. It was a product of a long process, much of which was linked with or parallel to developments south of the border, but one that emanated out of its own special interests and conditions. From the beginning Canada was a federation of four provinces – New Brunswick, Nova Scotia, Ontario, and Quebec – rather than a unitary state. In contrast to the United States, even the "French fact" – the special guarantees for language, religion, and civil law enjoyed by Quebec – which had some parallel with American states' rights – had less impact on the structure of its financial institutions. While Canada resembled the United States in that it was a federal form of government, the former was also different in that it was a monarchical parliamentary democracy rather than a presidential republican one, a product of constitutional evolution rather than revolutionary change. From the beginning, Canada's core values differed from those of America. Canada's mission of "peace, order and good government" reflected Canadians' desire to avoid some of the excesses that a pursuit of "life, liberty and happiness" might bring.

Initial Steps

Confederation had been the subject of much debate, especially in the Maritime Provinces and in Canada East (Quebec). When the announcement finally came, however, there was celebration. "The day marked the greatest state occasion in the history of British North America.... The Grand Parade at Halifax, Barrack Square at Saint John, Queen's Park at Toronto, and Victoria Square and the *Place d'Armes* in Montreal were rapidly filling up with citizens. And all over the country, in scores of market squares, parks and parade grounds ... the mayors, and town clerks, and reeves, and wardens, were about to read the Queen's proclamation, bringing the federation into official existence."[16] In contrast to reactions to America's independence movement, there was no massive human flight. Passage of the legislation through the British Parliament had been relatively smooth, "aided by ... the determination of both Colonial Secretary Carnarvon, and his Liberal shadow, Edward Cardwell, to carry it."[17] The new Conservative administration in Britain, led by Benjamin Disraeli, had introduced the legislation, but as the *Times* noted, the plan had been essentially worked out by Lord Palmerston, who had been in power from 1859 until his death in 1865.

Outside of Canada the day was largely ignored. The *New York Times* did provide a two-sentence description: "Reports from every city, town and village in the Dominion agree in the unanimity and heartiness with which Confederation day was celebrated. No previous event in the history of the country called forth such universal rejoicing."[18] Four days later the *Times* described the new prime minister, who held office for nineteen of the twenty-four years until his death in 1891: "Sir John A. Macdonald has played his cards well, and is clearly master of the political situation, and will keep it for some time to come."[19] However there was "little discussion and little interest in England."[20]

For many in the United Kingdom, granting more independence to and unifying British North America seemed like a natural, even obvious, development. This outcome would offer a solution to certain domestic and international political and economic issues. These included reducing military expenditures for defending Canada and financing investment there. Annual military expenditures for the defence of Canada had increased to £1.5 million during the American Civil War from £250,000, and British investors wanted to see a clearer government structure in Canada before lending funds for infrastructure, principally railways.[21]

The American Civil War brought those issues to a head by destroying some of the economic ties built up between Britain and the United States since 1814 and by unleashing America as a more aggressive economic and political competitor. On the basis of their many common interests after the War of 1812, Britain, its colonies, and America enjoyed remarkably amicable relations. Boundaries and trade sometimes had led to tensions, but both sides seemed to recognize that peaceful compromise was in their mutual interest. With successive agreements and despite hostile rhetoric over border issues, as settlement moved westward in the United States, post-Napoleonic generations on both sides of the

Atlantic tended to view prior Anglo-American conflicts as unpleasant and seemingly unnecessary incidents.[22] In 1818 the two governments agreed to disarmament on the Great Lakes, through the Rush Bagot Treaty. Thirty years later, they peacefully settled the long-standing dispute over the border between British and American western territories all the way to the Pacific Ocean.

In 1854, with help from the Canadian colonials, Great Britain negotiated a Reciprocity Treaty with the United States. This agreement allowed free trade in natural products and greater access of Midwestern products along the St Lawrence River. The Reciprocity Treaty resulted in an increase in trade between the two countries, with the United States temporarily surpassing the United Kingdom as Canada's major market and supplier. By 1860, the United States accounted for 51 per cent of Canadian imports and 57 per cent of exports, up from 37 per cent and 35 per cent a decade earlier.[23] However, in 1866 America abrogated the Reciprocity Treaty. Canada's trade with the United States quickly declined as a percentage of all trade, but the change was not evenly divided between exports and imports. While Canadian imports from the United States surpassed those of the United Kingdom in the 1880s, Canadian exports to the United Kingdom were greater than they were to the United States until the 1920s, when America passed additional tariffs,[24] discouraging Canadian exports. The problem was significantly compounded with the infamous Smoot-Hawley tariffs of the 1930s. As a consequence, Canadian exports to the United Kingdom were usually greater than those to America until the Second World War.[25]

Four years of the U.S. Civil War erased most of the positive attitudes and some of the agreements. With the war over, the British North American colonists were confronted by "the hostile attitude and aggressive expansion of the United States."[26] Successive waves of Irish Catholic immigrants to America added to the proportion of the population with little loyalty, or worse still, great hostility, to the British Empire. The Fenians, who were American supporters of Irish independence, launched raids on Canada from America. Americans of all ethnic backgrounds deeply resented British attempts to supply the South for profit and the use of Canadian territory by Southerners plotting to attack the North. Understandably, fear grew that America intended to abrogate the Reciprocity Treaty – which it did in 1866 – and that it planned to rearm the Great Lakes, which it did not.

As the Civil War drew to a conclusion Thomas D'Arcy McGee, the Irish nationalist Roman Catholic who was assassinated three years later – a rare occurrence in Canadian politics – expressed the feelings of many:

> Republican America gave us her notices in times past through the press, and her demagogues and her statesmen, but of late days she has given us much more intelligible notices – such as the notice to abrogate the Reciprocity Treaty, and to arm the Lakes, contrary to the provisions of the addenda to the treaty of 1818. She has given us another notice in imposing a vexatious passport system; another in her avowed purpose to construct a ship canal around the Falls of Niagara, so as "to pass war vessels from Lake Ontario to Lake Erie"; and yet another, the most striking of all, has given to us, if we will only understand it, by the enormous expansion of the American army and navy.[27]

McGee's life highlighted how the perception of social conflicts in the United States shaped Canadians' vision for their country. He first emigrated from Ireland to the United States during the potato famine and was strongly opposed to British rule in Ireland. But over time his views changed as he encountered anti-Irish feeling in the United States, where prejudices often erupted into violence, and where anti-immigration parties were commanding sizeable voter allegiance. In the 1850s McGee encouraged people in Ireland to immigrate to Canada rather than to the United States. He himself moved to Montreal in 1857 and was quickly elected to the legislature. British North America's diverse cultural and religious make-up, seen by some as a threat to unity, also served as a brake on anti-Catholic immigration pressures from the Protestant English, Irish, and Scottish communities. McGee saw in Canada a better balance between "natural freedom and the need for authority."

In spite of McGee's views and in spite of the turmoil of the Civil War, which caused a modest slowdown in American growth, the United States did much better than Canada in the decade of the 1860s (see appendix 2). The major growth occurred in the north central states, states such as Illinois and Missouri, and in cities like Chicago and St Louis, which became major hubs for both rail and water transportation. Canada meanwhile was suffering through a malaise, caused partially by a provincial political impasse, and partially because of the economic hardship caused by America's abrogation of the 1854 Reciprocity Treaty in 1866. While the British North American colonies continued to attract immigrants as well as experience high birth rates, particularly in the French Roman Catholic part of the colonies, the decade was marked by exodus as colonists from both Canada East and the Maritimes moved to the "Boston states," and colonists from Canada West moved to neighbouring Michigan and New York.

McGee, a great advocate of Canadian unification and western expansion, supported protective tariffs and extensive minority rights, which included uncompromising criticism of Irish Protestant and Catholic intolerance of one another. This stance led to his assassination, a rare event in Canadian politics, by Fenians in Ottawa in 1868.[28]

Winston Churchill (a man with shared American and British roots) wrote, "The American Civil War in the United States ... aroused their [the Canadians'] fears that the exultant union might be tempted to extend its borders.... How indeed could Canada remain separate from America and yet stay alive?"[29] Interestingly, Churchill did not note that the American Civil War had heightened tensions between the imperial authorities in the United Kingdom and the colonists. The dispute hinged on who was responsible for expenditures on defence, with the colonists contending they were imperial expenditures and British authorities contending the opposite. While he was chancellor of the exchequer, Gladstone was a leader of the Little Englanders in the Melbourne administration, who saw the colonies as a costly and strategic liability. The major expenditures at issue related to troops, militia in the case of the colonists, and the Intercolonial Railway. This last item was strategic – an all-British route would avoid passing through American territory. Since it was strategic and running through remote territory, it would require costly subsidization. Robert Lowe, a Liberal MP in the British Parliament, "predicted that while the Thirteen Colonies had 'separated from England because she insisted on taxing them,' England would probably 'separate from the colonies because they insisted on taxing her.'"[30] As Alexander Tilloch Galt, who first proposed Confederation in 1858 and served as Canada's first minister of finance, wrote from London in January 1867, "I am more than ever disappointed in the tone of feeling here as to the Colonies. I cannot shut my eyes to the fact that they want to get rid of us."[31]

Added to the mix were the dramatic changes in the world as the result of the new technologies of railway and telegraph. Not only did the railway hold out the promise to the colonies of a new country with year-round access to an ice-free port, but it also offered strategic protection from the United States with a railway running from Halifax to Montreal on an all-Canadian route. "The new means of transportation made possible a union of continental proportions in which all hoped to find escape from existing difficulties and stimulus to renewed expansion and prosperity."[32] As appealing as that may have been to Maritimers, the allure for the citizens of Canada West, present-day Ontario, was the idea of buying parcels of land from the vast territory of the Hudson's Bay Company in the West – Rupert's Land. This was a place for young farmers to go, work their own land, and remain British rather than migrating to the mid-western United States.

In addition to the American threat, British disinterest, and technological factors, increasing concern about purely Canadian political imperatives and administrative deadlock contributed to calls for a federation of all British North American colonies. One major issue was the cry in Canada West for "representation by population," a normal democratic aspiration, but for those from Canada East, particularly the French Canadians, this did not seem just. When the Act of Union was passed in 1841, Canada East and Canada West were given equal voting power, even though Canada East's population was at least 35 per cent larger, as calculated from early nineteenth-century censuses in the two Canadas. Prior to 1840, at the time of Union, Canada West had enjoyed an advantage similar to what the Southern states had experienced prior to the Civil War.

Men and Values: Cartier and Macdonald

Cartier once described himself as "an Englishman who speaks French."
                    Richard Gwyn, *John A.: The Man Who Made Us*

Macdonald was an unregenerate Anglophile: he loved Britain, its history, literature, legal system and political system, and London's bustle and buzz.
                    Richard Gwyn, *Nation Maker: Sir John A. Macdonald*

Confederation was not just a product of politics and economics but also of personalities. Like the creation of the American government, the Canadian owed much to some remarkable individuals, in particular George Étienne Cartier and Canada's first prime minister, Sir John A. Macdonald. While good friends and political colleagues, their background and experience were very different. Unlike the views of some of the most influential American Founding Fathers, their visions for their new nation were remarkably similar, despite their differences over many specific issues.

Cartier's family had arrived in New France two decades before the Battle of the Plains of Abraham in 1759. They accepted the transition to British rule. His grandfather had fought with the British during the American Revolution. When Cartier was born in 1814, his family named him George, not Georges, the normal French way of spelling the name, after King George III. During the 1837 rebellions, Cartier was one of the Lower Canadian rebels, although he contended that his participation was provoked by his objection to the Chateau Clique, the British establishment who had the ear of the British governor. Unlike some of the other rebels, Cartier did not wish to separate from Britain. During the short-lived protests of 1849 called the Annexation Movement, which will be discussed later, Cartier stoutly defended law and order and British institutions. Cartier's pronounced Anglophilia was reflected in his clothing tastes. Among European capitals, his favourite city to visit was London. He had a strong distrust of the United States and its institutions. In favour of Confederation he stated, "We, who have had the advantage of seeing republicanism in operation for a period of 80 years, of perceiving its faults and its vices, have been convinced that purely democratic institutions cannot assure the peace and prosperity of nations, and that we must unite under a federation so formed as to perpetuate the monarchical element.... The preservation of the monarchical principle will be the great feature of our confederation, while on the other side of the line the dominant power is the will of the masses, of the populace."[33] Like Macdonald, Cartier brought enormous energy to the governance of British North America and to Confederation.

Unlike Cartier, Macdonald was not a third-generation citizen. Young John was the five-year-old son of Scottish immigrants when his family arrived in Canada in 1820. The family settled in Kingston, the largest community at the time in Upper Canada and a centre for the Scottish community, whose immigration and Enlightenment traditions were vital to Canadian history and to Macdonald's tolerance for non-Anglo-Saxon communities. He claimed that during the 1837 Rebellion, as a militia private, he carried a musket as part of a force opposing William Lyon Mackenzie's rebels, although he later defended rebels in court. A moderate conservative in all things, Macdonald disliked extremism. And as a Canadian conservative he believed in a positive role for government, but in contrast to America's Founding Fathers, with a lesser ideological sense of mission.

Some have labelled Macdonald anti-American, but as Richard Gwyn, his most recent biographer, has noted, he was not anti-American but was instead indifferent to the United States. He felt the American central government was too weak, and he, like many others, did not favour universal suffrage, which he felt resulted in "a tyranny of the majority."[34] For Macdonald, such American notions as a secret ballot, separation of church and state, and direct democracy represented a threat to a well-ordered society, a view shared by most Canadians, liberal and conservative, at the time.[35] However, Macdonald liked America's Anglo-Saxon character and institutions and recognized the importance of economic relations. Although he could look across the St Lawrence River and see the United States, Macdonald preferred to visit the United Kingdom, the heart of one of the greatest empires the world had known. Above all Macdonald was a Canadian who knew that Canada was caught between the world's greatest power, an ocean away, and the world's future power, right next door. For Macdonald "*pro forma* deference to the shared Mother Country was a small price to pay for the deterrent power of being under the umbrella of the British Empire opposite the Americans. Macdonald early developed the idea that Canada could develop a distinctive and even superior form of government, but knew that it depended on the pillars of taking the best of American positivism and British political moderation; the subtle and not overly cynical invocation of the two countries against each other for properly Canadian ends while being faithful and inoffensive to both."[36]

A skilled politician, Macdonald, despite tragedies in his private life, knew how to work a room with charm and storytelling, and how to divide political spoils through patronage. First and foremost, he understood key realities of Canadian politics, especially the need to balance the interests of Canada's French and English populations, which entailed his compromising despite his preference for a strong federal government.[37]

Both Cartier and Macdonald were lawyers with successful commercial practices. Cartier sat on the board of directors of banking, insurance, mining, and railway companies. When Macdonald was only in his mid-twenties, he was elected to the board of the Commercial Bank of the Midland District, one of the two major banks in Upper Canada. Both Cartier and Macdonald became active in politics and supported the *bleus* and the conservatives respectively. Unlike their counterparts in the United States, during the period before Confederation, liberals and conservatives in Canada were not divided by fundamental economic and political issues. Rather they diverged over religious matters and specific issues of the day, such as support of separate schools for Roman Catholics, patronage appointments, and representation by population.[38] Both Macdonald and Cartier were elected to the provincial legislature in the 1840s, Cartier in Canada East and Macdonald in

Canada West; both entered their respective provincial cabinets in the 1850s and formed their first joint-Canadian provincial government in 1858. All governments in the province of Canada, which included East and West Canada, were double-headed ministries, with co-premiers, one English and one French.

In the mid-1860s Cartier and Macdonald approached Confederation from different perspectives, but with a willingness to compromise. Cartier articulated the need for a federal-monarchical form of government. His main interest was to ensure that the French province's right to its own education and justice system as well as guarantees of religion and language would be protected. Macdonald favoured a unitary state but bowed to his friend and colleague Cartier, who required a federation, in recognition of the "French fact" – the unique cultural and linguistic character of the citizens of Canada East.

The two men's parties formed a powerful coalition. In the first election in 1867 Macdonald's Conservatives won forty-nine out of eighty-two seats in Ontario, but Cartier's *bleus* did even better in Quebec, winning forty-eight out of sixty-two seats. "From 1867 until his death [1873], Cartier was Macdonald's principal lieutenant, and often replaced him as prime minister and leader of the government in the House of Commons. He was a kind of co–prime minister, practically the equal of Macdonald."[39] Their opponents were known as Reformers or Clear Grits in Upper Canada and the Parti Rouge in Lower Canada. Both the Clear Grits and the Parti Rouge favoured greater democracy and opposed patronage appointments but they had difficulty working together because the Upper Canadian Reformers favoured "representation by population," which the Parti Rouge did not. Moreover, the Reformers tended to be anti-French and anti-Catholic and made co-operation more difficult. In Canada fundamental issues of federalism and finance did not divide political parties, unlike in the United States.

Wrestling with Cultural and Physical Distance: The Achievement of Confederation

Canadian Confederation was a great political achievement. It was made possible by a remarkable conjuncture of events which brought each of the separate colonies to a crisis in its affairs at the same time and pointed to political union as a common solution to their difficulties.

Joseph Sirois, *The Rowell-Sirois Report*

While Confederation owed much to the wisdom of these two men, plans for creating a Canadian state built on previous agreements were plagued with many obstacles, many of which were part of a long historical process that can be divided into three distinct periods: (1) from the English conquest in 1760 until Pitt the Younger's Constitution Act of 1791, (2) from the Constitution Act to the Act of Union of 1841, and (3) from the Act of Union to Confederation in 1867.

French Roots

The first European-settled area that was to become Quebec was French-speaking. It was "discovered" in the early sixteenth century when the European Christian nations were turning their attention from the Mediterranean Sea to the "new world" across the Atlantic Ocean. This territory was settled in the early seventeenth century and expanded all the way to the Ohio Valley and the Gulf of Mexico, driven by the quest for furs and souls. By the mid-eighteenth century, there were 55,000 French in North America – Quebec, Illinois country, and the Louisiana territory. At the start of the Seven Years' War (1756–63), the third of many wars between France and the United Kingdom, the most important of the French trading posts in terms of fur and hide production was Detroit. The French and Indian War, as Americans called it, was the culmination of a sixty-year struggle between England and France, the "white tribes" in North America, for control of the Great Lakes region. From a British perspective the most important victory in Canada came in 1759, at the Battle of the Plains of Abraham in Quebec City, when Quebec fell to the British. In 1760, Montreal fell to the English as well, and with it, the huge province of French Canada. All of this was made official in the Treaty of Paris in 1763, ending the French dream of a colonial empire from Quebec City to New Orleans, including present-day southern Ontario, Illinois, Indiana, Michigan, Ohio, Wisconsin, and parts of Minnesota. More American territory changed hands in the first Treaty of Paris than in any other international treaty before or since.

At first the British handled the new territory of New France with great care. In 1774 the British government passed the Quebec Act, a generous piece of colonial legislation, which guaranteed to the conquered people their language and their religion, indeed their civil code, but not their criminal code. This was a departure in British imperial policy and marked a brief period of Canadian exceptionalism.[40] The

British settlers in the American colonies considered the Act antithetical to their interests. As discussed in chapter 1, the Act contributed to the American Revolution. The 1774 Continental Congress condemned the Quebec Act and invited Quebec representatives to the 1775 Congress. When they did not come, the Americans attacked, capturing Montreal. However, they were driven out of Canada a few months later by British forces and that most Canadian of opponents, *l'hiver*.

Waves of English-Speaking Inhabitants

The American Revolution had major consequences for Quebec and Canada. The British government quickly moved from a policy of Canadian exceptionalism to one of establishing good relations with the new United States rather than with their North American colony. The Second Treaty of Paris of 1783 deprived Canada of the natural commercial empire south of the Great Lakes, as well as bifurcating Iroquois lands. It also resulted in the arrival of 50,000 exiles from the United States – people who were called Tories and traitors in America, but in British North America were called United Empire Loyalists. As discussed earlier, the majority went to the Maritimes, but many came to Quebec or Lower Canada from the frontier area of nearby colonies, especially New York State. The future of those Loyalists lay not in the relatively well-populated areas but in the more empty western interior north of Montreal. With the arrival of the Loyalists, the basis of the Quebec Act was eviscerated. This colony would not always be French in cultural orientation, and colonial policy would not be focused almost exclusively on placating the interests of French-speaking colonists.

The Constitution Act of 1791, among other things, divided what was then the province of Quebec in two. Historic Quebec became Lower Canada. The newer lands to the west, which were being settled by United Empire Loyalists, became Upper Canada and later Ontario. This division into Lower and Upper Canada compounded the commercial problems of the 1783 boundary settlement by inserting a political division into the middle of a commercial empire. In addition, each part would contain an elected assembly, an appointed legislative council, and within the legislative council an executive council, or cabinet, for the governor. "Canada was to receive the blessings of a British constitution and to serve as a beacon for British political principles. The intended audience was the United States."[41]

Life carried on under the new arrangement. The Anglo commercial elite of Montreal were frustrated by the French-Canadian assembly, while in Upper Canada a new land was being developed with many American settlers, post-Loyalist immigrants. For a variety of reasons, in 1812 President Madison declared war against Great Britain. He was under pressure from the Western war hawks, such as John C. Calhoun and Henry Clay, but opposed by New Englanders. The war was fought primarily on Canadian soil. American priorities in the War of 1812–14 were Quebec City and Montreal, but much of the fighting was in Upper Canada or modern-day Ontario. York (Toronto) was attacked twice. The British captured both Detroit and Michilimackinac, an island in upper Lake Michigan. Much of the fighting took place in the Niagara Peninsula, but as noted earlier, British soldiers burned and sacked Washington in retaliation for similar treatment by the Americans at York. The war was settled by the Treaty of Ghent in 1814, which left the boundaries as they had been, depriving Canada once again of the Ohio Valley. The Rush Bagot Convention of 1818 demilitarized the Great Lakes.

The period from the end of the War of 1812 and the Napoleonic Wars to the mid-1830s was marked by population growth and expanding economies, as well as colonial rule. The growth was fuelled by large-scale emigration from the United Kingdom, reaching a peak in the 1830s, and a very high birth rate in Lower Canada. The reasons for the large-scale emigration included the release of manpower after the Napoleonic Wars and the expanding colonial economy, particularly that of Upper Canada. Timber production and the timber trade were major contributors to the expanding economy. Between 1800 and 1820 Canada's share of the British timber trade exploded, climbing from less than 1 per cent to 81 per cent and holding at 75 per cent into the 1830s. Timber accounted for 40 per cent of all BNA colony exports to the United Kingdom.[42] The period also saw the expansion of agriculture in Upper Canada, with wheat and flour being exported to the United Kingdom via the St Lawrence River. In addition to the traditional fur trade there was also the early beginning of a manufacturing sector focused on gristmills and sawmills as well as textile mills, tanneries, foundries, and shipbuilders.

However, this population increase and the expanding economy were not matched by movements toward responsible government. For Canada this meant government in which the executive was responsible to elected representatives, rather than to the British-appointed governor general. In both Lower and Upper Canada, a small group of "favoured individuals" had the ear of the British governor. In Lower Canada this group was referred to as the Chateau Clique and in Upper Canada as the Family Compact. The British governors were often military men who had difficulty contending with the deep tensions, particularly in Lower Canada, between French and English, Protestant and Catholic. In an effort to introduce change, the Earl of Gosford was appointed governor general of Canada in 1835. Gosford had opposed the Orange Order in Ireland and worked to satisfy the demands of the French-Canadian Lower Assembly without alienating the Anglo minority there, but his efforts met with limited success.

Frustrations and Rejuvenation

In 1837 frustration over the lack of responsible government boiled over into rebellions in both Lower and Upper Canada. The economy was a contributing factor. This was a period of contraction, with crop failures, falling land values, and suspension of specie payments. But the rebels' main complaint was about the form of government, particularly about the small inside cliques around the governor general. In Lower Canada, where the *patriotes*, or rebels, were led by Louis Joseph Papineau, the rebellions were particularly violent. In Upper Canada, the rebels were led by William Lyon Mackenzie, Toronto's first mayor. Both rebel leaders professed admiration for the United States Constitution and the democratic populism of Andrew Jackson. After the rebellion was crushed, Papineau fled to the United States, but stayed there for only two years. While professing admiration for the United States, Papineau was hostile to commerce and favoured a seigneurial regime. Logic was not his strong suit.[43] Mackenzie too admired Jacksonian democracy, but at least he was more consistent than Papineau. He too fled to the United States, but became quickly disillusioned and wrote, "The more I see of this country [the United States] the more bitterly I regret the attempt at revolution at Toronto."[44] Once Mackenzie was granted amnesty, he returned to Canada in 1857.

In summary, as Canadian historian H.V. Nelles has noted, "The Rebellion of 1837 turned into the American Revolution in reverse; authority triumphed and revolution was discredited. The forces of order quickly rallied. Moreover, the erratic behaviour of the two rebel leaders did nothing to advance their cause."[45] Nevertheless, the shock served as a wake-up call for Canadians and the British colonial authorities, who had neglected dealing with many issues in British North America.

A crucial outcome of the 1837 rebellions was the appointment of "Radical Jack Lambton," the Earl of Durham, as governor general of British North America in 1838.[46] Although the British government removed Durham the next year, "Radical Jack" stayed long enough to complete a famous or perhaps infamous report, which bore his name. He recommended that the two Canadas be united and the French Canadians be assimilated, a proposal that did not endear him to the French-speaking population in Quebec. In addition, "Durham reached the conclusion that from the perspective of a need for reform, the solution available within the framework of British institutions implied the introduction of responsible government as a key measure.... He believed that in granting responsible government to the colonies, far from inciting them to become independent, the British government would not only put an end to sterile struggles and violence but would also confirm certain enduring links between Britain and her dependencies."[47] In short, granting more autonomous government would quell demands for complete independence. Despite Durham's removal in 1839, his report served as the basis of the 1841 Act of Union passed by the British Parliament, which brought the formerly separate colonies together into one province with two equal parts Canada East (formerly Lower Canada) and Canada West (formerly Upper Canada).

To put the upheavals of 1837 in context and help explain why they led to reform rather than further revolution, it should be noted that while the vast majority of Canadians, both French and English, wished to remain loyal to Britain and the Crown, the benefits of joining the United States seemed to be mixed at best. And whatever benefits that might accrue came at a political and perhaps moral price, and, most importantly, depended greatly on one's point of view. Envy was held in check by concerns about the trajectory of American democracy. Even a frequently quoted statement by Lord Durham needs contextualization. While in Canada, he observed, "On the American side all is activity and hustle ... On the British side, except for a few favoured spots, all seems waste and desolate."[48] At first blush, this comment is surprising, considering the devastation caused by President Jackson's misguided policies, which resulted in hundreds of bank failures in the late 1830s. However, Durham's point of view may have reflected the diverse components of Canadian culture and economy. Durham did not have a full picture, geographically or temporarily, of life in the North American colonies. He was there for only a short time and spent virtually all of it in Lower Canada, which was more severely hit by a monetary crisis, and visited Buffalo in the United States only briefly.

In contrast to the United States, Canada experienced no banking failures during this period, although specie was suspended for longer in Lower Canada than in Upper Canada, but in neither was it suspended for as long as it was in the United States.[49] The crisis also highlighted the differences between the economies of Upper and Lower Canada, where different regional characteristics contributed to different degrees of contraction. What made this crisis unusual in Canadian history was that it provoked armed rebellions in both Upper and Lower Canada. Violent clashes with recognized authority are rare in Canadian history.

The Road to Independence

The future of Canada depended on many political and economic developments on both sides of the Atlantic. Events in Europe led to changes in immigration to British North America and in trade policy within the British Empire. Chief among these events was the Irish Potato Famine of the 1840s. As a result of starvation in Ireland, a tidal wave of emigrants left their homeland for North America, which increased social tensions considerably north and south of the border.[50] The threat of American annexation after the American Civil War led British North American colonists and the colonial administration in London to start thinking about a confederation of provinces, independent of Great Britain in domestic matters.

With responsible government attained in 1848, power shifted from colonial governors, advised by a small group of colonial insiders and responsible to a British minister, to a British-style elected legislature that answered to the people who elected them. The original Canadian leaders were Robert Baldwin and Louis Hippolyte Lafontaine. Both were Canadian born and both were lawyers. They supported reform policies and fought for responsible government. In the early 1840s they served in a government that did not report directly to Parliament, so they resigned. With the change in imperial policy, Baldwin and Lafontaine formed a new council in March 1848, which consisted of members from the winning party in the legislative assembly. Their time in office witnessed two important decisions, one by the British government and one by the newly responsible Canadian government, which led to an unfortunate and short-lived annexation movement.

Changes in British colonial policy, especially in response to the Irish famine, had a huge impact on Canada. In the United Kingdom Sir Robert Peel was in his second term of office when the famine struck. In spite of strong opposition from within his own party, Peel abolished the Corn Laws in 1846, one of the most significant legislative actions of nineteenth-century Britain. This move transformed Britain from a nation that had supported mercantilism for centuries into one whose official policy was free trade. The repeal of the Corn Laws was designed to reduce the cost and quantity of imported grains (called corn in the nineteenth century) by opening up more sources of foodstuffs outside of the empire. An unintended consequence was the removal of colonial preference, which had benefited Canada. Henceforth Canadian exporters of wheat and flour had to compete on equal terms with American exporters to the British market. Originally this did not go down well in Montreal, especially since Canadians had enjoyed "varying degrees of protection" under specific Corn Laws dating back to 1815, and most recently amended just four years earlier in 1842.[51]

Moreover, three years later the newly responsible government of Baldwin and Lafontaine passed the Rebellion Losses Bill, which exacerbated tensions. It caused outrage among British merchants who were loyal to Britain and the Crown, because the bill failed to distinguish between the claims of 1837 rebel sympathizers and 1837 loyalists. Lord Elgin, the governor general of the day, who not only believed in responsible government but was under instruction to see responsible government introduced, signed the bill into law.[52]

This unfortunate conjunction of events led to the creation of a short-lived protest movement. The businesses of a number of prominent Montreal executives suffered when they had to compete on equal terms with their American counterparts in the British market. They were outraged by provisions for reimbursement for financial losses to rebels approved by the new "responsible" government, and a group of prominent Montrealers signed an Annexation Manifesto to join the United States. They went even further, burning the Parliament Buildings down, resulting in the permanent removal of the capital from Montreal, as well as threatening the governor general, the representative of the monarch, with violence. But with the return of good economic times, the threat of British retribution, and American indifference, support for annexation quickly dissipated.[53]

Perhaps more importantly, within a few months the economic and political environment changed sufficiently to make consolidation with the United States far less appealing. By 1859, British free trade and its industrial revolution had already increased the benefits of close association with the United Kingdom. Great Britain's leadership in technology, finance, trade, and trade liberalization towered over that of other nations and entailed many advantages for Canada. A large and well-regulated financial market, which relied on a commitment to the gold standard, a multifaceted banking sector, as well as robust accounting and other capital market governance institutions, made Great Britain the largest source of foreign capital for the rest of the world. Canada was part of a colonial empire that stretched across North America through Asia and Africa. And even though its star was also rising, the United States was still beset with great social, political, and financial instability.[54]

Despite that instability, closer economic ties with the United States helped fill the gap of lost colonial privileges. Lord Elgin, the governor general, encouraged the colonists to work with him in seeking reciprocity in "natural goods" between the United States and the British North American colonies. It was said that the 1854 Reciprocity Treaty was passed on a sea of champagne, provided by Canadian-hired lobbyists, or "congressional agents" as they were called at the time, to assist in gaining congressional support. Canadians needed no champagne incentive to bolster their enthusiasm for reciprocity because of the drop in exports to Britain. Times were good after the passage of the treaty, and Canadians shifted much of their trade from the United Kingdom to the United States.

On the political front, too, wounds were healed. In early July 1858, Alexander Tilloch Galt brought forward resolutions in the legislature for the first time calling for the confederation of all British North American provinces. Galt was born in England, of Scottish descent, in 1817. His father was involved in land development with the Canada Company. Galt visited Canada with his father in 1828 and again in 1835. He settled in Sherbrooke in the Eastern Townships of Lower Canada. And when he went into politics he always saw himself as part of the Protestant, Anglo minority in what became Quebec. Galt was a business executive and a railway promoter who went into politics as an independent member of the House of Assembly of the province of Canada in the 1840s. At that time, as Canadians were fighting for responsible government, political parties were just being formed. Those in favour of responsible government were called Reformers, and those who were less enthusiastic were called Conservatives. Galt

was an up-and-coming member when he made his speech propos-
ing confederation. Later he would become not only a Father of Confederation but also the individual most responsible for the financial
arrangements of the new federation and, briefly, the first minister
of finance of the new Dominion of Canada.[55] When Galt spoke, the
"House ... listened skeptically.... In the ensuing debate, member
after member assented in principle, but few thought the time had
come, especially for the union of all British America."[56] Two months
later, a delegation left for England to press for acceptance of a British
North American union. It consisted of Galt, George-Étienne Cartier,
the new premier and the most influential of the French-Canadian
politicians, and John Jones Ross, chairman of the executive council
and also president of the Grand Trunk Railway. Not the least of the
reasons to advocate for confederation, in the mind of Ross, was "that
a wider basis of credit than Canada offered was most desirable, if
not imperative, to keep the Grand Trunk solvent."[57] That same fall,
delegations from Nova Scotia and New Brunswick also travelled to
London to press their views.

From 1858 to 1867, events did not proceed in a straight line to Confederation, but rather many factors produced twists and turns. An
important impediment to the effective functioning of government was
political deadlock, which imperilled Galt's ambitious idea of a union of
the Canadas. By the early 1860s, the Grits, led by George Brown, owner
and publisher of the influential Toronto newspaper the *Globe*, held most
of the seats in Canada West, whereas Conservatives were stronger in
Canada East. The difficulty of either Conservatives or Reformers controlling Parliament for a lengthy period, coupled with the anxieties
arising from the presence of a powerful Union army on the border, led
Grit leader George Brown to approach Cartier and Macdonald with the
idea of a Great Coalition to break the political deadlock in June 1864.
The Conservatives accepted Brown's proposal, clearing the way for
negotiations toward Confederation.

The process of reaching an agreement occurred at two conferences
in the fall of 1864 – one in Charlottetown, Prince Edward Island, and
the other in Quebec City. The conference resolutions were debated in
the individual provincial assemblies but were not subject to a popular
vote. A final conference was held in the fall of 1866 in London. These
conferences resulted in agreement on the division of powers between
the federal and the provincial governments, as well as a consensus on
the financial basis of Confederation.

Federal Responsibility for Banking and
Financial Arrangements for the New Confederation

The British North America Act expressly gives to the Parliament of Canada exclusive legislative power over "banking, incorporation of banks, and the issue of paper money." The Constitution of the United States contains not a word about banks or banking, hence the control of these institutions might be deemed to fall wholly within state institutions.

William Munro, *American Influences on Canadian Government*, 1929

From the very beginning, the colonists wrestled with the perceived strengths and weaknesses of American federalism. Any federation begins with a division of powers between the different levels of government. In British North America, the view was widely held that the American form of federalism was flawed because it did not give residual powers to the federal authority, nor did it make banking a federal responsibility. The Civil War demonstrated the dangers of a strong attachment to one's state or province. As John A. Macdonald, then attorney general for Canada West, said of the United States at the Quebec City Conference in October 1864, "No general feeling of patriotism exists in the United States. In occasions of difficulty each man sticks to his individual State."[58] In terms of financial stability, the Fathers of Confederation were aware that the United States was not only notoriously prone to financial crises, which occurred with remarkable regularity about once a decade (1837, 1848, 1857) but also that the U.S. dollar had been trading at a discount to the Canadian dollar since shortly after the outbreak of the Civil War. Indeed, just a few months before the Charlottetown Conference, the U.S. dollar had declined to less than 38 cents Canadian as a consequence of the closing of the gold room in Washington when Confederate troops under General Jubal Early approached the capital.[59]

By the time the Fathers moved on to the second conference in Quebec City in October, further evidence surfaced demonstrating the fragility of the American financial system. In spite of the passage of a National Currency/Banking Act, there was vicious fighting in Virginia and Missouri, with not only bank failures but also thousands of deaths. The Canadians were well aware of the strife and troubles south of the border. The Toronto *Globe* contended that there seemed to be little room for dispute about shifting the distribution of powers such as trade, navigation, coinage, currency, or banking to the federal level.[60]

The authors of Canadian Confederation sought to avoid America's mistakes. Consistent with Galt's original proposals back in 1858,[61] the first three federal powers proposed were trade, currency, and banking.[62] Therefore, it is not surprising that by the time the Act was presented and passed by the imperial Parliament, currency and coinage, as well as banking, incorporation of banks, and the issue of paper money were federal functions.[63]

There is little written on the financial terms of Confederation, in stark contrast to American debates over significant compromises about the Constitution. All meetings were held behind closed doors, but this alone cannot explain the difference. The absence of primary source documents is astounding. Somehow the diaries, letters, essays, detailed reports, and newspaper articles, items that form the basis of American historiography for the Federalist period, are non-existent for Canada.[64] W.L. Morton in his Canadian Centenary Series volume *The Critical Years, 1857–1873* devoted just one sentence to the topic: "The financial arrangements, providing for the equalization of the burden of debt assumption and for payments to the province in lieu of direct taxes, which everyone assumed ... would be lightly levied, proceeded rapidly under Galt's guidance."[65] Determining a fiscal structure was not that easy. As in the United States, some of the fiercest debates over the form of the new government revolved upon financial issues, but unlike its southern counterpart, Canada lacks historical accounts similar to the Secret Debates of the 1787 Constitutional Proceedings in Philadelphia. However, Christopher Moore's recent work on the Quebec City Conference adds to our knowledge of Galt's success in substituting federal subsidies for local tariffs.[66]

Like Hamilton in the United States, Galt wanted debt concentrated within the central government. He made his objectives clear: "It is desirable that all Provinces should enter the Federation with the same liabilities, and secondly that all should be admitted on just principles so that no claim can hereafter be advanced on account of claims now existing." Samuel Leonard Tilley, leader of the New Brunswick delegation, a good negotiator, and a future Canadian finance minister, rebutted Galt's statement: "The Federal Government would take all the public property and proposed nothing in return for this."[67] Using his negotiating skills, Tilley ensured that New Brunswick received a generous per capita grant on entering Confederation.

Since it was thought that the central government would have greater responsibilities and higher revenue sources, it was decided that the

Table 2.1 Provincial Assets and Liabilities Assumed by Dominion at Confederation,
1 July 1867 ($000s)

Item	Canada	New Brunswick	Nova Scotia	Total
Debt assumed by dominion	76,160	7,900	9,034	93,094
Total assets taken by dominion to offset debts	4,098	107	303	4,508
Net debt assumed by the dominion	72,062	7,793	8,731	88,586
Debt allowances as per BNA Act	62,500	7,000	8,000	77,500
Total assets transferred to dominion	62,763	4,754	6,123	73,640

Source: Sirois, *Royal Commission on Dominion-Provincial Relations*, 42, table 5A.

dominion would assume most of the outstanding $93 million debt. All of the provinces had heavy debts, incurred principally for transportation. In the case of Canada, costs were incurred to build canals on the St Lawrence River and for the Welland Canal, which permitted access between Lakes Ontario and Erie, bypassing Niagara Falls. In both Canada and the Maritime provinces, railways were a major expense. "These dead weight debts ... seriously endangered the credit of the provinces in the London money market."[68] As a consequence a formula was developed to calculate debt allowances on a roughly equal per capita basis (see table 2.1).

Seventy-six per cent of all the debt assumed by the new dominion was for direct debt. The assets taken by the dominion to offset debts were principally cash (only a small amount in the case of New Brunswick) and sinking funds (only in the case of Canada). The largest assets transferred to the dominion and the only ones that affected all three provinces were direct investments and loans to railways. Responsibility for canals, harbour improvements, public buildings, roads, and bridges was also transferred to the federal government in Canada.

In terms of expenditures, there were only small differences among the three provinces if provincial and municipal expenditures were aggregated.[69] Over 80 per cent of all expenditures were for development and "traditional functions." Development included debt charges as the biggest cost, but other expenses included transportation, roads and bridges, public domain, and agriculture. "Traditional functions" covered primarily justice, legislation, and general government, but also included national defence. In addition there were modest costs for education and public welfare.

As the *Rowell-Sirois Report* noted, "The revenue systems of the three provinces were markedly similar and chiefly notable for their simplicity. The provinces relied almost entirely on indirect taxation ... their principal revenues were derived from customs, excise."[70] Since the new federal government was to assume almost all of the debt and the large expenditure functions, the provinces were limited to direct taxation, although such an arrangement was not common at that time. The provinces would receive per capita grants from the federal government to cover any shortfalls in provincial revenue. As Christopher Moore concludes, "The financial terms gave blunt evidence of Canadian primacy.... Had these fiscal proposals been introduced at the start of the conference, they might have launched intense, even fatal, disagreement. Even in the last days, with confederation almost a *fait accompli*, the financial terms provoked hard bargaining."[71]

Evolution of the Currency and Banking Systems

The chronic coin shortage also encouraged the introduction of paper money. The most famous issue is ... the card money of New France. Introduced in 1685, card money initially consisted of playing cards cut to different sizes according to denomination and signed by colonial officials.

James Powell, *A History of the Canadian Dollar*

Canada had banks and currency before it had a formalized banking system and before it became a country. Its pre-British financial system was shaped by the fact that among the French there was a deep distrust of paper currency. When Canada was a French colony, English ships often blockaded the St Lawrence River. In desperation, people used playing cards for currency, from 1685 to 1719, and from 1729 to the 1750s, and the result was significant inflation, which further undermined faith in paper currency of any kind. While there were no banks in eighteenth-century British North America, merchants played the role of financial intermediaries.

After the passage of the Constitution Act of 1791, there was some progress in the standardization of currency among the colonies. After a few false starts a banking system was established. Dealing with currency first, a specific problem was that there were two different ratings for currency: one based in Halifax and the other in York (modern-day Toronto), and both were based on foreign coins. The Halifax rating valued one Spanish silver dollar, the most common coin in circulation at the time, at five shillings. The York rating, which was introduced into Upper Canada by Loyalists arriving from the United States, valued that same Spanish silver dollar at eight shillings.[72] Another issue that emerged in the early decades of the nineteenth century was whether to use dollars and cents or pounds, shillings, and pence. As banks were incorporated they tended to use both currencies in the province of Canada but the Atlantic colonies stayed with pounds, shilling, and pence.[73]

On the banking scene there were two early attempts to found banks in Canada before the first bank, the Bank of Montreal, was established in 1817. In 1792 a group of Montreal-based merchants tried to establish the Canada Banking Company. The attempt was premature in that in Lower Canada there was an objection among French Canadians, based on their experience with playing card currency, to any form of paper money. In the English settlements, while there was need for a bank, there was insufficient stability.[74]

In 1808 there was another attempt to establish a bank, and the Montreal merchants had support from Quebec City merchants. This attempt failed as well, but copies of the proposed charter survived and were compared with those of the First Bank of the United States (BUS) founded by Alexander Hamilton. "The Canadian bill is a copy ... of the American Act. It shows that the Canadians ... were quite under the influence of the American ideas as expressed in Hamilton's plan.... The subsequent history of Canadian banking shows clearly that these ideas were permanently adopted. They became the basis of the Canadian system."[75] As Adam Shortt noted in his classic *History of North American Banking*,

> The commerce of Canada ... was closely connected to the United States. Many ideas came through the United States to Canada, especially to Montreal. Quite a number of the merchants ... had come from the American colonies before the separation from England; many others came after the separation ... There was little change in the social, economic and municipal ideas in which they had been trained. These ideas ... were as well suited to the natural conditions of Canada as they were to those of the United States. Those who came directly from Britain found their circumstances so completely altered that they naturally laid aside their old ideas and adopted others better suited to the customs and conditions of a new country ... Montreal became the natural port of entry and outlet for Vermont and north eastern New York ... Montreal was thus the Canadian city which had most constant and intimate relations with the American Republic.[76]

During the early stages of Canadian banking, several hallmarks of Hamilton's ideas were accepted without question by Canadians. Meanwhile, some of these same ideas were only partly accepted – or some not accepted at all – by Scottish and other banking systems. The first was the importance of limited liability, joint-stock banking. Well into the nineteenth century, most countries allowed only partnerships, with full partner liability, to take deposits and issue notes. Hamilton was one of the first government regulators to encourage the formation of banks with capital from shareholders, some of whom were sufficiently passive and distant to tolerate full liability for a bank's actions. Although American and Canadian bankers instituted various schemes to protect the interests of depositors against unscrupulous or incompetent shareholders and managers, limited liability and widespread shareholding was accepted broadly in the United States and completely in Canada. The second key takeaway from Hamilton was the importance of some sort of national banking system. But whereas throughout American history, national banking was performed only by a central bank – and that only intermittently – in Canada commercial banks were never restricted to a region or province.

In contrast to the two earlier failed attempts, much attention has been paid to the establishment of the Bank of Montreal (BMO). The founding of the bank was prompted in part by a desire for paper currency, which had been whetted by the experience with army bills during the War of 1812. By 1816, all army bills had been redeemed successfully, creating an urgent need for a replacement currency. In November 1817 the Bank of Montreal opened its doors, with articles of association but without a charter, which it did not obtain for five years.[77] The key individual involved in the founding of the bank, although he never served on its board, was John Richardson. Born in Scotland, Richardson apprenticed in Schenectady, New York, and established a business in South Carolina. He was thirty-three when he arrived in Montreal in 1787. There he became involved in the western Great Lakes trade. He was also involved in the two earlier attempts to found a bank in 1792 and 1808. The original share capital was fixed at £250,000. Although the United States had 392 banks at the time,[78] it should be remembered that there were no banks in America when its population was 800,000, as was Canada's in 1817, and that BMO share capital was roughly ten times the American average capital at the time. This was probably due to understandable concerns about bank solvency in light of recent U.S. and British experiences and the lack of dependable regulation. BMO's founders were conservative in other ways, preferring to avoid the banking model that entailed investing in new speculative ventures rather than lending short-term funds to established companies.[79]

British North American and American economic affairs were conjoined, helping to tie the new bank to the United States in many ways. America's experiences with banking were proximate and well known, and they seemed more relevant to Canada than those in Europe. Before the building of the Erie Canal, Montreal served as the metropolitan centre for much of the trade with Vermont, New Hampshire, and New York. Montreal merchants did more business with the United States than Great Britain, and the region's readers looked to Boston journals. Nearly half of the new shares were sold to wealthy families in Boston, New York, and Philadelphia, but voting was restricted to Montreal residents and British subjects.[80] The bank founders also looked to the United States for staff training, their first notes, and the plates on which they were printed, as well as for personnel – the first teller was an American.[81]

Immediately following the establishment of the Bank of Montreal, a flurry of activity ensued with the founding of four new banks. Two were created in Lower Canada – the Quebec Bank in Quebec City and the Bank of Canada in Montreal, founded by American speculators trying to cash in on Montreal's post-war prosperity. The other two were established in Upper Canada – the Bank of Kingston and the Bank of Upper Canada. However, the first bank to receive a charter in British North America was the Bank of New Brunswick in 1820.[82] By 1822 all five banks in the Canadas had charters. But the Bank of Kingston failed to raise the necessary capital and therefore forfeited its charter. Meanwhile the Bank of Upper Canada, which was closely associated with the political establishment, did receive its charter, which was closer than any of the others to the Hamiltonian model in that it involved government investment in the bank.[83]

Over the next two decades, several banks came onto the scene with different ownership structures. In Nova Scotia the Halifax Banking Company was formed in 1825 as a partnership, without a charter, and operated for fifty years, even though two earlier attempts to charter banks – in 1801 and 1811 – had failed. The partners were members of the Halifax establishment and blocked other bank entrants until the Bank of Nova Scotia obtained a charter in 1832.[84] That same year the Commercial Bank of the Midland District was incorporated in

Kingston. The Commercial Bank became one of the two major banks in Upper Canada for the next forty-five years. Five years later, in 1837 the Bank of British North America, a Montreal-based British bank with a royal charter, arrived on the scene. It quickly established branches in all the colonies. The Bank of British North America was an example of a British overseas bank, a free-standing company.[85] Many others existed elsewhere in the empire. The Colonial Bank, for example, was established at the same time but focused on the West Indies, with agencies in Saint John and Halifax.[86] These British overseas banks were created in the 1830s. The owners were based largely in the United Kingdom, and the goal was to establish overseas branches that were managed from London.[87]

Other Canadian banks were incorporated. Some failed, while others had their charters repealed. By 1840 when the Act of Union was passed, there were ten banks in the Canadas – five based in Upper Canada and five in Lower Canada. The two largest were the Bank of Montreal and the Bank of British North America, with branches throughout British North America. Each of these banks had more than £500,000 in paid-up capital. In the next tier with £200,000 in paid-up capital were Ontario's Bank of Upper Canada and the Commercial Bank of the Midland District, and Montreal's City Bank.[88] BMO had three branches in 1840 – Quebec City, Kingston, and Ottawa – having closed its Toronto branch in 1823. In the 1840s it added twelve more branches. By comparison, in 1837 America had 729 banks for sixteen million people, but Canada's bank capital of $12.5 million was roughly equal to that of the United States on a per capita basis, a trend that would continue into the future.

During the period from 1791 to 1841, the Treasury lords in the United Kingdom controlled colonial banking laws, although in British North America the reporting format was based on the common practice used in Massachusetts. This inevitably led not only to slow decision making but also often to inappropriate decisions for lack of understanding of local conditions. In 1836, for example, in anticipation of problems from the speculative boom of the time, the lords acted. They did not merely disallow a number of bills. which would have significantly increased the banking capital of the province, they simply sent the bills back for reconsideration.[89]

The year 1837 was a difficult time in North America. President Jackson's decision to veto the extension of the Second Bank of the United States led to loose lending practices in the United States and a significant economic downturn. The contagion spread to Canada, accompanied by poor harvests and political insurrections. As a consequence, banks in Lower Canada, like banks in the United States, suspended specie payment, that is, they would not provide specie for paper currency on demand. This lack of convertibility came to Lower Canada earlier and lasted longer than in Upper Canada, although no longer than in the United States. However, the Canadian banks did contract credit, and that contributed to the economic downturn.[90]

As the period of the separation of the two Canadas drew to a close, the government of Upper Canada made an important decision: it sold its Bank of Upper Canada stock and thereby severed its formal link with it. The government did so because it was extremely hard-pressed financially and needed the money from the sale of the stock.[91]

But in the third and fourth decades of the nineteenth century, the Canadian banking system had other, broader problems. Many observers noticed great differences in the availability of credit, population density, and property values between New York State and Lower Canada, some of which probably resulted from banking practices. Lower Canada (Quebec) suffered from severe shortages of money. There, banknotes did not circulate beyond towns, interest payments were still forbidden by priests, and specie hoarding was commonplace. The British governor general blamed Canada's backwardness on its financial system, singling out the French influence.[92]

With political union in 1841, currency reform proceeded more quickly. This led to a new standardized rating in 1842 for both a British gold sovereign and a US$10 gold eagle. But two other questions emerged. Should Canada adopt a decimal-based currency, and should government-issued paper currency replace or be used side-by-side with chartered bank currency? In the early 1850s the colonies decided to keep government accounts in decimal currency, but the British government delayed passage of the legislation until 1854. In the end, the legislation actually allowed both decimal and British units but was amended four years later to permit dollars and cents only. The other British North American colonies followed suit, and by 1871 decimalization was the rule.[93]

In 1841 Governor General Lord Sydenham proposed a government issue of paper money, but the proposal was rejected by the assembly. Since Canada had achieved responsible government, the decision of the elected assembly overruled the wishes of the British governor general. In 1860 Alexander Galt, who was now finance minister for the province of Canada, again attempted to establish a government currency but was unsuccessful for lack of support in the assembly.[94] However, in 1866 the measure was approved but in a somewhat different form and with strenuous opposition. Unlike Galt's 1860 proposal, in this case the banks were not required to give up issuing their own currency.[95] Reform leader George Brown strongly opposed this measure because he felt it would be "ruinous to banks…. It was far more important that capital should be easily available to 'industrial interests' than it be kept for the exchequer through the government note scheme, just so that the finance minister need not borrow abroad."[96]

Throughout this period, while the Canadian banking system continued to be under the purview of the Colonial Office, carefully monitored by the Treasury lords, "not all of the regulations framed by the British lords of treasury in 1840, as norms of colonial banking legislation, were adopted by the Canadian committee on banking and currency."[97]

In 1850 Francis Hincks, who was the inspector general (minister of finance) and future minister of finance of the new Dominion of Canada, followed the example set in New York State by introducing free banking into Canada. Free banking permitted the establishment of a bank with no branches without an examination of the suitability of the applicant.[98] This measure was frowned upon in the United Kingdom, and few such banks were established. But the failure of free banking in Canada, compared to its success in the United States, relates less to imperial influence and more to the fact that in Canada free banks had to compete with chartered banks, whereas in America they did not.[99] Another indication of the growing autonomy in the Canadian colony was the decision of Galt, the provincial minister of finance, to appoint a select committee on banking and currency in 1859.

Canadian banks experienced two major economic downturns during this time – the crisis of 1847 and the collapse of 1857–8. While there were no banking failures in 1848, the banks' cautious approach to lending during the crisis contributed to hardships felt by farmers and merchants. Blame was cast on the banks. The collapse of 1857 and the following depression of 1858 are often referred to as the first worldwide depression. The boom in the mid-1850s and the subsequent crash in 1857 took a particularly harsh toll on banks in Canada. The banks restricted their operations in a move that allowed them to avoid suspensions, for a time at least. Adam Shortt argues that the banks' restriction of operations may have actually done more damage than a temporary suspension of payments would have, because it brought legitimate trade to a standstill, preventing a recovery. He contrasts this with the United States' banks, which suspended payments but managed to facilitate a recovery under normal trade conditions without abnormal restrictions of their discounts.[100] The Panic of 1857 is cited as the beginning of the end for the Bank of Upper Canada, the oldest bank in Ontario, which finally failed in 1866. All things considered, "its bankruptcy caused little concern."[101]

The Canadian banking system grew and prospered in spite of the panics, the bifurcated regulations between imperial authority and colonial legislature, abolition of the Corn Laws in 1846, reciprocity with the United States in 1854, and then the 1866 abrogation of reciprocity by the United States. While there were no new banks until the mid-1850s, by 1867 there were twice as many banks as there had been a quarter-century earlier, in spite of the failure of the original bank in Canada West – the Bank of Upper Canada. The other major Canada West bank, the Commercial Bank, was in suspension and would be absorbed by the Merchants Bank in 1868. There were a number of other smaller failures: the Zimmerman Bank; the Bank of Western Canada, which was wound up in 1860; the Bank of Brantford, withdrawing from business in 1863; and the short-lived International and Colonial Banks in 1859.[102] All of these failures were caused more by "mistakes and misapprehensions, peculiar to the institutions directly involved" rather than "world-wide ... financial and speculative upheavals."[103] Table 2.2 provides the reader with a picture of Canadian banking progress between 1841 and 1867. The dramatic growth as evidenced by the increase in paid-up capital stock is striking. A notable feature is the shift from British pounds to Canadian dollars.

On the liability side, what is most striking is the dramatic increase in deposits, particularly those bearing interest. On the asset side, what is noticeable is the increased diversification. While discounted notes and bills were still the major asset class, there had also been major growth in government securities. What is less obvious is the need for flexibility in notes because of the highly cyclical nature of the economy, with demand peaking in September and October and the trough typically occurring in May. Another striking feature is the dramatic increase in government securities, often to support railway enterprises. Breckenridge contends that this is evidence of the beginnings of "a financial as well as a commercial bank."[104]

Another notable feature was the dramatic increase in bank branches from just a handful in 1840 to well over 100 in 1867. Most of the branches were in Ontario, with fewer than a dozen in Quebec, nine in the

Table 2.2 Canadian Banks, 1841–71

	1841	1851	1861	1871
Number of banks	9	8	16	19
Currency	£	£	$	$
Capital stock paid up (000)	2,276.7	2,897.6	24,411.0	26.618.7
Capital stock authorized by act	0	0	35,266.7	37,466.7
Liabilities				
Promissory non-interest bearing notes	919.0	1,623.4	11,780.4	8,312.4
Cash deposits bearing interest	54.9	565.3	9,545.3	13,938.4
Cash deposits not bearing interest	786.5	1,623.4	9,176.0	13,938.4
Balances due other banks	340.8	271.6	444.1	2,771.9
Net profits or contingent funds	146.4	59.8	0	0
Dividends unpaid	21.0	0.9	0	0
Total other than stock	2,268.6	3,647.5	30,945.8	39,788.6
Assets				
Notes and bills discounted	3,282.2	5,574.0	39,588.8	48,158.4
Coins, bullion and provincial notes	392.5	413.4	4,960.4	7,384.2
Balances due from other banks and foreign agencies	203.6	218.5	4,157.3	5,068.6
Other debts due to the bank not included elsewhere	0	0	4,064.4	2,297.4
Government securities	24.7	43.8	2,736.0	6,142.6
Landed or other property of the bank	46.1	135.3	1,429.3	1,510.6
Promissory notes or bills of other banks	148.3	144.4	1,136.2	1,651.8
Total	4,097.4	6,529.4	58,072.4	72,213.6

Source: Breckenridge, *History of Banking in Canada*, 85.

Maritimes, and two in BC, which was not yet part of Canada, although it was a British North American colony. The Bank of Montreal alone accounted for over one-third of all branches – primarily in Ontario but by 1867 in Atlantic Canada, including St John's and Halifax.[105]

The First Bank Act of 1869

When I go into a bank I get rattled. The clerks rattle me; the wickets rattle me; the sight of the money rattles me; everything rattles me.

Stephen Leacock, *Literary Lapses*

The new government of Canada, created by legislation known as the British North America Act, now had legislative responsibility for banking in Nova Scotia and New Brunswick as well as in Quebec and Ontario. The minister of finance responsible for oversight of banking,

Alexander Tilloch Galt, the man who first proposed Confederation, resigned his office on 7 November 1867 – four months and one week after the new country came into being. He did so because he felt that the government should have provided financial assistance to allow the Commercial Bank, of which he was a shareholder, to continue. When cabinet refused, Galt felt betrayed and resigned.[106]

Prime Minister Macdonald turned to his closest friend in cabinet, Sir John Rose, to take Galt's place. Rose was one of those rare personalities in politics, more a businessman than a politician, with close ties to both the Hudson's Bay Company and the Bank of Montreal. "His two-year occupancy of the finance portfolio was dominated by a great debate over the nature of the dominion's first banking system. At issue was whether the individual Canadian banks should continue to possess the right of free note issue, a profitable activity, or whether there should be a state currency backed by government securities."[107] John Rose and Edwin King, the aggressive general manager (in modern-day parlance he would be called the CEO) of the Bank of Montreal, favoured the American National Bank Act of 1863. This approach provided that the government would issue all the currency rather than the banks. Indeed King had gone on record in regard to his views about the American Act as early as November 1867, and those views were shared by his counterpart at the Bank of British North America.[108]

In addition to favouring a replacement of banknotes with government notes, Rose also wanted to discourage branch banking – and encourage the creation of small country banks, leaving the Bank of Montreal in the pre-eminent position. Both the House of Commons and the Senate reviewed the alternative banking proposals. Neither body favoured the idea of the government becoming the sole issuer of paper currency.

On 1 June 1869 Rose introduced Canada's first Bank Act bill in the House of Commons. The bill was seconded by none other than the prime minister. The bill ignored "the recommendations of the experts who testified to the committee of the house ... called for Dominion bank legislation upon the model of the 'national bank act' of the United States. In substance it was identical to the proposal put forward by Edwin King, the general manager, and approved by the board of the Bank of Montreal in November, 1867."[109]

As explained in the *Dictionary of Canadian Biography*, "One day of debate, 1 June, confirmed the strength of the opposition.... The struggle has been interpreted as one between Montreal, seeking to maintain its position as the country's financial centre, and the rising commercial and financial aspirations of Toronto."[110] Thus the battle was joined. The lead story of 3 June in the *Globe*, a Toronto-based newspaper, was "The debate upon Mr Rose's Banking resolution ... proved that the Ministerial scheme is no more popular in the House than in the country."[111] A day later, the *Globe* continued its attack: "The Government Banking scheme has done a vast deal of injury by the alarm which it has spread throughout the country."

Opposition to the legislation was not restricted to the *Globe*. There was a strong feeling that the legislation was anti-Ontario. William McMaster was a prominent Ontario businessman and senator, a director of the Ontario Bank, the Wellington, Grey and Bruce Railway, the Canada Landed Credit Company, and the Toronto and Georgian Bay Canal Company (after 1865 the Huron and Ontario Ship Canal Company).[112] In 1864 he was appointed to the board of the Bank of Montreal, the most prestigious board appointment of the day. However, he felt that the Montreal bank was restricting credit to Ontario business in order to feed the provincial government, whose business the bank had acquired. In 1866 both McMaster and the Toronto branch manager of the Montreal bank resigned and started the Canadian Bank of Commerce. The new bank began operation in 1867 and by June 1869 had sufficient prestige in the Toronto community to raise $2 million in capital, which rendered it one of the two largest Toronto banks, although it was only about one-third the size of the Bank of Montreal. Rather than openly opposing the Bank Act, McMaster left that to George Hague, the cashier (general manager) of the Bank of Toronto, a relatively small Ontario bank with paid-up capital of only $800,000. The attacks of the *Globe* and the opposition of men like McMaster and Hague and indeed most of the Ontario business community, regardless of party, were enough to have the first Bank Act bill withdrawn "temporarily" on 15 June.

As the new Dominion of Canada approached its second birthday, it had legislative responsibility for regulating banks, but it did not have a Bank Act. What no one anticipated was that the fledgling country would soon lose its second minister of finance. "Rose, always closely identified with Montreal's interests, felt discredited by the rebuff to his legislation. It led directly to his decision, effective in September, to resign his portfolio, leave Canada, and enter the world of international finance."[113]

The demise of the first Bank Act also led to the departure of Canada's most powerful banker. "King's image as a ruthless businessman undermined his usefulness to the Bank of Montreal. It was no coincidence, then, that in October 1869 King submitted his resignation as general manager to assume the more honorary position of president."[114] Soon after, he left Canada for London.[115]

As the summer of 1869 approached, Prime Minister Macdonald faced important challenges, which included but were not limited to demands for "better terms" for Nova Scotia, the most separatist of the provinces, where many wished to repeal the union; troubles in the Red River country from Metis who were upset with Confederation and with the land surveyors on their territory, which would lead to armed resistance and place the West in jeopardy; and the desire of the Liberal opposition for a "Zollverein" (an economic coalition) with the United States. In addition Macdonald faced the challenge of finding a new minister of finance, one capable of getting a Bank Act passed, a daunting task to say the least.

Although the challenge to find the right leaders and adjust the balance of public and private responsibility would continue in both Canada and the United States, by 1869 each had laid the basic political framework for its financial system for decades to come. The events and actions of the 1860s had set the stage for a remarkable, albeit choppy, period of economic growth.

CHAPTER THREE

The Maturing:
1869–1914

Two Nineteenth-Century Emerging
and Maturing Markets

Between 1885 and 1914, Canada's development strategy began to yield dividends. The population doubled, economic growth skyrocketed, and the "last best west" came into its own. With cities emerging as buzzing hives of activity, nearly 40 per cent of Canada's 8 million inhabitants lived in urban areas by 1914. Such a massive transformation brought new tensions and exacerbated old ones.

Margaret Conrad, *Concise History of Canada*

The years between 1870 and 1914 were momentous in the annals of American and Canadian history, but the pace of change in the two countries was not always in sync. With some alternation of dates and populations, the epigraph above could have been written about America (see appendix 3).

In the United States, the end of the Civil War and the North's victory cleared the way for a "reconstruction" boom and the political will to advance growth based on immigration, infrastructure construction, western expansion, protectionism, export, and innovative technologies. From 1870 to 1914 GDP grew nearly fivefold; population increased by 150 per cent, and per capita GDP nearly doubled. The Dow Jones Industrial Average (DJIA) – a measure of stock market performance created in 1884 with twelve stocks, ten of which were railroads – nearly doubled in its first thirty years of existence, despite dividends considered high by late twentieth-century standards.[1]

To be sure, this period was not uniformly prosperous and harmonious. It was punctuated by panic, and throughout much of the 1870s was often referred to as the Great Depression or Long Depression, a term most economists reject.

For the United States, the opening of the West helped defuse social tension brought on by the downturn and a veritable revolution in business.[2] It was during this period that the two countries and much of the rest of the world experienced the transformation in distribution and production, a creation of large and vastly more complex business organizations, spirited by the construction of rail and telegraph lines, and accompanied by financial and management innovation.[3]

Although the basic rail network east of the Mississippi River had been laid down by the time of the Civil War,[4] from 1870 to 1910 the quantity of mainline railroad track in operation increased from 53,000 to 266,000 miles, requiring a huge investment of capital and management. With the help of government subsidies through financial assistance and land, productivity doubled with added scale and more efficient equipment.[5] As late as 1917, U.S. railroads possessed assets of more than $500 million, making them far larger in terms of assets than General Electric ($232 million), Ford ($166 million), and International Harvester ($265 million) – all firms created during this same vibrant era. Only U.S. Steel, the largest manufacturer in the United States, with assets of $2,450 million, approached the largest rail line in assets, the Pennsylvania, with $2,663 million in assets.[6] As Alfred Chandler argued, the last decades of the nineteenth and first decades of the twentieth century witnessed the birth of large, integrated distribution and manufacturing enterprises in many places. However, as others have pointed out, despite this transformation, America still had many farmers and small companies whose need for financing differed greatly from the new corporate behemoths.[7] Remarkably, all of this economic development occurred with little or no fundamental change in America's financial system.

If anything, this period was even more remarkable in Canada than it was in the United States, perhaps in part because of the soundness of the financial system. In 1869 the new Dominion of Canada acquired Rupert's Land from the Hudson's Bay Company, in the largest real estate transaction in the history of the world. Rupert's Land was nearly twice the size of the Louisiana Purchase.[8] Moreover, prodded by imperial authorities, the new dominion assumed responsibility in 1871 for British Columbia, on the West Coast, with its substantial debt, in return for a promise to build a railway to the Pacific in ten years. This new railway would add a third east-west rail line in North America to augment the two lines south of the border.

Many of the political changes in Canada paralleled those in the United States. In 1878, Sir John A. Macdonald announced a three-part National Policy, very similar to the policies approved by the Republican Party at its 1860 Convention in Chicago. The policies included a protective tariff, a railway to the Pacific, and free land given to citizens to promote settlement in the West. The tariff came first, quickly followed by the creation of the Canadian Pacific Railway. Although the homestead legislation was on the books as early as 1872, settlement of the West would take longer.

Despite these achievements, in 1896 the Conservative Party of Canada, which had been in power for all but four years since Confederation, was replaced by the Liberal Party under Wilfrid Laurier. The first French Canadian to be prime minister, Laurier was a sixth-generation Canadian who became a lawyer and a politician. Knighted shortly after becoming prime minister, Sir Wilfrid served a longer consecutive term (fifteen years) than any other Canadian prime minister. His political success should be seen in the context of the wheat boom, which began at about the time he was elected.

The years from 1896 to the First World War saw a huge increase in wheat and flour production, as the result of three factors: the closing of the U.S. frontier; the development of a new strain of wheat, called Marquis, which not only produced a higher yield but also developed faster in the short Prairie growing season; and technological change, specifically in the form of the Hungarian milling process, which permitted Manitoba #1 Hard to be ground into usable flour. The wheat boom ignited extraordinary Canadian growth. Whereas from 1870 to 1896 Canadian population growth lagged behind the American, from 1896 to 1914 its growth rate passed that of its southern neighbour (see appendix 3). In both countries, a shift in distribution accompanied the increase in population. New cities such as Winnipeg emerged on the booming Canadian Prairie.

By the First World War, approximately 40 per cent of Canada's and America's populations lived in urban environments (areas of more than 25,000 people). Whereas Canadian per capita income had fallen as a percentage of American during the first twenty years of Confederation, by 1914 Canadian income grew to 83 per cent of the American level, up from 65 per cent less than two decades before. During the wheat boom the Canadian economy grew nearly twice as fast as that of the United States, such that by the outbreak of the First World War the volume of Canadian wheat exports was as large as that of the United States. The period from 1896 to 1914 also saw manufacturing replace agriculture as the major industry as Canada urbanized; cities such as Montreal and Toronto experienced explosive growth. While the United Kingdom was still the main recipient of exports and source of foreign investment, the United States passed the United Kingdom in the 1880s as a source of imports into Canada.

While much has been written by Canadian historians about Canada's development strategy that resulted in what is popularly known as the Laurier boom or the wheat boom, relatively little has been written about the financial problems during the first decade of the twentieth century and the fallout of the "irrational exuberance" of those years. The first decade was second only to the 1940s in economic growth, but there were also problems, which included the stock market crash of 1902–4, the credit crisis of 1907, and bank failures in 1908. Although one of the worst economic crises of the twentieth century for Canada and well known in the United States, the 1907 Panic has not received much attention in Canada. In the mid-decade, Canada experienced several bank failures, the largest of which were the Sovereign and Ontario Banks. The dramatic railway building that contributed to the boom, a tenfold increase in trackage between 1871 and 1912, also contributed to the economic fallout during the First World War, which required government nationalization of two of the three transcontinental railways. Moreover, the boom contributed materially to the post–First World War bust and even to the Great Depression.[9]

Despite these problems, many Canadian companies had an international profile. Those such as the Canadian Pacific Railway and the large, international public utility Brazilian Traction Light Heat & Power were popular stocks traded on the London Stock Exchange.[10] Others, such as Montreal Light Heat and Power and Niagara Falls Power Company, were leaders in domestic and cross-border electrical utility development. This emerging field revolutionized production and people's lives around the turn of the century but required huge amounts of capital.[11] Domestically the major industries were coal and steel manufacturing on Cape Breton Island and at Sault Ste Marie in northern Ontario; mining on the Pacific Coast; and the manufacturing of agricultural implements manufacturer in the British Empire, Massey Harris, which exported product to Germany and the United Kingdom, was the largest such manufacturer in the British Empire. Circa 1910, however, many non-financial Canadian companies remained small, compared with American, even adjusting for the relative size of the economy and populations, and in some important growth sectors of the twentieth century Canadian companies were not represented at all. As will be discussed, banking organizations were a significant exception to this generalization.

Banking activity exploded in both countries, but in different forms. These two nations were well ahead of many countries in approving and expanding joint-stock banks. The increase in bank branches had a major impact on the Canadian financial system's extraordinary economic growth. During much of the nineteenth century, in many countries, small unit banks were still the norm. Canada may have led the world in branch banking. Without branching, except in California and some Southern states, U.S. banks tended to be much smaller than Canadian ones, but there were many more separate banks. At the turn of the century, nearly 10,000 state and national banks operated in the United States.[12] During this period, well ahead of the United States, Canada had already decided that banking and currency would be under federal authority. While those responsibilities were enshrined in the British North America Act, there was disagreement on the precise nature of the Bank Act. The powerful Bank of Montreal favoured the American model of the 1863 National Bank Act, while most banks in Ontario and the Maritimes were strongly opposed to it. It would take four years and three ministers of finance to pass the Bank Act of 1871, which, nearly a century and a half later, remains the basis for banking in Canada.

Attracting foreign capital was crucial for both American and Canadian economic growth. With both countries running trade deficits during most of the period, banks played an important role in managing foreign investor expectations, but in very different ways. Understandably investors were reluctant to invest in distant projects managed in far-off, unfamiliar places, thus creating opportunities for those individuals inclined to be strong intermediaries. During the last three decades of the nineteenth century Canadian and American interest rates fell and the spread between their rates and British rates fell, presenting a measure of success. The declines were choppier (as were short-term rates) in the United States, but yields generally were lower than those in Canada.[13]

The Battle of the Bank Acts, 1869–71

Out of virtual chaos which had been growing more complex and more embittered for years, Hincks alone proved his capacity to bring order, to reconcile conflicting interests, and to establish Canadian banking and currency upon a basis which has endured ever since, and is still the pride of the country.

Adam Shortt, *History of Canadian Currency and Banking*

While the first two years of his administration had been good politically and personally for Canada's first prime minister, there were clouds on the horizon. In spite of having attracted Joseph Howe, the leading Nova Scotia opponent of Confederation into the federal cabinet by offering Nova Scotia "better terms," Macdonald still faced a strong separatist sentiment in that province. In addition, trouble was brewing in the Red River settlement in the West with the Metis population. The Metis did not like the arrival of Anglo-Protestant settlers, who had begun to trickle in with the news of the acquisition of Rupert's Land by the new Dominion of Canada from the Hudson's Bay Company. Nor did they like the surveyors who arrived to resurvey their river lots. Louis Riel, the young Metis leader, placed his foot on the surveyor's chain and stopped the process. In a matter of months there would be armed resistance, and the whole future of the West would be in doubt. As if this weren't enough, efforts to renegotiate a reciprocity treaty with the United States were going nowhere.

In spite of these clouds, John A. Macdonald had to turn to his trade, what he called "cabinet making." He had to appoint a new minister of finance, his third in three years, as a result of the resignations of Alexander Tilloch Galt and John Rose. In the British parliamentary system, which Canada had adopted, the members of cabinet are selected from the legislative branch. So rather than having the whole country from which to choose, the prime minister was required to select someone from the 252 members of Parliament (180 MPs and 72 senators). In fact, his choice was even more limited, because cabinet members were normally selected from the House of Commons, and only 100 MPs were his supporters.

The task of cabinet making also required complicated trade-offs in terms of region (Maritimes vs Quebec vs Ontario), ethnicity (French vs English), religion (Roman Catholic vs Protestant), and perhaps most important of all, party affiliation. Macdonald's government was a coalition of Conservatives and Liberals, who used to be called Reformers. Of the original thirteen cabinet members, five were from Ontario, of whom three were Liberals and two Conservatives. Conservatives believed in a positive role for the state, the building of railways, and settling the West. In this regard, they were conservatives like Alexander Hamilton and Abraham Lincoln. They also believed in strong ties with Great Britain and the monarchy. In Quebec their supporters were known as *bleus* and they had the powerful support of the Roman Catholic Church. Liberals, sometimes called "Clear Grits," believed in small government, opposed patronage, and objected to Roman Catholic separate schools, which the Conservatives supported. The Liberal allies in Quebec were called *rouges* and were seen as radical in wanting to limit the influence of the Roman Catholic Church over politics.

Even with these limitations, Macdonald had options for the all-important portfolio of minister of finance. They included bringing back the first minister of finance, Sir Alexander Galt, who also represented the English Protestant minority in Quebec; Sir George Étienne Cartier, the leader of the French in cabinet; and Leonard Tilley from New Brunswick, who was minister of customs and would eventually become minister of finance in 1873. In addition there was Richard Cartwright, a future Liberal minister of finance, who was a Conservative Member of Parliament (MP) but not yet in cabinet.

The Montreal press endorsed Cartier as an excellent candidate to prevent the portfolio from going to someone from Ontario.[14] Originally "Tilley had been touted as the logical candidate for minister of finance since he was most senior in terms of service. He certainly thought himself competent for the position, but it is doubtful whether Macdonald gave a second thought to a non-Canadian for such an important position."[15] Nor is there any evidence that Macdonald gave any further thought to Tilley for the position in 1869. Among Conservative members in the House of Commons who were not in cabinet, one stood out, at least in John A.'s own mind, and that was Richard Cartwright, the MP for Lennox, a riding situated next to Kingston, which was represented by none other than John A.

The Contributions of the Third Minister of Finance

For a variety of reasons Macdonald chose to go outside Parliament and offer the position to Sir Francis Hincks, who happened to be visiting Canada at the time. Hincks had had a distinguished career having served as both inspector general (Minister of Finance) and as premier in the pre-Confederation province of Canada. He had been out of the country for fifteen years, having served successively as imperial governor of Barbados and the Windward Islands and of British Guiana.

Most historians attribute Macdonald's decision to a desire to beef up the Liberal side of his Liberal Conservative coalition. If that was his motive he failed miserably, because many Liberals, particularly George Brown of the *Globe*, attacked the appointment viciously. Meanwhile, the Conservatives were never more than lukewarm to Hincks. However Hincks had two important advantages. He was not from Montreal and he "had financial experience, which suited him for the position of Minister of Finance."[16]

When Hincks was sworn in as Canada's third minister of finance in just over two years, he faced a confused and complicated situation. In Ontario things were particularly unsettled because of the failure of the two largest, oldest Ontario banks, the Bank of Upper Canada and the Commercial Bank of the Midland District. There was a bitter and fractured relationship between Canada's largest and most powerful bank, the Bank of Montreal, and most of the other Canadian banks. A major issue was whether the banks would be allowed to continue to issue their own notes, or whether note issue would be taken over by the government. Furthermore the separatist-leaning province of Nova Scotia had views about currency that were different from those of the new government.

From the time of Hincks's appointment to the following February, when he tabled his proposals in the House of Commons, Hincks was in almost continuous motion. In addition to running for elective office[17] he held numerous conferences with the different stakeholders. The House reconvened on 15 February. The day before, Hincks had given the powerful Bank of Montreal six months' notice terminating its special status. No longer would BMO be (1) overseer of note issues, not just its own but those of others as well; (2) exclusive banker to the government, i.e., sole depository of government money; and (3) fiscal agent for the colony with the Treasury in London. As minister of finance, Hincks could open government business to all banks.

On 1 March 1871 Hincks "revealed the new policy of the government to an expectant House."[18] His challenge was not only to establish both a single currency and a general banking policy but also to settle the controversial issue of who could issue bank notes. "He had ... managed to get the general consent of the banks to these measures."[19] The biggest point at issue from the banks' perspective was the issuing of notes. Hincks favoured government issue of all notes, similar to what his predecessor had proposed, but knew that would not fly with the banking community. Therefore he compromised and permitted dual issuing of notes by government (one and two dollars) while allowing the banks to continue to issue notes worth more than four dollars (later raised to five dollars). Notes in circulation represented between 15 and 20 per cent of all chartered banks' liabilities and therefore were of great importance to the banking communities.

The Legislation

The next year a Uniform Currency Act was passed, which extended decimal currency throughout the dominion, including the last hold-out, Nova Scotia. "The British sovereign, rated at $4.86 2/3, became the standard coin and the United States Gold Eagle, a U.S. official bullion coin, was made legal tender for $10."[20]

The government also passed a general Bank Act, formally known as An Act Relating to Banks and Banking, devoted largely to consolidating and re-introducing legislation. The smaller banks, however, urged one change to the 1870 Act: reducing the amount of required capital from $1 million to $500,000. The Act consolidated federal regulation over banking by repealing all provincial Acts in conflict with federal currency and banking legislation – in clear contrast to the American system. The key provisions of the 1871 Act, many of which will play an important role in Canadian financial history, were:

1 Minimum capital of $500,000, of which 10 per cent was to be paid-up;
2 Power to issue notes in denominations of $4 or more, not to exceed paid-up capital and to be secured by gold or dominion notes;[21]
3 Double liability on shareholders, to be paid before realizing on the assets of a failed bank, a method used by some U.S. states to deal with the problem of limited liability of institutions whose risk of failure had broad economic impact;
4 Total bank liabilities not to exceed three times capital, which had not been part of New York or U.S. bank law; U.S. regulators focused on lending limits; the National Banking Act required reserves of 25 per cent of assets;[22]
5 Mandatory decennial revision by Parliament, an unusual feature for banking law; this provision called for regular review of banking law, with or without a crisis at hand;
6 One vote per share, which empowered large shareholder blocks;
7 Prohibition against extending credit on real property, which lasted until 1954;
8 Maintenance of a 6 per cent interest ceiling on loans advanced.[23]

Hincks's biographer wrote, "His success in the field of banking and currency earned him the title of 'Father of Canadian Banking.'"[24] The *Dictionary of Canadian Biography* noted, "Hincks had succeeded in ending the stalemate and in establishing the principle of general legislation applying equally to the banks and currency in the country."[25]

Hincks may not have been a financial genius but he was "a successful financial administrator ... as inspector general he helped to restore Canada's financial reputation by putting the province's finances on a sound footing. Baring Brothers and other British financial houses held him in high regard. He was given credit ... for establishing a favourable economic environment for railway building and development."[26] Nevertheless, Hincks's main legacy was gaining agreement between the government and the banks on the issuance of notes, and for the long term, establishing the principle of regular reviews of the Bank Act.

Overview of Canadian Banking, 1869–1914

Canada was fortunate that, by the early twentieth century, it had both a legislative framework for a sound financial system, and a healthy number of financial corporations in operation. Both were necessary in meeting the demands for capital that entrepreneurs and growing corporations required to carry on their activities.

Joe Martin, *Relentless Change*

Canadian banking regulation exhibited a rare ability to adapt with relatively little Sturm und Drang. In the period from the Bank Acts passage to the beginning of the First World War in 1914, there were four decennial revisions, which made modest improvements. The 1880 Bank Act Revision (effective 1881) laid out more detailed requirements for monthly returns. The 1890 Revision (effective 1891) set out directors' qualifications more clearly and reduced the requirement that all directors be British subjects and instead required that a majority of the group be British subjects. "The revision of 1900 (effective 1901) recognized the Canadian Bankers' Association (an organization of the banks) as an agency in the supervision and control of certain activities of the banks."[27] In 1913, after a series of bank failures, provision was made for the appointment of external auditors, although it was specified that the appointment had to be an individual auditor rather than a firm. And as a war measure, the provision for emergency circulation was extended to 1914.

During this period, Canada adhered to what was called the Four Pillars in finance: the separation of commercial banking, investment banking, trust services, and life insurance. The origin of this separation of financial services is unclear, but it was inherited from British traditions. As was the case in Australia, this separation was reinforced by the fact that the provinces or states came first and had the initial power to regulate. The Fathers of Confederation, however, decided that banking and life insurance corporations should be regulated federally, while they left the regulation of trust companies and investment dealers – neither of which was very important in the late nineteenth century – to the provinces.

Growth with Relative Stability

Throughout the period from the passage of the Bank Act to the First World War, Canadian banks did well, although there were failures as well as consolidations. Total bank assets grew more than fourteen-fold, to $1.6 billion, between 1869 and 1914.[28] But in spite of tremendous growth, the chartered banks' share of financial intermediation declined and was slightly lower than that of the United States.[29] While the number of banks declined from 35 to 22 as a result of the failures and consolidation, the number of bank branches, a characteristic of the Canadian system of banking ever since the Bank of Montreal began opening branches immediately after its 1817 founding, exploded. The count rose from 123 in 1868 to 750 in 1900 and then to more than 3,000 in 1914. Much of this growth was in Western Canada as a result of the wheat boom, which led to the settlement of the Canadian Prairies. Where there had been no bank branches by the beginning of the new century, there were 82, and by 1914, there were 800. The larger banks also had operations in the United Kingdom and the United States (usually in three or four different cities) as well as in France, Spain, Mexico, the Caribbean, and South America.[30]

From the time of Confederation in 1867 to the outbreak of war in 1914, a Canadian bank had suspended or ceased normal operation on average every other year, starting with the thirty-four-year-old Commercial Bank of New Brunswick in 1868. However there were two bad years in particular, 1879 and 1887, prior to the Credit Crisis of 1907, when more banks failed. In each of those years four banks ceased operation. In 1879 three of the bank failures occurred in Quebec and one took place in Nova Scotia. The most notable failure in terms of size and notoriety at the time was the Consolidated Bank of Canada, which had been created only four years earlier. With paid-up capital of over $2 million, it was the largest failure in post-Confederation nineteenth-century Canada. It was also notable because the president was Sir Francis Hincks. While his was largely a figurehead position, he was indicted and found guilty but acquitted on appeal and "censured for his negligence."[31] In 1887 two of the banks that ceased operation were in Ontario, while the other two failed in the Maritimes. Neither failure was as large as that of the Consolidated Bank. Their paid-up capital ranged between $200,000 and $500,000, and in the case of Pictou Bank in Nova Scotia the suspension was voluntary.

The first decade of the twentieth century was more tumultuous. The 1907 Credit Crisis was preceded and succeeded by seven bank failures. The first to fail was the Bank of Yarmouth in Nova Scotia in 1905, quickly followed by the Ontario Bank, which had thirty branches and $1.5 million in capital. The oldest bank in the province of Ontario, its failure was due to the behaviour of a dishonest general manager, which led to its absorption by the Bank of Montreal. Three banks collapsed in 1908. By far the biggest was the seven-year-old Sovereign Bank[32] with paid-up capital of $3 million and eighty-five branches, the largest failure in post-Confederation Canada to that time. The Canadian Bankers' Association judged that improper banking practices and poor management had caused its failure and recommended that more appropriate institutions take it over. Of the two small Quebec banks that went down, one, the Banque de St Jean, failed because of fraud and incompetence. The other, Banque de St Hyacinthe, collapsed for reasons attributed to its incompetence, and the latter voluntarily accepted its own demise. Two years later two more banks went under, a small bank in New Brunswick and the twenty-seven-branch Farmers Bank in Ontario. Once more the failures were attributed to mismanagement. These failures contributed to the additional requirement for external auditors in the 1913 Bank Act revisions.

In Canada, as in many countries, the two decades before the First World War witnessed many consolidations. Just as banks were failing, others were being absorbed. The major acquirers were Canada's two biggest banks, the Bank of Montreal and the Toronto-based Bank of Commerce. The Bank of Montreal, the more established bank, made three Maritime-based acquisitions in the early twentieth century, in addition to taking over the Ontario Bank. The Canadian Bank of Commerce added the Gore Bank in Hamilton as early as 1870 and began

Table 3.1 Assets of Canadian Chartered Banks, 31 December 1914

Bank	Total assets ($ million)
Bank of Montreal	265.5
Canadian Bank of Commerce	240.0
Royal Bank of Canada	178.4
Bank of Nova Scotia	95.7
Merchants Bank of Canada	84.4
Imperial Bank of Canada	81.8
Dominion Bank	80.5
Union Bank of Canada	80.3
Bank of British North America	60.9
Bank of Toronto	59.5
12 other banks	328.6

Source: *Canada Year Book*, 1914, 575.

the twentieth century by acquiring the royal chartered Bank of British Columbia, which was quickly followed by a couple of Maritime-based acquisitions as well as the Quebec-based Eastern Townships Bank in 1912. Some banks, such as the Bank of New Brunswick and the Union Bank of Halifax, found that they, too, were absorbed, even after they had taken over other banks.

As a consequence, there were fewer banks in 1914 than at any time in the previous sixty years.[33] Still the largest, although not as dominant as it had been at the time of Confederation, the Bank of Montreal was followed in size by the rapidly growing Toronto-based Canadian Bank of Commerce and the even more rapidly growing Royal Bank of Canada, which had moved its head office from Halifax to Montreal in 1907. The three leaders were followed by five banks with assets of anywhere from $80 to $96 million. The Royal Chartered Bank of British North America, which was the second-largest bank at the time of Confederation, fell to ninth place (see table 3.1). The smallest bank in Canada, the Weyburn Security Bank in Saskatchewan, had assets of only $1.6 million.

Other Forms of Financial Intermediation

While chartered banks were the major financial intermediary in Canada, they faced competition. Indeed their importance declined relatively speaking from a high point of nearly 80 per cent of all financial intermediary assets in 1870 to less than 60 per cent at the century's end. In the latter part of the nineteenth-century mortgage and loan companies showed dramatic growth, in large part because chartered banks lacked the legal authority to issue mortgages. Meanwhile, settlers were pouring into Ontario to take up the virgin lands and turn them into productive farms. In order to do this they needed mortgage loans. The concept of a mortgage loan company was imported from the United Kingdom, as was much of the capital (primarily from Scotland). By 1880 the mortgage and loan companies represented 25 per cent of the assets of all financial intermediaries, making them half the size of all chartered banks collectively. The oldest and largest of the mortgage loan companies, the Canada Permanent and Western Canada Mortgage Corporation, was formed by a merger of four companies in 1899. Though not as large as the biggest banks, Canada Permanent was the sixth-largest Canadian financial institution in the early twentieth century, larger than any of the life insurance companies and larger than some banks (e.g., the Bank of Nova Scotia and the Royal Bank of Canada). Other large loan and savings companies included the Huron and Erie Loan and Savings Company and the Central Canada Loan and Savings Company.

In the period from the turn of the century until the First World War, mortgage and loan companies lost financial industry share, not only to banks but also to the rapidly growing life insurance sector and, to a lesser degree, to the emerging trust company sector. By the beginning of the war their share of financial industry business was declining and continued to do so for several reasons as the century progressed. They relied heavily on British capital, which lost some of its interest in North American investment as interest rate differentials narrowed. And they failed to anticipate the huge demands arising on the Canadian Prairies in the early twentieth century. The mortgage and loan sector itself was centred in Ontario, which blinded companies in that business to the burgeoning opportunities in the West. As the century drew to a close and the westward movement began, the industry had 90 per cent of its outstanding mortgages in Ontario. This had been a sound strategy up to that point – total mortgages went from $35 million to $238 million in the quarter-century before 1900.[34] But with the wheat boom, the Western Prairies mortgage business boomed. Before the First World War, the volume of mortgages increased another $220 million. While the Ontario market grew by 60 per cent and still represented nearly 60 per cent of the Canadian market, the West had an almost infinite increase and would grow to account for over 10 per cent of the overall Canadian market – compared with 0.5 per cent at the beginning of the century, and Alberta had not yet become a market. In contrast to the mortgage and loan companies' continued focus on Ontario, the life insurance companies moved aggressively into the Western Prairie market, thereby gaining in overall market share.

A new, albeit still small, part of financial intermediation was the trust companies. They first appeared on the scene in the 1880s but blossomed in the twentieth century. Spawned by entrepreneurs and encouraged by the government in its attempt to separate commercial banking and trust services in order to avoid conflicts of interest, trust companies prospered and became an important part of the Canadian financial scene. At the beginning of the century trust companies represented 1.4 per cent of all financial intermediaries. By the outbreak of the war in 1914, they represented double that amount. Originally most trust companies were provincially incorporated in either Ontario or Quebec, but as some expanded across the country they opted for federal incorporation. In the early twentieth century only one trust company, the Toronto General Trust, was large enough to be counted among the thirty largest financial corporations in Canada. Incorporated in 1872, it was the oldest trust company in Canada. However, the company did not really start doing business for another decade. By the beginning of the twentieth century it had assets of $20 million and was slightly larger than the Royal Bank of Canada. In addition to their fiduciary activities, including investments in mortgages and government of Canada and other bonds, the growth of the trust company industry owed a lot to their intermediary business. As a consequence of these opportunities, a number of savings and loan companies converted to trust companies.

A clear difference between Canada and the United States was the absence of important domestic investment banks in Canada. Limits on state and national bank branching in the United States, particularly foreign branching, and U.S. dependence on multiple sources of foreign capital led to heavy reliance on a wide range of private banks to acquire and monitor foreign investment in America. Canada needed capital as much as, if not more than, the United States to finance the construction of harbours and canals, then later for railways and of course agriculture and manufacturing. Demand for capital in Canada was far greater than the local supply. Typically Canadians went to the London market, not only for its sophistication but also because interest rates were lower and capital more plentiful. In both the United States and Canada, Barings Brothers was an early major player, as was Glynn, Mills, Currie & Co. As the Canadian economy continued to grow, the

Figure 3.1　Early foreign investment in Canada
Source: Lockwood (n.d.).

United Kingdom provided most of the foreign capital, primarily as the result of interest rate incentives. By the turn of the twentieth century, nearly $1.25 billion of foreign capital was invested in Canada; the United Kingdom provided 85 per cent of that amount, the United States supplied 13.5 per cent, and only 1.5 per cent came from the rest of the world.[35]

The main Canadian bank to take advantage of the underwriting activities in the United Kingdom was, not surprisingly, the Bank of Montreal, which began underwriting debt in the London market as early as 1874. Five years later the bank underwrote a bond issue in New York. In 1893 the bank succeeded Baring Brothers and Glynn, Mills, Currie & Co. as the Dominion of Canada's fiscal agent in London. However, as Canada entered the twentieth century two trends were observable. One was the shift away from chartered banks to independent investment dealers as underwriters, and the other was the shift to the U.S. market as a source of capital. At the outset of the First World War, the United States was supplying nearly one-quarter of all foreign capital to Canada, up from only 13.5 per cent at the turn of the century. In the period 1911–15, foreign capital inflows into Canada reached over $1.5 billion, double the amount of the previous five years and five times the amount that flowed in five years before that.[36] Much of the U.S. capital was in the form of direct rather than portfolio investment, particularly in industrial and pulp and paper companies. British capital, on the other hand, was found mostly in portfolio investment, particularly in railroads and industrial firms.[37]

The late nineteenth and early twentieth century also saw the growth of domestic investment banks, called investment dealers, in Canada. Their activities differed in many respects from those of their American counterparts. Most Canadian investment dealers traded in bonds before they traded in equities, but by the time of the First World War most dealt in both for their own accounts or for customers. A key firm in the early development of Canadian investment banking was the Central Canada Loan and Savings Company – the creation of George Albertus Cox, the greatest Canadian financier of his era. In addition to having his own company, Cox owned and ran Canada's largest life insurance company (Canada Life) and was president of the country's second-largest bank (Bank of Commerce), and of two leading fire insurance firms. Cox was also the owner of other major life insurance companies,[38] as well as a member of the Senate of Canada. His son-in-law, A.E. Ames, who was with Central Canada, founded a stock brokerage house with funds provided by Cox. Later, former employees of A.E. Ames founded Dominion Securities and Wood Gundy, two of the earliest bond-dealing houses. The first major equity investment dealer in Canada was Royal Securities, founded in Halifax by Max Aitken (later Lord Beaverbrook) who transferred the operation to Montreal early in the twentieth century. Aitken was involved in a series of corporate mergers in Canada, including the creation of Canada's pre-eminent steel company in Hamilton (the Steel Company of Canada, the Canadian equivalent of U.S. Steel in Pittsburgh) and Canada Cement, before he left for England.[39]

Money and Banking in the United States, 1870–1913

The national banking system, however, did not correct the stability problem that surfaced after the BUS disappeared. Financial panics continued with greater frequency than they had in the early decades of U.S. history.
                    Richard Sylla, "Reversing Financial Reversals"

As in all countries, money, banking law, and credit were inextricably tied together and formed crucial components of the financial system in America. The Civil War altered the configuration of many of those elements, but the overall financial system itself remained fragmented, complicated, and vulnerable to crises.[40] From early in 1862 (when conversion of Union currency into specie was suspended) until 1 January 1879, known as the greenback period, the dollar was linked to other currencies at rates determined by the market, which fluctuated daily. The dollar was not guaranteed to be convertible into specie, but there were no restrictions on its use, including conversion into foreign currencies. Gold was a commodity like many others, except as it related to foreign payments, since many of the countries with which the United States did business were on the gold standard. Despite political pressure to keep a floating dollar rate, the official suspension of gold convertibility since 1862 was expected to be temporary. Official U.S. government policy was to resume payment in specie, which was finally achieved in 1879.[41]

During the aftermath of the Civil War, many new banks were incorporated into a system that still contained a substantial number of small institutions. Legislation during the period altered the rules about who could create currency and how. As discussed in chapter 2, national banking was stimulated by the combination of new federal banks created by the National Bank Acts and the 1866 tax on the banknotes of state banks – designed expressly to get state banks out of the currency business. With the passage of the National Bank Acts during the Civil War, many observers believed that state banks would soon be out of existence entirely. The state banks suffered, but they continued to play an important role in American banking.[42]

Despite the state banks' reduced capacity to create notes, demands for credit helped keep them alive. A desire for cheap money, as well as shortages of gold, stoked political pressure to decouple currency from gold, or at least to move toward bimetallism (a monetary system based on two metals, gold and silver) as well as many other financial techniques – such as greater use of chequing accounts – to get more money from any given level of gold. More money supply was related to the issue of more banking that was locally controlled. Regions and towns did not want the money supply and loanable funds determined by distant bankers. Moreover, a resumption of convertibility after the Civil War, an ambition of money-centre bankers and some politicians, required substantial price deflation and monetary discipline, and this ignited political discord. Although doubts about U.S. adherence to the gold standard rocked American financial markets and dominated political discussions during the forty years leading up to the First World War, new discoveries of gold and extraction developments eventually helped increase prices and secure U.S. adherence to the gold standard, but with much rancour and handwringing.[43]

Even the Supreme Court got involved. In a remarkable decision, Chief Justice Salmon P. Chase found that his own decision as secretary of the Treasury to retroactively make the greenback (paper dollars) legal tender – a truly official currency, not backed by specie – was unconstitutional.[44] Not until Ulysses S. Grant, the Civil War hero and eighteenth president of the United States, stacked the Supreme Court a year later with his supporters was the Chase decision overturned. In 1879 paper money began to circulate at par with specie, and banks resumed payment in gold, putting the issue to rest for a time at least.[45] In contrast to Canada, America ended the nineteenth century and began the twentieth without adapting many aspects of its financial system to modern demands, contributing to instability and uncertainty in what had become the largest economy in the world.

Despite huge capital needs, Civil War reforms, and many crises, America's financial system remained highly fragmented with thousands of small state banks, most of which had only one office. Even its new nationally chartered banks, forced to respect state rules, remained essentially one-branch institutions that were bound to just one state, thereby being relatively small compared to their foreign competitors, which themselves were highly restricted and therefore virtually non-existent in the United States. U.S. bank regulation was still very much a state affair. Even though some banking state regulations were less severe than the national rules, capital requirements were strict in most major states and banking activities very limited. Commercial banks in most states could not, for example, offer trust services or operate internationally. The main job of connecting public banks to the world was performed by private investment bankers, who, through a network of relations or family ties, provided cross-state or cross-national border financial transactions. Most regulation of public securities issuances, exchanges, and in general accounting practices – commonplace today – was not a fixture of the system for lack of consensus on best practice and specific legislation. Although the number of incorporated banks grew by a factor of 4.5 from 1870 to 1900, there was no central bank. State banking laws still guided banking practices. Even though the number of national banks skyrocketed after the National Bank Act of 1863, many state banks simply converted to national ones, primarily to avoid the tax on notes issuance, and most commercial banks remained state banks. Even national banks had to obey the laws of the states in which they operated. Excluding unincorporated and mutual savings banks, which will be discussed below, there were nearly 9,000 U.S. banks in 1900, of which 5,007 were state incorporated banks. Free banking and unit banking still dominated in most states.[46]

All banking was divided into the six categories of institutions described above; many performed services that we still need today, whereas other services have long since become obsolete. Each type of institution had specific advantages and constraints. Since each was limited in what services it offered, many of the different types of banks tended to work in networks to provide a broader range of services. As the geographic scope and type of banking services offered were narrow, banks participated more as intermediaries rather than targets during the great merger movement at the turn of the century. Despite, or perhaps because of, the fractured nature of American banking, deposits in the United States grew sixfold between 1870 and 1900 while money supply tripled, all during a period of great growth when wholesale prices were declining.[47]

National and State Commercial Banks

National banks were superimposed on the older state banking structure. To make them appear sounder, legal reserve requirements were mandated, along with double liability for the shareholders of national banks. Initially the conversion from state to national banks was slow, so the national government levied a 2 per cent tax on state banknotes (increased in 1865 to 10 per cent), quickly driving state banks out of this lucrative method of raising funds. By 1866, fewer than 300 state banks remained. They were in cities and towns where the issuance of banknotes was less important. But as the practice of simply extending credit by creating deposit accounts for the borrower had grown in all but very remote areas, the importance of issuing notes became less important, as did the importance of a national charter. From 1870 to 1900, the number of national banks grew from 1,612 to 3,731.

Commercial banks had to weigh the advantages of national incorporation against the disadvantages. To be sure, with the federal imprimatur, there was more prestige and the right to issue notes without the onerous tax. On the other hand, the costs of incorporation (stricter regulation) imposed a burden on profits.[48]

An examination of Citibank (City Bank and then in 1865 as National City Bank [NCB]) during this period provides a useful example of banking and business transformations in these years. Founded in 1812 with a New York state charter and designed to profit from the termination of the first BUS, NCB, like many banks of its day, was intended as a kind of credit union for merchant-politician owners. In 1837 it nearly collapsed in the financial panic of that year. Favoured by its location in New York – the most vibrant market of the American state banking markets – by the 1890s NCB was the largest bank in the United States. Although it was big in the United States, NCB was not among the ten largest banks in the world before the First World War, as measured by deposits.[49]

By that time NCB had operated under three regulatory regimes: from 1812 to 1852 under two state charters; from 1852 to 1865 as a state "free bank"; and as a national bank from 1865 onwards. Each regime imposed various restrictions. As a chartered bank, its minimum capital was over three times that of a national bank, but there were no minimum reserve requirements or deposit rate ceilings, and circulated notes did not have to be secured. The reserve requirements and deposit rate ceilings for national banks were 25 and 2 per cent respectively. As a national bank, too, NCB's notes in circulation had to be secured by federal government bonds. In 1890 it had no overall lending limits, which as a chartered bank could not exceed 2.5 times paid-in capital, but loans to a single borrower could not exceed 10 per cent of paid-in-capital and retained earnings. Under all three regimes, branching was prohibited. In addition to the prestige of being a national bank with the concomitant authority to issue notes, NCB could become a depository for the federal government and could accept as deposits the reserve balances of national banks in other cities. Perhaps the most serious impediment to growth, however, was not domestic, but rather involved international activity. Until 1914 national banks could not open up international branches or create international acceptances based on trade. According to the prevailing opinion, international transaction entailed too many risks. At the very least, opening international operations conflicted with the principle of unit banking and would further encourage the growth of big banks. In contrast, private banks continued to offer international services through their family or other foreign connections.[50]

But despite the foreign prohibitions, NCB focused on business connections that went well beyond New York. Limited to one branch and losing a great deal of straight loan business to the more lightly controlled state banks pushed the national banks into capital market transactions for their larger corporate clients, who themselves saw many advantages to disintermediation – the removal of the middleman.[51] NCB got into underwriting for securities and sought out America's largest corporations as its customers. With a broad network of important banks and individuals, NCB distributed new securities and made loans to large companies. Large corporations and wealthy individuals kept their deposits in the vaults of NCB and similar banks. In 1905 its deposits were eight times what they had been a decade earlier. Fifty-six per cent came from fourteen firms, ten of which were major railroads. NCB's chairman, James Stillman, was a close friend of William Rockefeller, who brought other powerful magnates onto the NCB board. Through its international network of correspondent banks, including important Canadian connections, NCB financed trade and cleared cross-border transactions.[52]

Canada's largest bank at the time, the Bank of Montreal (BMO), serves as an interesting contrast to NCB. In 1895 its capital was greater than that of NCB's with US$12 million, compared to US$4.2 million. Unlike NCB, which had no branches, BMO operated two branches in the city in which it was based, as well as forty elsewhere across the country, and one in London. It even had a branch in Chicago and an agent in New York, as well as many correspondent relationships. By the 1880s approximately 30 per cent of BMO's investments were outside of Canada, a substantial portion being in the United States.[53] In 1895 its president, Donald A. Smith, a key figure in Canadian and American railroad development, was still in Canada but would soon move to Great Britain, as Canadian high commissioner to the United Kingdom. Although he retained the title of president, as in many American companies, the role was largely ceremonial, with day-to-day operations handled by the general manager.[54] By 1914, NCB's assets were 35 per cent larger than BMO's ($352 to $260 million). However, NCB's capital had grown by then to over ten times its 1895 level.[55]

Whereas Canadian banks operated nationally with branches, there was less need for local banks in Canada. In the United States, state banks filled certain needs that their national counterparts could not or did not want to satisfy. Increasingly, during the last thirty years of the nineteenth century, proponents of the establishment of new banks relied on the state rules, which were often less onerous than the national ones. From 1870 to 1900 the number of state-incorporated banks skyrocketed from 325 to 5,007. By the time the Federal Reserve was created in 1913, approximately 25,000 commercial banks were operating in the United States, 70 per cent of which were state banks.[56] State banks offered broad banking services such as taking deposits and making loans, but on a less grand scale than many of the national banks.

Table 3.2 Assets of America's Largest Banks in 1913

Bank	Total assets ($ millions)
First National City Bank of New York	293.3
Continental and Commercial National Bank of Chicago	213.8
National Bank of Commerce New York	181.6
First National Bank (New York)	150.6
First Chicago Bank	142.0
Chase New York	134.3
National Park Bank of New York	122.5
Hanover Bank New York	105.9
Shawmut Bank Boston	102.3
First Boston Bank	92.2

Source: Comptroller of the currency

Many had already gotten out of the note-issuing business before the federal tax was put into place. Not only were the state banks easier to set up, they satisfied the financial needs of smaller firms and farmers, who had less interest in marketable securities and international transactions. These local banks tended to be more flexible and responsive to their communities by providing working capital and bridge financing for agricultural interests. In some states and localities, they operated with fewer restrictions, and their transactions depended less on large networks that entailed a greater geographic breadth.[57]

As evidenced in table 3.2, America's big banks were clustered in New York, Chicago, and Boston. Several Canadian banks were as large as – or even larger than – the top American banks, despite the far greater size of the U.S. economy. If a list of the top ten North American banks were created, Bank of Montreal, the Canadian Bank of Commerce, and the Royal Bank of Canada would be included, pushing the last three American banks off the ranking.

Other Domestic Lending Institutions

In some communities, groups of borrowers and investors went a step further. They organized mutual associations for their banking needs, entities that were often owned, not by shareholders, but rather by their members, with trustees managing the enterprises. For this section, we will refer to them as savings and loans (S&Ls). Under this rubric we will include what are sometimes called savings banks, thrifts, mutual associations, and S&Ls. Although they are not identical in their structures (for instance, some are incorporated), S&Ls share two characteristics: they are formed to serve the financial interests of a community, and they are focused on individual rather than commercial banking needs. S&Ls under different names operated for a long time in the United States. As in other countries, they were designed for social stability by promoting self-reliance and thrift, especially among the poor, but also among many skilled and semi-skilled workers.[58] Unlike many other smaller financial institutions, they (approximately 650) were concentrated in the Northeast. Those S&Ls, like insurance companies, often concentrated on helping widows and orphans. Some focused on recent immigrants, especially of one particular ethnic group or another. By the turn of the century, savings banks saw their market share dwindle in the face of extensive commercial bank competition. The increase of private savings and borrowing during the first decades of the twentieth century and restrictions on the provision of mortgages by commercial banks gave them a great boost. By the second decade of the twentieth century, S&Ls were taking business from life insurance companies, which had offered housing loans, by "offering innovative small-denominated amortized mortgage loans to members and took savings deposits."[59]

Trusts and other organizations filled another "hole" in the banking system. Unlike commercial banks, they could act as paying agents for the interest and principal of bonds (making money on the float), paying interest on deposits, and performing other trustee work. Like standard banks, trusts could take deposits from individuals and corporations, but they could also act as executives for wills and administrators of estates. These activities gave them control of many financial assets which until 1914 were prohibited to commercial banks, i.e., those that provide more general banking services. Eager to exploit the loophole in banking law that allowed the trusts to operate in this regulatory space, many large public banks and private ones founded their own trusts. Holding funds in trust made some of them very cash rich (perhaps too cash rich), adding sources of new liquidity for the commercial banks. Amazingly, unlike national and some state banks, the trusts, such as Bankers Trust and Guaranty Trust, both of New York, could and did create international branches and conducted extensive foreign exchange business. One foreign-owned trust operated in New York, the Transatlantic Trust Company. It was organized by three large Hungarian banks and served mostly as a conduit between Hungarian immigrants in America and their motherland.[60] One quasi-bank, American Express, made its reputation by providing financial services, such as transfers and traveller's cheques, to wealthy Americans domestically and abroad by establishing a branch network in many foreign cities, something large American banks could not do.

Foreign Commercial Banking

Foreign commercial banks were faced with restrictions in most American states. Like all banks, they were largely prohibited from operating multiple branches or crossing state lines. In New York, for example, the most logical place for entry, they could not operate branches until 1914. Other states restricted their right to take deposits, discount bills, or lend funds – in short, to do "banking business." Under the National Banking Act, directors of national banks had to be American citizens, making control by foreign head offices in the absence of many modern communication devices difficult. Most large foreign banks operated with U.S. representatives working with U.S. correspondent banks. There were some exceptions, driven by trade and U.S. investment.[61]

But soon after the War of 1812, foreign money started to make up a substantial portion of demand for bank and state bond investments in the United States. In the same year that the Second Bank of the United States obtained its charter, Canadian banks started to arrive in the United States. Founded in 1817, the Montreal Bank,[62] as it was initially known, was the first Canadian entry into the United States. In 1818, the bank appointed an agent in New York, Prime, Ward & King (later Prime, Ward & Sands), to handle species and foreign exchange (American and British) in New York. From the first, this bank served as a conduit for specie and foreign exchange between British North America and the United States. Bank of Montreal notes circulated in New England and New York, but in the 1830s these activities did not involve the bank in substantial U.S. investment. BMO's activities, though, were soon copied. In 1832 the Bank of Nova Scotia was in its first year of existence and appointed an agent in New York, and four years later the Bank of British North America chose Prime, Ward & King to become its agent in New York. Compared, however, to investment in American banks, these Canadian activities were only a small part of total foreign investment into the United States.[63]

By the 1850s several of these banks opened their own agencies in New York. According to some accounts, the Bank of Montreal was the largest New York player, conducting millions of money market transactions, perhaps sacrificing Canadian capital needs to earn returns on Wall Street. By this time, too, the Bank of Montreal was already considered one of the three most important banks in North America. After the Civil War, it reputedly became number one.[64]

While outright ownership of U.S. banks was rare, in 1853 foreign participation in the equity ownership of American banks was relatively common but not substantial to total investment. Although nearly 1,000 banks had foreign investors, foreign-owned banking common shares represented only 3 per cent of the total. Virtually all banks that permitted foreign shareholders were 90 per cent owned by Americans, testifying to the breadth but not the depth of foreign interest in U.S. banking.[65] Some increases in foreign ownership happened by default, through bankruptcy or as an add-on to their core activities. This happened to the Bank of Montreal when it acquired mortgage and trade debt through its financing of grain purchases in Illinois.[66] In the northeast, non-Americans held more than 10 per cent of four banks, and in the South these individuals held an even larger percentage of five banks, but none in this sample had a controlling foreign majority. Even in Louisiana, where the foreign equity investment was relatively heavy, it averaged only 28 per cent.[67]

Some states were more hospitable than New York to foreign direct investment in the banking sector. Illinois, for example, allowed foreign banks and banks from other states, demonstrating an openness that Canadian banks welcomed. By 1881 four Canadian banks were accepting deposits, rendering significant competition to American financial institutions, especially in the grain trade. Bank of Montreal was the first. The Canadian Bank of Commerce followed in 1875, with the British Bank of North America and the Merchants' Bank in 1881. For several years the new arrivals offered a variety of services, but the more recent entries shut their doors in 1886, leaving Bank of Montreal as the only Canadian bank in America's second city. In the 1890s several other foreign banks, including the Bank of Nova Scotia, tried their luck with the looser Illinois banking rules, but by 1914 only the Bank of Montreal and Bank of Nova Scotia had survived. Neither firm did regular commercial banking, despite the former's substantial size in the Chicago market.[68] In California, too, foreign banks played an important role. In 1876, six of the original members of the San Francisco Clearing Association were foreign banks, including two Canadian. Even though California law became more restrictive of foreign banks in 1913, a year later many foreign banks were active in San Francisco, including one from China called Hong Kong and Shanghai Banking Corporation, a free-standing company founded with British money, and one Japanese firm called the Yokohama Specie Bank.[69]

Although there was substantial European banking activity in American finance before 1914, there was little foreign direct investment by the big British and Continental European banks. European banks, including British, worked through correspondent banks in the United States. Two of the world's biggest banks at the turn of the century had tried and failed to establish U.S. subsidiaries before 1900. During the last quarter of the nineteenth century, Crédit Lyonnais, for example, operated agencies in London and many other cities in Europe, North Africa, and the Middle East. But the subsidiary that opened in New York in 1879 was closed three years later, ostensibly because its activities "were not adapted to the local legislation and customs," but perhaps also because of a crisis in France. Most of its business in the United States was done through correspondent bank relations with private and joint-stock banks administered by independent agents in the United States and employees in France.[70] Deutsche Bank met with a similar fate. An equity interest in a private American firm went bad because of speculative investments in trade instruments. First with a German-born journalist, an entrepreneur, and then with a dyed-in-the-wool Yankee banker, Deutsche Bank first sought out American securities to sell in Germany and later strived to mount bigger ventures there, nearly all in partnership with American private and joint-stock banks.[71]

Other foreign financial institutions exploited weaknesses or loopholes in American banking. National banks were not allowed to lend money against land or real estate, but state banks, trusts, and real estate investment companies, which accessed foreign money for the express purpose of financing mortgages, were permitted to do so. Several U.K. firms set up as a form of investment trust, but this initiative was for real estate lending in the United States, much as they did in Canada. Indeed, some of the companies were set up to do business in the United States and Canada. Although most of these companies came from Great Britain, some were incorporated in Continental Europe and Canada. Through most of the nineteenth century, insurance companies and savings and loans had been the main institutional lenders, but mortgage lending was still mostly a private business between individuals, not institutions. Like much of the money that comes from abroad today in the mortgage market, these new entrants bought some larger tracts of land directly, but they tended to avoid the additional paperwork of lending on many small properties. As writing mortgages was a very local endeavour, foreign investors worked through non-national American banks that had local expertise. Their activities were geographically varied and included farm mortgages.[72]

In short, a great deal of foreign banking activity was occurring, but there was relatively little direct investment by joint-stock firms.[73] Twenty foreign banking agencies in New York were established in 1914 (five with Canadian headquarters), which could be called foreign direct investment (FDI), engaging in vital international financing transactions under licences required as of 1911. However, it is unclear what the advantages of the licence were, since the agencies could not operate as bank branches. They could not take deposits, make loans, or discount bills. Some British and other important banks preferred privacy to registration with the New York superintendent of banking. Of all the banks registered, undoubtedly the Bank of Montreal was the most influential in the United States. But apart from the states of Illinois and California, no foreign-owned commercial banks (deposit taking and loan making banks) of any importance were operating in the United States.[74]

Investment Banking Partnerships

Given the myriad restrictions on domestic and foreign banks in the United States, the dependency of international investment banking on private bankers should not be surprising. Other countries housed major private banking players, but nowhere did private bankers play such a crucial a role in investment banking and the national financial system as they did in America. No other country combined such strict limits on commercial banking with relatively poor capital market protections, capital shortages, and vibrant growth opportunities. Some of these banking houses had their beginnings in U.S. merchant banking, such as Brown Brothers and Co. Some were offshoots of European banking houses. Most had ties to Britain, such as Kidder, Peabody & Co., or Germany, such as Speyer and Co. J.P. Morgan, son of J.S. Morgan, who was an American partner in a British firm, became a banker in New York and the American partner and correspondent of the Morgan bank in London. When J.S. died, J.P. became the head of the bank in New York, and the London house (later Morgan Grenfell) became the British subsidiary of the American bank. Some were tied by family bonds (Kuhn Loeb & Co.), some religious, some both. Some were based in Philadelphia, such as Drexel, and Boston, such as Lee, Higginson & Co. Nevertheless, New York was the epicentre of these private banking houses. Even the non–New York banks had a presence there.[75] They all belonged to a world that was at once bounded by a carriage ride in Manhattan and an extraordinarily cosmopolitan metropolis at the same time. With many financial services and regulation in their infant stages, for many years nearly all private banks played multiple roles for capital projects, making enormous capital flows possible into America's inchoate capital markets.

The structure of American banking and America's dependence on foreign funds contributed to reliance on inchoate commercial paper markets for short-term financing. Unlike in the United Kingdom, trade credit in the United States was not based largely on bank acceptances, but rather on bank facilities in the form of one-name, collateralized promissory notes that could be turned into cash relatively quickly. Restrictions on the size of a bank's deposit base (unit banking) and on the use of international bank acceptances contributed to another innovation, commercial paper, that is, general unsecured short-term securities traded on open, impersonal markets. The United States led the way in developing the markets for commercial paper for financing short-term business activity, which today represents a nearly $2.0 trillion international form of borrowing, a major means for firms to raise cash for under 270 days. Unlike private bank loans, by the last third of the nineteenth century, commercial paper could be traded, providing a new investment vehicle for commercial banks and geographical diversification of U.S. finance, which suffered from regional and seasonal cash shortages. This form of short-term financing was particularly useful for companies to escape the monopoly of small banks in rural areas in the West and South. Until 1913 (see end of this chapter) U.S. national banks were not allowed to accept bills of exchange, forcing purchasers, especially importers, to rely on commercial paper to borrow to make payments for goods. But commercial paper was (and is) traded in arm's-length transactions, without the information and relationship advantages associated with long-term banking contacts. Rates and availability for this form of funding, therefore, tended to fluctuate more than for bank loans.[76]

Railroads: The Agony and the Ecstasy
of Disruptive Technology

The railroads were the first private business enterprises in the United States to acquire large amounts of capital from outside their own regions.

Alfred Chandler Jr, *The Visible Hand*

Railroads were not only a powerful driver of demand, productivity, and managerial innovation, they were also a great source of financial instability.

The trouble with railroad construction in the United States was that it caused even more systemic financial risk than it did in other countries, for a longer period. At times the system was overbuilt and over-leveraged, exposing severe weaknesses in American governance norms, bankruptcy law, and other aspects of regulation. States and municipalities competed with one another to arrange for lines to pass through their jurisdictions by building terminal facilities, buying railroad bonds, and guaranteeing others. After 1860, federal subsidies increased beyond what states contributed. In addition to millions of acres of land grants, the federal government lent as much as US$175 million directly to companies for construction, especially of transcontinental lines. During and just after the Civil War, government money was crucial.[77] Despite the generous subsidies of land and capital during the forty years that preceded the First World War, the rail companies increased their financial risk, because American demands for investment and consumption exceeded the country's ability to generate sufficient funds from internal sources or domestic institutions.

In the last thirty years of the nineteenth century, America's need for foreign capital, especially for the railroads, grew immensely. In 1869 long-term foreign investment in the United States amounted to nearly US$1.4 billion, approximately 70 per cent in federal securities. Less than 20 per cent was in railroad debt or equity.[78] By 1914 the United States owed the rest of the world US$7.1 billion in long-term capital, twice what America had lent to others.[79] Of that sum, US$4.2 billion was for railroads.[80] Although other countries such as Germany increased their investment during the period, Britain still accounted for 60 per cent of the total. Only 4 per cent came from Canada, roughly half of which was connected with its North American rail system.[81] From 1890 to 1895, over 50 per cent of some of America's largest railroads were owned by foreigners. Though the percentage probably peaked in 1890 before the crises of the 1890s, 30 per cent of the nominal value of all railroad securities even in 1914 was held by foreigners. British investors in particular liked putting their money into railroads, but so too did German, Canadian, and Dutch investors.[82]

Railroads and Finance in the United States

America's dependence on foreign capital put it and its creditors on a rocky path. In 1893 more than 50 per cent of the long-term financing of rail lines was in the form of debt.[83] By 1900 America had experienced three waves of railroad defaults, coming in roughly ten-year intervals: 1873, 1884, and 1893. In the early 1870s twenty-one American railroad securities issued on the London exchange were in default. Some had been issued only a year before going into default.[84] "In 1893 alone an astonishing 74 rail companies with US$1.8 billion in capital and 30,000 miles of track went into receivership, nearly one-sixth of America's 1890 rail capacity and nearly as many miles of track in one year as during the prior nine years combined."[85]

Railroads desperately needed to be managed and restructured, and many management and financial changes resulted. The detailed managerial and public reports of rail lines set the standard for accounting in the era. The influence of railroads on accounting is well documented. More detailed reports and more sophisticated operational measures for usage were necessary because of the huge capital investment in land, rail lines, rail cars, and stations. The great distances between service and headquarters, as far apart as the West Coast and New York, increased demands for financial reporting that had spillover effects on other sectors.[86] However, the many financial crises exposed weaknesses, such as the quality or the lack thereof of consolidated financial statements of related lines, and the practice of not paying in full the par value of common and preferred equity shares, both of which disguised the degree of indebtedness of many firms.

There were multiple operating problems. Many of the lines were small and insufficiently connected to each other and larger networks. As in many sectors, they needed to be merged. By 1895 nearly 400 small lines had merged with others over a five year period.[87] But state and federal law often blocked consolidation.

The saga of the Northern Pacific Railroad serves as a good illustration. Founded in 1864 to connect shipping centres along Lake Superior in Minnesota to those in Puget Sound in the state of Washington, using ample rail and telegraph line rights, and land grant rights, it aspired to become America's second cross-continental line. The road was rocky. In its first thirty years the Northern Pacific went bankrupt three times. At the time of its second bankruptcy, as measured by track length, it was the tenth-largest line in the United States. In 1896 it controlled three times the amount of track it had owned in 1883, the year of its second crisis. Like most great lines, its financial structure added enormously to the risk it took. In 1893 interest expense on $380 million in debt accounted for over 40 per cent of revenues. Throughout its early history, it suffered from overly ambitious or corrupt management, overcapacity, and an inability to rationally merge with other lines in the region. When times were good as well as during crises, state officials and bankruptcy courts blocked the merging of subsidiary trunk lines. Each downturn in the U.S. economy, especially in farm production and credit shortages, threatened the Northern Pacific's existence. With substantial foreign investment and oversight in the 1890s and shortly after the turn of the century, owners and creditors sought but failed to get American regulatory approval for a merger, with its first competitor, the Great Northern, and then with the Union Pacific, which was deemed to be anti-competitive and was blocked by the courts under antitrust legislation. The efforts to manage and consolidate the Northern Pacific were truly international in scope, involving Germany's largest bank, leading New York bankers, and three key figures in the building of Canadian railroads, Lord Strathcona, Lord Mount Stephen, and James J. Hill, a Canadian-born American railroad tycoon.[88]

The financial distress of many rail lines required financial engineering, primarily a reduction of company debts and fixed outlays. Sometimes years of complex and delicate negotiations preceded bondholders' willingness to swap some of their debt for new bonds and equity, thereby turning some into shareholders. This process contributed to the creation of a more dispersed pool of investors who had to grow accustomed to contingent rather than fixed claims on a company's earnings and new attitudes about accounting information and other governance devices, what some have called the equity revolution. Perhaps most importantly, the crises exposed the weaknesses in the quantity and perhaps the quality of American management.[89]

Investors accepted financial restructuring on the condition that bankers provide strong oversight of companies. Distant foreign shareholders were often shocked by the incompetence of local management and shareholders, let alone by the more serious conflicts of interest. Investors, especially the foreign ones, seemed quite willing to turn over control of their shares to voting trusts led by private bankers, such as J.P. Morgan and August Belmont, rather than to allow the more "capricious" American shareholders control during crucial restructuring periods. Mostly private bankers, but also some public ones, such as NCB and Deutsche Bank, remained involved for many years in detailed management questions.[90]

Railways and Finance in Canada

One can observe similarities and differences in the development and financing of railroads in Canada and the United States. Railroad construction served an economic and a political purpose in each country. As in America, Canadian companies relied on foreign debt, a major exception being Canada's largest railroad, the Canadian Pacific, which strongly preferred equity financing. Relative to the United States, even more railway expenditure was undertaken in Canada. Vast sums of money were spent on the creation of three transcontinental railways, each with a vast feeder network and main lines running 4,000 miles from the Atlantic to the Pacific Ocean. All of this was happening in a country with a population of just eight million people. The bubble burst during the First World War, and two of the three transcontinental railways had to be nationalized. In both the United States and Canada, government was involved in railroad construction and operation, but that involvement before the twentieth century was less direct in America than it was in Canada. American railroad construction received much support from governments, especially in the form of millions of acres of land grants, and was involved in more than its share of scandals involving governments, but the Canadian government took more direct financial action, which spared Canada much of the turmoil caused by railroad failures south of the border.

Railways first came to Canada in the 1830s, originally as an attempt to combine water and rail transportation – understandable in a country with so many lakes and rivers as Canada. The first railway, the Champlain & St Lawrence (C&SLR), was financed by Montreal business executives, including John Molson, the Montreal brewer. Originally railway growth was slow, inhibited by lack of capital and a small population. It was also impeded by the financial panic of 1837. In 1849, only sixty-six miles of track had been laid in the whole of the province of Canada, which comprised the southern parts of modern-day Ontario and Quebec.

As in the United States, key private individuals played a decisive role, but railways in both countries received various kinds and degrees of support from politicians. The inspector general or minister of finance at that time, Francis Hincks, who would go on to become the Canada's third minister of finance, believed in the importance of railways as a tool for economic development. He studied the actions of governments in the United Kingdom and the United States. Hincks was particularly impressed with an observation he made in Massachusetts, where a government investment of $5 million had yielded a $400,000 profit to the government.[91] This success inspired Hincks to introduce the Guarantee Act of 1849, which provided a government guarantee of interest on bonds issued by railways that were at least seventy-five miles long and at least half constructed. He had faith in technology and British industrial ingenuity, a view that was prevalent at the time.[92] Hincks thought this legislation would be a sufficient incentive for investment by the private sector. To facilitate railroad construction, the government passed the Municipal Loan Act in 1852, giving municipalities the power to borrow on the province's credit in order to fund railways. While the programs were designed to attract private capital, they inevitably linked railroad construction to politics.

In the 1850s, the Grand Trunk Railway (GTR) constructed what was then the longest railroad in the world, running from Montreal over 500 miles to Sarnia in Canada West (present day Ontario) where it crossed over into the state of Michigan. This was Barings' first major issue of railroad bonds. It ended badly for Barings and for investors.[93] In response to operating problems, the Grand Trunk assigned Charles J. Brydges to run the railroad in 1852. Brydges was the first of a number of British and American (but mostly American) managers who ran Canadian railroads. In addition to supplying foreign capital and senior managers, the British and Americans provided railway contractors, engineers and artisans.

While the Guarantee and Municipal Loan Acts gave impetus to railroad construction, it also spawned a wave of financing that was heavily debt oriented – the ratio of debt to assets/equity was three-to-one in the Grand Trunk's case in the late 1850s.[94] When the new Dominion of Canada came into existence in 1867, 2,300 miles of rail covered the territory. Confederation was in part both a product of, and catalyst for, rail construction. Indeed, one key reason that the four original provinces agreed to join together was because of a promise, a condition that a railway, the Intercolonial, be built from Nova Scotia to Montreal. Shortly after Confederation, John A. Macdonald convinced the distant colony of British Columbia to join Canada by offering to have a railroad built to the Pacific Ocean.

The Intercolonial Railway and the Canadian Pacific Railway present dramatically contrasting pictures of railroad financing in Canada. The Intercolonial was a "strategic" railway in that it was originally conceived for defence against the Americans. Therefore it had to be situated well away from the American border and was by definition non-commercial. Problems were compounded by the fact that it was built and run by the government. The Intercolonial took nine years to build and cost nearly $80 million, almost four times the original estimate. It never made money and represented an ongoing cost to the fledgling Dominion of Canada until the railroad and its 1,500 miles of track were taken over by a new Crown corporation, the Canadian National Railway (CNR), during the First World War.[95]

The Canadian Pacific Railway (CPR) was a different story. An original attempt to build the railway resulted in a government defeat – what was known as the Pacific Scandal. The new government made little effort to fulfil the commitment made to British Columbia when it joined Confederation in 1871. But when Sir John A. Macdonald's government was re-elected in 1878, one of its highest priorities was the construction of a railway to the Pacific. The CPR was incorporated by special charter in 1881. The company took over existing lines and those under construction, and received a cash subsidy of $25 million as well as twenty-five million acres of land. The contract was signed by the government, five individuals, and two investment banks – one British, the other French. The five individuals were of Scottish birth and led by George Stephen, president of the Bank of Montreal, who resigned his position to become president of the railway.[96]

Deliberately excluded from the group was Donald Smith, later Lord Strathcona, who was not allowed to sign the agreement because the prime minister felt that Smith had betrayed him eight years earlier. But Smith, who rose from the lowest position in the Hudson's Bay Company to head up the firm, as well as succeeding his cousin, George Stephen, as president of BMO, was an essential member of the syndicate along with Stephen and Richard B. Angus, one of the five original investors. Financing of the railroad was complicated by efforts of Baring Brothers and the Grand Trunk Railway to paint a bleak picture of the CPR's financial prospects in London. And at times it appeared the CPR would fail. Initially it appealed to the New York market after being blocked in London. In 1885, on the verge of defeat, the CPR was saved when a rebellion broke out in the North West, and the railway was needed to get troops to distant territory to quell it. But in the direst moments the CPR had the great advantage of having shareholders – Stephen and Smith in particular – who pledged their "personal assets ... down to their gold cuff links."[97] After the rebellion was put down, things changed for the better for the CPR. In 1886 the company saw its first surplus. The financiers disliked debt and therefore sought to avoid it. Therefore the CPR did not incur debt charges as so many other railways had. In 1889 they paid their first dividend. The company quickly became the largest and most powerful in Canada, and with success came access to the London market. By 1914 the majority of common shares and almost all the preferred shares traded on the London market. Crucial to the company's success was the appointment of the American railroader Cornelius Van Horne as general manager. He achieved the remarkable feat of building in five years what was expected to take ten.[98]

As Canada approached the twentieth century with a population of close to 5.5 million, the young country had 18,000 miles of track and more than $1 billion of capital invested in the rail system. In the years between the beginning of the century and the outbreak of the First World War Canada would experience a flood tide of railway construction, including that of two more transcontinental railways, resulting in a doubling of trackage as well as capital invested. The first of the two companies authorized to build a transcontinental line was the Grand Trunk. The Grand Trunk had been moribund and had squandered opportunities in Canada, but in 1896 it recruited an American, Charles Melville Hays,[99] to run the company and "to introduce 'American' methods."[100] In 1903 Prime Minister Laurier, who wanted his own Liberal railway (the CPR was regarded as the Conservative railway), announced approval of the construction of a second transcontinental railway for Canada. The arrangement was unusual – a new company was created, the Grand Trunk Pacific (GTPR). The government was to build and own a line from Moncton, New Brunswick, to Quebec City, and then continue building west to Winnipeg across the bleak Canadian Shield. This portion would be leased by the government to the company. From Winnipeg the company would build a line to the West Coast. Not surprisingly this hybrid monster came crashing down during the war years and was absorbed into a Crown corporation – the Canadian National Railway.

Canada's railway picture was complicated when two entrepreneurs who had been contractors to the CPR – William Mackenzie and Donald Mann – decided to get into the railway business in western Canada in the late nineteenth century. In 1903 they felt they should have been authorized to build Canada's second transcontinental railway. When they were not, the two kept building anyway, moving east from their strong western base. Initially they were financed by a combination of government guarantees and their personal investments, relying heavily on the Canadian Bank of Commerce to finance their share. Like the GTR, the Canadian Northern Railway, having built a third transcontinental across the inhospitable Canadian Shield, had to be taken over by the government during the war.

By the war's outbreak, Canada possessed a remarkable network of railways: over 30,000 miles – all for a country with a sparse population of eight million. This was a system that was built using British capital, taxpayer money, the personal fortunes of self-made men, and managerial know-how. Many of the top- and second-tier Canadian managers were recruited from the ranks of experienced American railroad employees.

Capital and Controversy: Domestic and Foreign Insurance in North America

Whereas, the Insurance of Houses from Loss by Fire hath, where the same has been practiced, proved very useful and advantageous to the Publick; Now know ye, that we the said Subscribers hereunto, as well as for our own mutual Security as for the common Security and Advantage of our Fellow-Citizens and Neighbours, and for the Promoting of so great publick a Good as the Insurance of Houses from Loss by Fire, upon the most equal Terms, and apart from all views of private or Separate Gain or Interest; have of our own Motion offered each to the other, and have unanimously resolved and agreed, and by these Presents do covenant, promise and agree for ourselves severally and respectively, and for our several and respective Executors, Administrators and Assigns, to form, erect and settle an Office, Society or mutual ... for the Insuring of Houses from Loss by Fire.

Benjamin Franklin, Papers

The civilized man has built a coach, but has lost the use of his feet. He is supported on crutches, but lacks so much support of muscle.... His note-books impair his memory; his libraries overload his wit; the insurance-office increases the number of accidents.

Ralph W. Emerson, "Self-Reliance"

As business became more capital intensive, life more complex, and wealth more widely distributed during the latter part of the nineteenth century, domestic non-banking organizations that could harness capital and manage risk became more important to all of North America. Insurance was one of the most dynamic but complicated sectors of the American economy. Its growth helped finance American expansion by capturing and investing large amounts of American savings. As the epigraphs that introduce this section are meant to indicate, American attitudes and policies about insurance reflected a recognition of insurance's uses as well as fear of the moral hazard that it could engender.

Insurance and American Growth

With ocean trade essential to the colonies and the infrastructure of cities usually made of wood, maritime insurance – mostly from Britain and home-grown mutual companies – made its appearance in America even before the War of Independence. By the Civil War, American insurance expanded beyond maritime and local mutual insurance. In 1792 the first joint-stock company was founded (the Insurance Company of North America or INA) in Pennsylvania. By 1806, there were fifty joint-stock and mutual firms with capital of US$15 million. Nine of the ten largest fire insurance companies operating in America before the First World War had been founded before the Civil War. Moreover, in 1860 many foreign companies provided a variety of insurance services with their own agents or with American companies. The British presence was particularly strong in the South with the cotton trade. As late as 1913, eighty-nine foreign insurers were operating in the United States, of which nearly half were British, but thirteen other nations were represented. Germany accounted for thirteen insurance companies that experienced varying degrees of success. Some foreign insurers were larger in the United States than in their own countries. According to some estimates, between 1870 and 1914, 40 per cent of British property casualty revenue came from America. As in most countries, the business of life insurance developed more slowly than property and casualty insurance.[101]

After the Civil War, American demand for life insurance grew quickly. The expanding economy and booming population increased demand, and new forms of insurance, such as worker's compensation, came into existence. From 1870 to 1895 the life insurance business in the United States increased by a factor of six. By 1905 life insurance premiums accounted for 5 per cent of U.S. GDP, roughly $1.0 billion. With life expectancy growing by 25 per cent in the latter half of the nineteenth century, demand for insurance grew to protect individuals against the consequences of a premature death or conversely, a longer life. American companies were particularly creative with marketing new forms of life insurance such as tontines, as well as well as using agents who worked on commission. This helped them internationalize early, an "accomplishment" that brought them into conflict with foreign and even American regulators. From 1850 to 1880 American per capita insurance in force grew from one sixth that of Great Britain to an amount equal to Britain's, and with a much larger population. With an increasing number of American competitors and more regulatory obstacles placed on foreign ones, competition became more difficult for non-American companies. Eager to participate in the boom, firms from Great Britain, Canada, and Germany established even more agencies, branches, and subsidiaries during the post–Civil War period.[102] In fire and casualty, for example, there were eighty-nine foreign companies in 1913; nearly half were British, but the Germans, Russians, and French also had a substantial number of companies. Collectively, they held US$184 million in admitted assets.[103]

In 1905 the life insurance sector came under intense public scrutiny. Given its origins in community service and the special trust required to leave money with any organization for long periods, the charges brought against it threatened the sector's status as an innovative financial service and its national and even international viability. The concerns of bond- and policyholders as well as those of regulators led to the establishment of the Armstrong Commission, headed by Charles Evans Hughes, later chief justice of the U.S. Supreme Court. As a result of its findings, New York became the "gold standard" for underwriting insurance, and twenty-nine U.S. states had banned many life insurance practices, including investing in industrial equity by 1907. The commission also recommended new policies for marketing and managing policies.

Following the lead of British insurance companies, the United States had little home-grown reinsurance before the First World War. Ceding a part of a primary insurance company's risk (insuring the insurer) to a company specialized in helping other insurers diversify was discouraged by British law. In general reinsurance started slowly in the United States, despite a desperate need to diversify risks. American insurers tried to avoid the effects of catastrophic events with cumbersome devices, such as insurance exchanges and co-insurance agreements. Many aspects of reinsurance law remained unclear. For example, it was a point of debate as to whether the reinsurer was still liable if the primary insurer went bankrupt. Well into the twentieth century, virtually all companies providing reinsurance in the United States, such as Munich Re and Swiss Re, came from Continental Europe, where the practice had been commonplace since the middle of the nineteenth century. By 1900 these companies did extensive business in the United States, even before they had legal entities present.[104]

Had reinsurance been more developed in the United States, some of the catastrophic financial effects of the San Francisco earthquake in April 1906 might have been avoided. That event was an immense human and economic disaster, with far-reaching effects on American insurance and finances, even contributing to the 1907 Bankers' Panic that occurred eighteen months later. In a city of 400,000 residents, the same number of people died on the day of the earthquake as were killed in terrorist attacks on 11 September 2001. Ninety per cent of the buildings were wooden. According to some estimates, the quake caused US$20 million in earthquake damage and US$400 million in fire damage, for a total of 1.3 per cent of U.S. GDP. Many insurance companies went bankrupt. Even large reinsurance companies were threatened. Part of the problem lay in how risks had been defined and insured. Was the damage caused by the earthquake, which was not insured, or the fire, which was? If one building burns and collapses onto another, is the damage caused by a fire or by the collapse of another building? American regulators needed to grapple with these issues and encourage greater efforts to define risks and damages strictly, as well as to diversify over a broader geographic range, for which European reinsurers provided an exceptional source of capital and expertise.[105]

Two aspects of regulation were very American. First, the regulation of insurance was and is a complex mixture of state and national law. Against the arguments of the insurance companies themselves, the U.S. Supreme Court (Paul v. Virginia, 1868) ruled that insurance was not interstate commerce (covered by the interstate commerce clause of the Constitution) and therefore not a matter of federal jurisdiction. The decision has been challenged at times by regulators and legislators, through the Interstate Commerce Act 1887, the Hepburn Act 1906, and the Mann-Elkins Act 1910. All pushed the federal government into regulating some pricing decisions. The ruling led to an odd configuration of insurance regulation in the United States. Insurance companies, unlike banks for most of American history, could maintain operations and write business across state lines, even though their regulation was principally state by state. The rules for insurance companies, though, were and remain coordinated on a national basis by private insurance organizations and the National Association of Insurance Commissions. Moreover, from time to time, national regulators and the courts still threaten states and companies with more federal oversight if state regulations are deemed inadequate. The second peculiarity of the American market was the practice, prevalent well into the 1920s, of confining insurance companies to one type of activity, called mono-line insurance. If a company wrote maritime insurance, for example, it could not write fire insurance.[106]

Although the precise reserve restrictions and investment guidelines differed from state to state, we know that insurance was a major source of U.S. investment. Most of that investment came from life insurance companies. In 1905 the big three life insurance companies alone – Equitable, Mutual, and New York Life – held US$1.3 billion in assets, over 4 per cent of U.S. GDP.[107] In 1900 the assets of twenty-nine life insurance companies were mostly in mortgage loans (28.8 per cent) and government bonds (32.2 per cent).[108] Aggregate figures for the period before the First World War are almost impossible to come by, but in 1925 nearly 40 per cent of all life insurance assets went into government and corporate bonds, and nearly 45 per cent went into mortgages or directly into real estate.[109]

The Canadian Experience

Although Canada and the United States took very different approaches to banking, there were similarities in their respective insurance industries.[110] Not surprisingly, the first insurance mentioned in relation to Canada's history is marine insurance. At the time, merchants trading with the different Canadian territories usually bought their insurance in Europe (and in particular in London), with access to such insurance being one advantage of the European merchants over those based in Canada. The first fire insurance offered in Canada was also British in origin. The Phoenix Company of London started advertising in North America in the late eighteenth century and opened agencies in Montreal in 1804 and in Halifax in 1805.[111]

The Canadian life insurance industry, like the American industry, took off in the 1840s. In 1842 Mutual of New York (MONY) received a charter, and the next eight years saw a boom in the creation of other insurance giants like Aetna, Massachusetts Mutual, and New York Life. In 1847, in what was then Canada West (and is now the province of Ontario), Canada's first life insurance company, fittingly called Canada Life, was established in Hamilton. Over the next five decades other Canadian life insurance companies would be founded, but unlike in the United States the companies would be mostly joint-stock companies rather than mutual companies.[112]

In 1867 the new dominion moved quickly to pass legislation on insurance. In some ways the government's hand was forced because of the failure of the Western of England Fire Insurance Company. In May 1868 legislation was passed requiring a deposit of $50,000 with the government. This had the effect of making Canada a less attractive place for British and American insurers, opening the way for the development of Canadian life insurance companies. The legislation also adopted a system of inspection, copied from Massachusetts, and annual valuation, copied from New York State. At this time the insurance business, both fire and life, was dominated by British and American companies. Fire insurance premiums were double those of life insurance.[113]

Like the United States, Canada has had bifurcated regulation of its insurance industry. The federal government supervises both federally incorporated and foreign insurance companies, but provincial governments license the providers of insurance as well as the marketing of insurance products. In the mid-1870s the government of Canada passed additional legislation relating to life insurance. The office of the superintendent of insurance was established in the Department of Finance. The first superintendent was J.B. Cherriman, English born and Cambridge educated, who came to Canada as an assistant professor of mathematics at the University of Toronto.[114] Legislation was also passed requiring that federally incorporated companies provide annual statements, actuarial reserves, and mortality tables, and that companies doing business in Canada had to maintain sufficient assets to match liabilities.[115]

In 1869 Canada's life insurance industry was dominated by British and American insurers, who held over 45 per cent and nearly 40 per cent respectively of the business in force, with the remaining 15 per cent held by Canada Life. However, as a consequence of the legislative provisions requiring a $50,000 deposit, many foreign life insurers departed the scene, believing that they had better uses for their capital. This left a void, which was soon filled by new Canadian companies. By 1900 Canadian insurers held over 60 per cent of all insurance business, American firms possessed less than 30 per cent, and British firms held below 10 per cent. This pattern continued to the First World War, when the distribution of premiums was 63 per cent Canadian, 32 per cent American, and only 5 per cent British.[116]

Canada Life, which had moved to Toronto from Hamilton at the beginning of the twentieth century, was the oldest and largest life insurance company. By 1914, however, it was surpassed in size by Montreal-based Sun Life. Both companies had entered foreign markets, principally the United Kingdom and the United States.[117] Other insurers were making their presence felt, including Toronto-based Confederation Life and Manufacturers Life, Waterloo-based Mutual Life, and Winnipeg-based Great West Life.[118]

The distinguished Canadian historian Michael Bliss has noted that as the nineteenth century drew to a close a number of Canadian life insurance companies found the Canadian market too small and limited. By "the 1890s Canadian life insurance salesmen traveled the world, opening new markets for their policies, importing capital to Canada where their companies could invest it profitably." This was certainly true of Sun Life and Manufacturers Life. "It is often said that the first policy was sold in China by Sun Life of Canada which appointed its first full time manager in Shanghai in 1894…. Aside from Sun Life, pioneering development for an extensive market was made by Manufacturers Life (Canadian), which had a general manager appointed in Shanghai in 1897."[119]

Sun Life began to expand internationally in 1880 when it opened an agency in the British West Indies. This agency was followed by a flurry of international activity befitting the company's name. In the early 1890s it expanded into Asia Pacific and South America. In 1892 Sun Life was selling insurance in Japan, China, India, Malaysia, Hong Kong, and Singapore prior to its appearance in the United Kingdom in 1893. One reason for Sun Life's success was that it was prepared to sell insurance to Chinese nationals in China and to "freely accept native lives" in India. In 1895 it opened an office in Detroit, the first in the United States, and in the same year the company started selling life insurance in the Philippines, Vietnam (French Indochina), and Thailand. Manufacturers Life Insurance Company was like Sun in that it sought out opportunities in Asia Pacific. In 1897 the firm made its first sale in China. However, the board of directors was nervous about the market and passed a resolution stating, "No further business be accepted from the Chinese empire without approval of the Board."[120]

In 1899 regulations were changed to permit life insurance companies to invest in the burgeoning Canadian utility industry, a change that liberated hundreds of millions of dollars for investment in this emerging sector with its huge need for capital. For example, three life insurance companies owned all the bonded indebtedness of the Toronto Electric Light Company,[121] which had a distribution monopoly in Toronto.[122] American life insurance companies were particularly active in investing in stocks, bonds, and debentures and held two-thirds of their investments in these securities. Canadian companies balanced their investments between stocks, bonds, and debentures and loans on real estate. There were ample opportunities in real estate when Western Canada opened up and as the mortgage and loan companies failed to capitalize on that market.

An unusual feature of late nineteenth-century Canadian insurance companies was that they often appointed politicians to their boards, sometimes as president, to add a dimension of probity. Sun Life's first president was a prominent Montreal business executive who was also a member of Parliament, Thomas Workman. Similarly, Confederation Life appointed Sir Francis Hincks, Canada's minister of finance, as its first president. Not to be outdone, North American Life appointed former prime minister Sir Alexander Mackenzie, but Manufacturers Life trumped them all by appointing the incumbent prime minister, Sir John A. Macdonald, as president.

The 1905 New York State Armstrong Commission affected Canada as well as the United States. An enterprising sensationalist newspaper publisher, who was also a member of Parliament, highlighted the work of the commission and called for an enquiry in Canada. The government of Canada appointed a royal commission[123] to investigate. Although the commission shed light on some of these insurance company investments, it discovered little impropriety. Nevertheless, it sullied the reputations of many in the process. Among those whose reputations suffered was Senator George Albertus Cox,[124] the Honourable George Foster, and Dr Oronhyatekha, supreme chief ranger of the Independent Order of Foresters.[125]

The McTavish Royal Commission made recommendations similar to those of the Armstrong Investigation. These suggestions highlighted the need for greater transparency on investments, director interests and compensation, and restrictions on classes of allowable investments. The government acted on some of these recommendations, while extending more supervisory power to the government.[126]

Professional Spinoffs in North America: Actuarial, Consulting, Accounting, and Credit Services

The added complexity of business led to demands for new financial services. Many of these new service organizations had their origins in older financial companies that began to specialize, for regulatory or business reasons.

The growth of insurance was accompanied by an increased tendency to commercialize and professionalize the writing of its policies. This shift ran against the original intent of much of the earliest insurance activity, which was community service rather than profit. Many Americans resented this approach to insurance, which they conceived of as a private (non-government) activity that should not be designed for economic gain. Foreign insurers brought with them more pressure to be business-like and statistical with insurance, as opposed to the early mutual companies whose purpose was to provide insurance for all members of a community, often in perpetuity. Insurance companies used more complex math to assess losses and, later, the value of diversification. Other services developed along with actuarial science to help make insurance more professional. Companies and regulators turned to organizations like the General Adjustment Bureau, to advise and help adjust insurance losses with independent experts, an organization still used today.[127]

Other specialized advisory services came into existence. As early as 1884 Frederick Winslow Taylor, one of the earliest management consultants, was "appointed Chief Engineer of the Midvale Steel Company, there was only one university in the United States teaching management, formally."[128] Other early practitioners were the Gilbreths (a husband-and-wife team), Mary Parker, and Harold Smiddy. Although their early work focused on productivity improvement, they also advised financial companies on their holdings in industrial firms. They formed the nucleus of a new industry that began to boom in the 1920s and 1930s.[129]

Railroads and other big businesses suffered from a lack of trained managers to deal with the greater complexity of diversified organizations. They had to rely on engineers, especially those with military training. In the early stages of the revolutions in distribution and production, the experience and breadth of knowledge of bankers helped fill this management gap. Much of the managerial expertise provided by banks in the latter part of the nineteenth century was usurped in the early part of the twentieth century, at least in the United States, by specialized consulting firms and rendered less urgent by new management cadres trained at business schools like Wharton and Harvard, founded in the late nineteenth and early twentieth century.[130]

During the last twenty years of the nineteenth century, accounting came into its own. Efforts to enhance the professionalism of accountants moved from the local and state level to the national. Accountants debated whether to follow Continental countries where accounting rules and procedures were handed down by the state, or the British model of an independent professional organization that dictated rules. Consensus even among these groups was hard to build. Accountants wrestled with such issues as how to define the limits of competent practitioners, coordinate and control their activities, promote status and income, and build an effective interface with key elements of the accountant's environment – for example, companies, banks, and exchanges. Although few accountants had anything like a national or international practice, lines were delineated between elite and non-elite practitioners, those in big cities with big clients and those without. Much of the organizational effort tended to be concentrated in the Northeast, closer to the large banks, investors, companies, and exchanges, which were driving demands for more reporting and managerial accounting information. Unlike other professions such as law and medicine, accounting was not embedded in any university curriculum or tradition.[131]

Even natural alliances with their British colleagues, considered at the forefront of accounting knowledge and organization, were not easy to forge, because some Americans resented the "foreign" intrusion. Experienced British accounting firms were called in to investigate American "irregularities" and acquisition target companies, and this practice offended American accountants. It was not until 1883 that a British firm opened an accounting office in the United States: Thomas, Wade Guthrie & Co., which worked mainly with insurance and rail companies, including one with a Canadian connection. Price Waterhouse did not arrive until 1887, but Deloitte, which came in 1888, seemed to have the largest American business.[132]

Despite state and international rivalries, which impeded more unity, elite accountants had by 1886 formed the American Association of Public Accountants, which promoted a review of accounting standards, training, and licensing requirements. However, this group had rivals. During the first decade of the twentieth century, a new journal was founded, the *Journal of Accountancy*, dedicated to furthering "accounting science." It tackled many thorny economic and political issues, such as depreciation rates, whether the balance sheet or income statement contained more important issues, and how to calculate utility pricing. Not until 1916 did a new umbrella organization, the American Institute of Accountants, unify the different strands of the profession. Though the AIA's efforts included attempts to establish auditing and accounting standards for all public companies, the results were spotty. By 1914 company audits were still not required, and listed companies could still average several years of earnings.[133]

More complex financial relationships also required more sophisticated ways of assessing credit risk, or at least circumventing banks that sold expensive trade documents. As in the United Kingdom, Americans used merchant credit as a way of making up for specie and insufficient bank credit. Although the British did a great deal of credit reporting, America invented the credit reporting firm. Dun and Bradstreet, which was the result of the merger of two companies in 1933, is the product of two firms that have existed since the middle of the nineteenth century. That firm is almost synonymous with credit reporting. In both the United States and Canada, the Mercantile Agency Reference Books and Bradstreet's Book of Commercial Ratings became the standard references for credit rating. But in the nineteenth century their reports were at first based not on financial data, but on traits like honesty, punctuality, sobriety, thrift, and transparency. A new professional organization, the National Association of Credit Men even lobbied for greater sharing of debtors' payment records.[134] Surprisingly, banks, which had performed some of these functions in their issuance and discounting of trade bills, did not seem threatened, perhaps because the amount of each transaction was generally lower than those in a bill of exchange.

In Canada, as in the United States, the end of the nineteenth century saw the growth of accounting. As early as 1858, nine years before the creation of the Dominion of Canada, a young Scots immigrant to Montreal, P.S. Ross, established his own business as an "Accountant, Custom House & Commission Agent."[135] His accounting business originally focused on balancing books. An early part of the accounting business was calculating taxes as the result of the protective tariff. Another part dealt with insolvencies. By the mid-1870s the Ross family had a modest accounting practice, including clients in manufacturing and land development, and even the Montreal Protestant School Board. A major breakthrough for the firm was its appointment as auditors to the new Sun Life Assurance Company, which would go on to become one of the world's largest life insurers. There is an apocryphal story that Sun Life was so short of cash that the firm paid its audit fee with an insurance policy. Another early audit client was Bell Telephone Company of Canada.[136]

In the late 1870s Ross, who was concerned about professional standards, helped establish the Association of Accountants in Montreal, which received statutory recognition in 1880, being the first such professional body in North America. Ross served as its president for thirteen years. The Institute of Chartered Accountants of Ontario followed shortly thereafter. The two bodies were very different, with the Montreal body limiting its membership to those practising accounting and the Ontario body including not only those practising accounting but also those working in the financial sector and in wholesale trade. With the assistance of a senior U.K. accounting association, the two groups reached an agreement at a meeting of the American Association of Accountants in Atlantic City to create a dominion body for the profession. In addition to waging internal battles in Canada, the Ontario body fought with U.K. accountants who felt they should be recognized in Canada because they had qualified in the United Kingdom. The battle was sufficiently heated to involve the colonial office. By 1911 the field of accounting had its own professional magazine, the *Canadian Chartered Accountant*.

Government action helped regularize the profession. Long before the United States passed national legislation that led to national accounting norms, the government of Canada passed legislation incorporating the Institute of Chartered Accountants, Actuaries and Finance in 1902. A major boost for the accountancy business was the passage of the Ontario Companies Act in 1907. The legislation required that companies provide shareholders with a balance sheet, a statement of income and expenditure, an auditor report, and other information.[137]

Actuarial science was born in Canada in the mid-nineteenth century with the establishment of the country's first insurance company, Canada Life, in Hamilton, Ontario. The firm's founder held the title of fellow of the U.K. Institute of Actuaries. When the new Dominion of Canada was created, the appointment of an actuary to the position of superintendent of insurance indicated Canadian interest in actuarial science. The department also recruited actuaries to its staff. When the Actuarial Society of America was founded in the late 1880s, four of the thirty-eight charter members were Canadian. A Canadian organization was not established until 1907, and all twenty-four members lived and worked in Toronto.[138]

The Critique of the Gilded Age:
Progressives, Populists, and 1907

While the shock of the disasters in the United States can be heard in Canada, it must be remembered that the trouble that has arisen this week has been due in its financial acuteness to the defects of the banking system in the United States ... while our own stock markets are allied to New York, and our security list must sympathetically decline, especially in issues quoted both on the American and Canadian exchanges, there is, fortunately, no coterie of free booting speculative financiers in control of our fiduciary institutions, and there is no shadow for public doubt in the fidelity and soundness of our monetary trustees. Further, our Canadian financial public have not been given over to speculation in the same volume and purchases of our own securities on margin have been practically at a standstill for months.

Financial Post, 26 October 1907

Understandably, capitalism and the rapid growth of big business were not without critics. The great economic growth at the end of the nineteenth century was punctuated by serious depressions. The prices of many commodities remained stagnant, hurting farmers especially. Cities, and urban squalor, grew rapidly. From 1850 to 1900 the population of large eastern cities boomed. For example, Chicago's population grew from 30,000 to 1.7 million. From 1880 to 1910, the proportion of people living in an urban environment (towns of more than 100,000) quadrupled. As exchange became more complex, rules needed to be devised. Income inequality was on the rise and standards for product sale unclear.[139] Consolidations were not confined to the railroads. The creation of huge new companies and new means of distribution and production added economic efficiency but threatened the livelihoods and sense of independence of those wedded to smaller, more traditional enterprises.

Financial reformers were troubled by the lack of concentration of ownership and the over-concentration of control; they were fearful of bankers but wanted more sources of credit, and above all they wanted easy access to American exports, with no strings attached by those sending the dollars. Much of the reform movements' impact is beyond the scope of this book. We will not discuss meat safety standards, for example, but efforts to improve working conditions had some very direct financial impact, such as the creation of new forms of insurance.

Above all, populists and progressives shared a perception that business had become too big and powerful. Between 1895 and 1904 America witnessed the greatest merger wave in its history. The Standard Oil Trust was the first large consolidation, followed by others in several sectors. New Jersey's passage of a general incorporation law for holding companies in 1888 provided the regulatory framework. In those years, approximately 150 consolidations occurred. That meant that 1,800 firms disappeared into consolidated companies, and in a third of the cases these companies controlled over 70 per cent of their respective markets. Not surprisingly, the mergers created many concerns. Somewhat surprisingly, fewer concerns arose among the financial firms that were helping to fund and promote many of the restructurings.[140] While her 1985 study did not deal with banks, Lamoreaux filled this lacuna in the narrative with her 1994 study of New England banking. Despite the perception that the United States was over-banked, bank mergers were small by comparison to mergers in many other sectors and confined to certain regions that had much to do with particular regional issues. Against management and even owner resistance, the massively over-banked region went through a restructuring. The number of national banks operating in Boston dropped from the sixty that existed in 1895 to just twenty-three in 1910. In Providence, the number fell from twenty-five to nine during the same period, dramatically increasing average assets and profitability. But in contrast, the number of trusts actually increased in Boston.[141] Although many insurance companies also merged or simply failed during the period, America still had hundreds of joint-stock insurance companies writing property casualty and many others writing life.[142]

The merger movement was part of a larger process in American (worldwide) corporate governance, one of which witnessed control of major businesses ceded from owners to professional managers, agents of distant and dispersed shareholders, with little social accountability. By the First World War, the three largest companies in America each had more than 50,000 shareholders. This had mixed significance. By 1913 America had 7.5 million shareholders, nearly 8 per cent of the population, with the average size of shareholding per person dropping steadily.[143] The additional pool of shareholders helped American corporations reach huge scale and scope, even before the First World War. Seven oil companies alone had assets over US$500 million by 1913.[144]

Those who want major reforms in American capitalism are usually divided into two movements, populists and progressives. Each of these shared many common concerns but had distinctive orientations and electoral bases that evolved out of the critique of big business. The period witnessed an increase in agrarian unrest, which spawned several distinct political movements and led to the forming of the Populist Party, which eventually combined with the Democratic Party under William Jennings Bryan in 1896. The unrest expressed itself in political and legal pressure. Populists wanted to set maximum freight rates with the railroads, farmer cooperatives, increased circulation of greenbacks, government-issued paper money that would inflate prices, debt relief for farmers, an income tax, stricter controls on immigration, and more cooperative institutions to further agricultural interests. Although some research contends that their perceptions of narrower margins were not founded in reality, farmers tended to blame falling prices for their products and higher prices for their inputs on powerful industrial and financial interests.[145] These concerns contributed to legislation that controlled corporate consolidations and railroad pricing practices, but not to financial reform. For some of the reformers, however, profit-seeking finance was irredeemably flawed.

Progressives had a wide-ranging agenda for improving government and aiding the public good. They included reformist Republicans and future New Deal supporters, as well as muckraking journalists, labour leaders, intellectuals, and even business people. In fact, all three candidates for president of the United States in 1912 – Woodrow Wilson, William Howard Taft, and Teddy Roosevelt – identified themselves as progressives. Their wide-ranging proposals at many levels of government for reducing tariffs, reforming education, sanitation, health care, work rules, regulating public utilities, fighting corruption in public office, and in general creating infrastructure such as subways, electrical generation plants, and water reservoirs are beyond the scope of this chapter, except as they touch finance, as they often did. Many of these improvements had to be financed with large bond issues, paid out of government revenues, which made taxes increasingly important to finance, reinforcing demands for a progressive tax on corporate and individual income.[146] It is to the progressives, rather than the populists, that we owe most major changes in American financial regulation during the first thirty years of the twentieth century.

Not surprisingly, progressives pushed for better financial accounting. Considering America's leadership in providing financial information through much of the twentieth century, it was still behind several other countries in the 1890s in its requirements for providing public financial information. Hard as it may be to imagine, in 1900 even listed American companies were not required to provide annual audited financial statements. Some lumped many years together; others provided no reports at all.[147] In the last decade of the nineteenth century, accountants began to organize themselves to promote the use of clear financial information for the management and regulation of companies. They also promoted accounting theory and standards to help investors evaluate company operations. From the beginning, the process was highly influenced by British accountants, who worked closely with some Americans and helped found some U.S. firms, created accounting norms, and pushed for company audits. While foreign influences were not always welcome, Canadian accountants and economists were involved in the process too. "Blue sky" became the watchword for many reformers who believed that openness was a superior form of control over well-informed and well-placed "insiders," which had been the norm in the United States and other countries. Although this reliance on transparency had its financial critics on both sides of the Atlantic Ocean, eventually the process of establishing professional organizations and standards became a linchpin of American corporate governance from the 1930s to today.[148]

Given its increased urbanization and industrialization, Canada too suffered from many of the same problems that animated American progressive calls for reform in America. Nevertheless, at the turn of the century Canada did not have a progressive movement. That would come later, after the defeat of the Free Trade Agreement in the 1911 election.

In the summer of 1911, Prime Minister Laurier, who was now well into his fourth term of office, toured the booming West. Everywhere he heard the same thing. The Westerners did not like the protective tariff – they wanted lower tariffs and the ability to sell into the U.S. market. Laurier reminded them that in order to attain this goal the Americans had to agree. He had no inkling that they would agree when suddenly a request came from Washington to discuss freer trade. This was a complete change of attitude in Washington. The Americans were now willing to discuss freer trade, and Laurier returned from the American capital with a reciprocity agreement authorized by Congress. Originally, this issue looked like a sure-fire winner for Laurier's Liberals, and the prime minister called an election for September. The Conservative opposition was naturally against reciprocity. They were joined by the Group of Eighteen, a coalition of prominent Liberal businessmen that included former cabinet minister Sir Clifford Sifton. On election day the Laurier Liberals went down to defeat, as did the reciprocity agreement. However, in the newly admitted provinces of Alberta and Saskatchewan fifteen pro-reciprocity members were elected, compared with two opposed. In Saskatchewan the vote was close to 60 per cent pro and 40 per cent con. This defeat of reciprocity laid the foundation for the progressive movement, which would rise up in the late teens not only on the Prairies but also in Ontario and as far to the east as New Brunswick. The defeat of reciprocity in 1911 led to the end of the two-party political system in Canada and the creation of progressive political parties as farmers demanded equity. They did not like selling their products in free global markets while buying their inputs in protected domestic markets. Nor did they like the control exerted on the economy by "The Forty-two" – two groups of business tycoons. The first was based in Montreal and was associated with the Bank of Montreal and the CPR "group." The second was based in Toronto and had links to the Bank of Commerce and the Canadian Northern.

Meanwhile the reaction in the United States was shock and horror. The defeat of reciprocity received significant coverage in the *New York Times*, the *Chicago Tribune*, and the *Wall Street Journal*. It also adversely affected President Taft's election chances. As the *Boston Traveller* wrote, "It was very unkind of those Canadians to deprive President Taft of his best argument for reelection just when he needed it most."[149]

The 1907 Crisis

The 1907 Bankers' Panic helped shift progressive attention back to American banking. This was not the only crisis of the post–Civil War period. For many years, people felt as if they were living through a depression during the 1870s and 1880s, when some sectors were restructured and some commodity prices stagnated or fell. The country had witnessed severe shocks in 1873, 1884, 1890, and 1893, with large numbers of bank failures and in 1893 widespread failures of banks to convert deposits into currency. The crises had many immediate causes: for example, railroad leverage and overcapacity and foreign investor fears of the United States' weak commitment to the gold standard. The 1907 panic was the first that appeared to begin in the banking sector. Several of the lightly regulated New York trusts got caught out on commodity speculation, calling into question the solvency of others. In any case, the panic quickly spread to other regions, leading to a short but severe recession. J.P. Morgan, the leading investment banker of his day, stepped into the breach. He, not the state or federal government, organized a committee of bankers to determine which trusts were solvent and which were not, and to ensure the liquidity of the whole banking system. It was the last time a private banker would play this role. By and large, the public was not thankful but shocked that private bankers were needed and wielded this kind of power.[150]

During the panic, as in several other crises, widespread suspension of deposits into currency, took place, and the money supply declined, the only time this occurred between 1897 and 1914. With no federal bank to ensure liquidity, deposits declined sharply. Progressives were fearful of centralized financial power, but more fearful of private, centralized power, so they focused on the activities of joint-stock and private banks. Two intertwined problems had to be dealt with: the creation of money and the power of banks to control the economy. The panic led to the Aldrich-Vreeland Act in 1908, as a temporary measure. Passed by an overwhelming Republican majority, with no Democrats voting for it, the Act allowed national banks working in concert to start issuing currency backed by any bonds they held, not just government bonds, in times of emergency. The Act, considered by many to be a stopgap measure, also created the National Monetary Commission, whose recommendations ultimately led to the Federal Reserve Act of 1913.[151]

The panic and J.P. Morgan's role in quelling the 1907 crisis reinforced fears that powerful financial interests were controlling the American economy. Shortly after the crisis, the House of Representatives launched an investigation into "money trusts." The Pujo Committee, the subcommittee responsible for the enquiry, found that J.P. Morgan and other private bankers led a group of bankers that actually controlled eighteen separate financial corporations, which in turn sat on the boards of 112 companies with US$22 billion in assets (an amount equal to roughly half the U.S. GDP).[152] The findings of the Pujo Committee were publicized by one of America's most famous progressives and later Supreme Court justice, Louis Brandeis, in *Other People's Money – and How the Bankers Use It*, and influenced the legislation creating America's third central bank.

While not generally recognized, Canada too had a credit crisis in 1907, complete with bank failures. While not as severe as that of the United States, it still ranks as one of the worst years for the Canadian economy in the twentieth century. Much of the problem in Canada, as in the United States, was the commodity nature of the economy and the huge demand for cash to move crops in the fall. The problem was compounded by the enormous demands for capital from the prolonged capital infrastructure boom. With huge demands for credit, the banks started tightening their criteria for loans. This induced a period of near panic in the West. In Canada's case, the minister of finance, W.S. Fielding, saved the day by allowing banks to issue their own notes in excess of reserve requirements in the harvest season. Specifically, the banks were allowed to issue notes up to 15 per cent of their unimpaired paid-up capital and reserve fund, but only for the period from 1 October to 31 January.[153] This simple expedient got the Canadian economy through the "forgotten credit crisis" of 1907. It would take more than a quarter of a century and the Great Depression before the government in Canada decided on the need for a central bank to determine monetary policy.

America Gets Its "Third Central Bank"

Despite widespread agreement after the 1907 crisis that America's financial system was badly in need of repair, skilful political negotiations were required to enact legislation for America's "third central bank." Many ghosts that had haunted America's finance since the country's inception had to be addressed. The saga served as a veritable trial, exposing America's long-standing battles with regulation in general and its ambivalence about finance in particular. All the themes came to the fore: fear of central authority and plutocratic government; disdain for capitalists' infatuation with hard money, which ostensibly held back the common man in rural or urban settings from his natural birthright; resentment of foreign influences; and even reverence for past heroes. Indeed, framers of the legislation were even hesitant to call the new institution a central bank, for fear of what the term would conjure.[154]

In light of these challenges, the passage of the Federal Reserve Act was the major financial achievement of the progressive era. The Act, with features similar to those in a plan designed by Senator Nelson W. Aldrich, father-in-law of John D. Rockefeller Jr, in the end was passed by Congress, which was by then Democrat-controlled. The Act was signed into law by Woodrow Wilson, who had vigorously supported the idea of a Federal Reserve, despite heavy criticism from his own party. Since the original plan was conceived by a group of mostly private bankers, it was tainted in the eyes of many from its conception. Some key elements of the original plan had to be jettisoned. Sentiment ran high against powerful bankers by 1913, and in particular against the role played by Paul Warburg, a recent German immigrant and partner in M.M. Warburg & Company, the powerful investment bank. Warburg's participation inflamed suspicions of foreign domination, as the final legislation copied many elements of the German model. Warburg was even appointed to the Fed's first board. In contrast to the recommendations in the original plan, the Fed was a government-controlled central bank, rather than one run by private interests, as was the case with the Bank of England. But from the beginning, the highly concentrated New York bankers had a strong voice in Fed affairs. In deference to Bryan and other populist critics, the final act failed to centralize bank reserves and authority over the money supply, as most financial experts had wanted. Many opponents entreated the Democrats to vote against the legislation, as to do otherwise would betray the memory of Andrew Jackson. Some of the populist amendments to the bill, such as Federal Deposit Insurance, had to wait for the next major crisis for enactment. As one historian correctly put it, "The enactment of the Federal Reserve System, although a landmark in American history, was less an ending than a truce."[155] Indeed, as seen even in recent American election debates, many of the issues are still unresolved and remain active parts of America's current volcanic political landscape.

Nevertheless, the duties of the Federal Reserve were much more circumspect in 1913 than they are now and its governance was very different. The final bill gave control of the currency to the U.S. Treasury instead of private banks. Now the Fed could issue a new national currency, but for many years government currency existed side-by-side with private banknotes. Consistent with populist attacks on hard currency and private bankers, opponents of the legislation demanded that the issuance of currency had to be a public function, governed by the "needs" of the people, not in the interests of creditors. To ensure local voice and diversity in its tasks, the Federal System was divided into twelve regional banks, which would be responsible for the reserves and liquidity of the member banks in their regions. The Fed's mandate was to accommodate the commerce of the country and promote price stability (what was later dubbed and more clearly defined as the dual mandate), but this was even vaguer then than now. It clearly was to ensure liquidity for the banking system, but the degree to which it would use its bank reserves and ability to discount paper to serve as "banker of last resort" was also unclear. Although the Fed banks were empowered to discount bank paper (loans), those loans were intended to be short-term and connected to commercial transactions.

The decision-making process for discounting and types of loans covered – some wanted farm loans to be included – was left to a large extent in the hands of regional banks, with review from the national board. In theory the board could veto regional policies. This so-called real bills doctrine, along with America's commitment to the gold standard, was considered by most as a sufficient brake on an overzealous regional bank to ward off runaway inflation. However, the Fed's overall precise role as "banker of last resort" remained a thorny question into the twenty-first century. The six non-government members of the board were to be appointed by the president with the approval of the Senate. Until the 1930s, the Fed board remained tightly controlled by the federal government, with the secretary of the treasury and comptroller of the currency serving on the board, and the secretary as chair. All nationally chartered banks were required to become members of the Federal Reserve System, in which they would buy shares and leave non-interest-bearing deposits. State banks were given the option. The legislation also freed member banks from many of the constraints with which they had lived, such as underwriting international trade bills.[156]

It took a while to set up. Just determining the location of the twelve regional banks was no mean feat. It required political haggling. Like today, personalities counted. While William Gibbs McAdoo was secretary of the treasury, Paul Warburg, one of the original proponents of the bank, and Benjamin Strong, former president of Bankers Trust and first head of N.Y. Fed, were involved in Fed affairs and wielded influence beyond their positions. The original legislation left many levers of authority unclear, laying the groundwork for intense competition among the board, regional banks, and Treasury for determining policy and practice.[157]

Within eight months of the passage of the Federal Reserve Act, the untested new central bank was confronted with a challenge that was taxing to even its more experienced counterparts: the beginning of the First World War in Europe. The emergency currency created by the Aldrich-Vreeland Act, for example, was ostensibly no longer necessary after the creation of the Fed. However, it still played a major role in mitigating the financial crisis after war was declared in Europe, since the twelve new Federal Reserve regional banks did not open their doors until November 1914. Soon after America's entry into war in 1917, Paul Warburg, controversial from the beginning, felt pressured to resign his seat on the board as the result of his German heritage and various political clashes. Just when the war and new banking regulations catapulted the United States from a backwater to a leading financial market, the Fed lost its most experienced international banker.[158]

Canada would wait until 1934 to create a central bank, in spite of the examples south of the border as well as in the United Kingdom and fellow dominions, such as South Africa, Australia, and New Zealand. There were public policy reasons for this. Canada had monetary and fiscal stability. The "Canadian Bankers' Association (CBA) not only opposed a central bank but also provided a vehicle for informal policy guidance to the banking system … now called 'moral suasion.'… There was also the Bank Circulation Redemption Fund, for monitoring note issues. And the banks had … operated the clearing system." On top of that there was some form of monetary control as a result of the 1914 Finance Act, which will be discussed in chapter 4.[159]

Conclusion

I fancy the Canadians of 1850 did better by lending their money in the United States than they would have done in a rash and premature effort to surpass her advantages. It might even be contended that a presiding wisdom restrained Canada in the 19th century while America burnt her candle at both ends, and that in the 20th century Canada is having her turn. This implies that wisdom depends on what century one lives in.

Bray Hammond, *Banks and Politics in America*

The period beginning in the late 1860s was remarkable in the history of the two North American countries north of the Rio Grande River. With Arizona and New Mexico joining the Union in 1912, America consisted of forty-eight states. They were the last states to join the Union for a half-century. To the north, Canada had in 1869 acquired the vast territory known as Rupert's Land, and from this carved out the three Prairie provinces as well as expanded the borders of Ontario and Quebec. Canada also welcomed British Columbia on the West Coast and Prince Edward Island on the East Coast as new provinces. In addition to settlements, this period was marked by dramatic population growth through a combination of immigration and a high birth rate. Both countries more than doubled their populations, although the United States grew faster between 1871 and 1914 – to nearly 100 million by 1914, while Canada at that point reached just over 8 million, despite the fact that in the early twentieth century Canada's population was growing faster than that of the United States. And while the U.S. population ultimately grew faster than Canada's, by the beginning of the new century Canada's GDP was growing faster than that of the United States. By 1914, America was clearly the largest economy in the world, nearly double the size of its nearest rivals – China, the United Kingdom, and India. While Canada had a much smaller GDP, it was still the seventh-richest nation in the world in terms of GDP per capita.

Much of the growth in both countries was fuelled by the steam revolution, which required billions of dollars of investment. Much of this investment came from offshore, without which the thousands of miles of railway track that criss-crossed the continent would not have been possible. The railway companies were the giants in their economies, although obviously the American firms were much larger than their Canadian counterparts. The Canadian Pacific, Canada's largest railroad, for example, was roughly the same size in terms of assets as the Union Pacific, America's fourth largest. And, generally speaking, the large Canadian corporations were concentrated in the extractive sector and in electrical utilities. In the United States, giant industrial concerns had emerged and consolidated, especially in the areas of primary metals and petroleum (US Steel and Standard Oil), food (Armour and Swift), and emerging consumer sectors, such as automobiles (Ford and GM), cameras (Kodak), and appliances (GE and Westinghouse). In both countries, though, economic activity still depended greatly on individual farmers and small businesses.

In terms of political protest the United States was well ahead of Canada, with three progressive candidates for president in 1912. This is not surprising, because not only did the United States have a vast territory called the South, which obviously Canada did not, but America also had a settled West by this point. South and North Dakota and Montana became states of the Union a full sixteen years before Alberta and Saskatchewan became provinces of Canada. The defeat of the 1911 Canadian U.S. Reciprocity Agreement by the voters of central Canada would lead to a progressive movement in Canada in the early 1920s, centred on the Prairies.

In terms of financial systems, the two countries were similar in areas such as insurance, but could not have been more different in banking. In the United States thousands of banks existed without branches, while Canada hosted a few dozen banks with thousands of branches. By 1914, however, the United States had a central bank – which Canada did not – and 15 to 25 per cent cash reserves were required for banks. However, those facts did not ensure that the U.S. banking system was any more stable. Canada's minimum bank capitalization requirements were ten times higher than those of the United States. As well, bank shareholdings in Canada were more widely distributed, interest rates were equalized across the nation, regular review of the banking system was mandated by law, and, most importantly, Canada's currency was more elastic and thereby better able to deal with seasonal variations in loan demand.[160] The First World War and the ensuing economic and political chaos would change much but not all of the building blocks of each country's financial strengths and weaknesses. As with most transformations – if we might be allowed an agricultural metaphor – seeds are sown and fields are watered long before the crops are harvested.

CHAPTER FOUR

"The Great Disorder" and Growing Social Demands: 1914–1945

The Effects of the First World War: Short and Medium Term

It is curious to note how the European situation is judged here and surprising how little is understood. Even bankers who have every means of getting at the root of things as they are in Europe do not seem to get there, a fact which I can only explain by the lack of comprehension of the European psychology and European ways as well as an unlimited confidence of Americans in their own judgment. They are entirely ignorant of economic conditions on the continent and seem to gauge everything in Europe by what they know about England.

E. Hürlimann, Bericht über Amerikanreise

The "most remarkable" development of 1915 was the expansion of the domestic capital market…. "Thus after having figured year after year as our constant and heavy debtor, Canada has suddenly transformed herself into a creditor of Great Britain," observed *The Economist* in December 1915. "That perhaps is the most surprising economic *volte face* caused by the war."

Richard Roberts, *Saving the City: The Great Financial Crisis of 1914*

Finding a country or region that was not heavily affected by the First World War (August 1914 to November 1918) is impossible. Some countries ceased to exist, others came into existence; some acquired radically new forms of government, while in others a desire for independence was awakened or reinforced. The "Great War" ushered in a three-decade-long period comprising war, depression, boom, depression, foreign exchange and interest rate volatility, and then war again. The level of turmoil during those thirty years had not been seen in Europe or

North America since the French Revolution and the time of Napoleon I. Some have dubbed it, or a part of it, "The Great Disorder."[1] The shock and impact was due more to the length and severity of the war than to the fact that a "civil war" among European nations occurred. Few if any observers in the summer of 1914 foresaw a four-year conflict with 17 million civilian and military deaths and untold property damage.

The immediate effects were dramatic in Canada and the United States, but not equal in timing, extent, or value. On 4 August King George V declared the British Empire, including Canada, at war, a commitment Canadians accepted at first with enthusiasm. However, that passion waned as controls were introduced and casualties mounted. Even before war was declared, the stock markets in Canada's five major financial centres closed. Financial panic was prevented by prompt federal action, including a major step toward a central bank with the passage of the Finance Act, which provided the government with the authority to issue new dominion notes without gold backing to finance the war effort and to lend to the chartered banks at their request.[2]

While many important effects were experienced within months, many later ones had even more long-term significance. The year 1917 proved to be the most eventful in twentieth-century Canada: food and price controls were introduced; manpower was conscripted for overseas service, and riots ensued; two of three transcontinental railways were nationalized – one completed that year, the other begun; women's suffrage was introduced; and a coalition unionist government was created. The government was made up of Conservatives and English-speaking Liberals. It was also the time when the first election in six years was held,[3] a prohibition of alcoholic beverages was introduced (ahead of prohibition in America), and a "temporary" Income Tax Act was passed. The war saw not only a massive increase in borrowing but also a shift of indebtedness from the United Kingdom, briefly to the United States, but ultimately to Canadian citizens. It also marked a continuation of the shift within Canada from Montreal to Toronto, where leading bond houses with closer ties to New York played a greater role in raising funds. Shortly after the war, a depression led to a major bank failure and several bank consolidations.

In the United States, too, news of war was destabilizing, even though the United States did not enter the conflict until 1917. Even before war was declared by Europeans, the British Empire, and Japan, deposits were withdrawn from the United States and sent to England. Financial facilities for American bankers in Europe were curtailed and U.S.

securities were sold, with funds repatriated to European countries. Only the closure of the New York Stock Exchange on 31 July 1914 – for the third time in its history – stopped the haemorrhaging of foreign sales. It did not reopen until 28 November, and then only with restricted trading until April 1915. Despite the added risks, gold[4] was shipped from New York banks to Europe, putting upward pressure on the pound in much the same way as the dollar rose in the aftermath of the 2008 Bankers' Panic. The problems lasted for months, challenging the newly minted U.S. Federal Reserve Board officials and even their more experienced British counterparts.[5] Despite the potential for greater European demand for new war-related products, financial turbulence and other factors threw the United States into a deep recession, which nearly doubled the unemployment rate and lasted nearly a year. In 1914, over 100 U.S. banks failed – more than in any year since the Civil War except 1893, when 500 banks closed. The closures amounted to over 2 per cent of all the state and national banks.[6]

The war dramatically changed America's financial relationship with other countries. For the first time, America allowed, indeed encouraged, its commercial banks to go out into the world and do business elsewhere. America's seizure of enemy property propelled American companies in many sectors into dominant positions on their own shores, such as in insurance and reinsurance, as well as making some formidable international players. Despite isolationist reluctance, the war thrust America into the financial affairs of the rest of the world, contributed to a boom and bust, and created new demands for services from public and private institutions. At times the two sectors were working in an uncomfortable partnership, a harness in which they would ride for much of the next 100 years. Indeed, according to some anti-war activists, German bankers, and even historians, financial issues contributed to America's entry into the 1917 conflict on the side of the Entente (an informal alliance between Britain, France, and Russia).[7]

Unlike many developed countries, the United States emerged from the conflict relatively unscathed. It was indeed energized with fledgling confidence and a new but tentative willingness to export its sense of exceptionalism. The First World War had mostly positive effects on America, unlike its impact on Canada and most other participating countries. America lost relatively few soldiers (less than what Canada lost), relative to its population and the losses of other countries, saw no battles on its shores, enjoyed a boom in exports, and transformed itself for the first time from a debtor to a creditor nation.

Table 4.1 Shift in Canadian Bond Financing, 1913–1918 (% of Total Borrowing)

	1913	1914	1915	1916	1917	1918
In Canada	12.2	12.0	43.7	33.5	74.6	94.9
In United States	13.5	19.7	42.1	64.8	24.7	4.7
In United Kingdom	74.2	68.1	14.1	1.5	0.6	0.4

Source: Macmillan, *Report of Royal Commission on Banking and Currency*, 107.

The direct and indirect impact of the First World War on the U.S. financial system was vast, but precise estimates are probably incalculable.

The resulting changes in Canada and its financial system, although not as well-known, were even more profound than in America. Within a few years Canada's initial war buoyance morphed into a more sober mood, partially for financial reasons.[8] Even the end of hostilities was marred by a devastating depression, much more severe than the downturn in the United States, and a banking crisis that saw the largest bank failure in Canadian history to that point.

The war produced two parallel changes to the two countries' financial systems: greater reliance on capital markets and the imposition of federal income taxes. Most of the war was financed in Canada using borrowed funds[9] and inflation, not increased taxes. As was the challenge in all countries, Canada's ability to fund the war with taxes faced severe restraints. In 1914 the dominion government received nearly 80 per cent of its revenue from indirect taxes – customs and excise duties. Federal income taxes were not introduced until 1917. Until the war was nearly over, virtually no revenues were derived from income taxes, other than a business profits tax. [10] In order to finance the war, the Canadian government looked to the bond market, just as its southern neighbour did. This approach would have major implications for Canadians, bond dealers, and capital markets in Canada, just as it had in the United States (see table 4.1).

The U.S. government also relied on the general public to finance the debt, which increased the public appetite for buying securities. The government used an aggressive campaign to encourage war bond purchases. Many individual and small business investors who had never bought any securities, now held financial assets. Converting this interest into stock purchases was a relatively small step. From 1913 to 1929, not only did stock market capitalization as a percentage of U.S. GDP nearly double but the number of shareholders increased even more.[11]

Between March and November 1917 in Canada, the "bond market had deteriorated badly, and funds were urgently needed to finance the war ... Something special in bond selling seemed to be necessary. As a consequence of this, the Bond Dealers Association suggested a plan that would involve a country-wide organization."[12] The plan was executed, and bond sales far exceeded expectations. From 1915 to 1919 $2 billion was raised. Perhaps most important for the long term, the bond sales contributed to the shift of financial activity from Montreal to Toronto, one of the most important changes in Canadian finance during the twentieth century.[13]

The introduction of federal income taxes, however, was the most significant long-term change to both countries' financial systems. There was little resistance to a federal income tax for war purposes. In 1917 Canada passed the Income War Time Tax Act. Funds from the Act would not be collected until the 1918/19 fiscal year. Income tax was not new to Canada, but it had never been collected by the federal government. Some provinces and municipalities already levied income taxes. The tax was modest, and it is ironic in retrospect to consider that income tax, which is now such a fixture of the economy, was introduced as a temporary measure. It yielded only $9.3 million, or 3 per cent of all dominion revenue,[14] but this would quickly change.

The United States also ended the war with an increased reliance on income tax. Apart from short periods during the Civil War and in the 1890s, no federal income tax was collected until 1913. Indeed, many believed that the Constitution did not empower the federal government to impose one. Fiscal demands and expectations for more services and a more progressive tax led to the Sixteenth Amendment, which allowed the federal government to collect income tax for the first time. The amendment was ratified by the prerequisite number of states in 1913. Even with the new constitutional power, tax rates were initially very low, but they increased as fiscal needs during the war were covered in part by several upward revisions of the marginal tax rates on all sorts of income. Those rates were lowered in the 1920s but increased to First World War levels during the Great Depression. Today income taxes – corporate, individual, and payroll – account for nearly all federal revenues in the United States, but only 65 per cent of those collected in Canada. A long-term difference between the two countries is that the United States allowed mortgage interest deductibility for income tax purposes from the beginning and Canada did not.

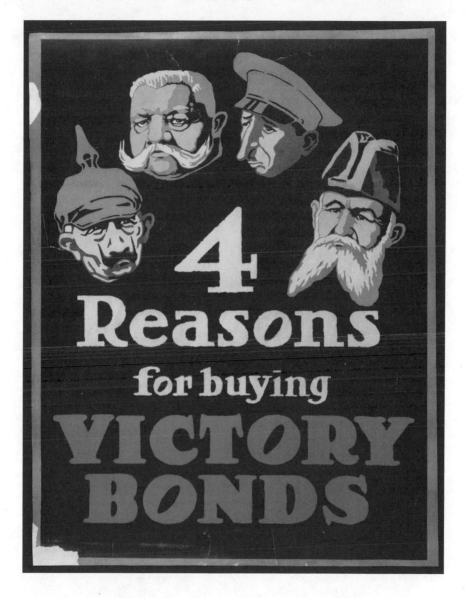

Figure 4.1 WWI Canadian recruiting poster
Source: World Digital Library (1917).[15]

The Boom Years in the United States and Canada

The twentieth century by contrast is a confusion of emergencies, disasters, improvisations, and artificial expedients. One passes in a few weeks in 1914 from a quiet stream, as it were, to white water.

David Landes, *The Unbound Prometheus*

It is essential to recognize that the twenty years following the First World War were not one unified political, financial, and economic period,[16] but rather several. As Charles Dickens described a similar era, "It was the best of times, it was the worst of times." The period 1914 to 1945 was marked by significant changes in the role and place of the United States and Canada in the world economy. In the late nineteenth century the United States passed China and became the world's largest economy. At the beginning of the twentieth century the United States passed the United Kingdom as the richest economy in the world. And that was just the beginning. In spite of the devastation of the Great Depression, the United States emerged from the Second World War as the world's dominant superpower, with an economy 60 per cent larger than all of Europe's combined, while the Chinese economy was diminishing rather than expanding. In keeping with this dynamic change, the United States moved from its earlier isolationist role to become a world leader in promoting freer trade, a stable global currency, and a secure world order. After the First World War, the United States had refused to join the League of Nations. However, after the Second World War, America truly entered the global sphere. Now not only was the United Nations organized in San Francisco, but also its headquarters was situated in New York City. A major financial capital before the war, New York surpassed London as the world's most important financial centre by many measures.[17]

The period 1919 to 1939 was marked by a maturation of the Dominion of Canada, a period when it became self-governing in foreign as well as domestic policy and developed closer links with the United States. During the war American outward foreign investment increased in volume – as well as geographic and sectorial dispersion – by nearly 50 per cent overall, but Canada by only a third. Banking foreign investment from the United States quadrupled but remained around 3 per cent of the total and inconsequential in Canada. Despite the Depression, U.S. investment in Canada grew nearly 30 per cent as measured by book value by 1940, making up 30 per cent of the U.S. total foreign direct investment (FDI).[18] During the Second World War, Canada became the largest single destination for U.S. foreign investment.[19]

The war had a profound impact on American demographics and the economy. Undaunted or perhaps even encouraged by the Eighteenth Amendment prohibiting the manufacture, sale, and shipment of liquor, Americans dedicated themselves to social and economic change. Mass production accelerated, and consumer goods, electrical power, new appliances, suburban housing, and city skyscrapers reflected seemingly endless opportunities for growth. Before the First World War the automobile was considered a novelty. By 1929 it seemed like a middle-class necessity. From 1920 to 1930 the number of families with indoor flush toilets grew from 20 to 51 per cent, central heating from 1 to 42 per cent, lighting by electricity from 35 to 68 per cent, washing machines from 8 to 24 per cent, vacuum cleaners from 9 to 30 per cent, and automobiles from 26 to 60 per cent. By 1930 home mechanical refrigerators and radios, which were virtually non-existent before the First World War, were found in 8 and 40 per cent of American homes respectively. During the Roaring Twenties, automobile production tripled, contributing to a boom in the construction of roads and suburban homes. All of this had a major impact on the U.S. financial system, not the least of which was the boom in consumer credit with the notion that one could "buy now, pay later." Strong demand for labour not only led to improvements in work hours and wages but also greater demand for banking services such as chequing accounts. Above all, the period 1922 to 1929 is associated with one of the great bull markets in history. During that period, the S&P index climbed from 100 to 309 and the ratio of stock price to stock dividends from less than nineteen to more than twenty-seven.[20]

But the news during those years was not all good. Farmers were plagued by deflation and high debt levels even as demand for agricultural products was high. They felt that they did not share in the general prosperity of the 1920s, even though their real incomes remained steady. The number of Americans living in urban environments swelled between 1920 and 1930, as many moved to cities for jobs and more opportunities. Those Americans living in towns of more than 2,500 people increased to 50 million, feeding social tensions. Hate crimes directed toward blacks, Jews, and other minorities abounded. Legal restrictions on immigration, especially from countries outside of Northern Europe, were strengthened. Despite the economic boom and political turmoil in much of the world, immigration declined from over 1 million per year in 1910 to fewer than 300,000 in 1929. Women won the right to vote and entered the work force in great numbers, but birth rates dropped and restrictions on work activities for married women remained in many sectors. By some measures, income inequality increased, although the impact of this development, if it was real, is hard to assess.[21]

During these years some American industrial companies grew larger in assets and market value than the railroads, attracting millions of new shareholders. Some U.S. firms had morphed into the world's largest, as measured by assets and market values. These thriving enterprises included Armour and Co., International Paper and Power, DuPont, Standard Oil, United States Steel, General Electric, and several transportation equipment and utility companies, such as GM and AT&T.[22] From 1913 to 1928 the capital stock of all American corporations grew from $65 billion to $92 billion, and the number of shareholders more than doubled. In 1928, 18 million Americans owned stock. In that year, too, the three largest American corporations, AT&T, Pennsylvania Railroad, and United States Steel, respectively, had 454,000, 158,000, and 101,000 separate shareholders. This raised new questions about the governance of public companies. From 1913 to 1929 daily trading volume on the five leading U.S. exchanges climbed from 20 million to 180 million shares. During the 1920s America's OTC market (stocks not listed on organized exchanges, a nascent NASDAQ) grew from 6 to 14 per cent of total stock trading. However, America was still behind the United Kingdom and some other countries in the percentage of corporations listed on exchanges. It also lagged behind its counterparts in the governance of public companies, such as accounting rules and audits. By 1926 all companies on the New York Stock Exchange submitted detailed balance sheets, but only 55 per cent listed their sales, and fewer still reported expense details. In addition, the ability of the exchange to enforce rigorous compliance became more and more limited as stock listings increased quickly during the 1920s.[23]

A first glance at comparative numbers for the Roaring Twenties could lead one to conclude that Canada "roared" louder than the United States, but that would be false. It is true that from the low point to the high point, Canada's economy improved more than that of the United States, but that does not take into account the severity of Canada's post–First World War depression. A comparison reveals that from Canada's economic high point in the First World War (1917) to its apex in the twenties (1928), GDP per capita improved by only 7.7 per cent, whereas the U.S. economy improved by 21.9 per cent (1918 to 1929). Although the image of the post–First World War period is one of boom and then bust, the reality is more complex. Between 1918 and 1921 the Canadian economy, for example, declined by 30 per cent in GDP per capita. In 1921 alone GDP per capita dropped 13.1 per cent.[24] Not surprisingly the political scene reflected this economic turbulence as populist governments were elected in Alberta, Manitoba, and Ontario[25] and won the second-largest number of seats in the House of Commons, pushing the Conservatives to third, in a historical first.

During the war years and through the 1920s and the Great Depression Canada did not experience anywhere near the same dramatic economic growth as the United States (see appendix 4.3). But while Canada's economic growth did not match America's, it did exceed that of most other countries. By 1945 Canada had not only surpassed Spain to become the seventh-largest economy in the Western world, but in GDP per capita it passed both the United Kingdom and Australia to become the third-richest economy in the world after the United States and Switzerland. Internationally, Canada had become a nation in its own right, not just a British colony, in recognition of its contributions to the war effort. The passage of the Statute of Westminster on 31 December 1931 by the imperial Parliament gave the self-governing dominions such as Canada independence in foreign as well as domestic matters.[26]

Large corporations in Canada were much smaller than those in the United States and were often subsidiaries of American parents, companies like General Motors of Canada and Imperial Oil (Exxon). One Canadian company that demonstrated dynamic growth across the border and beyond was Distillers Corporation Seagram.

Canada was shifting politically and economically away from the United Kingdom and more and more toward the U.S. orbit during the 1920s. A puzzling aspect of this trend was that, although Canada bought far more goods from the United States than vice-versa, Congress passed the Fordney McCumber Tariff in 1922, a protectionist measure and precursor of worse things to come. As a consequence, in some years Canada sold more to the United Kingdom than to the United States, although Canada was always a major buyer of U.S. goods and services.[27] In 1922 the United States surpassed the United Kingdom as the largest foreign investor in Canada and by the end of the 1920s was investing a third more in Canada than was the United Kingdom. Furthermore, American investment was direct, rather than portfolio, particularly in manufacturing, utilities,[28] mining and smelting, and pulp and paper.

Banking in Canada and the United States, 1914–1929

I think it only fair to say that in my view the Secretary of the Treasury and his colleagues at Washington adopted as generous a policy towards purchases by Britain in Canada from monies borrowed from the American Government as we could have reasonably expected in view of all the conditions at the time.

Thomas White (Canadian minister of finance),
The Story of Canada's War Finance

For Canadian banks the 1920s was a period of consolidation and merger, although it was also a time when the banks' share of the total financial intermediation pie fell from over 60 to 50 per cent.[29] In 1925 there were two major mergers, with the Royal Bank acquiring the Winnipeg-based Union Bank, which enabled it to surpass the Bank of Montreal for the first time. This shift occurred despite the Bank of Montreal's acquisition practices, which included the Merchants and Molson banks in 1922 and 1925 respectively. Not to be outdone, the Canadian Bank of Commerce acquired three banks, and perhaps the most interesting of all was Alloway and Champion in Winnipeg, the most important private bank in Canada.[30] At the beginning of the decade there were twenty banks. By the end of the decade only eleven banks remained.[31] As the *Canada Year Book* observed, "The elimination of weaker banks or their amalgamation with more stable institutions has been a progressive move toward greater security and confidence."[32]

In addition to consolidation, nearly 600 of Canada's more than 4,000 branches were closed, particularly in Western Canada; nearly two-thirds of those closures were in the recently settled Prairie provinces. All of the large banks, though, also maintained branches, subsidiaries, or agencies in the United States, Great Britain, and usually France. The Royal Bank also had a large presence in Latin America with fifty-four branches in Cuba, twenty in the British West Indies, and at least one in a dozen other countries, including Spain.[33]

Consolidation in banking met with the general approval of both citizens and government, not dissimilar to attitudes in California. However, Western cries for government bank inspection could be heard, but they were rejected on grounds of cost. The decennial Bank Act revisions in 1923 resulted only in a series of administrative changes and inaction by Finance Minister Fielding, Canada's longest-serving finance minister.

No sooner had the Bank Act been revised, including a rejection of the idea of government inspection of banks, than a bank failed. The Home Bank, a Toronto-based bank founded for Irish Roman Catholic immigrants, collapsed in the largest bank failure in Canadian history until then. "What made the Home Bank failure such a celebrated political case was that a handful of self-dealing speculators in Toronto had used other people's money which had been collected in small deposits across the country.... And there was a good deal of justifiable western anger at manipulations from the east."[34]

Despite the bank failure and partial government payments to small depositors (35 per cent of those under $500), general deposit insurance was not enacted. The subject of reimbursement led to a serious debate in both the House of Commons and the Senate. Concern about moral hazard resulted in restrictions of the proposed payments to small depositors, those with $500 or less. The focus was on compassion for small depositors, rather than a general insurance program.[35]

A major consequence was that the government finally introduced legislation in 1924 that created the Office of the Inspector General of Banks, decades after a similar position had been created for the Supervision of Life Insurance. Since the government was concerned about the cost of this new position, the matter was resolved by exempting branches from inspections and all costs borne by Canadian banks.[36]

Another problem in 1923 was the extension of the Finance Act of 1916. "Under the revised act, provision was made for an automatic return to the gold standard after three years unless the government took steps to the contrary."[37] In his history of the Department of Finance, former deputy minister Robert Bryce contends that the legislation was passed without sufficient understanding by parliamentarians and almost no debate in the House of Commons.[38] But it did permit the Canadian dollar to return to something close to par with the American dollar until 1932 (see appendix 4.4).

In contrast to Canada, where there were relatively few major structural and regulatory changes, the United States implemented four major changes in American banking during the first fifteen years of the Fed's existence. Obviously the first was the creation of a central bank to operate at the heart of American finance. Neither of the next two was completely dependent on the Fed's existence, but neither were they completely independent. The second change was the internationalization of American banking, and the third was the huge increase in the relative size of some American banks compared with their international rivals. The fourth change was the increase in activities at domestic banks.

The Fed had in some sense been born in the Bankers' Panic of 1907, as discussed in chapter 3. Within a year of its establishment in January 1914, the Fed found itself in a new, different, and vastly more serious crisis. The final bill, signed into law in December 1913, gave the new Fed relatively specific duties for American monetary policy. It would serve as a clearing house for cheques and as a banker of last resort, provide for ample currency, and discount bank commercial papers. The Fed's ability to deal with financial crises may have been hampered by what is called the real bills doctrine – the idea that central banks should discount only bank IOUs involving trade transactions. Over the next 100 years, the Fed's role in the financial system's long-term stability has expanded to include regulation of banking and other services, as concerns about centralizing monetary functions gave way to the need to coordinate policy on a national level.[39]

Although debates about its purpose endure to this day, the Fed possesses a governance structure that has changed over time and is still unusual. As early as the 1920s individual reserve banks moved from discounting bank loans to an open market operation of trading short-term Treasury securities. In 1923 these banks established the Open Markets Investment Committee, which became the Fed's chief means of influencing interest rates and credit conditions. Although these activities moved it closer to becoming a real central bank, confusion over the relative power of the board and reserve banks persisted. American inexperience and Europe's financial problems at various times between 1914 and 1945 made global coordination of financial matters more difficult, adding more strain to economies on both sides of the Atlantic. Ineffective crisis management in the 1930s, for example, contributed to the first major alteration in the Fed's governance. The Banking Act of 1935 removed the executive branch from direct board membership and lengthened the terms of the other members to fourteen years. Appointments, most importantly for the board of governors, are still in the hands of the president of the United States and Congress, to which Fed officials must report regularly, but over the years monetary policy has become more complicated. Responsibility for financial matters in the United States is still rather diffuse. In various ways, regulation of banks is still divided among states and a host of federal agencies.[40]

The final 1913 legislation included several provisions important to the international activities of U.S. banks. Under the provisions of the Federal Reserve Act, national banks could finally open foreign branches and engage in international bank acceptances. The war opened the way for the dollar as well as for currency trading in sterling, mark, and franc acceptances for the first time. Not only did American banks establish foreign affiliates, they also bought equity interests in banks that had been established to do international business, such as National City Bank's purchase of the International Banking Corporation, with branches in China, India, Japan, England, and elsewhere. A 1919 amendment to the Federal Reserve Act, the Edge Act, gave a short-term boost to foreign banking by granting a federal charter to banks engaged in foreign banking and investment in order to spur exports. The total amounts were small compared to other U.S. foreign direct investment, and interest in the Edge Act's banking advantages diminished in the 1920s.[41] The number of American banks abroad grew from a handful before 1914 to 180 in 1920, falling back to 107 by 1925, before climbing again in the late 1920s.[42] First National City Bank alone increased its total number of affiliates from one in 1914 to 90 in 1925, and then to nearly 100 by 1930 – a number that later declined by approximately 20 per cent during the Depression.[43]

Even before the war, some state bank regulators, most importantly those in New York, began to loosen restrictions on foreign banks. There was no federal law for foreign banks, only state law. The minor regulatory changes that were made during the interwar period did little to address the dearth of foreign banks in the United States, especially in light of the weakened position of many of America's trading partners. Some foreign banks, such as the Bank of Montreal, even reduced their U.S. investment.[44]

No sooner was the Fed up and running than its international inexperience was challenged. By 1 August 1914 U.S. banking officials had to deal with stranded Americans abroad, where hotels and banks were refusing to take dollars or travellers cheques. Extreme shortages of cash at home compounded the problem. Fearing that the dollar might lose value, many rich tourists were cashing cheques at seventy-five cents on the dollar. With the outbreak of war, conversion and transfer of gold was under threat. Meanwhile, the Fed was still hiring staff to deal with the day-to-day problems, and its executives lacked experience with monetary affairs.[45]

Nevertheless the windfall effects of the war on America were soon evident. France and the United Kingdom alone borrowed $2 billion a year from American markets, a total of $9 billion by war's end. Massive influxes of gold were arriving in the United States, doubling the nation's reserves and worrying Benjamin Strong, first president of the Federal Reserve Bank of New York and others that this new imbalance would destabilize the post–First World War economic environment.[46] After years of financial chaos following the war, Americans helped arrange a financial plan for reparations, plausible enough to encourage public and private loans into defeated countries.[47] American banks led the way in engineering large amounts of portfolio and direct foreign investment. By the late 1920s over $15 billion in public and private investment from the United States had been channelled into Germany alone, much of which went unpaid as capital markets collapsed in the 1930s, contributing to international political friction.[48]

In addition to the burgeoning international profile of American banking, other changes were afoot. From 1914 to 1929, the number of U.S. banks declined and their size increased, but the American banking system retained many of the structural weaknesses Hamilton had sought to avoid. Despite the 10 per cent decline in the number of banks (roughly 27,200 to 25,000), bank assets continued to grow, nearly tripling from the Fed's foundation date. In 1929 only a third of America's banks were members of the Federal Reserve System, with its liquidity and stability benefits.[49] Whereas no U.S. bank was among the top ten in the world as measured by deposits, by 1925 two such banks were larger than any other Continental European rival.[50] First National City Bank's assets grew by a factor of five from 1914 to 1929.[51] Even before the 1929 Crash, the pace of bank failures picked up, mostly due to exposure to agricultural loans as commodity prices dropped. Banks also started to offer some new services while dropping others. Banks got involved in new types of lending for housing and other consumer loans, as well as margin accounts for securities purchases. As credit reporting became more widespread and sophisticated, domestic letters of credit became less important to bank business.

Insurance in an Era of Political and Economic Instability

The world is entering a period of social and business reconstruction greater than anything of the sort in human history, and the time is past when it is possible

for persons engaged in any business which touches closely great numbers of
people to consider only their self-interest in disposing of day to day problems.

Alfred M. Best, *Best's Review* speech to the Association
of Insurance Agents, 18 September 1918

The First World War set in motion a series of changes for American insurance companies and the market. Some were merely an acceleration of
pre-war trends, while others were wholly new ventures. The interwar
period did not witness a sharp decline of overall inward and outward U.S.
insurance investment, but it certainly saw a major shift of interests, segments, structures, and, most importantly, the nationality of recipients and
providers of American insurance coverage.[52] The First World War hardly
changed Canadian insurance investment in the United States as measured
by number of companies, but their business became more volatile. During
the war, premium income and admitted assets increased substantially, for
example, but during the 1920s they declined, both in absolute terms and
as a percentage of insurance written by non-American companies.[53]

The outbreak of war in Europe had immediate and long-range effects
on U.S. insurance. A year into the war, American insurance companies
found themselves under considerable pressure to invest in European
war loans. At first the war disrupted American production and capital markets, but as American exports to belligerent nations picked up,
the country experienced a huge boom that affected insurance. The war
increased demand for and business restrictions on the delivery of insurance and triggered a restructuring of the insurance sector and concerns
about flows to and from foreign entities.[54]

Measures taken shortly after the U.S. declaration of war in 1917 drove
German companies out of the market. Meanwhile, the Russian Revolution the same year cut off Russian reinsurance companies from their
roots, creating a destabilizing vacuum in the U.S. insurance market.[55]
But as can be imagined, the American government's policies toward
foreign insurance companies were more complicated and slower to be
implemented than they were toward enemy-owned manufacturing or
banking facilities. Those businesses were fairly quickly brought under
U.S. control. The insurance departments of several important states
recommended that German companies in particular be exempted
from "trading with the enemy measures" to protect the two million
American policyholders who held insurance contracts with these same
foreign companies. Moreover, the German companies employed thousands of agents and office workers who were American citizens. Well

into the fall of 1917 German insurance companies continued to operate in the United States, with restrictions. But in the face of hostile reaction from many parts of the insurance sector, which claimed the German insurance companies' businesses could be easily absorbed by American companies, the initial policy was modified to liquidate business under the supervision of federal authorities.[56]

The conflict and its aftermath helped shift investments and create new insurance needs. Fire and marine insurance remained the most common types of insurance, but now political risk insurance, for example, was sometimes added to the portfolios of more than 300 domestic and foreign companies writing fire, marine, or some combination of both.[57]

A budding consumer culture also helped reshape insurance and other sectors. From 1910 to 1920 the four top fire insurance companies in the United States, Aetna, Great American, Hartford Fire, and Home, had collectively increased their premiums by 150 per cent. During the 1920s investment valuations became more important for insurance companies, but prosperity and international contacts brought many different sorts of challenges. Progressive and populist politicians questioned the justice and social value of America's rapid and chaotic economic growth. Charges of unfair competition, sloppy regulation of some segments, and unauthorized foreign entry into the insurance market abounded even during the early 1920s and continued during the boom economy. Regulatory authorities questioned the levels and methods of calculation on insurance company profits.[58]

Life insurance companies came under pressure from a tragic worldwide outbreak of influenza. Thirty per cent of all American workers became ill; 2.5 per cent of the American population died. An event of that magnitude today would cost the American economy around $700 billion. Not only life but also health and fraternal societies took a huge hit, but the health crisis led to increased interest in life insurance policies and premium charges.[59]

Nevertheless America was still seen as a relative safe haven. The war and subsequent financial turbulence may have slowed and certainly changed the national configuration of foreign investment in the U.S. insurance market, but it did not block it altogether. In 1929, despite the withdrawals, there were ninety-nine foreign fire and marine companies – the area in which foreign insurers were concentrated. The companies that remained ended up working with more complex structures and tended to have lower profits. Even considering the exits, foreign companies remained a powerful force in reinsurance, accounting for a majority of the premium income in the 1920s, but with a declining share and disappointing profits. In spite of the war, disease, and populist pressures, even vulnerable foreign investors felt that America's growth prospects compared favourably with those of their own domestic markets.[60]

As early as 1920 the sector's competition and configuration had already become more complicated, with many additional types of policies, new and restructured companies, and significant shifts in the ways older companies did business. Many troubled, pre-war companies disappeared. But despite many setbacks, mutual funds played a significant role in several of the big insurance growth areas of the twentieth century. These areas included casualty, health, and workers' compensation, in part because they enjoyed a distinct advantage in cost control and, therefore, profits.[61] Seemingly having put many scandals and the influenza behind them, life insurance companies continued their robust growth. The First World War reduced competition from German companies, but it also made some aspects of business in central Europe harder for American companies. Moreover, some American companies had lost substantial amounts of value on the European securities they had purchased.[62]

For many, the period was the beginning of a very American phenomenon, mass culture and mass marketing – a development from which insurance was not exempt. In the 1920s insurance advertising came into its own. Although small in comparison with post-1945 expenditures, for the first time advertisements were placed in major magazines, aimed at target markets. Even the Great Depression did not divert companies from investing in these greatly increased ad campaigns.[63]

Growth sectors posed new problems too. Automobile insurance policies increased with the dramatic rise in the number of American car owners. Automobile theft, a relatively new phenomenon, became an important issue for fire companies writing automobile insurance. Car owners resisted taking out insurance because of the high premiums; car manufacturers began to consider offering their own insurance for new car purchasers. One eastern U.S. state even considered creating its own fund to provide liability insurance for its own citizens.[64]

The popularity of the automobile served as a great stimulus to general liability insurance. Some liability insurance was sold much earlier, but these policies were usually specialty-type risks.[65] By the 1920s some companies – such as INA and Aetna, based in states that allowed multiline insurance – began to underwrite different kinds of risks.[66] Some states that had required monoline business in order to improve performance by specialization and to protect firms from competition in other insurance lines began to relent. Incrementally, multi-line insurance, adapted to the needs of auto and home owners, became commonplace in the United States, but it made underwriting and regulation more complicated for those used to dealing with finite, separate risks.[67]

In contrast to other financial sectors, the Canadian life insurance industry experienced dramatic growth, more than doubling in size. Within the industry, Montreal-based Sun Life continued its extraordinary growth. Sun Life tackled foreign expansion with a passion and made forays into more countries than its competitors. In particular Sun Life developed a very large business in the United States. While that business included all lines of life insurance, the company was prominent in the fixed annuity business, even when measured against its American competitors, never mind Canadian companies. Sun Life had the capital to support the annuity business, a product line that brought in assets in large volumes.[68]

The good and bad news was that the proportion of assets Sun Life invested in equities, particularly American equities, during the first three decades of the twentieth century was much higher than it was in the rest of the industry. In the thirty years prior to 1929 – during which Sun Life built its lead – the stock market generated capital for the company at a faster rate than its competitors; the capital was reinvested in the business, funding a faster rate of growth. And everyone knows what happened in 1929. The stock market crash almost destroyed Sun Life.

Before the 1929 Crash, Sun Life was thriving. In the 1920s it was taking market share from all the other major insurers, particularly Canada Life and Mutual Life. At the beginning of the century Canada Life had nearly 30 per cent of the market. Thirty years later Sun Life was in that same enviable position, while Canada Life was down to 12.5 per cent, still good enough for second place but well below its historic highs. Mutual Life also faced a setback, dropping from third to fourth. The other major life companies, Great West, Manufacturers, and Confederation, all increased their sales but suffered a loss of market share, not only because of Sun Life but also because the life insurance industry was fragmenting – unlike the banking industry, which was consolidating.

Canada has had a national tradition of protecting industries, particularly in financial services. But for some reason that has never been true in the non-life (property casualty) insurance sector. Whereas other countries are often protective of the non-life sector, Canada has never been. This was one sector of the financial services industry where British companies continued to play the largest role, with a market share in excess of 40 per cent, double the market share of domestic Canadian companies, while other "foreign" companies, primarily American, possessed a 36 per cent market share. In the late 1920s three British companies could boast premiums in excess of $2 million while only one American company had reached that level and no Canadian insurer had done so. Seven more British companies had premiums in excess of $1 million, as did two American and two Canadian companies. During the decade the amount of risk nearly doubled.[69]

This was the period when trust companies came to play an important part in the Canadian financial intermediation system. One unique aspect of trust companies is that they play a fiduciary role. Trust companies were not common in Canada in the late nineteenth and early twentieth centuries, a different story from that of the United States. Chartered banks in Canada were never given trustee powers, another difference between the two countries. The Ontario Loan and Trust Company Act[70] changed that. In 1921 this legislation granted chartered banks the authority to make unsecured loans. This legislation affected future laws both federally and in Quebec. The Act also permitted the trust companies to take deposits; as a consequence they became "near banks." The result was nearly a fourfold increase in their assets in the 1920s as they became larger than fire insurance companies and nearly as large as mortgage and loan companies.

In contrast, the mortgage and loan companies had negligible growth, primarily because their principal source of capital had been the United Kingdom. That source was no longer as attractive as the interest spread between North America and Europe narrowed. Domestically trust companies in the 1920s began providing mortgage loans, which were the trust companies' major assets.

The Causes of and Remedies for the Depression

The statistics of those times are appalling. At the nadir of the Depression, half the wage earners in Canada were on some form of relief. One Canadian in five was a public dependent. Forty per cent of those in the workforce had no skills; the average yearly income was less than five hundred dollars at a time when the poverty line for a family of four was estimated at more than twice that amount.

Pierre Berton, *The Great Depression*

The Depression of the 1930s was a watershed in modern history and modern economics. Whether the crisis was brought on by imbalances caused by the First World War, poor bank and financial regulation, overly zealous adherence to the gold standard, financial manipulation, over-reliance on the real bills doctrine,[71] inexperienced central banks, weak commodities prices, income inequality, a reaction to "irrational exuberance" of the 1920s, or most likely some combination of all of the above, is still a matter of dispute.[72] According to many economists, central bank policy failures, fiscal frugality, and American protectionism, with the passage of the Smoot-Hawley 1930 Tariff,[73] helped turn a stock market correction into a worldwide depression.[74]

The effects of the Depression were widespread but varied. Between the peak of prosperity (1929 in the United States and 1928 in Canada) and the trough in 1933, U.S. GDP declined by 28.6 per cent, Canadian by 29.6 per cent.[75] On a GDP basis per capita, the effects were even greater. The United States declined by 31 per cent and Canada by 35 per cent. The worst-hit countries in Europe – Poland, Austria, Germany, and France – declined by 25, 24, 17, and 16 per cent respectively. The eight major economies in Latin America declined by just over 18 per cent, while the twelve major European countries declined by a little more than 11 per cent. The U.K. economy contracted only 6.5 per cent.

With different causes, degrees of suffering, and in different historical contexts, the pain of the Depression was translated into political change that differed greatly among nations and regions. The U.S. response, for example, came mostly in the form of major financial reforms, fiscal stimuli, and a rethinking of trade policy, the impact of which was felt more after the Second World War than in the 1930s and will be discussed in depth in the next chapter. Despite significant national differences, in most of the world the Great Depression still plays a central role in policy discussions, sometimes kindling heated controversies about parallels between that event and the 2008 Panic. Through movies, literature, and family stories it is etched into the popular consciousness of much of the industrialized world like few other periods in history.

The effects on both Canada and the United States were devastating. From its 1929 peak, by 1932 the American S&P index of stock prices fell by 85 per cent.[76] On the Canadian market stocks fell 70 per cent, with the pulp and paper sub-sector declining by 97.5 per cent. In the United States consumer prices, which had been flat for five years, fell by 5 per cent and more per year for the next three years. U.S.

unemployment, which had been 3.2 per cent in 1929, reached 24.9 per cent, and remained above 10 per cent until 1940.[77] At the depth of the Depression Canada's unemployment rate reached 32 per cent. In Windsor, Ontario, an automotive city across from the river from Detroit, the jobless rate ascended to 50 per cent.[78]

The severity of the Depression in Canada owed much to not only the worldwide collapse in commodity prices, some of which preceded the economic crisis, but also to its proximity to and economic connections with the United States. The Smoot Hawley Tariff, signed into law by President Herbert Hoover in 1930, increased the rate on dutiable-good imports from 39 to 53 per cent, the highest in history. Canada's exports to the United States plummeted by 70 per cent, sales of agricultural and vegetable products declined by 93.5 per cent, animals and animal products dropped by 81.5 per cent. Wood and paper, although still Canada's largest export to the United States, declined by over 60 per cent. The full force of the Great Depression fell upon Canada's staple exports – hardest hit were the markets for cattle, dried codfish, copper, and wheat – all of which was compounded by a dramatic decline in the value of the Canadian dollar as the country went off the gold standard (see appendix 4.4). Average incomes declined by 48 per cent, but in the Prairie province of Saskatchewan they declined by 72 per cent.[79]

Although both countries were economically savaged by the Great Depression, significant differences can be observed in the way governments reacted and economic sectors were affected. Many incumbent politicians at all three levels of government were turned out of office by voters, but election results produced curious symmetries and asymmetries in the two countries. In the United States Franklin Delano Roosevelt defeated Herbert Hoover and remained in office throughout the Depression until his death, shortly before the end of the Second World War. His party held the White House for another seven years. In Canada William Lyon Mackenzie King was defeated in 1930, two years after the downturn had begun. However, he was re-elected as the economy was recovering in 1935 and he served again until the late 1940s. Thus Roosevelt and King were the two longest-serving leaders in the history of both countries. Their longevity was similar, but their politics were vastly different. While Hoover was a Republican and Roosevelt was a Democrat, both were activist presidents. King was a Liberal, and R.B. Bennett, who defeated him in 1930, was a Conservative, but both Canadian prime ministers were anything but activist in public policy.

The financial sectors in the two countries took dramatically different courses. The divergences are, of course, closely linked to public policy. In the United States thousands of banks failed, whereas no failures occurred in Canada. In the United States a national securities regulator (the Securities and Exchange Commission) was introduced, whereas regulation in Canada remained at the provincial level because of a decision of the law lords of the Privy Council in England. While in the United States the relatively new Fed struggled to get its bearings, in Canada the government moved to create a central bank for the first time.

Particular Issues in the United States

From 1929 to 1932, in several phases and for different reasons, over 5,000 American banks went under, nearly one in three, and 7 per cent of total U.S. deposits were lost. In 1933 alone, the final year of the crisis, 4,000 banks with $3.5 billion in deposits closed. A banking suspension was called in March of that year, which lasted sporadically for many months in some states, the dollar was devalued, and the hoarding of gold forbidden.[80]

The political fallout was also immense. The Democratic candidate for president, Franklin Delano Roosevelt, trounced his Republican rival, President Herbert Hoover. With the slogan "A New Deal for Americans," Roosevelt took nearly 60 per cent of the popular vote and won the all-important Electoral College vote by 472 to 59. In addition, the Democrats took control of the Senate and extended their majority in the House. Hoover has been tagged in perpetuity with the economic collapse, even though he had been in office only for six months before the crash.

Within five years the new administration passed a series of bills designed to stimulate growth and stabilize the economy, a move that transformed America. The social and financial impact of the New Deal was not really felt until after the Second World War. Despite his party's platform promise to the contrary, Roosevelt launched a host of infrastructure spending projects. The New Deal featured the creation of work and welfare programs, the Federal Emergency Relief Agency (aid to states for welfare), Works Progress Administration (anti-flooding and other projects), Tennessee Valley Authority (electrical projects), the Agricultural Administration Act (farm price and output regulation), and the Civilian Conservation Corps (conservation projects employing young men). All of these projects added to the government bureaucracy, but they substantially reduced unemployment and economic misery.

The New Deal also included huge reforms of American labour and financial practice. The National Industrial Recovery Act tried to raise prices and wages by limiting companies' ability to cut prices. The Act also sought to reduce working hours and establish a code of practice for economic sectors, which included policies about minimum wages and output. It was followed by the Fair Labor Standards Act of 1938, which created federal standards for a minimum wage and maximum work week. Turnover at the Supreme Court and Roosevelt's impressive electoral majorities led to the high court's removal of many of the constitutional impediments to the New Deal.[81] The Social Security Act of 1935 provided for federal old-age insurance and other benefits, based on employee contributions of 1 per cent of wages up to $3,600, along with employer contributions.[82]

For finance, the two most important measures involved banking and securities regulation. In addition to measures designed to allow the Fed greater powers to serve as "lender of last resort" for troubled banks and establish a quasi-government agency for federal deposit insurance, the Federal Deposit Insurance Corporation, in 1933 Congress passed the Glass-Steagall Act. This legislation, named after its Democratic and Republican co-sponsors, effectively eliminated the relationships between investment banks and commercial banks, which had developed over fifty years. For many Americans and legislators big, international finance had "stacked the cards" in capital markets against "the little guy" and were responsible for the financial distress in which the nation found itself. Not only did it prohibit commercial banks, such as Chase, from investment banking activities, it also forbade ownership interests and certain alliances among private and joint-stock banks for issuing and distributing securities.[83]

The Depression will always be linked, perhaps unfairly, with the boom in stocks during the 1920s and the failure of exchanges and the government to provide better governance. In addition to increased valuations, over $9 billion in new securities were being issued in 1929, approximately three times the amount in the early years of the decade. Fifty-four per cent of the securities were in common equity, up from 20 per cent in 1920. On 29 October 1929, the day of the final crash, over 16 million shares changed hands, up from the March 1926 record of 3.8 million shares.[84] Detailed records for the Curb and other exchanges are less well known.

Corporate governance and exchange governance did not keep up with added volumes. From 1900 to 1930 the number of shareholders in the United States grew from 500,000 to 10 million. As early as the 1890s industrial securities began to compete with the still-dominant railroad stock for capital, but most investors were very wealthy and guided by private financial advisers who served as gatekeepers between those with excess funds and those in need. That was changing. As the importance of exchanges increased and the number of shareholders swelled, so too did demands. Numerous examples of market manipulation became part of the popular folklore, reinforcing impressions that the stock market was merely an arena for vile speculation. Investors, even sophisticated ones, could find no solace in economic or financial theory to help explain price movements and their relationship to the underlying economy. The New York Stock Exchange was the largest in the United States, but it was not the only financial exchange. Boston, Pittsburgh, Cincinnati, and even Salt Lake City had exchanges. Some specialized in particular kinds of stocks – for example, mining – others in different kinds of transactions, such as commodities.[85] Accounting rules were vague at best. Some publicly traded companies did not provide income statements and balance sheets, while others provided only annual averages. More progress was made on tax accounting norms, but investors required different kinds of information.[86] Brokers and banks offered liberal margin financing to large and small investors, with few limits and little or no collateral. Efforts by the NYSE to add requirements to its brokers and listing companies produced relatively limited results. Even with New Deal reforms the level of confidence in capital markets that was reached in 1929 would not be restored until the 1960s.[87]

Consistent with the conviction that a lack of access and transparency contributed to the crisis, the government created the Securities and Exchange Commission (SEC), which was responsible for regulating exchanges, determining the accounting information that should be provided by public firms, and approving all securities for public sale. In two sweeping acts, the Securities Act of 1933 and the Securities Exchange Act of 1934, the government mandated accounting reports, certification, and federal filings, and created the SEC to enforce publicly traded corporate compliance and listings on exchanges. By 1938 even over-the-counter transactions came under SEC control. Empowered by Congress and well ahead of most other nations, the SEC turned to the accounting profession to define requirements for public firms and to design audit procedures, measures now demanded of all public firms. Indeed, certification by public accountants became mandatory.[88]

But these measures were not the last of the reforms, and indeed their impact was felt much more after the Second World War and will be dealt with in greater detail in the next chapter. By 1941 Congress created new vehicles for financing mortgages. These took the pressure off small banks to provide funds, averted many mortgage defaults, and in general gave the average person more access to borrowing in order to buy a house. In addition to public retirement insurance, Congress changed mutual fund rules to encourage citizens to save for their retirement. Collectively the housing measures of the 1930s and early 1940s stimulated demand for housing and saved many small banks from financial collapse by reducing mortgage defaults with a mixture of direct and indirect government intervention.

The Depression North of the Border

In Canada the origins and path of the Depression were very different from those of the United States in both public policy and finance. The Canadian economy was improving from the terrible depression after the First World War until 1928, when the Great Depression began. A major reason for the Canadian economy's descent into depression a year before other countries was the dramatic decline in the wheat crop in that year. Wheat was by far Canada's major export product. Although the United States produced more wheat, Canada was the larger wheat exporter. The 1930 crop was smaller than the year before, but the price collapsed by more than 60 per cent and continued to fall until it sank to 0.35 cents a bushel in the 1933/4 crop year, a depth not seen in 300 years. The overall price declined a staggering 75 per cent in Manitoba from 1924/5 until 1933/4 in a province that was the third-largest supplier to the U.K. market.[89] The punitive 1930 U.S. tariff exacerbated an already weak grain market for Canada. This protectionist tactic was introduced in the midst of a Canadian election campaign. The U.S. tariff became a major issue, particularly in agricultural areas that historically favoured free trade. The agricultural sector was particularly hard hit by the U.S. legislation. The result was a resounding defeat of the Liberal government of William Lyon Mackenzie King and the election of a Conservative government led by R.B. Bennett,[90] a former bank director and the richest man to ever hold the office of prime minister of Canada.

The new government was ill-prepared to deal with an economic catastrophe of such magnitude: for some basic and fundamental reasons, Canada did not have a national fiscal policy. Income tax was collected by all three levels of government, and custom and excise duties – the federal government's main revenue source – declined by 65 per cent during the Great Depression. Moreover, Canada lacked a central bank. In addition the prime minister was also minister of finance and he had no deputy minister (permanent head) in that all-important department.[91] Bureaucratic weakness was compounded by the fact that the assistant deputy minister of finance was in a penitentiary. It was two terrible years before the prime minister appointed the legendary William Clifford Clark as deputy minister of finance, greatly strengthening that key department. Clark, among others, favoured the creation of a central bank.

In addition to these fundamental problems, the government had to deal with the huge financial challenges of assisting with industry survival, more specifically the burden of overhead costs of the government-owned Canadian National Railway. Appeals to government also came from Western wheat farmers and Maritimers who sought subsidies for the movement of Eastern coal to Central Canadian markets. As if this were not enough, provincial municipal revenues were hopelessly inadequate to finance the cost of relief.[92]

Unlike its southern ally, Canada did not initiate a dramatic set of social projects during the Great Depression. Bennett introduced New Deal legislation in his last year of office. His successor referred the matter to the Privy Council, which declared it unconstitutional. Canadian policy throughout the 1930s favoured British-style strict budget balancing rather than U.S.-style pump priming. Despite dramatic increases in taxes, budgetary chicanery, and significant opposition to Keynesian measures, the U.S. Treasury, in contrast to the Canadian federal government, ran a deficit through much of the New Deal Era.[93]

However, on the fiscal side, growing awareness of the shortcomings of the division of taxing powers led to a royal commission, the most important in Canadian history, on dominion provincial relations. It was commonly known as the Rowell Sirois Commission, appointed to re-examine the distribution of federal provincial powers and responsibilities in relation to social and economic changes over the previous seventy years. Its report recommended changes in taxation powers, adjustment grants, and national programs, such as unemployment insurance, that were implemented in the 1940s.

On the monetary side, the deepening Depression stimulated discussions about the need to establish a central bank and provide more
liquidity in the system.[94] In July 1933 the government announced the
appointment of a Royal Commission on Banking and Finance as the
means whereby the decennial review of the banking system would be .
carried out. The chair of the commission was Lord Macmillan, a British jurist.[95] Unlike many other royal commissions, whose structures
reflected Canada's close economic ties to the United States, no American served on the Macmillan Commission. It began its public hearings
in August and finished two months later. It visited many Canadian cities and heard nearly 200 submissions from a wide variety of groups,
although the members conducted no original research.[96]

By a vote of three to two[97] the commission recommended the creation
of a central bank, a proposal the government accepted. It introduced a
bill to create a privately owned central bank.[98] The only division in Parliament was over bank ownership. There was no discussion of the objections
raised by the two dissenting commission members. The legislation was
passed in 1934 and began operations in the spring of 1935. Graham Towers
was appointed the first governor, or chief executive officer, who wielded
significant power because he had to concur in all board decisions.[99]

In the 1935 election the Liberals were returned to power. They proceeded to nationalize the central bank in stages and by 1938 the process
was complete.[100] The bank's principal role was to control the volume
of currency and credit in use.[101] It also assumed a number of functions
one would expect of a central bank. It became the clearing agent for
the chartered banks and it took over that part of the note issue function
that had previously been handled by chartered banks. The new central
bank also launched the publication of a monthly statistical summary
and refused to make a loan to the province of Alberta.[102] In addition the
bank provided advice to the government on monetary matters.

While the establishment of the Bank of Canada was the most obvious
change in Canada's financial system, another significant shift was the
advent of new housing policies. These had long-lasting effects on the Canadian market, particularly in the Great Recession of 2008. The key individual
who shaped Canada's housing policy was W. Clifford Clark,[103] the newly
appointed deputy minister of finance. Clark's philosophy was "Having a
home of your own … should be the reward of saving and sacrifice and not
a gift of a benevolent government."[104] Clark drafted the Dominion Housing
Act (DHA) with input from the Dominion Mortgage and Investment Association. Prior to the DHA, private lenders were prohibited from making

loans in excess of 60 per cent of the appraised value of the home. Under the new rules, approved loans were eligible for an additional 20 per cent loan from the state.[105] "The legacy of the DHA ... was in ensuring that the government would not ... get into the business of direct lending, but would focus primarily upon ensuring the health of the housing and mortgage markets."[106]

Just as Canada took a path different from that of the United States in housing legislation, which will be discussed in chapter 5, the country also took a radically different approach to securities regulation. This outcome was not the result of domestic choice but rather because of a decision by England's Privy Council. Within Canada the federal and provincial governments disagreed on the regulation of securities. The federal government launched a legal challenge over the provincial right to investigate companies and individuals suspected of misconduct under the provincial Security Frauds Prevention Act of 1930. "At the trial of *Lymburn v Mayland* ... it was ruled that provincial laws could not interfere with the actions of federally-incorporated companies ... Therefore, the SFPA was ruled *ultra vires* (beyond the powers) of provincial legislators. The federal government had won. Refusing to accept this rebuff ..., Alberta and Ontario immediately appealed the decision ... to the Privy Council in London, which ... ruled in their favour. This victory in the appeal of *Lymburn v Mayland* awarded jurisdiction for the regulation of securities markets to the provinces."[107] The appeal court's reasoning was that securities related more to property and civil rights, which were provincial responsibilities.

The Great Depression also resulted in a major realignment of Canada's stock exchanges. Montreal's heyday as the financial hub of Canada was on the wane. It had been the major stock exchange in Canada since trading began. The Montreal Exchange was hard hit during the Depression, just like the NYSE. The Toronto Stock Exchange was also affected, but other factors came into play. Another exchange was also operating in Toronto called the Standard Stock and Mining Exchange, specializing in mining stocks. Concerns were voiced about the SSME's operating practices. The newly appointed head of the Ontario Securities Commission, encouraged by the provincial attorney general, used moral suasion to convince the TSE to take over the SSME in 1934. Earlier that year the United States passed the Gold Reserve Act, which resulted in a 70 per cent increase in the price of gold, leading to good times on the newly combined Toronto exchanges and resulting in the third historic shift of the financial centre of Canada, from Montreal to Toronto.[108]

Coming Out of the Crisis

Many thought that the United States and Canada did not do enough to combat the Depression. In 1936 American Gross Domestic Product was still below its 1929 level, but it had climbed enough to relieve some hardship. The United States then entered a new downturn in 1937, "a recession within a depression."[109] The government had increased its spending, but not enough to take up all the slack in the economy. The only country that practised John Maynard Keynes's eponymous economic remedy was one that Keynes himself hated, Nazi Germany. Moreover, some observers were concerned that many of the measures, and perhaps more importantly anti-business rhetoric adopted during the 1930s, actually discouraged commercial investment and offset the effects of even positive reforms. In any case, only the surge in demand associated with preparation for the next war ended this extraordinary period of low growth and high unemployment.

The Depression and the violent international conflicts that followed vividly indicate the break caused by the financial and political turmoil of the 1930s. In the wake of the Crash and Banking Crisis, the U.S. insurance sector, for example, was heavily hit. Direct casualty premiums fell 30 per cent from 1929 to 1933, a trend that was even more pronounced among reinsurers because the loss in total volume prompted many primary carriers to raise their retention rates, especially in areas with low expected losses.[110] Like domestic companies, foreign ones had their investments and related income pounded by the collapse of capital markets. Several mostly recent corporate arrivals left the country. Nevertheless, in 1934 no single sector accounted for more inward U.S. foreign investment than insurance.[111] By 1934 fire insurance premiums had fallen to their lowest level in twenty years, and the U.S. devalued its currency, effectively reducing the cost of foreign companies' liabilities but reducing their revenues in their own currency.[112]

Perhaps most importantly the length and depth of the Depression reshaped American attitudes and political debates about risk and the means for delivering a host of insurance functions. Those for and against the New Deal recognized its connection to broader protection of the working class through some sort of insurance. The U.S. response was not only a particularly American mixture of expanded public and private action – an unholy alliance for some – but also required a huge increase in data collection and statistical analysis. For some this represented a threat to liberty, or, at the very least, made ours the "Age of

Statistics."[113] Although much of the landmark legislation was passed in the 1930s, its greatest impact was felt in the decades following the Second World War. For insurance companies, increased demand for protection against adversity and enhanced capacity to calculate risk could lead to opportunities for new customers and products. These could be served by increasing health, pension, and worker's compensation services. Higher demands for government insurance, however, were accompanied by an increasing sense that insurance was a public good, one that should be provided with little profit to service providers and with expanded protection beyond what contract or common law had envisioned. During the Roosevelt administration, insurance sector regulation came under closer government scrutiny, leading to a Supreme Court case in 1944 that threatened insurance's antitrust exemption.[114] Like the Armstrong Commission before the First World War, reformers of the 1930s and 1940s, through several pieces of legislation, attempted to reduce the power of financial institutions by limiting the products they could sell and where and how they could invest. Along with new investment vehicles, these measures produced many unforeseen consequences, both positive and negative.[115]

In Canada the reaction to the Depression was different, perhaps because of the soundness and multifaceted nature of the banking system. The Canadian and American economies reached bottom in 1932 but the Canadian economy recovered faster, although GDP did not surpass 1929 levels until 1939.

While Canadian banks had a rough time, none went broke. No Canadian banks suffered runs, which were commonplace in the United States. Although Canada rejected explicit deposit insurance until 1967, there is evidence of confidence that public and private regulators would intervene to prevent a complete meltdown of the financial system. In times of trouble it was not unusual for the government to encourage stronger banks to help the weaker ones. Since the first Bank Act in 1871, which included double shareholder liability, repeated amendments had bolstered explicit tight capital requirements, conservative lending, and public and private oversight. The Canadian banks, like those in California,[116] had the advantage of branch banking that was spread across a vast swath of land. This gave them a diversified base. Given their national and international scope, Canadian banks had to be well managed.[117] On the liability side, greater emphasis was placed on time deposits than on demand deposits, while on the asset side there was a dramatic increase in dominion and provincial government securities as well as a dramatic reduction in call and short loans.[118]

This is not to say there were no difficulties in Canada. Although the banks did not go broke, one-fifth of all branches were closed in the 1930s, and in the hard-hit Prairies it was worse: fully one-third of all branches shut their doors.[119] A review of the histories of the Commerce and Imperial banks indicates that as a priority expenditures were curbed and "rigorous control of costs was demanded."[120] Directors' fees were cut 15 per cent and the number of directors was reduced. Dividends were cut. With demand for private credit dropping, banks invested in government securities, which lowered profits.[121] The Bank of Nova Scotia postponed construction of its Toronto head office at King and Bay Streets. That bank's history noted, "On March 4, 1933, the day all U.S. banks were ordered to close, the Canadian Minister of Finance issued the reassuring statement that 'the Canadian banks are in a very strong and exceptionally liquid position, and wholly capable of meeting any demands upon them.'"[122]

The Royal Bank of Canada, one of Canada's two largest banks, had a particularly bad time, partially because of its extensive operation in Cuba, and "technically tottered on the brink of insolvency throughout 1932–33."[123] Only the tiny American-owned Weyburn Security Bank, in the heart of the Saskatchewan dust belt, disappeared. It was acquired by the Imperial Bank, which was doing reasonably well because of its strong presence in the gold mines of Ontario. Meanwhile Barclay's Bank, the recently established Canadian subsidiary of the British bank, enjoyed greater success than any others after more than tripling its assets between 1930 and 1935. Although the literature says little about how this was achieved, the board chair was Robert Borden, a former prime minister, who found his position frustrating because the bank was not treated or regarded as a distinctly Canadian institution.

Great Depression contemporaries were understandably proud of the achievements of Canadian banking and regulation. The CBA president in 1934, J.A. McLeod, suggested five factors behind the relative Canadian stability: (1) "the operation of the banking system under a single legislative authority," (2) freedom from "meticulous regulations in detail," (3) minimum size and strength of banks "prescribed for Canadian banks in The Bank Act," (4) systemic training of bank managers through a branch system, and (5) orderly distribution of banking funds for local needs through a branch system.[124] Three years earlier, in the House of Commons, Prime Minister Bennett, who also served as minister of finance and who had once served as a director of the Royal Bank of Canada, noted that the Canadian banking system "is predicated upon the assumption that the amount of money borrowed from the people – who are the depositors – by the banks will enable the banks to use it as to have it safe for the depositors when they require it." He went on to make the point that the Canadian "system of branch banks, with the mobility that is possible in the movement of credit from one portion of the country to the other, makes possible loans being made on a large scale by a branch with very indifferent deposits, insured by the easy mobility of credits from a point where there is a demand for loans with limited deposits. That is the strength of our branch bank system."[125]

There was nervousness in the life insurance sector about the future of Sun Life, by far the largest of the insurers and a company that was larger than most banks. Its growth had been spurred by massive investments in U.S. equities, which was not the normal pattern for Canadian insurers. By 1929, just in time for the stock market crash, Sun Life held 54 per cent of its assets in U.S. equities. As a consequence, the company was close to insolvency, particularly when its net surplus declined by over 90 per cent. The number plummeted from $60.3 million in 1929 to $5.9 million in 1934. The government of Canada, presumably deeming Canada's largest life company as "too big to fail," stepped in and amended the legislation governing the insurance industry. Prior to the amendment, securities of insurance companies were required to be taken into account at market value as published by the superintendent of insurance. However, the minister of finance was permitted, under section 67(2) of the Act, to authorize "the use of values in excess of the market value for companies desiring to use the same."[126]

Not surprisingly, the three largest provinces elected populist governments.[127] A socialist party called the Co-operative Commonwealth Federation was founded, dedicated to socializing the banking system. Voters elected members to the federal Parliament and to the Saskatchewan legislature. In Alberta the populist Social Credit Party was born. Elected to power in 1935, the party held power for thirty-five years. Originally it issued "prosperity certificates," which quickly depreciated and came to be known as "funny money." The Social Credit Party also passed legislation regulating banks, which was either prohibited by the federal government or ruled ultra vires, with the exception of a provincially owned bank that exists to this day. "In the history of Canadian monetary development, the Social Credit experiment in Alberta represents one of the most interesting aberrations."[128]

The Second World War and Its Impact
on North American Finance

Canada's contribution to victory in the Second World War was incredible considering her population of only eleven million people. In the spring of 1939, there were 10,000 men in her armed forces; by the end of the war, over one million had served in them.... The Royal Canadian Navy had 500 ships in service by 1943, and at one point was the third largest Navy in the world. No fewer than 125,000 Commonwealth air crew were trained in Canada.... Financially, the Canadian support of Britain was staggering.... Canadian contribution equated to a quarter of the total commitment to Britain under Lend-Lease, despite Canada having a population less than 9% that of the USA. The burden on individual Canadian taxpayers was nearly four times that of the Americans.

Andrew Roberts, *A History of the English Speaking People since 1900*

Twenty-one short years after the conclusion of the First World War, Canada and much of the civilized world found itself at war once again. While there were similarities with the previous war, there were also profound differences. In 1914 King George V declared the British Empire was at war, and Canada, as part of that empire, was at war as well. In 1939, a week after Britain declared war, the Canadian Parliament declared that Canada was also at war.[129] This was as a result of the Statute of Westminster, which gave Canada independence in international as well as domestic affairs. Although the Second World War was ten times more costly than its earlier counterpart in constant dollars, it cost fewer Canadians lives. Another key difference was the approach to conscription. While initially there was conscription for domestic service, a national referendum on the issue was called before conscription was imposed for overseas service. While opposition to conscription for overseas service endured, particularly in Quebec, no riots or deaths were caused by the decision, as had occurred in the First World War.

Another key similarity to the United States was that Canada was once again militarily unprepared for war. However, the country was financially more ready to finance a major war. Lessons had been learned from the Great War two decades earlier. This time, the Second World War would not be fought using debt and inflation. It would be fought using taxes and restraint, a policy of "pay as you go." Finance Minister James Ilsley was able to execute such a policy because not only had a dominion income tax been in place since the end of the First World War, but also because the federal government was able to negotiate the

Dominion Provincial Tax Agreement in 1942, helped by earlier recommendations of the Rowell-Sirois Royal Commission. This agreement gave the federal authority almost unrestricted access to the income tax, which had previously been a shared source of income. During the war federal income taxes grew dramatically – a 7.3-fold increase between 1939 and 1944. In addition the dominion government introduced an Excess Profits Tax, "the most spectacular aspect of taxation in World War II."[130] As early as fiscal year 1942/3 the new tax was generating over $400 million – between income taxes and excess profits, the dominion was receiving over half of the budgetary revenues necessary to fund the war – a far cry from the financial picture in the First World War.[131] In addition, the Bank of Canada co-operated with the private sector to facilitate borrowing through War and Victory Loans. Total new borrowing came to $15 billion ($1.3 trillion in constant dollars). All but $100 million of that amount was raised in Canada.[132] And as soon as war was declared, exchange controls were introduced (see appendix 4.4).

At the war's onset, Canada was Britain's partner in defence. Canada's position shifted to a strategic link between the United Kingdom (not always to Britain's liking) and the United States. Once the United States entered the war in 1941, Canada moved increasingly into the orbit of the United States but continued to play an intermediary role between the two larger powers, although at times, particularly at the Quebec City Conference, Prime Minister King served as little more than a glorified host.

In December 1939 Canada entered into an agreement with Great Britain that resulted in the British Commonwealth Air Training Program. "Undertaken, and principally paid for, by Canadians, the BCATP eventually trained 130,000 aviators – nearly half of the Commonwealth air crews. It was with good reason, therefore, that President Franklin Roosevelt later termed it the 'aerodrome of democracy.'"[133]

The next year Canada entered into the Ogdensburg Agreement with the United States, which created the Permanent Joint Board of Defence between the two countries. The following year the Hyde Park Agreement was reached, whereby the United States increased its defence purchases in Canada. This enabled Canada to make its own purchases of war equipment in the United States, requiring U.S. currency. In addition to these North American agreements, negotiations led to the Bretton Woods Agreement, a landmark 1944 contract that established an international monetary and exchange rate system. These were all contributing factors to the development of Canada's stronger ties with the United States and distancing from Great Britain.

As for the private sector in the Second World War, the stock exchanges did not close. Toronto was by now the dominant Canadian exchange,[134] and in number of stocks traded Toronto was even ahead of New York, although Toronto's value was only a fraction of that of New York. In contrast to the First World War, the financial markets were prepared from the beginning to channel Canadian savings into War and Victory loans.

The war was good for the chartered banks. The Royal Bank of Canada continued jockeying for position with the Bank of Montreal to be number one, and the former emerged from the war as Canada's biggest bank. The insurance sector did not fare as well, and its product offerings appeared to have reached maturity. Sun Life, in spite of its problems in the Depression, was still the dominant insurance company by a wide margin. A significant increase in the number of non-life companies occurred, probably because of limits faced by U.S.-domiciled companies to the acquisition of Canadian charters.[135] Trust companies and mortgage loan companies also struggled too during the war. In the latter case it was part of a longer-term trend. At the outset of the war there were 123 members in the Investment Dealers Association, while this number declined to 101 in 1944.

The Canadian government fully anticipated a depression, or at the very least a recession after the war. However, the lessons learned from the First World War were applied and, with a national fiscal system, a decade-old central bank and a sound private sector financial system, Canada did not suffer a post-war economic setback. Rather Canada embarked on a quarter-century of almost continuous growth, at a rate significantly greater than that of the United States.

In contrast to sentiment in Canada, resistance to enter another "wasteful European war" ran extremely high in America. Both candidates for president in 1940 pledged to avoid America's involvement, even though the moral issues in 1939 were much more profound than those of 1914. Only the Japanese attack on America's base in Pearl Harbor galvanized American emotions for war, and then only against Japan. On 8 December Canada and Great Britain declared war on Japan, and three days later Germany declared war on the United States, paving the way for united Allied action against the European and Asian combatants.

Even before war in Europe was declared, let alone America's entry, the threat of war had an economic and financial impact on America and its relationship to the world. Once again demand for American goods stimulated the economy, finally bringing the United States out of a decade-long depression.

All sorts of financial interactions between foreign company headquarters and their subsidiaries became more difficult. All over the world the state became more involved in business and generally favoured its own firms over those from other countries. Permission for visas and cash transfers became harder to acquire. Home-office personnel were not allowed to direct U.S. activities, and the transfer of files and other information from the United States to other countries was strictly controlled. Some U.S. journalists highlighted the dangers of foreign-owned insurance and other industries. Some foreign companies created complex holding-company structures. Some of these were based in the United States to protect their assets, cross-border cash flows, and confidentiality from government interference.[136]

For example, when the Second World War broke out, especially after America's entry, relations with foreign-owned insurance companies, much more numerous than banks, became more influenced by politics. Canadian companies profited from ever-closer ties with the United States. British firms provided vital intelligence. The branches and subsidiaries of eighty-two British insurance companies in the United States were used to collateralize $425 million in Reconstruction Finance Corporation loans in 1941.[137] Unlike the controversy First World War period, however, the debate over American versus foreign insurance companies was more subdued. Even compared with 1929, there had already been a great deal of attrition among foreign insurers due to regulatory restrictions, consolidations, and bad economic conditions. Most of the remaining companies were of British origin. Although there were no German companies among the foreign firms, there were several Japanese, one Italian, and many from countries that would end up under Axis control.[138]

The worldwide conflagration reinforced America's role as a safe haven, bringing home some American investors who had been making their way in other parts of the world. U.S. insurance investment abroad had a long but chequered past. One U.S. "associated-company," though, took the lead in the internationalization and innovation of insurance. The story of the American insurance giant AIG is dramatic and, if not unique, at least not representative of U.S. insurance history. In a sector with relatively few flamboyant figures, it had two at the heart of its narrative. Although one of the most international U.S. companies – and certainly the most international U.S. insurance company – AIG did not start as a U.S.

company. Its nearly 100-year international odyssey is a testament to the multinational and political dimensions of insurance. Founded in Shanghai shortly after the First World War by Cornelius Vander Starr, AIG began as an insurance agent in China for U.S. companies. Within a decade, Starr was representing many American companies with ten offices across Asia. Fascinated by Asians and Asian opportunities – long before it was in vogue – Starr sought out Asian clients, as opposed to Western ex-pats, and integrated locals into management and onto the board. During the troubled 1930s he made his first U.S. investments, buying up some troubled American insurers – acquisitions that set the stage for the company's move of headquarters to New York and an international diversification – a policy that saved the company after the Second World War and was successfully continued for decades by his legendary successor, Hank Greenberg.[139]

Not all of the effects of the military conflict were negative for the insurance sector, but most were. In a war environment profits were hard to achieve. Public demands for low-cost insurance continued to be translated into political pressure. With property values increasing and many policies written for three- and five-year periods – during which time policyholders failed to raise the value of their policies – many properties remained seriously underinsured, thereby increasing the loss ratio, but providing at least some hope for better times after the war. Threats of greater federal insurance regulation and state pricing pressures suggested, however, that the sector was in for a shakeout to a degree that might rival the effects of the San Francisco earthquake.[140]

In short, even prosperity and victory had a downside. They led to new responsibilities without necessarily comparable institutional changes. For the United States, the Second World War and the Cold War did not directly alter its financial system. They transformed the United States into an even more dominant economic and financial power than it was after the First World War. Once again, like the aftermath of the First World War, the effect of the Second World War was for decades confined mostly to altering that system's relationship to the rest of the world. Before and after the First World War, the United States rejected concerted world efforts to stimulate growth and encourage stability. However, in the years after the Second World War, few U.S. leaders shied away from accepting the necessity of America's central role in shaping world politics, economics, and finance. Indeed, in some countries American regulators tried to impose America's brand of financial management on even recalcitrant countries. Although much had changed about America's sense of international responsibility from 1914 to 1944, many observers feared that its knowledge of the world had not kept up with its new commitments since Hürlimann, president of Swiss Re, made his observation in 1920 that begin this chapter.

Although both Canada and the United States were hit very hard by the Depression, and more adversely affected than other Western economies, their political responses were different. American leaders introduced, for example, a Social Security Act, which contained provisions for old age and unemployment insurance, and several measures to encourage home ownership. Canada did not institute unemployment insurance for another five years and old age security for another twelve.[141] In addition, Canada has never adopted America's unique subsidies for housing. Perhaps the better performance of Canada's financial system – where, in contrast to the United States, no major bank or insurance company went under during the Depression – helps explain the different paths taken. However, Canada finally did create a central bank more than two decades after the American precedent. What is most startling is that neither country succumbed to one of the prevailing "isms" – communism and fascism – that appeared as panaceas for the ills of many countries, even those better off than North America.

CHAPTER FIVE

The Short Pax Americana: 1945–2000

Continuity and Discontinuity after the Second World War

Being left to the mercy of an all-powerful United States was intolerable, particularly as the U.S. government had been determined to show its people that American boys had not been sacrificed to perpetuate the moral abomination of empire. Yet here at Bretton Woods was the American Treasury Secretary tethering the historic event to the mast of his country's superpower ambitions. The British had been anxious to see themselves as partners with the Americans in creating the ground rules for the postwar order, yet at every step to Bretton Woods the Americans had reminded them, in as brutal a manner as necessary, that there was no room in the new order for the remnants of British imperial glory.

Benn Steil, *The Battle of Bretton Woods*

The financial history of this period is in some respects easier for the authors to tell and for readers to understand than those of previous chapters. Many aspects still colour our financial landscape and current events. But in other respects, communicating the importance of this period is more difficult. Finance became a much larger part of our economies, even more interwoven with other countries by giant multinational firms, and more influenced by complex and quickly developing economic theories and technologies. The borders between and among financial institutions became increasingly blurred and various activities intertwined in complex ways. While we have divided this chapter into chronologically organized sections, many connections between the sections require the reader to go back and forth in time and across functional activities.

Like the interwar period, the second half of the twentieth century witnessed distinct macroeconomic and political phases, with changes to North America's financial architecture and the relationship between Canada and the United States. Although these environments were essentially more conducive to sustainable growth and stable finance than those of the interwar period, they too shifted abruptly, challenging financial and political actors. World trade became a more important part of world GDP by growing at a faster rate. As a consequence exports represented 17.2 per cent of world GDP by the mid-1990s, up from 5.5 per cent in 1950.[1] Between 1950 and 1975, world GDP grew, albeit from a low base, 3.1 times. In the next twenty-five years the world GDP increased 2.2 times.[2] For those same quarter-century periods Canada grew, again from a low base, 3.2 times, while U.S. GDP grew 2.4 times. In the last quarter of the twentieth century both countries' economies more than doubled, but the U.S. economy grew slightly faster than did that of Canada[3] (see appendix 5.2).

For most of the period from 1945 to 2000 the United States was by far the world's most important economic and political player, but its macro- and microeconomic performance fluctuated a great deal.[4] Nevertheless, by most macroeconomic measures, the twenty years following the end of the Second World War compared favourably with the preceding years and many of the decades that followed, if not in economic growth alone, which tended to slow, but as measured by volatility and financial crises. During the 1950s and 1960s, the rate of inflation in the U.S. was less than half that of the next two decades.

The post–Second World War world order differed radically from that following the First. Despite the Versailles and Genoa conferences in 1919 and 1922, no summit after the First World War seemed able to re-establish the old financial order or even a consensus about how to build a new one. In contrast, by the mid-1940s most of the liberal industrial nations got behind new political and economic institutions and organizations, many of which, such as the United Nations, survived into the twenty-first century. This unity among nations may have been motivated by fears of reliving the economic and political chaos of the 1920s and 1930s, as well as the rise of totalitarian regimes.

Rebuilding a liberal world order began even before the war ended. Representatives from around the world gathered in Bretton Woods, a small resort town in New Hampshire, chosen for U.S. domestic political reasons. This important meeting took place in July 1944, when 700 economic and political leaders from Europe, North America, and other regions (forty-five nations in total) tried specifically to devise a monetary system that would prevent the currency chaos, premature and unrealistic adherence to the old gold standard, blocked funds, "beggar-thy-neighbour" devaluation, and protectionism that characterized the interwar period. While the delegates shared many motives of a common political-economic mission, they were divided by others. The United States, for example, was bent on dismantling the British Empire and its imperial trade preferences, forcing repayment of war debts, and in general shifting the financial centre of gravity from the United Kingdom to the United States. Understandably, America's closest ally, Great Britain, led by the most distinguished economist of the times, John Maynard Keynes, resisted.[5]

Despite different political agendas, the nations at Bretton Woods committed themselves to tying their currency to a fixed value of the U.S. dollar, which was convertible into gold at $35 an ounce, and to working toward a gradual decrease in impediments to trade and capital flows. This project required new organizations: the International Monetary Fund (IMF), to help national central banks manage their exchange rates and the World Bank, to stimulate investment projects, which would help alleviate balance of payment difficulties. In short, the countries committed themselves to giving up some of the economic prerogatives of independent nations, which set the stage for world finance for over twenty-five years.[6] From the outset, ensuring that participating countries had sufficient dollar reserves was one of the greatest challenges. Ironically, in some sense, the system collapsed nearly thirty years later because of its success.

Canada was one of the few countries in the "Free World" that floated its exchange rate for much of the period. Canada's delegation to the conference and its leader, Louis Rasminsky (who later became governor of the Bank of Canada), played an important role in mediating between Britain and America. The irony was that, despite Canada's role in facilitating a compromise between the two principal nations, Canada's special relationship with both countries made its own adherence to the rate constraints particularly difficult. Canada's ability to convert its foreign currency receipts earned by trade surpluses with other nations into U.S. dollars to fund its chronic U.S. trade deficit was undermined by the devaluations of the 1930s and by the strong dollar established under Bretton Woods.[7]

In the face of heavy criticism from the IMF and other institutions, Canada was the first major country to break away from the system.

From 1950 to 1962 Canada maintained a flexible exchange rate system.[8] Just after the Second World War the Canadian dollar was reset to parity with the U.S. dollar. In September 1949 it was revalued to 91 cents, but continued balance-of-payment difficulties led to domestic price and wage shocks as well as further speculation about further reserve losses and devaluations. In short order American foreign direct investment (FDI) increased and the Korean War stimulated demand for Canadian products, which at first amplified pressure on the central bank to find a new rate to head off inflation. Rather than trying to peg a new rate, Canada decided to float the Canadian dollar, letting the market determine a new "par value." Its currency appreciated 12 per cent to US$1.02. The Bank of Canada's limited direct monetary tools for managing monetary policy were bolstered by moral suasion and hands-on bank regulation, involving close scrutiny of bank activities. The float functioned reasonably well (see appendix 5.4). From 1953 to 1961 the Canadian dollar traded between $1.00 and $1.06 to the U.S., foreign investment doubled, and consumer price increases stayed below 4 per cent. During that same period, Canadian per capita GDP growth outpaced that of the U.S. In the face of a deteriorating economic and foreign exchange situation, greater capital mobility, and political conflicts over the role of monetary policy, in April 1962 the government restored the peg at US$0.925 with the help of a rescue package of just over US$1 billion from the IMF, the United States, and United Kingdom.[9]

Despite these problems, Canada attracted great interest from Europe after the Second World War. Siegmund Warburg, for example, felt that Canada offered some interesting opportunities. He was a German-Jewish refugee, a leader of the London investment banking community who was often credited with the idea of Eurobonds. For him, Canada was still in a pioneering stage of development, compared to its larger southern neighbour. In addition, its business environment, with career civil servants rather than politically appointed ones, was more familiar to Europeans. Warburg devoted substantial attention to Canada after the war. His first venture, Lamont Corporation, ended in disaster, but his initiative, called Triach, met with more success. Warburg launched Triach with Tony Griffin, a prominent Canadian businessman. Triach, was designed to harness British and other countries' financial and technical resources for Canadian investment, met with more success. Sadly, for many reasons, including his disappointment with Canada's management vision and opportunities he found elsewhere in the 1950s, Warburg felt that Canada had lost much of its lustre for him.[10]

Interestingly Canada's macroeconomic difficulties and policies, though out of step with its allies at the time, foreshadowed later problems with maintaining fixed rates and their perceived solutions, namely a floating rate system. By the 1960s many global economists cited Canada as an example of how a floating rate system might function smoothly and correct unsustainable imbalances in the international flow of goods, services, and capital.

As the Bretton Woods system came under pressure at the end of the 1960s, Canada broke away again from its fixed rate system and in 1970 returned to a floating rate system, well ahead of most other Western countries. Curiously, its decision to remain outside the system has received little or no attention from historians and economists. In contrast, contemporary economists noticed and praised Canada's ability to maintain steady rates during at least part of the period, confirming the views of James Meade and Milton Friedman. Despite its non-participation in the fixed-rate system for most of the period, Canada profited from the economic growth and stability produced by the Bretton Woods system, and from its own experience managing a free-floating exchange rate once the fixed rate system collapsed in 1973. Indeed, Canada's experience contributed to macroeconomic theory and policy for all open economies, which in turn also adopted floating rates after 1973. That experience highlighted how floating rates could help a country, enabling it to adjust more easily and cheaply to external shocks. It also demonstrated how an independent monetary system could also achieve low and stable inflation.[11]

For other countries as well, Bretton Woods helped produce prosperity. The system evolved. By 1958, most currencies became convertible. The role of central banks changed during the period. Several currencies devalued, and one, the deutsche mark, revalued. U.S. liquid liabilities were growing quickly as the result of America's balance of payments deficit, brought on by the war in Vietnam and the refusal of the Lyndon Johnson administration to curb its "Guns and Butter" campaign pledge, which favoured military over civilian spending. In this context, doubts arose as to whether all foreign dollars could be converted into gold. Moreover, for trade reasons, many countries wanted their currencies to remain weak against the dollar. Some foreign central banks reneged on their pledges to avoid buying U.S. gold with the dollars they held. Despite the creation of a new type of foreign reserve (special drawing rights from the IMF, or SDRs), the situation was not sustainable. In the face of anti-dollar speculation, loss of faith among foreign central bankers, and U.S. election pressures, in August 1971 the Nixon administration closed the "gold window," meaning foreign governments could no longer exchange their dollars for gold. This effectively ended Bretton Woods, although no one was quite sure what would follow. While some economists advocated floating rates, regulators harboured hopes that price and capital controls could create enough confidence in new, stable rates – even without the promise of U.S. gold conversion. Within two years, however, inflation in the United States jumped, and the U.S. foreign exchange rate began going into what appeared to be freefall.[12]

In one sense, Bretton Woods collapsed because it worked too well. Western countries lost the sense of desperation following the Second World War that contributed to a sublimation of national interests in the name of a common good. An extraordinary increase in the movement of goods, services, and capital led to a corresponding reduction in the ability of the government to control financial actors. Moreover, strides in the economy and economic theory led policymakers and private actors to believe that there were sufficient tools to manage risk by private entities and public authorities. Governments, companies, and central banks, above all, approached issues with greater confidence in their ability to use fiscal and monetary techniques to optimize the trade-offs among conflicting economic and social goals.

In addition, economic growth hid some structural problems. One steady development from 1950 to 1990 greatly affected central bank activities. With the Cold War and increasing social demands, U.S. government spending as a percentage of GDP grew from 24.5 to 35.0 per cent. The ratio of government workers to total workforce hardly changed from 1945 to 1990, but the activities of these workers altered significantly. But during the same period, federal government expenditures for income security, health, and education increased between twofold and threefold. Despite the war in Vietnam, from the mid-1950s to the end of the Cold War, military spending as a percentage of government expenditures (the "guns versus butter" equation) declined from nearly 50 per cent to around 20 per cent at the end of the Cold War, reflecting both a decrease in the absolute amount and the increase in other expenditures.[13] Other OECD countries had similar experiences.

With high government debt levels after the Second World War, pressure mounted on the Fed to keep interest rates low. The ensuing inflation following the war led to demands on the Fed for more independence.

Nevertheless, despite a 1951 agreement between the Fed and U.S. Treasury, the Fed's primary concern was still macroeconomic stability and growth, which meant supplying enough liquidity to avoid unemployment increases. Nevertheless, until the late 1960s there was relatively little pressure on the Fed for an interventionist monetary policy. The economy was booming and inflation low. The Fed simply had to follow a script: increase interest rates when the economy was growing quickly and reduce them when it slowed.

The challenge came in the mid-1960s. Inflation increased and growth slowed, for which the Fed was held partly responsible. Inflation had been below 2 per cent for most of the 1950s, but it climbed to 4 per cent per year from 1965 to 1969, and then surpassed 6 per cent from 1970 to 1978, rising to 12 per cent in 1979 and 1980, without any corresponding economic growth. This phenomenon was dubbed "stagflation" at the time. Suddenly the Fed was no longer the solution but rather part of the problem. As one recent head of the Fed wrote, "Policymakers became a little bit too confident about their ability to keep the economy on an even keel," or, as some said in those days, to "fine tune" it.

By 1980, bringing down inflation required aggressive Fed interest-rate action, which led to the steepest U.S. post-war recession until the 2008 Bankers' Panic.[14] Joblessness reached nearly 11 per cent in 1982, but inflation dropped from over 12 per cent in 1980 to 4 per cent in 1982, ushering in what some have called the "Great Moderation." This was a two-decade period with greatly reduced volatility of prices and economic growth, a success that may have reinforced the view of central bankers and others that the social sciences had mastered the secrets of managing economic cycles.[15]

During the post-war decades the relationship between Canada and the United States changed substantially. Many business leaders in both countries began to think of the pair as nearly one country for business purposes, despite growing fervour in each nation for a more nationalistic economic policy. In the 1950s and 1960s American investment in Canada grew and the Canadian government emphasized a continental investment policy, which meant greater ties to the United States. Canada remained open to foreign investment, especially American. Canadians even offered rich subsidies to attract American firms.[16] By 1970 Canada was the second-largest destination for American foreign direct investment, trailing all of Europe by a few billion dollars.[17]

In general, investment patterns in both countries changed enormously. American prosperity and the privatization of much of health care and retirement contributed to revitalization of equity markets, but individuals jumped back into equity markets on their own. The idea that common stocks were the best long-term investment once again took hold, as long as exchanges and security rules ensured a level playing field. Many factors encouraged this growth: a lengthy bull market following the Second World War; faith in the New Deal securities regulation; and tighter rules for NYSE members. Later these trends were bolstered by government measures to stimulate stock ownership: in 1974 the Employment Retirement Income Security Act (ERISA), which will be discussed later; 1975 commission deregulation; and the 1978 creation of retirement plans sponsored by an employer, called 401(k). The NYSE relaxed its rules on the advertisement of services by members and on stock ownership in general, which was especially important with small shareholders.[18] From 1952 to 1990, the proportion of individual Americans that owned stock climbed to one in four from one in sixteen – more than 51 million Americans.[19]

Banking: A Regulatory and Technological Revolution

The banking system of the United States is staggeringly large and complex. So too is the banking regulatory system.

> Willard Z. Estey, *Report of the Inquiry into the Collapse of the CCB and Northland Bank*

Understanding the development of American finance circa 2000, indeed finance as practised in much of the world, is impossible without understanding the complex regulatory and technological transformation that separately and interactively refined our financial architecture in the second half of the twentieth century. Indeed, U.S. banking history became world banking history after the Second World War, to a much larger extent than ever before. Regulation and technology allowed banks and other financial organizations to pursue their activities and service their clients, who themselves had become more diverse and spread over larger geographic areas and service functions. Whereas American banks had fewer than thirty foreign branches in 1950, many of the U.S. megabanks now had thousands of entities operating in every corner of the world. But as Richard Sylla has pointed out, what appeared as an influx of American banks into Europe was actually more of a flight from American regulation. During the quarter century following the Second World War,

American bankers had an enviable position in many respects, but their ability to use their natural dollar-based advantage combined with managerial and technical innovation was fettered in the United States. Foreign expansion was a welcome escape from the tough restrictions they faced at home over their domestic product and geographical growth.[20]

The Offshore Market

The increase in foreign direct investment by banks and the huge increase of offshore (euro) banking had important political and financial implications for Europe, North America, and Asia. It set the stage for a new supranational financial order that helped shape American and even Canadian finance.[21] Although many of these developments began in banking, they sometimes affected other segments of finance directly or by spillover effects. Much of our current financial architecture, our instruments and methods of trading, owe their existence to the development of the offshore market and the multinational presence of major banks.

In the 1950s some national regulators began allowing deposits in currencies other than their own to go substantially unregulated. They chose a narrow path to escape national regulation that turned into a four-lane highway after the fall of Bretton Woods. This decision was particularly important in the 1950s and 1960s for British and American banking. After the Second World War, the weakness of the British economy and the instability of the British pound, which had been the main currency for international transactions, threatened London as a financial centre. London bankers looked to lending U.S. dollars as a solution, but to do this they needed dollar deposits. Although small amounts of dollar deposits had existed before, the banks' new interest in having dollar deposits coincided with an upsurge in demand to keep dollars outside of the United States. For many reasons, depositors welcomed the opportunity to keep dollars with reputable banks in a market with excellent legal protection, but outside of the United States. Customers from countries with potential or actual conflicts with America especially found less political risk in the offshore market. Moreover, well into the second half of the twentieth century, euro deposits offered American banks a way of avoiding New Deal interest rate restrictions (Regulation Q), including forbidding interest on corporate chequing accounts, some of which were not fully repealed until the twenty-first century. British and other bank regulators turned a blind eye to the practice, which seemed at worst a harmless exercise and at best a useful way of ameliorating the dollar shortage outside of the United States. By the 1970s, for many governments, the existence of euro-funding was a welcome addition to their own domestic financing needs.[22]

By the time many of the original conditions that spurred the growth of offshore accounts disappeared – such as U.S. restrictions and taxes on capital flows as well as the dramatic increase in petrodollars – the offshore market had come to dominate international finance, not just because of its size but also because of its ability to innovate. The offshore market served as a hotbed of new financing ideas as well as a competitive pressure driving down transaction costs. Its self-regulating practices were dominated by large corporations and banks, which suited companies' hunger for hedging methods and flexible financing in the post–Bretton Woods period. In the topsy-turvy financial world of the 1970s, banks and their customers demanded new instruments to combat risks such as the huge increase in foreign exchange and interest rates. Euromarkets facilitated smooth, easy, short-term exchanges among banks and their clients.

In the decade before the collapse of Bretton Woods, the euro-currency market increased fifteen-fold, but its most dramatic growth occurred during the 1970s. Eurodollars reached a staggering $132 billion as early as 1973.[23] In just one five-year period, euro deposits grew tenfold, slowing in the 1980s to 100 per cent increases every five years, albeit from a higher base. Although the U.S. dollar is still the main worldwide currency, nearly all major currencies are involved in offshore banking. Its centres have spread from London to New York, Luxembourg, many Asian cities, and several Caribbean islands. Today much international banking activity is short-term inter-bank, and, in the last decade, intrabank, largely outside government control via the exchange of euro-currency accounts. These eurocurrency bank loans, based mostly in London and New York, grew tenfold from 1982 to 2004 to nearly $10 trillion, dwarfing international bonds by a factor of six, while foreign exchange daily transactions climbed from $60 billion per day to an almost unimaginable $1.9 trillion.[24]

Foreign Direct Investment and the Breakdown of New Deal Regulation

The development of offshore banking facilities was both a cause and effect of increased foreign banking investment. However, this was not the only piece of the puzzle. Increased trade and the distribution of Marshall Plan funds played a role at the early stages, but large banks were drawn to the financial freedom of eurocurrency centres as well as the need to follow their clients who demanded services there. From 1960 to 1975, U.S. banks, for example, increased the number of their foreign branches six-fold.[25] Investment also flowed in the opposite direction. From 1975 to 1999 the assets of foreign banks operating in the United States grew from less than $50 billion to $1.2 trillion, nearly 20 per cent of all U.S. bank assets. By 1996 U.S. bank foreign assets reached $1.1 trillion. The ascent of non-U.S. banks was similar, but it started a little later.[26]

Offshore competition forced changes to American domestic banking. At the end of the twentieth century, U.S. banking regulation was still a fractional affair, with states and several federal agencies taking on various roles, including the Comptroller of the Currency, the Federal Deposit Insurance Corporation (FDIC), and the Federal Reserve Board (Fed). Nevertheless, the United States witnessed the crumbling of two pillars of the U.S. banking system: limits on national banking and the division between commercial and investment banking. New Deal reforms had rendered domestic American banking safe but stodgy. Although the removal of limits on the combination of commercial investment banking was an important change, it was not by any means the only pillar of American banking that fell after 1970. Long before the Glass-Steagall Act (1933), American banks had restrictions on branching, especially interstate branching. During the 1950s and 1960s several federal laws increased those state powers, leaving a fragmented, patchwork banking system that forbade money-centred banks from developing a national retail network.[27]

The impetus for abolishing the New Deal and earlier restrictions on banks came to a large extent from a growing recognition that U.S. banks were losing their competitive edge. In the United States and in the rest of the world, foreign banks were apparently capable of performing a wider range of services over larger geographic areas. American banks sought to tap into new sources of funding. Citibank and other U.S. banks turned to the growing interest in dollar deposits in London to circumvent constraints in the United States. They established branches there, found customers eager to deposit with them, and lent funds back to the parent.[28] Many traditional activities were drying up.

Some of these changes paralleled developments in Canada. In Canada, as in most countries, the banking sector remained relatively sheltered through much of the post-war period. During the 1980s, foreign bank assets rose from 2 per cent to a high point of nearly 10 per cent of all Canadian bank assets. Sporadically U.S. and Canadian banks tried to enter each other's markets. In the 1990s Canada seemed very promising for international expansion to Citibank (initially called FNC and later Citi). Canada's economy was growing, and banking was still dominated by the Big Five chartered banks, which controlled nearly 90 per cent of all bank assets. Although other smaller banks existed, the Canadian Bank Act, like banking regulation in most countries, afforded protection from new entrants, both domestic and foreign. Profits were high.

In 1963 First National City (FNC) bought a controlling interest in Mercantile Bank (MB)[29] from National Handelsbank of Holland. FNC's decision contravened the warnings of both the minister of finance[30] and the governor of the Bank of Canada[31] that it should not make this purchase prior to the completion of the Bank Act's regular decennial review. With the purchase of Mercantile, FNC thought it could enter the whole Canadian market, an access other American banks would find difficult to duplicate. When the Bank Act review was finished, it imposed a 10 per cent ownership limit, foreign and domestic, on shares of banks,[32] but Citi was given an exemption allowing it to own 25 per cent of Mercantile. Although ownership constraints affected Citi's entry strategy, the general limits also prevented some potential American competitors, such as Chase, from entering the Canadian market to buy one of the big banks.[33] International investment helped Citibank address not only its funding needs, but also the revolution in banking caused by new business information systems. This sea change was monitored by a wave of new business school graduates armed with computers and a host of new competitors, including their customers themselves.[34] The expansion of branches included more centralization and a wider range of services. In the early 1970s American banks' foreign operations accounted for approximately 30 per cent of the activities in France, for example.[35]

Some banks chose a compromise between correspondent banks and direct investment in order to enter foreign markets. German, French, and even British banks in particular needed to overcome their initial reservations about setting up affiliates in London and other eurocurrency centres to enter this lucrative market. Well into the post–Second World War period, European bank entry or re-entry into the U.S. market was more tentative, often coming in the form of joint ventures and strategic alliances. By 1971 five big groupings of banks had clustered

Table 5.1 Largest "Free World" Banks by Assets, 1962

Rank	Bank	Country	Assets, US$ (millions)
1	Bank of America	USA	13,417
2	Chase Manhattan Bank	USA	10,932
3	First National City (Citibank)	USA	10,280
4	Manufacturers Hanover	USA	6,532
5	Barclays Bank	UK	5,756
6	Morgan Guaranty Trust	USA	5,312
7	Midland Bank	UK	5,276
8	Chemical Bank	USA	4,811
9	Royal Bank of Canada	CA	4,678
10	Lloyds Bank	UK	4,648

Source: *American Banker*, 7 August 1963.
Note: At the height of Bretton Woods, with a very strong dollar and increasing growth of eurocurrency accounts, American and British banks dominated the league tables, but one Canadian bank was among the top ten. Another was in the top twenty. Some Continental European and Asian banks, which would ascend in the 1970s, had not yet broken into the top ten but were among the top twenty.

for international investment. Most groups included only European banks, but some also comprised Japanese, Canadian, and American banks. Several established branches in many countries. Although their principal aim was servicing the foreign needs of domestic clients, some offered a wide range of services to foreign and domestic clients directly or through affiliate organizations, such as the American subsidiary of EBIC alliance, European American Bank (EAB). But whether by direct investment or through joint ventures, all of this was just the beginning.[36]

The 1960s and 1970s was a rocky period for American banks in terms of size. The relative financial clout of American banks changed radically, compared to their foreign competitors. As seen in tables 5.1 and 5.2, in the early 1960s American banks were by far the largest in the world. By the end of the next decade, changes in exchange rates and foreign investment had dropped their relative size compared to Asian and Continental European banks. In the 1980s and 1990s they would recoup much of their loss in relative size, but perhaps at the price of safety.

The dissolution of Glass-Steagall's separation of commercial and investment banking and the imposition of other limits on long-time U.S. banking practices had many causes and passed through many stages. As early as the 1950s banks formed holding companies to avoid

Table 5.2 The Largest "Free World" Banks by Assets, 1979

Rank	Bank	Country	Assets, US$ (millions)
1	Crédit Agricole	France	104,997
2	Bank of America	USA	103,919
3	Citicorp	USA	102,742
4	BNP	France	98,859
5	Deutsche Bank	Germany	91,188
6	Crédit Lyonnais	France	91,085
7	Société Générale	France	84,914
8	Dresdner Bank	Germany	70,331
9	Barclays Group	UK	67,474
10	Dai-Ichi Kangyo Bank	Japan	66,581

Source: *The Banker*, June 1980.
Note: By the end of the turbulent 1970s, many American, British, and Canadian banks had been overtaken by Continental European and Japanese. No Canadian bank was among the top twenty, which was rounded out by mostly Japanese and Continental European banks.

interstate and other restrictions on their activities. Increased foreign banking investment in the United States, as well as an American desire to establish a level playing field for their investments abroad, contributed to the International Banking Act of 1978. The Act put foreign and American banks on a level playing field but it required reciprocity from any country whose banks sought permission to enter the United States. The Federal Reserve's long-term policy of allowing commercial bank subsidiaries to underwrite and trade securities not exceeding more than 10 per cent of the bank's overall revenues was upheld by the Supreme Court in 1988. By the 1980s, too, most states had already passed or were planning legislation to remove state restrictions on interstate banking. Federal restrictions on national banks' interstate holdings were effectively eliminated by the 1994 Riegle-Neal Interstate Banking and Branching Efficiency Act.[37] The Gramm-Leach-Bliley Act (also known as the Financial Services Modernization Act of 1999) opened the market among banking, securities, and insurance companies by permitting formal consolidation of commercial banks, investment banks, securities firms, and insurance companies. By the end of the 1990s, then, U.S. restrictions on combining investment with commercial banking were effectively dead. For many years, the existence of eurocurrency accounts and their foreign subsidiaries had allowed the banks to circumvent domestic constraints.

American banks brought many advantages to Europe, including a focus on investment banking services and greater access to U.S. dollar financing. Until recently, American and British financial markets were considered the best in the world, with the trade-offs between liquidity, safety, and return enticing foreign investors.[38] The depth of those markets is produced in large part by innovation and the existence of private funds for long-term savings. Paradoxically, these "innovations" later also included allowing banks to trade complex instruments internally, a step that would contribute to the 2008 Crisis.

Many regulatory changes allowed American and British banks to trade in the lucrative ends of finance, some of which increased rather than diminished the risks they were intended to thwart. The United States and the United Kingdom led the way, for example, in the creation of derivative instruments and markets, and in turning a blind eye to banks trading derivatives. By December 2000 the Republican Congress and President Clinton had signed a bipartisan bill that allowed banks to trade in derivative instruments outside the scrutiny of normal capital market regulators. The Commodity Futures Modernization Act (2000) moved a huge portion of derivative trading beyond the oversight of the Commodities Futures Trading Commission (CFTC) and the Securities Exchange Commission (SEC). The Act was passed after a decade-long debate about how to regulate derivatives and had been highly promoted by Treasury Secretary Robert Rubin, Federal Reserve Chair Alan Greenspan, and other members of the "Dream Economic Team." Its supporters based their views on several beliefs: that the huge increase in over-the-counter (OTC) derivatives would continue; that existing OTC trading and products formed necessary linkages for derivatives users for whom standardized contracts were insufficient; that OTC derivative trading gave U.S. banks a huge competitive advantage; and, most importantly, that self-regulation among banks provided adequate control and had blurred the distinction between organized and private markets.[39] Although many promoters of the Act came to regret their support, and many blamed the Bush White House for reducing financial regulatory budgets, the effect of the latest reforms on OTC trading is not yet clear.

By 2000, for many market and regulatory reasons, the United States not only led the world in large investment banks, but it had also established a group of universal banks with a national and international network of retail and wholesale clients. Moreover, U.S. and U.K. financial leadership was bolstered in part by the strength of non-banking financial institutions. New Deal financial reform had included encouragement of private savings outside of banking institutions. Through a series of legislative acts, pension and mutual funds received favourable tax and other treatment, a strategy to promote diversification as the primary means of ensuring prudent investment. While the managers of these funds were given wide leeway in what to invest, the funds faced relatively strict limits on the percentage of any company's equity they could own and on the amount of their own capital that could be invested in one company.[40] Under these rules, active supervision of companies was discouraged, but it was not until several decades after the creation of these institutional investors that the influx of individual and corporate funds rendered them huge players in financial markets. When pension and mutual funds came into their own, they reinforced the growing tendency to rely on diversification and mathematical modelling as a governance tool.

Technological and Other Regulatory Changes

Every statement there is correct. It's not economics; it's not mathematics; it's not business. It is something different. It's finance.

Harry Markowitz, "Portfolio Theory"

The scope of banking was also affected by technological change. Increases in computing power and communication speed allowed banks to handle many more transactions over larger distances and to add new retail and wholesale services. Banks replaced many traditional transaction vehicles with automated services. Credit cards and cash machines are merely the aspect most visible to consumers of a revolution in wholesale and retail services. Letters of credit and cheques were virtually replaced in many areas of the world by electronic transfers within and between nations. Financial institutions became among the biggest users of computing power. American banks were not alone, but they led the way with many of these innovations.

In Canada, as the rest of the world, banks needed to make major investments in technology. American firms tried out some of their innovations in Canada. IBM tested some of its latest mainframes in Toronto, where the RBC ran ten applications on one machine while Citibank ran one application on ten machines. RBC was proud of its "robust technology infrastructure." "We were one of 100 companies worldwide recognized by *CIO* magazine, a technology publication for IT professionals,[41] for our excellence in customer relationship management (CRM) strategy and the resulting innovative customer service capabilities."[42] By the end of the century, CIBC even housed an Electronic Commerce & Technology Operations as one of its four business lines, accounting for over 14 per cent of all revenue. In 2000 CIBC invested $100 million in technology to assist its staff in dealing with customers. Today Canadian banks are preparing for the advent of smart cards well before their U.S. counterparts and are among global leaders in automated individual trading. They are also considered among world leaders in computerized securities trading, a new business segment that highlights both the importance of technology and the expansion of banking activities into related financial services.

Computing power helped make possible – and then was furthered by – advances in financial theory. With American financial reforms, traditional ways of measuring and controlling risk were replaced with new, more complex, statistical ones, many of which were dependent on large numbers of securities traded with relatively few transaction impediments. New Deal financial regulations made active corporate governance of public corporations by powerful financial players more difficult. The goal of these regulations was to create institutions and large organizations that allowed small investors to diversify easily as a way to minimize risks. By the 1970s several new financial theories developed for the management of risk and reward around securities with dispersed owners. In the 1950s Harry M. Markowitz, an American economist, made advances in optimizing portfolios by showing exactly how investors could reduce standard deviation (risk) at a given level of return. Conversely he also showed how they could increase return while maintaining a given level of risk.[43] Building on some of his insights, W.F. Sharpe and J. Lintner developed the capital asset pricing model, a major step in pricing risk.[44] At about the same time, financial theorists gathered evidence for various forms of what has been called the efficient market hypothesis. The idea that stock prices embody all available information and move in a random walk implicitly, if not explicitly, encouraged statistical analysis of individual asset movements in relation to the market, and discouraged fundamental analysis to beat market returns, putting a premium on optimizing returns from random fluctuations in market values.[45] Later work by F. Black, M. Scholes, and R. Merton seemed to unleash the power of options and other complex financial instruments, by articulating a quick and relatively easy formula for calculating with a computer what option prices should be (with a computer, obviously) in continuous time.[46] Coupled with increased market volatility after the end of Bretton Woods, these technological changes created an opportunity for banks and other financial institutions to design and trade new instruments, shifting their activities away from traditional commercial banking services into more investment banking and advising, thereby increasing the size of the financial sector.

The sheer volume of financial transaction and size of markets are impressive. Some numbers from the end of the twentieth and beginning of the twenty-first century clearly indicate the trajectory. From 1980 to 2005 world debt and equity holdings climbed from $3 trillion each to $35 and $44 trillion respectively. Both government debt and bank deposits grew at similar paces.[47] By 2007 the financial sector accounted for 7.7 per cent of U.S. GDP, nearly three and a half times the percentage in 1947. While bank assets as a percentage of GDP remained relatively unchanged in both countries from 1980 to the end of the century, stock market capitalization as a percentage of GDP grew by a factor of 2.5 in Canada and by a factor of three in the United States.[48] Although much of the growth came in markets and institutions outside of banks, changes in regulation allowed banks to participate in other financial growth areas.[49]

At the heart of these changes in finance over the last forty years has been the immense growth in the complex area of derivative instruments, many of which are not bought or sold on public exchanges and are only lightly regulated. A derivative instrument is a financial product whose value is based on some other instrument. There are many kinds: futures, options, swaps, and forwards. They have existed for many years but financial as opposed to commodity derivatives came into prominence as an antidote to the financial volatility following the demise of Bretton Woods. Although the value of global financial assets (bank deposits, government debt, private debt, and equities) rose to roughly $140 trillion in 2005, the derivatives world was even rosier. By 2006 the notional value of derivative instruments (value of the underlying assets, not market value of derivatives) soared to a number nearly four times greater than all of these other instruments (underlying assets) combined. Of those, over 80 per cent were over-the-counter – that is, traded in private and relatively unregulated – and mostly bank rather than organized market transactions. Much of the growth in bank-traded derivatives involved certain technical issues over the way interest rate derivatives are traded, as well as gaps in hedging caused by the standardization of market-traded derivatives.[50] Commodities and foreign exchange transactions had dominated derivative trading, but now interest rate contracts occupy by far the largest share. The greatest growth, however, occurred in a relatively recent entry, the now infamous credit default swaps (CDS). These CDS have been instrumental in the growth of securitization and the creation of public financial instruments supported by assets such as mortgages, which have played a key role in cross-border finance and the recent crisis. In the decade before 2006 securitized assets increased fivefold in the United States and fifteen-fold in Europe.[51] The increase in bank-based derivative and securitized instruments has been an integral part of a shift in bank business away from straight lending and toward services and trading. From 1984 to 2003 the non-interest portion of credit institutions as a share of their total income went from 36 to 46 per cent in the United Kingdom and from 25 to 45 per cent in the United States. In some countries, the increase has been even more dramatic.[52]

With these changes in bank products and geographic reach came new international banking regulation. However, increased international and European regulation has not prevented transnational banks from taking advantage of "regulatory arbitrage" and their own disproportional resources. The international standards of capital adequacy were set by the Basel Banking Committee on Banking Supervision, a forum created in 1975 to facilitate coordination of central banking. Under pressure to reduce bank failures and near failures – that called for more public support of banking systems after the end of Bretton Woods, national regulators turned to the banking committee. The committee focused almost exclusively on capital adequacy and credit risk, two measures that hardly dealt with the issues that produced the bank problems. The exclusion of other means of containing risk played to the strengths of two financial powerhouses reluctant to accept international control, the United States and Great Britain. This soon led to bank activity in jurisdictions without other controls to shift their business models toward riskier endeavours not captured by the Basel ratios. Moreover, the Basel committee and other supranational agencies have scant monitoring and enforcement authority with which to apply the international standards.[53]

During the 1980s both America and Canada experienced two contradictory regulatory trends, one toward greater international regulation and the other toward more self-regulation. Along with the international regulations, many large commercial banks turned away from traditional lending and moved into product design, advice, and trading.

They helped develop and employ new statistical techniques for assessing risk, such as Value at Risk (VAR), to which regulators also turned to control banks, while stretched the limits of old accounting rules, such as Marked to Market. All of these tasks depended greatly on computing power, bankers' internal control, and faith in sophisticated models.[54]

Moving funds across borders became easier and more profitable because cross-border transactions helped absorb large fixed costs. The last decades of the twentieth century witnessed the near elimination of controls on international capital flows for most OECD countries and the increase of computing power, which increased the speed of transactions and the ability to move money quickly. High computing investment increased fixed costs, which in turn needed more transactions to justify their economic value. That IT investment made it easier to handle vast numbers of transactions automatically. The same was true for pricing and risk evaluation, with complex statistical models based on cutting-edge financial innovations, such as the Black-Scholes-Merton Options Pricing and Value at Risk models. Many countries offered foreign banks the capacity to borrow cheaply from their respective central banks – a new feature of international banking – which extended transnational banks' ability to borrow cheaply in one country and lend more dearly through affiliates in another.

Canadian Post–Second World War Banking

Changes in Canadian banking during this period must be seen in the context of Canada's original banking legislation. Since Confederation in 1867, the responsibility for regulation of banking rested with the federal government. Since the 1871 Bank Act, Parliament has been required to review its provisions regularly, originally every ten years, since 1992 every five. In the post–Second World War period, this provision of the Bank Act has resulted in a number of mostly evolutionary changes. Beginning in 1954, banks were allowed to make mortgage loans for the first time to help satisfy Canadian post-war demands for housing. The most significant review of Canadian banking occurred in the early 1960s when a Royal Commission on Banking and Finance was appointed, chaired by Dana Porter, chief justice of the Ontario Court of Appeal.[55] The 1980 revision resulted in a loosening of restrictions on foreign banks. However, the most dramatic change occurred in 1987 when Canada experienced its own "Little Bang," as distinct from the "Big Bang" of the United Kingdom, which was focused on ending demarcations among financial institutions. The Little Bang began dismantling the four historic pillars of Canadian finance: the separation of banks, trust companies, insurance companies, and investment dealers. Five years later, in 1992 legislation was passed that effectively ended the four pillars. Henceforth the pillars were not separated, and the banks quickly acquired both investment dealers and trust companies. As the century drew to a close, the government took measures to restrict the growth of big banks, denying four of the Big Five the right to conclude further mergers, because of a concern about creating banks "too big to fail."[56] There were also political considerations, such as the impact of branch bank closures in the local constituencies of members of Parliament.

Post-war Canadian banking contained elements of both change and continuity. Although in 1945 ten Canadian banks enjoyed total assets of $7.2 billion ($100 billion in current dollars), dominating the financial sector with 60 per cent of all financial assets, none of them owned trust companies or investment dealers. The largest of these was the Royal Bank of Canada (RBC). The second-largest was the Bank of Montreal. Both were Montreal based and had been trading spots for first and second place in the league tables for the previous twenty-five years. The third-largest bank, only 60 per cent the size of the Royal, was the Toronto-based Canadian Bank of Commerce. Those three, along with the Bank of Nova Scotia and the Imperial Bank, were the "Big Five" of Canadian banking and accounted for 84 per cent of all bank assets. In 1945 the ten largest banks in Canada ranged in size from the Royal Bank of Canada with assets of $3 billion to the Montreal District and Savings Bank with assets of less than 7 per cent of those of RBC.[57] At century's end RBC, having been prevented from merging with its long-time rival Bank of Montreal, was still number one in a more crowded field of eleven domestic banks and forty foreign banks. In 2000 the Big Five still dominated Canadian banking, but by then regulatory changes allowed the banks to enter all phases of finance – insurance, trust, and securities dealing, in addition to banking. Moreover, all five were active beyond Canada's borders, principally in the United States. Together these banks represented less than 50 per cent of all financial sector assets because of the dramatically increased presence of trusteed pension plans and mutual funds.[58] As the century ended, the Big Five Canadian banks employed nearly 300,000 people and possessed $1.3 trillion in assets, with a net income of $8.9 billion and a market cap of $113.5 billion.[59]

Another major change was the continuing shift of the financial centre from Montreal to Toronto.

Housing in Canada, as in the United States, played an important role. In the post–Second World War era, demand for housing continued, especially with the post-war baby boom. The supply of mortgage funds began to outstrip the supply from traditional lenders. As a consequence, the government of Canada amended the National Housing Act to permit banks to write mortgage loans. Initially, the banks opposed the measure, "a curious role-reversal in the traditional relation of Canadian bankers and politicians" – curious in the sense that the bankers resisted new business the politicians were foisting on them.[60] Soon after the amendment passed in 1954, though, banks quickly became the second-largest source of mortgage financing after life insurance companies. By 2000 banks underwrote more than 70 per cent of all Canadian mortgages, which accounted for 20 per cent of all bank assets.[61]

But while there are similarities, there are also significant differences. In Canada there was virtually no subprime mortgage market or housing bubble before 2008. In 2000 Toronto, one of the two markets with the greatest demand for housing, had only recently turned the corner from a decade-long slump in housing prices. By 2008 Toronto prices still had not reached the levels attained in the late 1980s. In contrast to banks in the United States, banks in Canada carried the mortgages on their balance sheets with five-year renewals for matching purposes, which gave those banks much greater incentives to select and monitor borrowers. Moreover, in contrast to mortgage loans in America, most mortgage loans in Canada are recourse loans, that is, all of a borrower's property, not just the mortgaged house, is at risk. Non-recourse loans protect debtors from loss of other assets and reduce pressures to repay housing debt.

Many measures were taken to strengthen banking regulation in this period. As in many countries in this era, the issue of central bank independence became more important in Canada, but there was a clash of personalities that was uniquely Canadian. The Coyne Affair of the early 1960s unleashed a serious dispute between the government of Canada and the governor of the central bank over who was responsible for fiscal and monetary policy. As a result, a Royal Commission on Banking and Finance, the Porter Commission, was appointed, which served as the normal decennial review.[62] After two years of deliberation, the government took another two and a half years and two finance ministers before acting on its recommendations. The Porter Commission was the most wide-ranging review of Canada's banking system in Canadian history. The commission's goals were efficiency, competitiveness, and independent prudential regulation. It recommended continuation of self-regulation, whereby the inspector general of banks relied upon the work of independent auditors, who in turn relied upon the banks' own inspection staff.[63] Moreover, it recommended the removal of restrictions on the free flow of funds and advocated for greater competition, prohibition of interest rate agreements between the banks, and a strengthening of the office of the inspector general of banks. The commission made many other recommendations, the most important being removal of the 6 per cent ceiling on interest rates, a 150-year old restriction unimaginable for Canadian banking going forward.[64] During the Bretton Woods period, interest rates were also curtailed in the United States. Banks used many devices to circumvent this restriction, some of which contributed to the development of offshore markets and later shadow banking, but the U.S. restrictions on interest rate policies were gradually reduced in the 1970s and 1980s,[65] but not completely eliminated until the twenty-first century.

Incremental changes in the banking system gave way to more sudden and dramatic changes during the 1980s. The first occurred in 1980 with the regular Bank Act revisions, which flowed from the White Paper on the Revisions of Canadian Banking Legislation released in the late 1970s. Passage of the 1980 Bank Act ushered in a new era of financial services and competition, as foreign banks were now officially allowed into the Canadian market.[66] More specifically, the Act made provision for a new type of bank – foreign-owned subsidiaries – which were called Schedule B banks. (The existing banks were categorized as Schedule A banks.) Within the next four years, sixty Schedule B banks came into existence.

In spite of this increase in the number of banks, the government made no provision for an increase in staff at the Office of the Inspector General of Banks. As will be discussed in more detail in chapter 6, this omission would have implications for the bank failures of the mid-1980s, which in turn contributed to the creation of the Office of Superintendent of Financial Institutions (OSFI). OSFI integrated all financial oversight, a necessary step in light of the most important change in the integration of financial functions.

As discussed, financial institutions in Canada had been segregated by law and tradition into four pillars (see Figure 5.1) long before Glass-Steagall was enacted in 1933. One reason for this division was

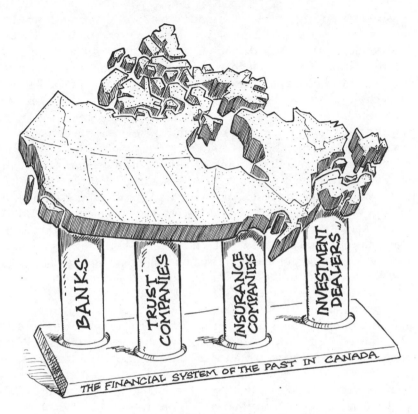

Figure 5.1 The Historic Four Pillars of the Canadian Financial System

Source: Canadian Foundation for Economic Education,
Money and Monetary Policy in Canada (Toronto, 1994), 7.

the structure of regulation. Banks were federally regulated, whereas investment dealers and trust companies were provincially regulated.[67] All this began to change when on 30 June 1987[68] the federal government passed legislation that permitted investment dealers to be wholly owned by other financial institutions, in part because senior Department of Finance officials were concerned about the possibility of relying on American underwriters for Canadian government debt issues. The consequences were immediate and dramatic, intensified by the market crash of 1987, which hurt all investment dealers. Within one year of the new Act and the market crash, five of the six largest banks acquired Canadian investment dealers.[69]

The process of breaking down the four pillars accelerated when the period for bank regulation review was reduced from ten to five years. Some observers believed this move was a thinly disguised measure to help the banks. They were the "big boys," and the view was that the new legislation was actually designed to permit the banks to dominate. As one authority on Canadian banking observed,[70] limitations on investments in non-financial businesses still prevented the Canadian banks from becoming German-style universal banks, but toward the end of the century even the Germans found aspects of that model prohibitively expensive in global financial markets.[71]

In December 1996, in anticipation of the quinquennial revisions, the government appointed a Task Force on the Future of the Financial Services Sector, which was expected to report by September 1998. Understandably, the government was embarrassed when two major banks tried to merge before the report came out. It learned in January 1998 that two of Canada's largest banks, Royal Bank of Canada and Bank of Montreal, intended to combine.[72] The BMO-Royal team gave a heads-up to Paul Martin, then federal minister of finance, just hours before their announced merger. In the view of many, the bank leaders had misread the politician. When asked to comment, Martin appeared angry. In a press conference, Martin called the merger plan "somewhat premature." The banks' merger announcement, he said, had pre-empted an ongoing bank review requested by Canadian bankers that was already underway. Known as the MacKay task force after its chair Harold MacKay, its mandate was to report on the future of the financial services industry. Martin said he feared the merger would derail the task force. Others thought the finance minister was put off because he had barely been forewarned about the deal. "It was an ominous beginning for a process that took almost a year."[73]

Three months later two more of Canada's five big banks, CIBC and TD, announced their intention to merge. Only the Bank of Nova Scotia opposed both mergers. On 14 December 1998, almost a year to the day after the infamous "eggnog agreement,"[74] Martin announced the government's decision to prohibit the mergers.[75] But as the century drew to an end the government did allow the merger of TD and Canada Trust, the largest independent trust company. And Peter Godsoe, CEO of BNS, the only banker to oppose the mergers, was quoted as saying he expected to see more merger attempts in the twenty-first century, once federal legislation was overhauled.[76]

At the same time, the global role of Canadian banking seemed to be changing. Among the big banks at century's end, there was some concern expressed that Canadian banks were slipping in international standings. In fact, not all banks had dropped; some had risen. The low value of the Canadian dollar contributed to reduced rankings based in U.S. dollars. Most importantly, Canadian banks continued to be among the world's most profitable, in part because of competitive restrictions that have helped make the system more stable.[77]

As has been discussed, some of the large Canadian banks had gone beyond Canadian borders almost from their beginning, but, as Neufeld noted, the big banks were quite passive during the interwar period.[78] A nadir in international activity was reached in 1949, when foreign loans comprised hardly more than 5 per cent of the total and there were only 105 foreign branches of Canadian banks.[79] By the late 1950s, however, external opportunities were once again being sought out, as the "low-hanging fruit" at home had been picked, such as retail and commercial markets. Canadian banks moved rapidly into Western Europe throughout the 1960s, shifting focus from traditional short-term trade financing to servicing medium- and long-term credit needs of multinational firms as well as governments. In the 1970s they became strong players in the eurodollar market, much to their chagrin later on.[80]

Circa 2000 all the big banks cultivated some sort of international strategy. The percentage of non-Canadian assets ranged from a low of 30 per cent for RBC, closely followed by TD, to a high of 44 per cent in the case of BMO. However, the strategies were very different with four of the five focusing on the United States, albeit in different regions and lines of business. The bank best known for its international operations was BNS, the only bank that segregated financial data of its international operations. It operated in a number of lesser-developed countries. At century's end, BNS had 39 per cent of its assets outside of Canada and earned 37 per cent of its net income in 2000 from non-Canadian operations.[81]

As in most countries, Canada during the post-war period witnessed a gradual relaxation of restrictions in foreign bank entry. Canadian Bank Act revisions in 1980 opened the way for foreign banks. By 1990 foreign banks held nearly 10 per cent of all assets, but their share slipped back to half that in the 1990s. In spite of the decline in assets, in 2000 HSBC[82] was the eighth-largest bank in Canada, with Citi in tenth position, followed by Deutsche Bank, Bank of America, BNP

Paribas, and ING.[83] Although regulations pertaining to foreign banking subsidiaries and branches have been further liberalized since the end of the 1990s, these foreign entities operate with many restrictions that do not apply to domestic ones, including restrictive choices in activities, limits on deposit taking, and exclusion from government deposit insurance.[84] Despite these restrictions, by the end of the century, over fifty foreign banking entities operated in Canada.[85] Despite reports of fewer restrictions in the new century, as recently as 2008 foreign bank subsidiaries and branches accounted for only 4.9 per cent of all Canadian bank assets. In 2009 foreign banks accounted for approximately 5 per cent of Canadian bank assets, compared with 18 per cent of U.S. bank assets. In many American states, foreign banks, including some Canadian, are important players in the retail bank market, which is not the case for foreign banks in Canada.[86]

The Shift from Montreal to Toronto

Canada witnessed a major geographic and activity shift after the fall of Bretton Woods, when the financial centre of the country finally moved from Montreal to Toronto. Although both the United States and Canada witnessed political turmoil in the post-war era, Canada's had more effect on the configuration of its financial system. At the end of the Second World War, Montreal was still Canada's largest city and the commercial centre of the country, a role that it had enjoyed for two centuries. Montreal served as headquarters for the lion's share of financial players. It was home to four of Canada's five largest financial institutions, including two of the three biggest banks, RBC and BMO. It also hosted Canada's largest insurer, Sun Life (nearly four times the size of its closest competitor, Canada Life). And the country's two largest trust companies, Royal Trust and Montreal Trust, were also situated in Montreal. Montreal Trust, the smaller of the two, was as large as BNS and larger than the Imperial Bank, the Toronto Bank, and the Dominion Bank, all Toronto-based. Many point to the election of René Lévesque's separatist Parti Québécois (PQ) in 1976 as the catalyst for Montreal's decline. But by 1976 the shift of the commercial centre of the country was already a fait accompli.

The beginning of the shift of the country's financial centre from Montreal to Toronto can be traced back to Toronto's victory over Montreal in the battle of the Bank Acts, which transpired from 1869 to 1871. During the First World War, Toronto-based investment dealers led the drive to sell billions of dollars of Victory Bonds. The financing of the war effort established Toronto as the main centre for the bond market. Toronto suddenly surpassed Montreal as the home of the country's largest stock exchange during the Great Depression. This was partly because Toronto pioneered mining stocks, which boomed when President Roosevelt raised the price of gold from US$20.67 to US$35.00.

After the Second World War, insurance companies, including Prudential of America and New York Life, began moving from Montreal to Toronto. Another subtle measure of the shift was the decision on location by those handmaids of business – law, accounting, and public relation firms. By 1961 five of the top six law firms were based in Toronto. Moreover, nine of the top ten advertising agencies could be found in Toronto.[87] Finally, six of the then "Big Eight" accounting firms were also Toronto-based.

The decline of Montreal and the rise of Toronto as Canada's financial hub was the result of a combination of economic and political factors. Montreal hosted the head offices of the major railways, Alcan, and Bell, but Toronto was the magnet for U.S. foreign direct investment in the twentieth century, especially Big Auto and Big Oil. In addition, Toronto had a dynamic retail sector. By the mid-1970s Toronto hosted twice as many headquarters of major non-financial corporations as Montreal.

Politics played an important role in the shift. The post-war period was one of unprecedented political turmoil. In spite of the large francophone population in Quebec, English was the language of commerce. The Montreal Stock Exchange and bank head offices (the Royal Bank and the Bank of Montreal) were located on or near St James Street, now known as Rue St Jacques, then known as "the Wall Street of Canada."

In the 1960s French-Canadian activism was on the upsurge, marking the start of Quebec's Quiet Revolution, a period of intense social, political, and economic change. "Maîtres chez nous" (master of our own house) became a popular slogan during provincial elections. At the federal level of government a Royal Commission on Bilingualism and Biculturalism was appointed. In 1960 the Front de libération du Québec (FLQ), a militant Marxist-Leninist separatist group, began its seven-year campaign of violence, which included bombings, bank hold-ups, kidnappings, and killings by bombs and by gunfire. In 1964 Queen Elizabeth was booed on a visit to Quebec City.

The political and linguistic turmoil in the province of Quebec in those years led many Montreal-based companies to transfer staff from elsewhere in Canada to Toronto rather than Montreal, as well as to relocate their headquarters. And in February 1969 the terrorist FLQ directed their attention to the financial community, specifically the Montreal Stock Exchange, with their largest single bombing. It caused extensive damage, injuring twenty-seven people and discouraging future capital deployment to the area.

During the 1970 provincial election, what became known as "le coup de la Brinks," a convoy of nine Brinks armoured trucks rushed billions in Royal Trust securities from Montreal to Toronto. More trauma followed when a British trade commissioner was kidnapped, along with the deputy premier of the province. The government proclaimed emergency regulations under the War Measures Act, the only time the country has used these powers during peacetime. "Habeas corpus was suspended, political rallies were banned, and membership in the FLQ was declared to be a criminal offence."[88] The FLQ killed the deputy premier, only the second political assassination in Canadian history.

By the time the PQ was elected to the provincial Quebec government in 1976, international economic historian Charles Kindleberger posed a question. He wondered "whether Toronto is emerging as the single financial center of Canada by a process drawn out at much greater length than in other countries, or whether the two centers have been stabilized in an exceptional cooperative relationship."[89] Kindleberger answered his own question: "It now appears ... that Toronto has overtaken and surpassed Montreal. It must be clear however that while this shift may have been partially driven by politics and culture it was a shift of an Anglo group of financiers from one Canadian city to another."[90]

The election of the separatist PQ party in 1976 accelerated the shift from Montreal to Toronto. No other North American city gifted as much capital, both financial and human, as Montreal gave to Toronto during this period. As people and businesses left Quebec in droves, so too did the Canadian dollar move down, from just above par with the U.S. dollar to the mid-$0.80s. The PQ government called for a referendum on separation in May 1980. Although it was defeated 59 to 40 per cent, along with the highly ill-advised National Energy Policy, which penalized producers and rewarded consumers, the vote contributed to another downward spiral for the Canadian dollar before it bottomed out at U.S.$0.69.

Throughout this turmoil in Quebec, Toronto solidified its position as the financial centre of Canada, just as New York replaced Philadelphia as America's financial centre over a hundred years earlier, and as

Frankfurt bested Berlin in Germany just three decades earlier. Like the United States and Germany, as well as many other countries, Canada's financial centre is not its political capital.[91] The Big Five banks were all headquartered in Toronto, and by 2000 the chartered banks owned the major investment dealers and trust companies as a consequence of the Little Bang of 1987 (see below). In addition most of the major life insurance companies, which had demutualized, consolidated, and gone international, were also Toronto based. The Toronto Stock Exchange was just demutualizing in preparation for a period of expansion that would see it acquire the Montreal Exchange in the twenty-first century.

Les caisses populaires and Credit Unions

Alphonse Desjardins established the first credit union, or *caisse populaire*, in Canada in 1900 in Lévis, Quebec. He was a Quebec journalist and newspaper owner, as well as a Hansard reporter of government proceedings. Desjardins also played an important role in establishing the first credit union in the United States in Manchester, New Hampshire.[92] Desjardins relied on European models from Germany, France, and Britain. The notion was to establish a cooperative-like organization that would permit citizens of limited means to borrow money at a reasonable rate. The *caisse populaire* proved popular in Quebec and later in Western Canada where the cooperative movement was particularly strong.

By the turn of the twenty-first century, *caisses populaires* and credit unions had assets of $131 billion, nearly 10 per cent of all the assets of deposit-taking institutions in Canada. Canada has the world's highest per capita membership in credit unions, with about one-third of the population belonging to a credit union. In Quebec 70 per cent of the population belongs to a *caisse populaire*, while in the Prairie province of Saskatchewan 60 per cent of the population belongs to a credit union. The largest credit unions by assets, however, are based in British Columbia. In contrast to all other "banking," the sector is mostly regulated at the provincial rather than federal government. In all cases the main business of credit unions is in residential mortgages financed by members' deposits.[93]

Credit unions first came to America via Canadian emigrants. Inspired by Desjardins, who actually attended the opening of the first, a group of French Canadians founded a credit union, St Mary's of Manchester, New Hampshire, in 1908. The more than 6,000 credit unions in the United States with approximately $1 trillion in assets are now regulated at both state and federal levels and play an important role in American finance. Over 100 million Americans are members of credit unions, ranging from those connected with military service, to religious groups and private companies.[94] With relatively conservative investment procedures and monitoring systems, credit unions survived the 2008 Crisis reasonably well, although a few ended up in government hands.

New Demands to Manage Risk and Provide Services Revolutionize Finance

It is strange to witness the fervent ardor that Americans bring to the pursuit of well-being and to see how tormented they always seem by a vague fear of not having chosen the shortest way of getting there.

Alexis de Tocqueville, *Democracy in America*

Not only did American demand for goods increase after the Second World War, calls for services did as well, perhaps even more so. Some needs were satisfied directly by the government; others by quasi-private and public measures. Although these expectations and the means for satisfying them were important in much of the developed world, they reshaped American finance in ways that made the economy in general and the financial system in particular very distinctive. American exceptionalism and innovation in finance have earned both fame and infamy for its financial institutions and organizations.

U.S. Pension and Mutual Funds

The legislative groundwork for these investment vehicles was laid during the New Deal, but their first sizeable impact on America's financial system came after the Second World War. Pension and mutual funds trace their roots back hundreds of years. Many governments provided retirement income to some citizens, especially soldiers and civil servants. Diversified funds for investment were popular in Great Britain, the United States, and several other countries, but the New Deal and post-war policies brought them together in a unique way in the United States, setting the stage for growth and a different governance relationship between investors and companies. Mutual funds required SEC listing and bolstered the governance of these funds through the Investment Company Act of 1940. Mutual funds were also exempt from

U.S. corporate tax on dividends if they distributed 90 per cent of their earnings to investors and maintained a diversified portfolio (owning no more than 10 per cent of the stock of any one company), which was intended primarily to keep them out of the governance of the companies into which they invested.[95] Some of the U.S. methods used for insuring retirement, health care, and housing were uniquely American, utilizing financial innovation to insure against new forms of risk and making for an unusual partnership of private and public sector initiatives.

With the help of U.S. securities laws and tax deductions, private American pension funds grew by leaps and bounds in the second half of the twentieth century. Large American companies offered lucrative pension plans, often in lieu of salary increases. The pension benefits were immediately deducted against corporate income, but taxable only when paid out to retirees. During the later years of the New Deal, mutual funds were made more attractive for pension funds by forcing diversity and by eliminating taxes on gains made by the funds until the funds were dispersed. Two institutions, pensions and mutual funds, are linked in their development. Mutual funds of various kinds – stock, bond, and even money market or open- versus closed-end – serve as the primary investment vehicle for group or individual pension funds. Together they have contributed to substantial capital market innovation. From 1945 to 1965 mutual funds grew by 18 per cent per year. The holdings of new institutional investors (pension and mutual funds), which were an insignificant amount of total U.S. equity twenty years earlier, accounted for 16 per cent of the $0.9 trillion value of U.S. equities in 1970. The transformation continued unabated through the end of the century. By 1998 that figure rose to 31 per cent.[96]

The investment strategy of institutional investors changed. Nearly 50 per cent of all pension assets were in common stock, up from 5 per cent in 1948. Whereas in 1948 roughly 75 per cent of these investments were in government, government agency, or private bonds, by 1990 that percentage had fallen to 30 per cent. By the late 1980s, too – even though 160 million Americans were covered by Social Security, federal obligatory retirement for all workers, and another 20 million by public state, local, and federal plans – 42 million U.S. citizens had private pension plans sponsored by employers or unions. Not all of these plans were funded – that is, with assets equal to the present value of future liabilities or some sort of insurance – leading to some scandalous failures and calls for new regulations. Unlike many other investors, these new institutional investors were relatively unconstrained in where they invested, as long as they respected limits on the amount of the fund or the assets they controlled. By the end of the century they were diversified both internationally and in terms of the type of investment activity, such as venture capital.[97]

During the 1970s and 1980s most private plans were restructured, and new opportunities for creating personal plans were added. Until then, most private and public pension funds were defined benefits (future benefits were guaranteed) instead of defined contribution (plans in which the amounts of contribution would be spelled out but benefits depended on investment results). As will be discussed, changes to the tax and pension law in the 1970s and 1980s reinforced a switch from defined benefit to defined contribution among private pension funds, the primary driver of which was risk. The issue of funding an increasing but unknowable future liability haunted many American companies, unions, and other organizations. Apart from Social Security, public retirement funds were unfunded and exempt from disclosing the degree of liability they had. Some of the largest pension funds in the United States were those for state and local workers.[98]

By the 1980s, too, most American households participated, directly or indirectly, in capital markets through some sort of private pension fund, even though (or perhaps because) the structure of the private funds had changed greatly. Two major reforms transformed pension funds by shifting the cost benefit relationship between defined benefit and defined contribution plans. The Employee Retirement Income Security Act (ERISA) of 1974 extended tax benefits to companies with a public insurance guarantee paid by the company, depending on the plan's degree of funding. It left those holding the plans largely free to invest how they pleased but bolstered limits on investments in a company's own stock, set limits on the quality of debt instruments, and added new fund governance requirements. However, ERISA exempted public plans. The Tax Reform Act of 1986 added limits to the tax deductibility of defined benefit plans and expanded the tax deductibility of defined contribution plans as well as personal retirement accounts. The number of defined benefit plans created in the United States surged from 3,000 per year in 1956 to nearly 35,000 in 1973, but in light of the new perceptions of risk, these numbers subsequently dropped radically.[99] By 1987 most companies had switched from pure defined benefit plans to defined contribution or defined contribution supplementary plans. The public sector did not participate in this trend. As late as 1998, 90 per cent of state and local government workers were covered by defined benefit programs. As early as 1987, two-thirds of all pension plans were still defined benefit, but three-quarters of those were government-worker plans.[100]

The shift to defined contribution and private accounts did not slow the growth of pension funds. By 2005 pension assets amounted to 121 per cent of U.S. GDP, nearly twice the percentage in the United Kingdom, twenty times that in France, thirty times that in Germany, and three times the world level.[101] Although pension and mutual funds are distinct financial organizations, regulations of one have had a huge effect on the other. There are many types of mutual funds, but all entail allowing smaller investors to diversify their risk by pooling their funds into a larger portfolio of securities.[102] By 2007 more than 88 million Americans owned mutual fund shares. Over half the assets of 401(k) plans and almost half the assets of individual retirement accounts were in mutual funds. They controlled assets of over $11 trillion.

The growth of mutual funds was both a contributing cause and a benefit of the rise of securities markets. Mutual funds adapted to changing consumer needs and regulations and gave a growing middle class a useful vehicle for investment, especially for retirement. Investment companies first became popular in the United States during the bull market of the 1920s. In 1924, a new type of investment company, known as an open-mutual fund or mutual fund, was introduced. Open-end funds were prepared to buy back (redeem) their shares at a shareholder's request at a price based on the current value of the fund's portfolio (current net asset value, or NAV) and continuously offered new shares based on that price. The Massachusetts Investors Trust (MIT), the first true mutual fund, was managed by its own trustees, issued only common stock, and continuously offered new shares to its investors. Late in the 1920s a closed-end fund boom began. Between 1927 and 1929 shareholding in this area grew nine-fold. During the same two-year period, the number of funds grew from 75 to 181, assets quadrupled from $600 million to over $2.7 billion, and annual sales soared from $188 million in 1927 to over $1.6 billion in 1929. By the end of 1929, 143 of 162 funds were closed-end. Investors preferred closed-end funds to mutual funds, possibly because of greater returns due to the leverage and history of their shares trading at premiums, albeit at high risk. There were problems, though. The cost of raising capital was often high. Capital structures were unduly complicated. Inter-company holdings were apt to be like a Chinese puzzle, allowing profits to be more easily hidden.

The Depression led to many reforms. The first were the Securities Acts of 1933 and 1934. They gave the federal government broad powers to regulate issuing and trading securities. The 1933 Act designated the Federal Trade Commission (FTC) as the regulatory body for securities. The Securities Exchange Act of 1934 created a new federal agency, the Securities and Exchange Commission (SEC), to administer the Securities Act of 1933 and gave the Federal Reserve Board the authority to establish margin requirements. It also authorized the SEC to take some (not all) of the direct federal control over the exchanges.

The results of this legislation contained a number of ironics and unforeseen consequences. Although the legislation had little direct impact on mutual funds, its indirect effect was profound. The 1933 and 1934 Acts mandated disclosures regarding new issues of securities and the markets where they were listed. The Acts also protected investors by regulating the markets in which they invested. But the 1934 Act proved to be vitally important to the mutual fund industry by creating an independent agency whose sole responsibility was the administration of the federal securities laws in the interest of investors. This contributed to an enhancement in public trust in institutions and markets, but more needed to be done. In 1935, in the Public Utility Holding Company Act, Congress directed the SEC to study the investment company industry and submit recommendations to Congress. The Revenue Act of 1936, however, was the most important event for mutual funds. It excluded all dividends received by a qualified trust (open-end mutual), effectively eliminating a double taxation of dividends from corporations to a qualified mutual fund and finally to trust investors.

The whole package of legislation is an indication of the goals of the New Deal: to provide small investors with the means to diversify and to protect investors against speculative activities. However, by providing tax relief to mutual funds only and not to closed-end funds, the Revenue Act of 1936 was instrumental in leading to enactment of the Investment Company Act of 1940. This is the statute that governs the structure and day-to-day operation of mutual funds and other investment companies and defines funds and investment restrictions, including the total percentage of a fund that can be invested in any one company and the total a fund can hold in any one company's equity.

The overall effect of New Deal reforms in the second half of the twentieth century was dramatic and multifaceted. Pension funds, which accounted for just under 4 per cent of overall American financial assets in 1950, soared to almost 15 per cent by 1990. Other alternatives to commercial banking and insurance companies for gathering savings, such as money market accounts and federally sponsored mortgage pools, jumped to 34 per cent of all financial assets in that year, up from 15 per cent in 1950, leaving commercial banks with only 27 per cent of the assets (down from 50 per cent in 1950).[103]

Canadian Pension and Mutual Funds

By 1970 pension plans as a group became among the fastest growing financial intermediaries in Canada, reflecting a widespread desire to enjoy a guaranteed level of income after retirement.[104] The growth rate since 1970 has been even more rapid than it was between the Second World War and 1970, with pension plans surpassing life insurance companies in size in the early 1980s. Back in 1945 most pension plans were sold by life insurance companies, and governments offered only means-tested plans. Today Canada has a tripartite system of retirement income, which consists of government plans, employer/employee plans, and individual savings and plans.

In 1951 the government of Canada introduced a universal Old Age Security Act, as part of the post-war reconstruction plans. As in the United States, provisions were made from time to time for retiring soldiers from British regiments. And when Canada Life, Canada's first life insurance company, began business in the 1840s, deferred annuities were part of their product offerings.[105]

In 1957 the government of Canada introduced registered retirement savings plans (RRSPs) in order to encourage individuals to save for their own retirement. Prior to that point only individuals who belonged to employer-sponsored registered pension plans could deduct pension contributions from their taxable income.

In the mid-1960s the governments of Canada and Quebec introduced government pension plans, which provided universal retirement pensions in Canada for the first time. The plans were and are compulsory and contributory. The funds collected were distributed to the provinces for investment as they saw fit. In Quebec, the money is invested through the Caisse de dépôt et placement du Québec, which was created to invest the funds of the Quebec Pension Plan. Subsequently the Caisse was entrusted with other Quebec funds, e.g., government and public employee pension plans, and has grown to become the largest purchaser of shares on the stock exchange. By 2000 the Caisse possessed assets of over $100 billion, making it larger than any Canadian financial institution other than the

Big Five banks and representing one-fifth of the giant Canadian pension market.

A recent article in *The Economist* described Canada's pension funds as "maple revolutionaries" and as "depoliticized sovereign wealth funds."[106] The new Canadian model emerged in the mid-1990s when the usually fractious federal and provincial governments finally came together to save the CPP from bankruptcy and put the plan on a solid financial footing.[107] Other initiatives included the creation of the independent CPP Investment Board, the Ontario Teachers' Pension Plan, the Public Service Investment Board, and the Ontario Municipal Employees Retirement System. In addition to being large (among the largest pension plans in the world), these groups manage the money in-house[108] and invest in assets all over the world with a focus on maximum rate of return without undue risk of loss.

The first open-ended mutual fund arrived in Canada in the depth of the Great Depression. It was called Canadian Investment Fund Ltd., but was established by the American firm of Calvin Bullock.[109] In the immediate post–Second World War era 89 per cent of funds were closed-end funds, but a quarter of a century later, 76 per cent were open-ended mutual funds.[110] The open-ended funds continually issued new shares, and customers could redeem their outstanding shares at the current net asset valuation.

The American and Canadian markets were different in two respects – the American market in mutual funds, as in most areas of economic endeavour, was much more specialized than the Canadian market. Furthermore, the U.S. market was much less concentrated. The 1964 report of the Porter Royal Commission on Banking and Finance the commission noted "the dominant position of a few houses" and observed that eight large firms represented half the industry in 1962.[111] Seven years later those same eight firms represented nearly 80 per cent of the industry.[112]

By far the largest of the mutual funds was Investors Syndicate. It was established in 1926 as the Canadian office of the Minneapolis-based Investors Syndicate (IDS, or Investors Diversified Services), not as a mutual fund company but rather as a provider of scheduled savings plans. In 1940 the parent company sold its first mutual fund in the United States.

In 1950 the Canadian Investors Syndicate[113] entered the mutual fund business. The 1950s saw a number of new small mutual funds established by entrepreneurs. Investors was different because, unlike the rest, it had its own tied sales force, much like a life insurance company, rather than relying on independent financial planners. Growth in the industry did not take off until the mid-1980s.

Initially mutual fund companies invested almost exclusively in common stocks. From the end of the Second World War through the 1960s, the market price of equities rose at a steady pace, and the performance of mutual funds mirrored that upward trend, although, unlike the United States, Canada introduced a universal pension plan in the mid-1960s and as a consequence individuals did not have to focus on retirement savings as much as they did in the United States. In the 1970s the equity markets stalled in both countries, and mutual funds found themselves treading water. In the 1980s the emergence of money market accounts – market mutual funds that took advantage of the high interest rates as per Paul Volcker's inflation-fighting initiatives – gave a tremendous boost to the sector.

In the 1990s activity in the industry soared, increasing from $25 billion in 1990 in assets under management (AUM) up to $426 million at the turn of the millennium,[114] surpassing the life insurance companies in size as interest rates declined and mutual funds became more attractive. No other segment of the financial system experienced near that level of growth, not even the pension sector. A contributing factor for this phenomenon was that once Canada experienced the "Little Bang" of 1987, Canada's huge chartered banks entered the mutual fund field. Initially the banks were not interested in the mutual fund sector, concentrating their efforts on acquiring trust companies and investment dealers, but with the decline in interest rates and their huge distribution network through their thousands of branches, they later pursued mutual fund business with a vengeance.

While ownership was more diffuse than it had been – by century's end twenty-five firms controlled 95 per cent of assets under management. The largest mutual fund company was still Investors, which had been acquired by the Desmarais family's Power Corporation in 1986. But by 2000 all Big Five banks had gotten into the mutual fund business, along with National Bank and HSBC. Moreover, three of the top five banks – Royal, TD, and CIBC – were among the eight largest mutual fund companies in Canada. Much of the bank business was in money market funds. In addition to Investors and the three banks, four independent Canadian companies[115] and two American firms[116] rounded out the Big Ten of Canada's mutual fund industry and represented over 70 per cent of the AUM in Canada.[117]

Housing in the United States

Americans have long placed high value on home ownership. That view is epitomized by Frank Capra's classic movie *It's a Wonderful Life*. Government policies have been created to help finance and bolster private ownership of housing, with multiple objectives. For nearly 100 years these policies bailed out home owners, banks, and the construction sector, pushing the financial system in directions virtually unknown in the rest of the world. As well, housing loans were used to finance many other purchases, some connected with homes, others not. But as in many aspects of American finance, the Great Depression served as a stimulus for activity. Housing loans were designed to buy and refinance longer-term mortgages of hard-pressed owners from their bank creditors, who were also financially strapped in the early 1930s after the housing boom of the 1920s. Between 1929 and 1933, 5,000 banks failed, mostly small rural ones. Empowered with the ability to issue bonds, at its peak Home Owners' Loan Corporation held 10 per cent of all U.S. mortgages. By 2005 government and private securitization of non-farm mortgage debt had climbed to 40 per cent and 20 per cent respectively.[118]

State involvement in house purchases predated the 1930s, but the Great Depression and ensuing New Deal revolutionized home buying. Until then, debt financing to buy a house was also variable rate and short-term, through a local financial institution. It relied on local deposits and required large up-front payments (around 50 per cent of the purchase price). With the collapse of the housing market and general financial distress in the 1930s, two institutions were established to intervene, the Home Owner's Loan Corporation (HOLC), for buying and restructuring mortgages in default into twenty-year facilities, and the Federal Housing Administration (FHA), to provide default insurance on new mortgages, effectively shifting all but interest rate risk from thrift institutions. By 1936 HOLC was wound down and in some sense replaced by the Federal National Mortgage Association (FNMA, later known as Fannie Mae) to purchase FHA-backed mortgages from thrift institutions with funds provided by long-term bond investors such as insurance companies and pension funds.[119]

Housing policy in both countries is a wonderful example of the differences between Canada and the United States. In particular, one can contrast the effect of foreign models, social policy on finance, and path dependencies. Home financing in the United States circa 2000 represented a complex mixture of foreign models and domestic expectations. Most American colonies began as property of the colonists and shareholders. Those who arrived as indentured servants, not slaves, received a piece of land with their liberty, making them tenant farmers to those landowners, but they were not full members of the colony until they owned land. Those colonists who paid their own way, in contrast, were rewarded with a plot of land. Many territories in later generations used land grants to attract free, white immigrants, a practice that caused political conflicts with slave states, whose economic model was threatened by small land ownership and waves of freed labour. Land ownership was also connected with emancipation. Northerners encouraged former slaves to demand from the government "forty acres and a mule" – part symbol and part reality of the slaves' new freedom.[120]

With cheap land and wooden houses in colonial America during the early years of the new republic, there was virtually no mortgage market in the United States. Loans, if needed, were private contracts among individuals. Therefore, the impact of mortgages on America's financial system was minimal until well into the twentieth century. Although British immigrants had brought the "building society" concept to the New World, only US$1.5 billion of mortgage debt (approximately 5 per cent of U.S. GNP) was by 1900 in the hands of institutional investors, mostly associations. Looking to French and German models after the First World War, Americans increasingly called for U.S. government entities to take collective action to address housing shortages. Some U.S. government incentives to purchase homes, such as tax benefits, were unusual in America. From the beginning of the U.S. experience with income tax and mortgage interest, there was a deduction against income for computing taxable income. This was different from Canada and virtually all other countries. Moreover, until 1951, thrifts, the main institutional conduit for mortgages, were exempted from federal taxes.

The Depression served as a policy watershed on housing, as in so many areas. However, housing measures had much greater effect after the Second World War. Aiding in the securitization of mortgages was, in the long run, probably the greatest step the government took to provide assistance to home ownership.

Although earlier attempts were made to involve the federal government in securitization, the collapse of the U.S. housing market in the 1930s led to many measures to buttress home lending. The federal government created several organizations to allow small banks to lend more by establishing a secondary mortgage market. The measures were designed to help both the borrowers and the lenders, which helps explain later problems. In the late 1920s and early 1930s, the number of non-farm private homes in foreclosure tripled. The first measure passed in 1932 created the Federal Home Loan Banks to lend to thrift organizations to encourage their lending, but it failed to have the desired effect for lack of resources. The Homeowners' Loan Act of 1933, passed when nearly half of residential mortgages were in default, added management resources and funds to refinance loans. The new agency could borrow with tax-exempt bonds to buy up distressed mortgages. Once the loans were bought, they and other debts were restructured. The next year, following the enactment of insurance for bank deposits, the federal government instituted an insurance program for qualified mortgages. Even with the insurance fees that were paid, given the fact that down payments were relatively low, the insurance scheme was very popular. In 1938 these efforts were stepped up with the creation of the Federal National Mortgage Association (FNMA), which later morphed into Fannie Mae, with the mission to buy up mortgages.[121]

During and after the Second World War, the federal government expanded these activities to support veterans directly. In 1954 Fannie Mae was given an additional mandate to create a secondary mortgage market using federal and private funds and to facilitate acceptable housing for segments of society that had been unable to obtain adequate housing. By that time many of these activities were privatized, but a decade later, in an effort to reduce government outlays, the Johnson administration lobbied Congress to privatize FNMA's secondary mortgage activities, leaving the Special Assistance and Management and Liquidation Functions, GNMA (Ginnie Mae), with the federal Department of Housing and Urban Development (HUD). Fannie Mae required that the original issuers buy stock in that organization. Privatization did not sever the government connection completely. Fannie Mae retained its mission to advance housing support for low- and moderate-income earners. With HUD's approval, Fannie Mae could attain advantages for raising funds on debt market. In 1971 securitization began in force. Moreover, over 30 per cent of all "one-to-four" family houses were insured by the government. In 1982, 45 per cent of all residential mortgages were purchased by Fannie Mae or Freddie Mac, the additional privately funded organization created in 1970 by the government to help spur the secondary housing mortgage market.

During the last twenty years of the twentieth century, nominal housing prices had doubled. In the next eight years, those prices doubled again. In 2008 one-third of all new mortgages were subprime, or owned by less-qualified buyers who could not get insurance or mortgages under older standards. Down payments dropped from 20 per cent to nothing, or virtually nothing in many cases. By 2007 a full 60 per cent of nonprime loans contained little or no documentation about the borrower's creditworthiness. A year earlier, nearly one-third of all new mortgages were subprime. Something had to give. In 2006 mortgages with negative equity began to climb quickly, reaching 6 per cent in 2007, and a year later, delinquencies doubled.[122]

When the crisis hit the housing bubble, it arrived in full force. In October 2008 the premium on interbank lending went up sevenfold. With massive injections of liquidity and other stabilizing measures, by 2009 it dropped back to its pre-crisis levels. But the crash in housing dragged down other sectors. The S&P lost half its value in a year. From 2007 to the end of 2008, unemployment rose from under 5 to over 10 per cent.[123]

Canadian Housing, 1945–2000

The two countries' housing policies run counter to images in both countries of how and how much public support each provides for social programs. Differences in housing policy between Canada and the United States have had an immense impact on each country's financial system. But despite very different housing financial policies, during the second half of the twentieth century, American and Canadian home-ownership rates were similar, with the United States having a slightly higher ownership rate until 2008, when Canada's rate surpassed that of the United States.[124] Indeed, despite greater housing subsidies in the United States, through much of that period, Canadian rates were actually higher. Canada's housing policy was established in 1935 by one of the most influential deputy ministers of finance in Canadian history, W.C. Clark. He wrote, "Having a home of your own ... should be the reward of saving and sacrifice and not a gift of a benevolent government."[125] The public policy that flowed from this philosophy was the promotion of market health rather than the promotion of private home ownership, as in America, with only a minor deviation in the 1970s.

While Canada did not have a "New Deal" in the 1930s, it did have a post-war reconstruction plan, which saw increased government involvement in the economy. After the Second World War a large number of returning veterans were spurring a demand for mortgage financing. At that time, banks were not allowed to lend money for mortgages. Life insurance companies were the major source of mortgages, followed by the trust companies. As a consequence of this demand, the government created a new Crown corporation (a state-owned enterprise) called the Central Mortgage and Housing Corporation (CMHC), later renamed the Canada Mortgage and Housing Corporation. Its basic function was "to administer the National Housing Act ... and provide discounting facilities for loan and mortgage companies."[126]

The creation of CMHC did not signal a shift in federal policy away from a private market approach. Rather, the primary mandate of the CMHC was to aid and assist the private market in the Canadian housing field. The first president of CMHC was a former mortgage inspector at Sun Life who had worked with Deputy Minister Clark in drafting the DHA in 1935. His direction of CMHC focused on developing the Canadian housing industry by "eliminating risk" for private builders and lenders.[127]

The demand for housing continued, especially with the post-war baby boom, and a problem with the supply of mortgage funds began to surface. Traditional lenders could not keep up with demand. As a consequence, the government of Canada moved to amend the National Housing Act to permit banks to make mortgage loans. The Act also instituted a system for insuring mortgages, twenty years after the Federal Housing Administration and Veterans Administration launched one in the United States. The amendment was passed in 1954, and the banks quickly became the second largest source of mortgage financing after life insurance companies.

By allowing chartered banks into the mortgage market and providing a system for insuring loans, the bill's authors hoped to channel a much greater pool of funds into the marketplace.[128] The insurance system would be administered by CMHC and therefore was explicitly backstopped by the federal government. The effects of these changes were immediate and significant. The year 1955 saw a one-third increase in housing loans issued by lending institutions, the bulk of which was due to chartered banks.

Further refinement of mortgage market policies took place in the 1960s as the government removed yield ceilings that up to that time had restricted the market's ability to set its own mortgage rate. Simultaneously, the government reduced the minimum term for government-insured mortgages.[129] This was in response to both a recommendation of the 1964 Porter Commission and to a dramatic jump in interest rates. Because interest rates climbed above 6 per cent in the late 1950s, the banks could not lend because of the ceiling. CMHC was slow to respond to the situation. As a result, it was "more difficult for the construction industry to plan ahead, and unnecessarily forced building costs and wages upwards."[130] In 1967 additional changes allowed banks to lend "conventional" mortgages (those not insured under the NHA).

From the late 1960s to the early 1980s there were some signs that the Canadian government was shifting its focus from promoting market health to promoting private home ownership as a primary goal. In 1967 Prime Minister Lester Pearson stepped down and was succeeded by Pierre Elliott Trudeau. One of Trudeau's opponents for the Liberal leadership and position of prime minister was Paul Hellyer. Trudeau tasked Hellyer with developing a new approach to housing. Hellyer quickly produced a report calling for a more activist federal government role. Trudeau disagreed, arguing with Hellyer's central premise that it was the federal government's role to provide housing for those in need. Trudeau, an expert in constitutional law, viewed housing as a provincial responsibility.[131]

However, in spite of Trudeau's stance, federal initiatives were introduced that were aimed at public housing construction and assistance to new home buyers.[132] In addition Canadian tax policy was revised to include a capital gains tax on all real estate other than a primary residence, thus focusing on home ownership rather than real estate as an investment. Problems arose in the late 1970s with the costs of supporting assisted home ownership, so the program was wound down, mirroring a broader reduction in the federal role in directly promoting private home ownership. By the mid-1980s Canada had returned to a "market steward" role.

The last two decades of the twentieth century saw a continuation of Canada's federal role as market steward. This period was marked by a significant yet passive role for the federal government in Canadian housing. Activity has been generally limited to the mortgage insurance program and the development of a modest mortgage-backed security market. CMHC has continued to focus primarily on mortgage insurance, dramatically increasing the value of insured mortgages. In 1985 CMHC outlined the direction of future housing policies, indicating that the federal role would be to support the private market in delivering housing solutions, a reaction to the failure of the interventions in housing markets in previous years. The experiences of the 1970s, combined with growing economic challenges in Ottawa, made this an attractive position. While the scope of CMHC's mission was thus restricted, the depth of its financial involvement in the market continued to grow. In 1980 CMHC had assets of $10.6 billion. By 2000 this figure had grown to $22 billion. Its home owner insurance in force had skyrocketed tenfold to more than $200 billion.

Securitization has been one of the most notable developments in Canadian housing policy but has represented a much smaller source of capital in Canada than in the United States. Mortgage-backed securities (MBSs) were introduced in a 1986 amendment to the NHA in an attempt to keep mortgage costs low. These amendments allowed NHA-insured mortgages to be bundled and resold to investors. This securitization process is similar to what provides a large proportion of the capital for residential mortgages in the United States; however, MBSs play a much smaller role in Canada. In 2000 mortgage-backed securities represented just 10 per cent of residential mortgages in Canada, compared to close to 60 per cent in the United States.

Several factors may explain the differing securitization levels in the two countries. First, it has been suggested that Canada's strong and concentrated financial system has played a key role in ensuring stability. Canadian home owners have had consistent access to capital from large, well-established national lenders. Prior to the 1954 amendments the large national insurance and trust companies provided this source of funding. Since the introduction of those amendments, chartered banks have increasingly assumed this role. This concentrated lending environment reduces the need for securitization when compared to the more fragmented financial system of the United States.

Another factor that may explain the different levels of securitization between the two countries is the regulatory environment in Canada since the late 1980s, when the Office of the Superintendent of Financial Institutions (OSFI) was created. Canadian lenders (banks, insurance companies, and mortgage and trust companies) and their investments are regulated by OSFI, who actively restricts securitization. OSFI sets capitalization guidelines for these lenders and supervises risk management. This has been pointed at as a source of fundamental strength in the Canadian system.[133]

In short, Canadian policies differed from those of the U.S. in several key ways. Going back to the introduction of income tax in both countries in the second decade of the twentieth century, mortgage interest in America was deductible, but not in Canada, costing the U.S. Treasury $75 billion a year. Innovation in the United States has often been a euphemism for less rigorous repayment schedules. "Freddie" and "Fannie" promoted home ownership in the United States, whereas CMHC promoted market health in Canada. Canadian borrowers have historically had access to a broad and deep pool of capital from large national insurance and trust companies, and, since the 1950s, from national chartered banks. There was not the same opportunity in the more fragmented American financial system. More than the creation of Freddie Mac itself, its use in solving multiple social ends made it important to American financial history. A 1992 bill legislated quantitative goals for the issuance of mortgages refinanced by Fannie and Freddie. These goals were expanded in the new century and opened opportunities for the private sector to take advantage of the appetite for mortgage-backed instruments and the willingness of many layers of regulators to ignore sloppy standards in mortgage origination.[134]

The Canadian housing system and federal housing policy have developed with a relatively consistent focus on facilitating healthy private market conditions, with the belief that such markets will provide optimal housing solutions for the majority of Canadians. This tradition can trace its roots to W.C. Clark, who wrote the nation's first housing legislation. His ability to shape this legislation was facilitated by the aspects of the Canadian governmental system, including the crucial role of a permanent bureaucracy, as distinct from the provisional role of elected politicians. Occasionally federal policies have promoted a more active role in the housing market for the national government; however, these policies have been sporadic and short lived.

This position contrasts with the American system, which places greater emphasis on the affordability of housing and the promotion of home ownership. The origins of these divergent motives are beyond the scope of this analysis, but the effects can be traced to recent housing-related crises. The more active role of elected members in the American governmental system has also been a contributing factor.

Other Forms of Consumer Debt

Many other features of American finance in the second half of the twentieth century designed to ensure that all Americans had access to a growing list of "necessities" had their beginnings long before World War II. America was well ahead of the rest of the world in its accumulation of private debt and consumer financing. Indeed, in many ways the American financial system encouraged debt by favouring the interests of eager debtors, as opposed to optimistic creditors. In the nineteenth century, American retailers, such as Abraham and Strauss and Macy's, pioneered instalment sales. During the 1920s GM established its General Motors Acceptance Corporation (GMAC) to help stimulate borrowing for its cars. Other companies applied the same model, using bank loans to finance their own customer credits. Some, like GM, Frigidaire, and Maytag, even used this selling device internationally.[135]

The fall of the Bretton Woods system and the stagflation that followed occasioned an explosion of other forms of private debt. It helps explain public policies to encourage consumer debt to stimulate the economy, long an American antidote to financial downturns, and to make up for sluggish growth in personal income. Personal lending had existed before the Second World War, but the ability of lenders to borrow against these funds or sell them off expanded greatly in the twentieth century, turning it into a big business with high margins. Financing the American dream with debt was the modus operandi of the system. And it was not just housing that profited – banks, governments, and individuals were all complicit. The policies that helped define the American financial system contributed to instability long before 2008. In the post-war heyday of economic growth from 1945 to 1970, few participants foresaw any danger in financing greater amounts of debt in banks and public markets, because the consumers could pay back their debts for cars, television sets, and houses with ever-increasing incomes. Until the 1980s interest on all types of debt was tax deductible, and tax rates were high, making their after-tax cost relatively low. Income stagnation and higher health and education costs increased the incentives to borrow in the last quarter of the twentieth century, just as the tax benefits declined. During the last decade of the twentieth century, outstanding consumer credit climbed eightfold, from $200 billion to $1.6 trillion. Given America's low savings rates during this period and weaknesses in its banking system, this level of consumer debt would not have been possible without securitization.[136]

Financing of U.S. demand for consumer credit would have been impossible without financial innovation, especially securitization and other derivatives. With U.S. savings rates falling and institutional investors facing regulatory restrictions over the kinds of securities in which they could invest, directing funds to those in need and managing investor risk became harder. The once close geographic and ethnic bonds between debtor and creditor disappeared. Moreover, with foreign investors looking for high dollar returns and much of American savings in the hands of institutional investors in search of high returns but limited to high-quality, bundled securities, securitization was a godsend. The problem was that these efforts to salvage the thrifts and keep mortgage and other lending activity up had huge hidden costs to taxpayers. The mortgage market's dependence on explicit or implicit government guarantees was a source of short-term private strength but long-term social vulnerability.[137]

By securitizing debt and creating public debt instruments, bankers freed the American consumer credit market from its reliance on local deposits. Investors from many other countries were enticed not only by higher yields, but the comparative safety of these instruments. Not only did they have implicit government guarantees, a host of new derivative instruments helped shield them from risks they could not control, or at the very least helped them choose carefully which risks they wanted to bear. Again, using data leading up to the 2008 Panic, one observes that these innovations came from humble beginnings to form an integral part of the financial system. From 1996 to 2006, securitized debt jumped from under $700 billion to nearly $3.2 trillion.[138] These amounts included many kinds of securitization, but housing made up a substantial portion and helped drive other kinds of consumer borrowing, which also profited from securitization. This additional borrowing fuelled consumer needs and painted a false sense of confidence in the borrower's ability to repay unsecured debt. The latest stage in the surge in home buying and prices became intertwined with other forms of debt formation. In short, by 2008 a huge debt-creation network had been established, in which oversight of the debtor had given way to a system of insurance contracts (derivatives) and "automatic, numeric benchmarks," whose ostensibly great advantage was easy application at a distance from the real assets from which the securities derived their value.

Insurance during and after Bretton Woods

America's post-war economic development represented an opportunity and a threat to insurance companies. The new stability, coupled with liberalization, produced results that even surpassed those achieved before the First World War. Sales of consumer goods requiring insurance were booming, and the new American private pension sys-tem, bolstered by the negotiation of generous corporate contributions, promised to bring multifaceted, revolutionary applications to Ameri-can capital markets. Already the wealthiest country in the world with a strong insurance market before the Second World War, America was on the verge of establishing a new kind of equity and insurance culture, albeit one with many fragilities.[139]

But as Bretton Woods came to an end, the outlook became less encouraging. The favourable loss picture and investment environ-ment of the 1950s and 1960s left companies unprepared for the loss and inflation turmoil of the 1970s. With multiple-line legislation came new forms of coverage and more insurance company merg-ers. Rate wars, though, came close to extinguishing home insurance, and riots in American inner cities contributed to red-lining insur-ance risks, which helped bring in greater government involvement in insurance coverage.[140]

In the post-war decades American life insurance companies focused on opportunities in the home markets, in contrast to their foreign expan-sion before the First World War, and their interest in other commercial sectors after the Second World War.[141] There were plenty of opportu-nities at home. In 1945 Congress had passed the McCarron Ferguson Act, which not only legislated the transfer of responsibility for regula-tion of insurance from the federal to state governments; it also softened provisions of the Sherman Act to allow insurance companies to share information for rating. New lines, such as hurricane insurance, were developed, and regulations on combining different forms of insurance were loosened. By 1965 total life insurance contracts were nearly three times higher than their 1945 levels. In the twenty-five years following the Second World War, automobile insurance premiums (theft, damage, and liability), for example, rose eleven-fold with little inflation. Mean-while life insurance, including health and annuities, grew eight-fold.[142]

For much of the second half of the twentieth century, companies seemed to prefer working with foreign companies to avoid national barriers and additional cost of foreign direct investment. Building on their ventures during the interwar period, some American compa-nies, such as INA and AFIA, pursued foreign business.[143] In the mid-1980s CIGNA, for example, the resulting company of the merger of two major American insurers, purchased AFIA and operated nearly 100 foreign entities to exploit what it anticipated to be greater overseas insurance demand. But as late as 1984, American insurance companies lagged behind companies in other sectors in foreign direct investment. Although the sector maintained more foreign branches and employees than did the banking sector, American insurance companies possessed far fewer foreign revenues and assets (as a percentage of their total) than banking, manufacturing, and other services firms.[144]

There were two notable and interrelated exceptions to America's relatively weak outward insurance direct investment. The first was American International Group (AIG), with its operations in ninety-two different countries and particular strengths in Latin America and Asia, and the second was the creation of offshore captive insurance companies. During the decades that followed the end of the Second World War, AIG acquired new companies and restructured a complex collection of enterprises in a holding company structure that first grew out of many companies' interwar experiences with political risk. The group consisted of thousands of entities that were public and private. For many years it was owned by a Panamanian company managed out of Bermuda. AIG's name became a watchword for international diversification and innovation, as well as opacity and recklessness, in a sector struggling to deal with a series of broad challenges.[145]

During the 1970s domestic U.S. reinsurance competition stiffened and shifted. Although many American firms started their own reinsurance departments, and some home-grown pure life companies ventured outside of the United States, foreign companies continued to play an important role in the sector, which in the post-war period quickly developed to a size that corresponded to that of the U.S. economy.[146] But America's influence on insurance was felt in less tangible ways too. American emphasis on business education, technological development, and specific aspects of its regulation pushed the creation of specialized professional know-how and standards.[147] Early in the twentieth century, insurance leaders began to invest in the education and certification of managers. Although not as successful as some other activities, insurance profited greatly from advances in professionalization of risk management, technology, and theory in the second half of the twentieth century.[148] As an extremely information-intensive domain, insurance was one of the first sectors of the economy to benefit from the digital revolution. Technological developments went hand-in-hand with a revolution in risk management, whose methodology depended on extensive computing power. For many reasons, virtually all of the new pricing risk theory emanated from the United States but affected insurance underwriting and investment worldwide.[149]

. In short, the breakdown of Bretton Woods in the early 1970s stimulated insurance demand and innovation, but competition and instability eventually undermined profitability. "Stagflation" and macroeconomic instability led to frustrated expectations and a seemingly desperate and inconsistent series of government policies with a wide range of uneven effects on insurance.[150]

The Liability Crisis and Beyond

By the mid-1980s, for many reasons, insurance companies were faced with a host of new types of liabilities and a huge increase in awards, a U.S. phenomenon with global ramifications. A range of legal changes made liability suits in the United States easier. From medical malpractice to product liability, the broadening of evidential standards and doctrines of culpability dramatically increased the number of lawsuits and the size of awards. Manufacturers were no longer held to the standard of negligence but rather to one of strict liability. Even the state-of-the-art defence was disallowed in the famous Beshada v. Johns-Manville asbestos case. Companies were not only required to use existing knowledge, but they also had to foresee future knowledge. Moreover, they no longer had to be completely responsible. A small degree of "guilt" opened them up to a lawsuit, leading the legal profession to pursue anyone vaguely connected with an injury who had money. Some steps to hold down costs, like no fault insurance, actually added to fraud. By 1982 some segments of the insurance sector spent 25 per cent of their premiums on legal expenses, up from 5 per cent in 1960. During the second half of the twentieth century, U.S. tort costs went from 0.6 per cent of GDP to 2.2 per cent. Insurance companies had underwritten risks with completely different assumptions about the number, type, and amounts of lawsuits. In addition, some companies became trapped in the vicious cycle of underwriting more risk to capture more cash from premiums written in the vain hope that high investment returns would offset higher future losses.[151]

The economic and legal turmoil rekindled old and new regulatory issues. Large property and casualty insurance failures attracted public and congressional attention. The National Association of Insurance Commissioners (NAIC), whose budget came largely from insurance companies, could not build an industry or public consensus around proposals to make regulation more effective and consistent. Although general attitudes toward limiting federal power at the time favoured keeping states central to insurance regulation, much of the public became convinced that state governments were altogether too weak or too cosy with insurance companies to resist pressures for lax regulation. Although natural disasters of the early 1990s, like Hurricane Andrew and a series of earthquakes in, compounded the already bleak long-term trend toward higher insurance losses and lower profits, some of the proposals targeted insurance pricing. Even before the new swell of regulatory zeal, Europeans especially tended to find American insurance regulations astoundingly pro-consumer, adding to the administrative costs of providing insurance and reducing profitability. Stricter investment standards, designed to improve solvency, also increase expenses. In some places private insurance became unavailable at politically imposed prices. Increasing direct public involvement in insurance included government organized and subsidized funds, such as those for residual automobile and workers' compensation, as well as mandated disaster and health insurance proposals. Even exiting a market was a complicated option for insurance companies. The news was not all bad, however. More insurance got sold, with higher premiums, and for new kinds of risks. Some companies added new limits on coverage or dropped some high-risk segments altogether.[152]

The growth in captive insurance represented a related but relatively distinct, larger response to the liability crisis and regulatory changes. Like securitization, this form of disintermediation also represented an opportunity for insurance companies and led to new and greater forms of financial foreign investment. Unable to get liability insurance during the worst of the "crisis," companies with the help of insurance company advisers opted for more self-insurance, often with offshore entities and third-party insurers and reinsurers that took on excess risk. By the early 1990s self-insurance accounted for 75 per cent of the alternative market. The highest growth came from workers' compensation, but increasingly, general liability and commercial auto coverage became part of self-insurance. As with banking, much of the disintermediation in insurance originated in the United States, in response to some special circumstances there, due to the increasing ability and willingness of commercial companies to internalize financial functions.[153] Many clients began to see property insurance as a needless expenditure that reduced insurance company margins. American insurance premiums paid to captives doubled from 1986 to 1992 and amounted to 40 per cent of all premiums paid. Although some of the growth came from insurance companies' decisions to get out of certain lines and some regulatory changes, the companies were driven primarily by cost and other considerations to use captives and self-insurance.[154] The development of captives entailed a huge transfer of insurance activity and expertise offshore, to Bermuda and other destinations, a move that realigned the American and even the worldwide insurance landscape. Reinsurance companies were particularly active in helping captives shed unwanted risk, and also to assume much of their parents' property, workers' compensation, liability, health care, and even employee life insurance. Although they siphoned off traditional business, offshore insurance was one of the most important growth areas for the insurance sector. Some insurance firms turned adversity into opportunity by advising and helping their clients set up captives. By 2002 captives accounted for over $60 billion in net premiums and over half of the total commercial risk expenditures.[155]

Still one of the least concentrated markets in the world, U.S. insurance in general witnessed further consolidation and new entries. Although the distribution of insurance remained fundamentally unchanged during the last decades of the twentieth century, regulation (or deregulation) encouraged new entries. Many new financial intermediaries, such as pension and mutual funds, reached maturity during the period. Many commercial companies and individuals were emboldened to perform services for themselves for which they once turned to insurance companies, such as ordinary property insurance and retirement planning. Life insurers were beset by new competition, capital shortages, and customer preferences for cheaper products. Much of the decline was relative, not absolute. Many large companies used more liberal regulations to switch back from the mutual form to joint stock and to diversify into an array of new financial services and real estate as well as into insurance coverage that was new, or new to them, such as disability and group pensions. While some companies were forced out of the business, better times always attracted new competitors.[156]

In general, the increase in the 1990s of service sector acquisitions, especially cross-border deals, was quite striking. Strong equity markets served as both a catalyst for and product of a wave of consolidation. To be sure, U.S. and other insurers had long used various methods, some hard to measure with international statistical flows, to go global – such as reinsurance and partnerships with foreign insurers – to gain the benefit of international scale while avoiding national restrictions and minimizing the cost of direct marketing. As with multinational banking, M&A activity represented the most direct way to increase focus and scale in the insurance sector. During the past thirty years, several international commercial treaties removed many of the obstacles to cross-border deals, making foreign direct investment in the sector a more palatable growth option. The boom in acquisitions was part of a worldwide stock market boom, which left many American mutual funds at a distinct competitive disadvantage and led to the demutualization of many companies. In 1990 Allianz bought Fireman's Fund Insurance Company for $3.3 billion. The biggest reinsurance deal was Munich Re's purchase of American Re from KKR for $3.3 billion in 1996. The deal catapulted Munich Re into the number three spot on the American reinsurance market. Earlier that year, Zurich Insurance Group, which already had acquired Maryland Casualty Group in 1989, bought Kemper Corp. for $2 billion and followed that purchase with another a year later. The combined company would have a sales force of approximately 15,000 people to sell insurance and other financial services in the United States. Between 1995 and 1998, nearly fifty M&A property-casualty reinsurance deals were done.[157]

Insurance in Canada: From Demutualization to Mutualization

For many reasons, Canada was spared much of the liability crisis. Nevertheless, Canadian insurance lived through several significant regulatory changes during the period. In the life sector, the federal government introduced mutualization in 1957 as a nationalistic, protectionist measure against mostly American incursions. Four decades later the government reversed that policy and permitted demutualization. And in the late 1980s and early 1990s, two other important actions also affected the insurance sector. As discussed, they were the creation of the Office of the Superintendent of Financial Institutions (OSFI) and the destruction of the "four pillars" of the Canadian financial system.

The provisions for the mutualization of life insurance companies must be seen against the background of a wave of American acquisitions of small companies. At least five small Canadian companies[158] had been taken over by foreign investors in the 1950s. There was a concern that some of the biggest Canadian companies would soon face the same fate. The Canadian Life Insurance Officers Association (CLIOA) promoted the view that Canadian life insurance needed mutualization to protect Canadian companies from foreign (American) takeover. In November 1957 the Canadian government moved to block the possibility of takeover by amending the governing legislation to permit mutualization. In addition, the legislation stipulated that the majority on the board of directors of every insurance company had to be Canadian citizens and that the board could prohibit the transfer of shares out of Canada.[159] Major Canadian life companies, representing 25 per cent of insurance sold in Canada, took advantage of the provision to mutualize, including the largest company, Sun Life, as well as, Manufacturers, Canada, and Confederation, while Great West Life and London Life did not. Ironically and largely ignored is the fact that Canada was, on one hand, among the most welcoming of all jurisdictions to foreign direct investment (FDI), particularly from the United States in the non-financial sector and, on the other, the most hostile to foreign ownership of life insurance companies and banks, although not non-life insurance companies. In 1965 the Canadian government further protected national interests against foreign counterparts in the life insurance sector by restricting total foreign ownership of federal incorporated Canadian life insurance companies to 25 per cent and restricted foreign ownership of any one shareholder to 10 per cent.[160]

Consolidation of financial regulation in Canada also affected insurance. When the government of Canada created an Office for the Supervision of Financial Institution in 1987, the superintendent of insurance, an office first established in 1875, was placed under the new regulatory body, along with the inspector general of banks. Acting in accordance with many recommendations, Canada's regulatory framework was adapted to the country's financial system with increasing demands for integration of financial functions.[161]

As discussed in the banking section, Canada experienced its own Little Bang in 1987. In addition to giving the banks immediate permission to buy investment dealers, which four of the Big Five did, "liberalizing" legislation introduced later removed all remaining restrictions on institutions from any of the "pillars" entering any other.

On the defensive and in the need of capital in the 1990s, some large insurance companies wanted to demutualize, reversing the 1950s policy, in order to consolidate and gain greater economies of scale to absorb large investments in technology. The government first indicated its receptivity to demutualization in June 1996, emphasizing its desire for companies to access capital. OSFI's Regulatory and Supervisory Practices Division began working on the development of a new supervisory framework in response to the legislation that followed in 1997. The framework, which outlined a comprehensive, risk-based methodology for the supervision of federally regulated financial institutions in all industries, was approved and put into practice in 1999. The Act specifically outlined how large and federally regulated mutual life insurance companies could demutualize, with OSFI's framework spelling out the government's role in insurance industry oversight.[162]

Government policies affected insurance in other ways. In contrast to the United States, where health care and workers' compensation were largely privately funded – though in the case of workers' compensation it was state-mandated – in Canada these insurance areas were largely run by the government. As early as 1914, the Ontario government passed a workers' compensation act that resulted in the creation of a provincial Crown corporation (a state-owned enterprise) that provided workers' compensation insurance. Within four years of the passage of legislation in Ontario, four other provinces followed suit – Nova Scotia, British Columbia, Alberta, and New Brunswick. The other provinces did the same later on. As a result Canada has a nationwide system of government-provided workers' compensation insurance. By 2000 the Compensation Boards in Ontario and Alberta and the Insurance Corporation in British Columbia had between $4 and $10 billion of assets, making them as large as the largest private non-life insurance companies such as IOF and ING.[163]

Government competition and mutualization were not the only obstacles to private insurance growth. In the immediate post-war era, the life insurance sector continued to fragment but grow. Although there was growth, however, life insurance became a less important part of financial services, with pension plans and then mutual funds surpassing them in size. Non-life, by contrast, while smaller to begin with, retained its more modest share. Extraordinarily, the top seven life insurance companies held their same respective spots in the ranking in 1980 that they had a quarter century earlier.[164]

However, as the century drew to an end, the formerly somnolent sector was in the midst of dramatic changes. Where there had been seven large players a decade earlier, now there were five, and in short order there would be only three. Confederation Life, a victim of poor management, failed, and London Life was acquired by Great West Life. Sun Life demutualized, as did Manufacturer's, Canada, and Mutual (now called Clarica) Life.[165] These five companies accounted for 85 per cent of the assets of the industry – the remaining 15 per cent was split almost evenly among forty-nine Canadian companies and sixty-seven foreign branches. Among the smaller Canadian players were Quebec City–based Industrial Alliance and Halifax-based Maritime Life. But the two major U.S. companies, Metropolitan and Prudential, were no longer among the larger companies. Metropolitan had been acquired by Clarica. The three largest companies, all with assets of $55 billion or greater, were Manulife, Great-West Lifeco, and Sun Life Financial Services. All three of these companies had significant presence outside of Canada.[166]

Each of them had a different international strategy. Great West Life pursued a specifically North American strategy, with 60 per cent of its assets in Canada and 40 per cent in the United States. The company entered the U.S. market in 1906 in North Dakota. In 1979, it established a separate U.S. operation, headquartered in Colorado. In 2000 there were two co-presidents and two co-CEOs, one based in the United States, one in Canada. Manulife and Sun Life pursued other strategies. Both conducted only one-quarter of their business in Canada, and both did nearly twice as much business in the United States as in Canada. Sun Life had a large presence in the United Kingdom as well, almost equal to its presence in Canada, while Manulife kept 12 per cent of its assets in Asia, principally Hong Kong, but with the intention of significantly increasing its Asian presence in the twenty-first century. As part of that strategy, Manulife became the first Canadian insurer to open a representative office in China in the early 1990s. Four years later Manulife entered into a joint venture with Sinochem, a Chinese conglomerate. And in November 1996 Manulife-Sinochem's joint venture opened its first office in Shanghai. Although Sun Life Financial had an Asian Pacific[167] legacy dating back to the nineteenth century, it had only a modest presence there. It held just over 1 per cent in the region at the end of the twentieth century with operations in Hong Kong and the Philippines, where it was the number one life insurer in the country based on premium income. In 1995 it entered the Indonesian market. However, it too had eyes set on expanding into Asia in the twenty-first century.

In some ways, the Canadian non-life sector retained its profile throughout the period. Fragmented among 200 companies, this sector comprised twice as many Canadian companies as non-Canadian, but the non-Canadian companies were larger and accounted for nearly two-thirds of all assets. Unlike the life sector, non-life not only grew in absolute terms but also maintained its 2.5 per cent share of all financial sector assets. Eighty per cent of the insurance sold was for automobile (54 per cent) and personal and commercial property (29 per cent). Four provincial governments were involved in the auto insurance business, representing 25 per cent of all auto business. While there were no really dominant players, eight companies wrote 50 per cent of the business, down from twenty-six companies in 1980. Of those eight, three were British, three were Canadian, and two were Continental European (one Dutch and one French). In addition there were twenty-seven fraternal benefit organizations that sold non-life insurance.[168] At century's end, the two largest non-life insurers were IOF, a Canadian fraternal organization,[169] and ING, a Dutch insurer that had been active in Canada since shortly after the Second World War.

Financial Exchanges and Equity Financing

In addition to the explosion in and internalization of derivatives trading and growth of institutional investors, several other major transformations in equity holding and the structure of markets occurred after the fall of Bretton Woods. Although the changes were more dramatic in the United States, Canada felt the aftershocks of some and led the way in others. Each of these transformations will be dealt with separately, but none can be seen in isolation from the other and from other changes in the environment, such as developments in financial theory. The story of financial exchanges illustrates not only how different elements of the financial system are connected to one another, but also how tied they are to both domestic and international technological, political, and economic change.

For virtually all of American history, "Wall Street" has not only served as shorthand for all U.S. financial exchanges and "America's equity culture" but also for the entire American financial system, as our book title suggests. This exaggerates Wall Street's role. It began its life in response to scandal. In order to clean up their trading operations, dealers and auctioneers created the Buttonwood Agreement in May 1792, meeting under a tree at 68 Wall Street, to create a formal exchange for buying and selling securities. As late as 1818, the exchange listed five U.S. government securities, one New York state security, ten bank issues, thirteen insurance securities, and several foreign exchange deals.[170] For the first three decades of the new nation's life, Philadelphia was a more important financial centre, as seat of America's first two central banks and home of many of its earliest banks and insurance companies.[171] Boston was one of the largest homes for banks, and Chicago hosted the largest commodities futures exchanges.

Wall Street's current status owes much to many towering figures, such as J.P. Morgan and John D. Rockefeller, as well as developments in four critical periods. Despite Philadelphia's early primacy, it was New York that became America's largest port by the 1840s, which contributed greatly to its status as the most vibrant centre for trading many kinds of financial instruments, not just equity. For much of the next sixty years, the trading was highly concentrated on railroads. The markets were restricted to large investors with a high tolerance for risk and a capacity for skulduggery.

The late nineteenth and early twentieth centuries witnessed some of the first steps toward market maturity, such as inchoate accounting standards and antitrust legislation, but with much turbulence. The expansion of Wall Street was driven by the combination of American first-movers of new sectors, the consolidation of small and large companies, and the exit of entrepreneurs, all of which created new offerings of public shares just as the rise of middle-class wealth created potential new shareholders and financial institutions. Many large companies were still controlled by small groups of intermediaries and investors (trusts), which simultaneously added to the confidence of distant investors and aroused suspicion of conflicts of interest. Symbolized by J.P. Morgan, America's largest companies were controlled in large part by syndicates of large investors, which helped stabilize markets but also contributed to calls for a reduction of insider control and monopoly power. From 1900 to 1920, the net effect seemed to be positive. At its peak before the crash, the Dow index repeated that growth rate in less than ten years. The Dow index grew by 66 per cent, despite a downturn after 1920. The boom of the 1920s added demand and brought in smaller shareholders, many of whom financed themselves through debt. The crash resulted in reaction and regulatory control with measures designed to limit the power of inside investors. As discussed earlier, that control reduced the special relationship between banks and the securities business and added to the financial clout of other intermediaries on capital markets, setting the stage for another boom in the 1950s and 1960s.

Moreover, the crash exposed domestic accounting inadequacies and conflicts of interest, while revealing that the crisis had international dimensions. The worst culprit turned out to be a colourful Swedish financier, Ivar Kreuger, whose ability to hide his financial liabilities with complex holding structures fooled investors on both sides of the Atlantic.[172]

Despite the reforms, the Dow did not return to its 1929 peak until 1954. There were still many obstacles to a new rally and market-maker prosperity. In the mid-1930s the economy and stocks revived, only to collapse again in 1937. Some on Wall Street blamed the reforms enacted by the SEC that were then forced on the NYSE, which limited the power of exchange members. Other New Dealers continued to blame the domination of monopolies and financial plutocrats who controlled vital industries. War clouds in Europe also affected trading, but brokers became less profitable as new issues fell off and competitive bidding was introduced.[173]

New Bulls, Bears, and Motives: The Conglomerate Wave, Private Equity, Venture Capital, the Dot.com Bubble, and Hedge Funds

In the 1950s the U.S. stock market began one of its longest and most vibrant bull markets. From 1945 to the end of Bretton Woods, the Dow Jones index increased approximately ninefold.[174] The rebound in prices and trading was spirited by many developments. Company profits and yields increased. Inflation was increasing but still low. Government spending increased faster than overall economic growth. Despite all this growth, the structure of exchanges changed little until the 1980s. One important change was the increase in M&A activity. High-flying companies, some selling at forty to fifty times earnings, discovered that in the strong market they could use their high stock prices to acquire companies with dimmer prospects, whose low book-to-market ratios made them seem like "bargains." These deals represented a cheap way to increase growth.[175]

The upsurge of M&A activity serves as a wonderful illustration of how various elements of finance, such as theory, banking, and technology, are tied together to produce change. The acquisitions owed a lot to shifting views of financial theory. Diversification, a term borrowed from financial portfolio optimization theory, became the watchword for large corporations. Beginning in the 1950s and continuing into the 1960s, giant conglomerates formed, serving as an umbrella for many activities in one sector and perhaps more importantly in different sectors. Leaping from the financial idea that owning inversely correlated securities would reduce the volatility of a portfolio, the corporate theory postulated that losses in one sector in a business cycle would be balanced by gains in another, smoothing earnings. It ignored the fact that, unlike securities, the company correlations had not been determined by long-term statistical analysis and the companies themselves had to be managed.

Some combinations were friendly, others hostile. Harold Gineen of ITT and W.R. Grace were corporate names associated with this conglomerate movement. The growth of consumer credit also helped finance demand for stocks. Easily acquired debt helped fuel stock ownership. Brokers began to tout these "diversified" firms as secure growth opportunities.[176]

By the late 1960s the bull market ran afoul of a series of economic and political realities. Government spending contributed to inflation and a loss of confidence in the dollar, which led to the breakdown of fixed exchange rates, unleashing a period of more inflation and more foreign exchange volatility. A surge in raw material prices increased input prices for manufacturing countries. Many of the darlings of the stock market conglomerates became targets of their host and home country regulators for their abuse of market power. Moreover, their "diversification benefits" seemed to rob shareholder value rather than create it. As interest rates increased and banks developed new products with higher yields and more security, stocks lost much of their lustre and competitive advantage. As demand for stocks waned and a variety of pressures reduced commissions, brokerage firms began to fail or consolidate.[177]

The bear market lasted well into the Reagan administration. From the end of the 1960s to the beginning of the 1980s, stock prices were volatile but ended up back where they began. But that long decade and a half might be viewed as a mere pause in one long bull market, a prelude to what were probably the best fifteen years in Wall Street's history. Once again, financial theory contributed to restoring the bulls' optimism.

Academics were not the only contributor to the stock market turnaround, but they helped. New financial theory attacked some of the core concepts behind the consolidation movement. The ability of markets to discover reasonable prices and manage risk was praised. Two of the best-known ideas of the time, the capital asset pricing model and the efficient market hypothesis, undermined the idea of diversification through purchasing businesses in different sectors by reminding investors of how easily they themselves could diversify and by undermining the idea that buying "cheap" companies was not an easy way to enhance shareholder value. Advances in options pricing relied on many of these financial insights. The theory showed market participants how they could invest, hedge their bets themselves without even owning the assets that underlay the derivative instruments, and even help build public and private markets to trade them. Along with these views came another idea, agency theory, which emphasized the costs of ownership by distant, passive shareholders, and conversely the merits of hands-on management.[178]

Many acquisitions and divestitures of the 1980s were connected to agency theory. Whether product or cause of market changes, this theory will always be connected with a new wave of acquisitions, leveraged buyouts (LBOs, or high debt raised by borrowing against the target company's own assets) and their subset, management buyouts (MBOs). The theory postulated that companies would gain in value if shareholder and management interests were reunited, as had been the case during early industrial development. Private equity firms – which specialized in taking over widely held firms owned by passive shareholders, selling off some of their parts, and carefully controlling the cash flows of what was left by managers and active shareholders – had little difficulty finding a slew of undervalued targets. Firms such as KKR were particularly adroit at finding, buying, and managing public companies with low Tobin Qs, which are a low ratio of share price to replacement cost of assets per share.

Much of the acquisition binge was connected to developments in debt, which was often used to finance them. Under pressure from the vibrant eurobond markets in the 1970s and 1980s, which attracted banks and customers from outside of North America and Europe, U.S. regulators made the syndication and underwriting of debt in the United States and by American firms easier. Congress held firm on repealing Glass-Steagall until the end of the 1990s, but the Fed created a path for companies and banks to issue securities without holding them for a long time through shelf registrations under SEC Rule 415. The decision allowed U.S. and foreign financial institutions to get pre-approval for an issue, without having to actually go public and sell immediately. This added flexibility by allowing investment banks and their clients to wait until the time seemed most appropriate and reduced the banks' need to hold the securities for a long time. Commercial banks were getting involved on Wall Street again, working more closely with brokers and pure investment banks. Here too financial practitioners found justification in financial theory, which at this time emphasized financial benefits of the tax shield provided by interest, even if other supposed benefits were illusory.[179]

The most infamous debt innovation connected with acquisitions, especially for LBOs and MBOS, was a new form of junk bonds. Junk bonds had been around for a long time, but they were not financing vehicles. "Fallen angels" were normal debt sold at deep discounts, with high yields, below investment grade. The innovation that Michael Milken and the investment bank Drexel Burnham first created in the 1970s was to use new issue high-yield bonds as part of complicated financing for acquisitions in the 1980s. Their strength in this segment, compared to that of many competitors, was not just the novelty but also their selling and distribution capacity. By the end of the 1980s, sophisticated financing using complex layered debt with little equity was being used to buy many small companies and even some of the largest companies in America. RJR Nabisco (US$24.6 billion), led by Canadian businessman F. Ross Johnson, was an example of an organization whose collection of assets seemed more valuable separately than together and whose management over-invested in projects whose returns did not cover the cost of capital. Many more transactions exceeded multiple billions of dollars. In 1989 nearly US$200 billion in LBOs were conducted (over 400 separate deals), up from virtually nothing at the beginning of the decade.[180] The amount of outstanding junk debt went from US$7 billion in 1983 to US$250 billion by 1992.[181] Many companies ceased to exist and many shed jobs, at least in the United States, igniting a chorus of criticism, but high economic growth rates and low unemployment prevented the critique from turning into restrictive legislation. Even the insider trading scandals that brought down Drexel and imprisoned Milken only slowed but did not end the tidal wave of debt-financed acquisitions.[182]

The exchanges themselves adapted and thrived too. In addition to restructuring old companies, new firms required capital, and founders once again sought exit. With the United States running large trade deficits, many foreigners were interested in buying U.S. equities. Indeed, many of the acquisitions during the last three decades of the twentieth century were instances of American companies being bought by foreign ones. Venture capital thrived. From 1984 to 1997, the amount of venture capital commitments to private firms alone soared from US$3 billion to $10 billion, with pension funds, insurance companies, individuals, foreigners, endowments, and corporations all jumping in with both feet.[183] The bull market of the late 1980s and 1990s will always be associated with the rise of the National Association of Securities Dealers Automated Quotes (NASDAQ), which was founded in 1971 to take advantage of computer advances to speed up price discovery. It was originally conceived as an electronic network, the first of its kind, a means of comparing quotes among dealers for 2,500 securities not traded on other exchanges, known as over-the-counter (OTC) stocks. It soon became a quasi-exchange itself, increasing confidence in OTC stocks. Securities had to be approved by the SEC, but participant companies needed only three market makers in their securities – brokers and dealers willing to transact business – and to fulfil some minimal requirements in assets, capital, and shareholding.[184] Despite charges that investors could not rely on the NASDAQ's 545 market makers, the NASDAQ prospered. It helped reduce transaction costs and buy/sell spreads. A wave of initial public offerings (IPOs) of tech and biotech companies drove much of the growth. While the Dow surged tenfold from 1980 to 2000, by the end of the millennium the NASDAQ 100 index seemed on an inevitable ride to 5,000, an increase of more than fifty times.

The growth of equity values, trading, and profits for investment bankers was not without setbacks. During the 1980s stock markets suffered their worst shock since the 1930s. On Black Monday, 19 October 1987, following significant drops in Hong Kong and Western Europe, the New York Stock Exchange lost 508 points and 23 per cent of its value. The crash had many causes: fears of inflation and speculation, market drops from their August highs, as well as technical, macroeconomic, and political concerns. Temporary losses for investors were staggering, but no general banking collapse ensued. The Fed announced that it would provide emergency funding for banks. The overall economy was hardly affected, although some financial activities such as leveraged buyouts suffered setbacks. Stock prices rebounded relatively quickly. Even though many economists feared that the crash was signalling the beginning of a new depression, by the spring of 1989 the Dow reached it pre-crash high, part of a long bull market. The two major changes coming out of the crash were brakes on trading (circuit breakers) and faith in the "Greenspan put," the Fed's ability to calm markets by injecting liquidity.[185]

Despite or perhaps because of prosperity and technology, not only were brokers consolidating, the ownership structure of exchanges also changed greatly. In 1990 most exchanges were owned by market participants (brokers) and were national exchanges. By 2010 most were publicly traded, cross-border enterprises. In 1992, for example, the NASDAQ linked up with the London Stock Exchange, creating the first intercontinental linkage for securities trading. In 2000 the National Association of Securities Dealers spun off the NASDAQ to form a public company, which later was transformed into the NASDAQ OMX Group. The NASDAQ experience with emerging companies and its international connections was soon being emulated throughout much of the world. Europe formed the EASDAQ. The NYSE merged with Euronext. Other mergers were contemplated, including the NASDAQ with all or parts of the NYSE.

Trading in Canada

As discussed in chapter 4, Canadians also created exchanges before the First World War. The development of exchanges in Montreal and Toronto during the last three decades of the nineteenth century enhanced the confidence of Canadians in their new country. In both cities, brokers organized themselves into exchanges. These networks gave the brokers a forum for gathering and exchanging information as well as securities. Dealing with fellow members of the exchange reduced competition and increased reliability. Although many stocks did not trade on the exchanges, gradually more and more corporations saw the value of trading on exchanges. New exchanges appeared, specializing in speculative mining and oil companies. Gradually stock ownership expanded to something that was no longer the sole domain of the very wealthy. Although arguments for increased regulation to prevent fraud and misrepresentation had many supporters, Canadians tended to opt for loose or rather self-regulation. Additional self-regulation generally followed crises. By 1912 Manitoba became the first jurisdiction to pass a blue-sky law, modelled on the state of Kansas legislation that established tribunals to oversee new issues offered to the public. New technology such as the telephone reduced transaction costs. The Canadian government had to borrow heavily during the First World War, thus contributing to the public's appetite for securities. During the prosperous 1920s, Canadians plunged into capital markets with great enthusiasm, until the 1929 Crash reminded investors of the prevalence of scams.

Many of the changes in Canadian financial markets paralleled those in the United States, but there were also many departures. As discussed, one major difference between the two countries is on banking supervision and policy; another is securities regulation, which is a provincial responsibility in Canada. Securities regulation played an increasingly important role in post–Second World War Canada. As in the United States, share prices in the 1920s boomed in Canada and collapsed in the early 1930s. In 1939 share prices still hovered around their 1926 levels. As the Canadian economy grew rapidly after the Second World War, share prices increased tenfold by some measures. Growth was driven in part by a greater number of investors with more disposable income. Canadian turned not only to "blue chip" companies with reliable dividends but also to "unproven" non-dividend paying oil and mining shares, many of which were traded only over the counter in Toronto. Demand for more transparency and reliability led to new federal and provincial laws to vet the quality of new issues and add to required disclosures.[186]

But even before the Second World War and the creation of the SEC, most Canadian provinces had enacted security fraud prevention legislation, forcing brokers and salesmen to register and specify practices that may be deceptive. As discussed in chapter 4, in 1931 Ontario created a special board to oversee securities dealings, an agency that was later renamed the Ontario Securities Commission. A few years later, the OSC forced a merger between the Standard Stock and Mining Exchange, which had a "gambling den" atmosphere, and the more reliable Toronto Stock Exchange (TSE).[187] Also discussed in chapter 4 are the results of the 1929 stock market crash, which saw the shift in trading from St James Street in Montreal to Bay Street in Toronto.

After the Second World War, the pace of reform sped up. Following U.S. practice, the OSC rewrote securities law to require "full, true and plain disclosure of all material facts about new issues." The law further directed the OSC to review the registration of brokers and salesmen, giving the OSC the power to cancel those whose behaviour was contrary to the public interest. American views influenced Canadian measures, but Canadian authorities were given fewer resources than the SEC. During the 1940s and 1950s Americans complained about lax controls on dubious shares and selling practices in Toronto. Twenty years after its creation, the OSC was viewed by many in Canada and the United States as too passive and too hobbled by those whom it was supposed to control.[188]

Until 1977 all foreign firms were barred from New York Stock Exchange membership. In 1950 Wood, Grundy and A.E. Ames & Co., two Toronto-based firms, were exempted from the NYSE prohibition and ranked among the top underwriting firms in the United States.[189] Once the ban on Canadian bank security trading was lifted in the late 1980s, Canada's big banks started trading directly in New York.

In the 1950s both countries loosened some of their regulatory controls. However, self-regulation proved to be inadequate in Canada, as it was in the United States. The OSC probably remained more active than its American counterparts, but the TSE did not tighten its own internal controls, such as listing requirements, until 1958. A series of scandals and concerns in both countries in the late 1950s and early 1960s, including examples of insider trading, led to securities law changes in the United States. In turn, the Ontario government established the Kimber Commission in 1963 to consider the effects of unscrupulous transactions. It recommended several changes to securities law, including a rule that any bid for more than 20 per cent of a company's shares should remain open for twenty-one days to allow shareholders more time for serious consideration of a tender offer. Its recommendations led to a new Securities Act in 1966, which also called for more disclosure of executive and large shareholders' interest in a corporation.[190]

Whereas American law actually encouraged mergers by making borrowing for takeovers easier, despite a requirement to disclose purchases of over 10 per cent (later reduced to 5 per cent), renewed acquisitions in Canada in the 1960s led to concerns about financing acquisitions with debt. These worries had more to do with the weakness of disclosure requirements for potential mergers. Nevertheless, resistance from the financial community blocked legislation. With the number of mergers continuing to mount in the 1970s, the OSC tried again to bolster investor protection, especially against special deals made by large shareholders.[191]

Antitrust regulations in the United States propelled discussions about fixed-fee commission, but Canada's antitrust laws were less strict. The 1966 Securities Act gave the OSC responsibility for overseeing stock exchange by-laws, but few regulators and market makers understood that this included rules about commissions. By the early 1970s, the OSC became extensively involved in rate setting. Within a few years, the cost of participating in the markets had increased sufficiently such that regulators on both sides of the border were forced to consider amending strict rules about banning corporations from owning seats on exchanges. Longstanding market participants were threatened by acquisition, which raised concerns about unqualified exchange members, especially foreign ones. Institutional investors were responsible for issues such as special market privileges and market manipulation.[192]

In the 1930s, the Toronto Exchange had become Canada's dominant equity trading exchange. It went from strength to strength and was the dominant Canadian exchange for most of the twentieth century. In 1977 it introduced the world's first computer-assisted electronic trading system and twenty years later became the first fully electronic major exchange in North America, after which the traditional, physical trading floor was shut down. By 1980 the TSX accounted for 80 per cent of all equity trading in Canada, with annual trading volume of 3.3 billion shares worth close to $30 billion.[193] In the mid-1990s the TSX became the first exchange in North America to introduce decimal trading and in 1997 became the largest stock exchange to choose a floorless, electronic (or virtual trading) environment when its physical trading floor closed.[194]

As the new millennium dawned, technological demands and globalization resulted in dramatic changes to security trading in Canada. By 1999 there were exchanges in five cities in Canada, each trading a fragmented mix of security types. Being member-owned, their primary goal was to keep trading costs low, an orientation that limited innovation and competitiveness in exchange management. Issuer services were poor, with little available in marketing to attract new issuers or demonstrate value to existing ones; the response to data requests was slow, and infrastructure investments were put off in favour of offsetting commission fees for members.

As trading volumes and complexity increased, cracks began to show. There was general agreement among the stakeholders that they did not want to fund the capital improvements that were needed to varying degrees at all five exchanges. Many also feared that if Canadians did not make a bold effort to develop exchange-traded derivative products in Canada, others would. The development of interest rate products was particularly critical, because they play a central role in the determination of other prices used by the Bank of Canada and other financial institutions to set interest rate policies. A deal was struck that consolidated Vancouver, Calgary, and later Winnipeg into a Vancouver-based Canadian Venture Exchange, with centralized large cap equities and derivatives trading in Toronto and Montreal, respectively. The arrangement would allow each exchange to specialize, increase liquidity, and reduce costs for market participants, and had specific benefits for all parties. Toronto received a material boost to its trading volume, improving liquidity and increasing efficiency by leveraging its existing infrastructure. However, derivatives were not a material part of its business, and index products were barely on the horizon. Montreal received an equalization payment to compensate for its lost trading revenue, giving it a much-needed cash infusion to replace an aging trading system. It also became the sole shareholder of the Canadian Derivatives Clearing Corporation, which would become an increasingly strategic asset in its efforts to develop proprietary new products. Focusing junior listings in one place, on the

CDNX, created an ecosystem for early-stage companies that would facilitate their ability to attract investors and increase liquidity in a thinly traded market. Reflecting the market structure and opinion climate at the time – with all stakeholders not-for-profit entities – no thought was given to assigning a finite term to the agreement. Lawyers advocated introducing some time limit, and a ten-year term was agreed upon.[195]

The Canadian markets did well in the latter part of the twentieth century, essentially mimicking those of New York, albeit with greater strength in the 1980s and early 1990s and weaker during the dot.com bust of the early twenty-first century. Canadian banks experienced tremendous growth during this period, far greater than their American counterparts, especially after the "four pillars" of the Canadian financial system were dismantled in the late 1980s and early 1990s. The banks first acquired investment dealers, then trust companies, then entered the consumer finance, insurance, and mutual fund sectors. As spectacular as the growth was in bank assets, pension plans increased nearly fivefold between 1990 and 2008, while mutual funds increased more than twenty-five-fold, in large part as the result of lower interest rates and increased distribution through bank branch networks.

As in the United States, though not to nearly the same degree, impressive financial gains in Canada masked several structural weaknesses. As will be discussed in detail in our conclusion, Canada's financial system and markets avoided most of the excesses that beset the system south of the border, although Canadian security regulation is seen to be weaker than that of the United States.[196] To be sure, America spawned many new companies and financial instruments, but with insufficient recognition of the costs. Too many observers, including trained economists and financial analysts, blithely ignored many warning signs, such as increasing bank failures, unrealistic stock valuations, and unregulated financial institutions and practices. Much of the innovation and dynamic growth in the United States was purchased with no regard for existing risks and even with the addition of some new ones.

CHAPTER SIX

Conclusion:
Continuities and Discontinuities in
North American Finance Leading to 2008

In the United States, fortunes easily collapse and rise anew ... Now, any bold undertaking risks the fortune of the person who attempts it and of those who place their trust in him. Americans who make a kind of virtue of commercial recklessness, cannot in any case stigmatize the reckless.

Alexis de Tocqueville, Democracy in America

The Risk of Complacency

The last decades of the twentieth century and the first of the new witnessed a reputational roller coaster for North American finance, albeit with unequal dips and bends in our two countries. Despite its relative stability, Canada was not immune to some of the negative consequences of seductive new economic opportunities. As in earlier periods, Americans and Canadians, while sharing many financial and other experiences, differed greatly not only in number and depth of financial crises, but also in how they reacted. Not surprisingly, both the crises themselves and the ensuing reactions to them were conditioned by historical and attitudinal differences, which we have tried to highlight. Whereas Americans structured a system to achieve maximum access and innovation, Canadians showed more willingness to sacrifice some of both for stability. Whereas financial issues were and still are matters of heated public debate in the United States, Canadians have more faith in their political and financial elites' ability to find socially useful compromises between the rights of creditors and debtors. Perhaps most importantly, Canadians from their earliest history seemed quite willing to learn from the vigour and foibles of their southern neighbour.

In light of the 2008 Panic and "Great Recession," we tend to forget that many of the twenty years that preceded them, while rocky, also stoked optimism and perhaps even complacency about how much we can control economics and politics. Especially in the last decade of the twentieth century, events seemed to justify exuberance until at least 2000. For some it was the beginning and end of an era.[1] These events include the fall of communism; the spread of democratic capitalism throughout much of the world; moderate inflation; technological developments; buoyant stock markets; successful handling of emerging and developed country financial crises; a general loosening of border constraints on travel, capital, goods, and service flows in much of the world; the birth of a new currency zone; and a willingness of former rivals to work together to ensure world peace. Despite Japan's "lost decades" – its poor economic performance since 1990 – increasing inequality in many countries, several financial crises, the bursting of the dot.com bubble, the attack on the World Trade Center, higher raw materials prices, and the war in Iraq, much but not all of the optimism endured into the new century and found its way into political and regulatory discourse.[2] For many policymakers and even the general public, the turbulence of market mechanisms was more than outweighed by the economic growth it promised and the advances in economic theory that could explain and control it.

The revival of faith in American capitalism after the Second World War, its very position as the "capital of capital," rested on several pillars. These included the U.S.'s reputation as the world leader in accounting reliability and transparency, rating agencies, and the general governance of its capital markets. With the Glass-Steagall Act and other measures that separated investment and commercial banking, America took investment and commercial banks out of the corporate governance business, substituting other government and private organizations as intermediaries to control information and provide diversity. New Deal reforms led to the creation of independent audits and the development of professionally mandated accounting rules, giving America's accountants more scope and authority to do their work than those of virtually any other country. Rules governing mutual funds required the use of standardized measures of the quality of securities. That ruling gave American rating agencies an advantage in evaluating companies and their securities, a function which became a worldwide business by the end of the twentieth century. The SEC had the power in the United States to set rules on trading securities for exchanges and corporations, despite America's fragmented incorporation rules, which were still well ahead of other countries'. However, before 2008 these pillars showed many cracks.[3] As the Alexis de Tocqueville epigraph states, Americans have always exhibited a tolerance for recklessness in commercial innovation, which appears curious to much of the rest of the world, including Canadians.

The funding of public goods and private consumption is a helpful illustration. Surprisingly, Americans and Canadians spend approximately the same percentage of GDP on public goods such as housing and income support (in 2005, America spent 15.5 per cent versus 16.2 per cent in Canada).[4] On education and health care, America spends vastly more per capita, but its priorities (in matters of quality, equality of access, balance between private and public spending, and cost control) are very different, as is the method financing. In Canada most social services are funded by tax revenues. In 2000 tax revenue in Canada as a percentage of GDP was more than 20 per cent higher than it was in America. In the United States, a much larger percentage is funded by debt, and perhaps most importantly, complicated and risky financing schemes that involve some dangerous "partnerships" between the public and private sectors. Shortly before the 2008 Crisis, aggregate debt as a percentage of national income was over 25 per cent higher in the United States than in Canada.[5]

Bank failures picked up through much of the world after the fall of Bretton Woods and accelerated through much of the 1970s and 1980s, reflecting a worldwide increase in debt financing and macroeconomic instability. American banks led the charge in lending to less developed countries (LDC debt), but Canadian banks were also all-too-active in this new banking segment. Recycled petrodollars were at the centre of the eurodollar food chain. During the decade following the end of Bretton Woods and oil shocks, banks and their clients were looking for new business and higher yields. They therefore lent out nearly a trillion dollars to emerging markets such as Brazil, Argentina, Mexico, and Nigeria, some of which were oil producers themselves, but whose expenditures exceeded revenues, especially as oil prices began to drop. Led by Citibank, whose chairman, Walter Wriston, famously and incorrectly stated that "countries don't go bust," British, Swiss, American, and even Canadian banks found themselves with mountains of bad loans to countries with high inflation and not enough dollars to repay their mostly U.S.-dollar debt. By the mid-1980s the inability of these countries to service their debt led to defaults, quasi-defaults, debt restructurings, and painful bad debt write-offs, mostly for large banks, but also some medium and small ones.

Apart from international investment, many old domestic weaknesses in American finance came to the fore. America's fragmented banking system once again threatened the whole financial system. One group of financial institutions that did well after the New Deal legislation, Savings & Loans (S&Ls), doubled its share of financial assets during the four decades following the Second World War.[6] In the late 1970s the American government increased the size of deposits that the federal government would insure and deregulated many restrictions on how S&Ls could invest funds. The resulting mismatch of sources and uses of loanable funds became a classic illustration of moral hazard. Small depositors lost much of their motivation to check the quality of banks and S&Ls. The managers of S&Ls found that they could easily increase margins by paying low interest on safe deposits and investing in high-yield risky assets, such as junk bonds and LDC debt. By the end of the 1980s this resulted in a wave of bank defaults and a massive government program to take over and restructure a large segment of the American banking system. Although the final cost of the bailout was not as great as originally feared, the cost to taxpayers for liquidating the 744 S&Ls amounted to US$87 billion.[7] In the late 1980s bank failure rates approached 10 per cent, a level that had not been known since the 1930s or through many years in the nineteenth century, but the banks tended to be small. Failed bank deposits as percentage of total deposits were around 1 per cent, nowhere the 8 per cent rate at the nadir of the Depression.[8] Exchanges were also troubled. As discussed in chapter 5, in October 1987 a mass panic hit the New York Stock Exchange. The market lost 23 per cent, in absolute value the greatest single-day loss in its history, a fall of 40 per cent from peak to trough,[9] although there was modest growth for the full year.

The 1980s also witnessed a number of financial disasters in Canada, which have largely been forgotten. They included but are not limited to the LDC problem, the oil shock at home, trust company failures, and even bank failures.[10] All of these led not only to a total reform of the regulation and supervision of the Canadian financial system but also to an end of the four pillars of Canadian finance and the creation of universal banks. While the story of the LDC crisis with its recycled petrodollars is well known, Canada's role in it is not. Canadian bank LDC lending was double that of the United States when measured in loans as a percentage of country GDP, second only to Switzerland and greater than that of the United Kingdom, France, and Japan. Encouraged by the federal government, Canadian banks "drank the Kool-Aid"; they believed foolishly in the concept of obtaining easy money from oil exporters and relending those same funds to both oil exporting and importing countries. As the former CEO of the Canadian Bankers Association wrote, "The economic analysis employed by the new generation of hot-shot lenders in the international divisions of banks to justify the loans was trivial or non-existent, and based on inadequate data."[11] In the late 1980s the Office of the Superintendent of Financial Institutions (OFSI) required Canadian banks to make loan-loss provisions for their LDC debt. Canadian banks took different routes to restructuring. Collectively, in 1989 they took $5.26 billion in provisions – some, such as RBC, worked through the crisis over time, others dealt with the losses immediately.[12]

As Canadian banks put themselves into jeopardy with international loans, the government of Canada undermined the banks with a misguided[13] "National" Energy Policy. Since the banks had made extensive loans to the oil and gas sector before the policy was announced, the banks suffered, along with the oil and gas sector. In the early 1980s, the Canadian economy suffered the worst economic decline since the Great Depression,[14] and a period of greater economic damage than that associated with the 2008 Panic.[15] Much has been written about two bank failures in Alberta in the mid-1980s, which were in part fallout from the "National" Energy Policy. These were the first Canadian bank failures in six decades. Generally ignored is the fact that three other larger banks had to be taken over by other banks.[16] Although Canadian regulators spearheaded attempts to ease the system strain that might be caused by further bank failures, as discussed in chapter 4, they did not save banks – indeed they let two fail – or depositors as much as they directed their efforts throughout the 1980s to preventing system contagion.[17]

Trust company issues compounded these problems. Historically Canadian banks had not been allowed to have trust divisions, leaving this fiduciary role to specialized trust companies. Gradually the trust companies became more like banks, taking deposits and performing other bank functions. They did not face the same ownership restrictions as the banks, and some owners exploited the trust companies for their investors' purposes. Between 1982 and 1985 there were ten major cases that led to pay-outs of $3.2 billion by the Canadian Deposit Insurance Corporation.[18]

Amid the chaos of the Canadian banking system at that time, a Commission of Enquiry, chaired by Supreme Court Judge Willard Estey, was appointed to investigate the bank failures, which recommended significant changes in the regulatory system. There was a general sense that the system was sound, but the commission concluded that Canada needed to move beyond self-regulation. This led to legislation in 1987 that created an Office of the Superintendent of Financial Institutions (OSFI). The new body combined and strengthened the roles formerly carried out by the inspector general of banks and the Department of Insurance. The first superintendent, Michael Mackenzie, who had been a senior partner with Clarkson Gordon,[19] the leading Canadian auditing firm, moved quickly, forcing the banks to take significant loan loss provisions and requiring a higher standard for capital adequacy than was demanded by the Basel Concordat, the set of recommendations known also as Basel I.[20]

In addition, the Financial Institutions Supervisory Committee was created to bolster oversight of the system and encourage a greater "will to act." This was a major change from Canada's century-old practice of self-regulation. This change was followed by the dissolution of the traditional four pillars of Canadian finance: commercial banks, investment banks, life insurance companies, and trust companies – initially giving permission to banks and insurance companies to acquire investment dealers.[21] This dramatic change in the way Canada supervised its financial system contributed to Canada's relatively mild experience with the markets from 2007 to 2009, when other countries such as the United States were experiencing severe market trauma.

But surviving these crises gave rise to a new and perhaps exaggerated optimism, at least in the United States, sometimes dubbed the Washington consensus centred in the United States, but stretching out to much of the world. Its fundamental tenets were a deep faith in the value and spread of liberal capitalism, in the potency of collective action to ward off financial crises and other economic challenges, and in the ability of open markets to increase economic growth and reduce risk through well-informed rational actors and high-tech solutions to ancient financial problems. Many developments fed this faith. The first was surviving the challenges of the 1980s. By the 1990s the LDC debt crisis, if not resolved, was under control, although banks in Toronto, New York, and Boston all experienced a commercial real estate setback in the early 1990s. Many of the hardest-hit countries had managed to get their macroeconomic woes under control. Large banks had restructured their balance sheets and activities sufficiently so that they no longer seemed on the verge of collapse. Major financial powers had agreed to international regulatory standards for capital adequacy based on the riskiness of loans (Basel I), designed to ward off another lending frenzy, and were in the midst of refining those standards still further (Basel II), with more sophisticated risk measurements. Alan Greenspan's handling of the October Crash received widespread praise and held out hope that similar shocks could be easily absorbed with the aid of clever monetary policies. Liberal democracies became the norm in much of once-communist Europe. The economies and politics of Asian countries came closer to resembling those of North America and Europe, and dangerous financial panics, exacerbated in part by fast money from Western countries, were met with a solid, united financial response by OECD countries.

As discussed earlier, the financial markets of most major countries seemed to converge, reducing the regulatory and institutional differences among countries. Great progress was made in developing a global accounting system, and the Big Eight became the Big Four as major international accounting firms merged. Perhaps the most important development was the rapid growth of technological innovation. Fuelled by biotech products and electronic connections, the changes promised great improvements in health care and economic productivity and fed a sustained stock market boom through most of the 1990s.

Even the collapse of a large and innovative financial hedge fund company, Long-Term Capital Management (LTCM), seemed to vindicate policymakers' faith in market mechanisms and cooperative efforts. LTCM provided a poignant illustration of the dark side of financial theory – its overconfidence in statistics and models – which contributed to the 2008 financial crisis. Despite its two Nobel Prize–winning partners – or perhaps because of them – LTCM followed up a few years of high profits with increasingly risky positions, greater leverage, and disastrous losses, when Russia defaulted on its loans. A concerted effort by the Fed and major banks prevented failure of LTCM's business model, built on cutting-edge financial theories and state-of-the-art trading, from bringing down other financial institutions. Indeed, before 2008 American politicians and regulators showed little concern about controlling many new financial institutions and organizations that were on the edge of, or completely outside of, government control. Despite convergence and the globalization of finance, Canada has been relatively free of so-called shadow banking. Wealthy private Canadian individuals and institutions can access organizations outside of Canada, but Canadian banks have provided a wide range of services. Moreover, Canadian regulators, especially since the creation of OSFI, had put in place oversight measures that extended over all financial services. Before the twenty-first century, Canadians seemed to understand the importance of coordinated public supervision of financial organizations and that a culture of private sector restraint provided long-term social benefits.

Around 2000, additional cracks appeared in the edifice of world financial architecture. Even before the end of the millennium, Y2K fears undermined faith in high-tech and market exchanges. The Nasdaq index hit a peak of 5132 on 10 March 2000, plunging 60 per cent within a year. A few months later the 9/11 attacks closed exchanges and raised the question of future financial market attacks, in the United States and elsewhere. A year later two large American companies, once the darlings of market makers, Enron and WorldCom, were in disgrace, destroying the reputations and the existence of some of America's most important financial gatekeepers. Although there were some accounting irregularities, Canadians witnessed nothing comparable to the American frauds. In short order the United States passed legislation designed to shore up control weaknesses.

The Sarbanes-Oxley Act became law in the summer of 2002. It created a new oversight board for accountants, the Public Accounting Oversight Board, putting greater onus on accountants to find errors and demanding more personal responsibility by executives, but stimulated criticism on both sides of the Atlantic. Accountants were probably the first of America's financial gatekeepers to come under fire, reversing a long period of faith in the profession. The period from 1946 to 1961 had been called a golden age of the accounting profession, with confidence in accounting firms and standards spreading throughout the free world. Some of the accounting firms whose origins were British and American, what was called the Big Eight, were products of cross-border mergers and achieved international recognition, even among the general public. As firms grew and diversified into other areas, especially consulting, competition and conflicts of interest grew. By the 1970s a series of scandals shook the accounting sector. By 1974 the Big Eight accounting firms were fighting off 200 lawsuits and came under government investigation. This led to the Metcalf Report, which contained many damning charges. Inflation and other changes in the macroeconomic environment of business called into question many accounting norms. By the 1990s the Big Eight had been whittled down through mergers to the Big Six, and after Enron and other litigations, they dropped down to the Big Four. Worse still, some critics raised the question of whether audit firms, as they were then constituted, had outlived their usefulness.[22]

These shocks to the accounting profession, centred in the United States, could not but help affect Canadian firms, even though the latter had avoided the most egregious activities. In addition to the restructurings that resulted from deals done outside Canada, the Canadian Touche Ross firm strongly encouraged its American counterparts to find a merger partner. The Canadian firm referred more work to the United States than vice versa, and the Canadians wanted their American counterpart to be stronger in the U.S. market. While somewhat taken aback by the U.S. firm's proposal for a merger with Deloitte, the Canadians agreed to merge, unlike the Australians, who went with KPMG, and the U.K. Deloitte firm, which went with Coopers & Lybrand. The Canadian member firm of Arthur Young, which, like Touche Ross, referred more work to the United States than it received in return, refused to join with the Canadian Ernst & Whinney firm. As a consequence the Canadian member firm of Ernst & Whinney went with KPMG. When Arthur Andersen's Enron audit led to its dissolution, in most parts of the world the Arthur Andersen partners moved over to Ernst & Young, but in Canada they merged with Deloitte & Touche, further strengthening Deloitte's pre-eminent position in the Canadian market.

Although the U.S. Sarbanes-Oxley Bill came into existence in 2002 ostensibly to correct many perceived deficiencies in the relationship of auditors to management, the independence of accountants was still under fire, especially in the United States. The bursting of the dot. com bubble, and worse still the accounting frauds of Enron and World Com, and other examples of misconduct, called into question the transparency and utility of public accounting information. Moreover, Sarbanes-Oxley included other provisions to bolster what was perceived to be a severe weakness in America's board and oversight system in general: the insiders who were ostensibly entrusted to watch out for the interests of shareholders.[23] It was a case of the proverbial fox guarding the henhouse. In response to concerns about conflicts of interest, all of the large firms except Deloitte & Touche sold off their consulting arms. By 2008, though, accounting firms were rebuilding their consulting practices.

Different Roads to the 2008 Financial Crisis

But as illustrated by the Panic of 2008, these reforms hardly addressed the driving forces of American and global financial instability. Few if any American political or financial leaders realized that a sea change had occurred in the financial institutions and organizations of America and the world, severely endangering world financial stability. Even those leaders who were well versed in financial history, such as Ben Bernanke, continued to focus on interest rate policy and cross-border flows, rather than on the mechanisms to transmit them.[24] Slowing economic growth and increases in economic inequality seemed to justify loosening requirements for mortgage and other consumer credit. As discussed in detail in chapter 5, this phenomenon, coupled with shortages of direct bank financing, meant funding had to come from institutional investors and foreign sources, which increased securitization of mortgages and other consumer debt. It represented financial engineering with great benefits but even greater risks, given how the products were created, sold, managed, and regulated. The financing of mortgage and other debt with securitized instruments set the stage for the 2008 Bankers' Panic, a threat that regulators essentially underestimated if they considered it at all. With the Reform of Commodities Futures Trading Act (2000), creating and trading even more derivatives outside of public markets helped satisfy the need for managing interest rates, foreign exchange, and credit risk, as well as opened opportunities for hedge funds and speculation. The entire incentive system of much of the world's financial practices encouraged actors to ignore, indeed often to cultivate, sloppy lending practices to individuals, governments, commercial companies, and other financial institutions. It encouraged the players to seek out dubious methods of evaluating risk, such as reliance on conflicted rating agencies, and finally to use opaque pricing methods afforded by large-scale internalization of trading. Market reliance on rating agencies serves as a wonderful illustration of misplaced incentives. Many institutional investors, restricted in their investments to high-grade instruments and eager to obtain higher yields, turned a blind eye to the fact that rating agencies were competing for fees from the very issuers of the securities they were rating.[25] The ability of banks to internalize capital markets was aided by the SEC's decision to allow banks to leverage up to forty times their equity. By 2007 total outstanding derivatives amounted to ten times world output.[26]

Like its neighbour and some other countries, Canada used derivative instruments and variable-based compensation – both listed among the causes of the 2008 Crisis – but it handled both in a more measured way. Despite Canadian expertise in derivative pricing, Canadian banks and their regulators showed little inclination to build up big positions in new and relatively untested assets and liabilities for which there was no organized market, and whose prices (values) could be divined only by using complicated mathematical modelling, entailing substantial exposure to counter-party risk. The bankers' incentives were different in the two countries. While the compensation for Canadian bankers was comparable in amount and structure to their American counterparts (at least among commercial as opposed to investment bankers), the mission for which the bankers were being rewarded seemed different. Whether compensation comes in the form of salary, bonuses, or stock options, compensation cannot be seen in isolation from the organization's overall aims and implementation. Whereas American executive and trader compensation seemed skewed toward short-term profits with little adjustment for risk, the Canadians appeared to have struck a better balance between short-term shareholder value and long-term social stability.[27] That said, history warns us that perhaps the next crisis may reveal a Canadian Achilles heel, such as a housing bubble, which both regulators and compensation systems overlooked.

Although Canada participated in some of the financial activities that added turmoil to the last thirty years, it avoided many others, especially the heavy reliance on securitization and derivatives. Its experience with financial trauma over the last thirty years was less intense than America's, but it did undergo a challenging time in the 1980s and as a consequence adopted a new integrated supervisory system for financial institutions. According to the IMF[28] and other global authorities, few, if any, OECD countries fared better than Canada did during the recent crisis. Nevertheless, Canada did encounter a serious issue with credit default swaps (CDS), triggered in late 2007, known as the asset backed commercial paper (ABCP) problem. The ABCP crisis has received little attention outside of Canada.

The 2008 Crisis led to fewer reforms in Canada than in the United States. It needed fewer, perhaps because people remembered the chaos of the 1980s and the commercial real estate crisis of the early 1990s. Canada's banking system was on a much sounder footing in 2008 than it had been twenty years earlier. With a more rational system of home financing, the Canadian mortgage market was based on a much more solid foundation, with neither mortgage interest nor real property tax deductibility nor recourse mortgages. Although Canadian mortgage financing grew dramatically in the eight years leading up to the 2008 Crisis, Canadian banks with loans on their books had fewer incentives to ignore credit unworthiness or fiddle with devices such as tricky interest rate gimmicks.[29] A national banking network rendered Canada's banks less dependent on wholesale funding and securitization of all sorts of loans. In general, Canadian banks tended to be less leveraged than those of many other countries. Unlike that of the United States, Canadian financial regulation was not fragmented among a host of competing organizations.[30] This reality was a result of the changes made in the 1980s in response to the LDC crisis, multiple trust company defaults, and some bank failures.

Most academic observers attribute Canada's financial strength to path dependencies – the continued use of a product or practice based on historical preference or use – traced back to wise decisions in the nineteenth century.[31] There is some truth to this explanation, but it ignores the fact that Canada's success was also the result of valuable lessons learned from and corrective action taken after the financial debacles of the 1980s. The Canadian banking system was lightly regulated historically. The first Bank Act, passed in 1871, made no provision for an Office of Inspector General of Banks (OIGB). It took a major bank failure in 1923 before this regulatory step was put into place.[32] Indeed, the Canadian government had specifically rejected the idea of an inspector general in the decennial Bank Act revision the year of the failure, even though there had been a superintendent of insurance dating back to the 1870s. The Porter Royal Commission of the early 1960s recommended that the OIGB should continue to rely on independent bank auditors, who would in turn rely on internal bank inspectors. This was a system of light rather than intrusive regulation. When the Bank Act was amended in 1980 to encourage the creation of more banks, including foreign ones, there was no provision for additional staff in the office of the OIGB and the regulator was swamped, having difficulty keeping up with the increased workload. However, the disasters of the 1980s resulted in the establishment of the Office of the Superintendent of Financial Institutions (OSFI) in Canada that oversaw the financial system as a whole.

Despite these measures, which strengthened financial supervision in Canada, problems arose as financial markets deteriorated in the United States and Europe. In September 2007, $32 billion of asset-backed commercial paper was frozen in Canada, triggered by the U.S. sub-prime crisis. ABCPs were short-term instruments backed by the repayment of short-term commercial loans, much like the mortgage-backed securities. The real issue was not the ABCP, but rather the credit default swaps (CDSs) that were used to insure them. As discussed in chapter 5, CDSs were complex derivative instruments used to insure the value of other instruments. One institution, the Caisse de dépôt et placement du Québec, a Quebec government agency established in 1965 to manage different government pension plans, used CDSs extensively. By 2007 the Caisse was the sixth-largest financial corporation in Canada (after the Big Five banks). It held $13.2 billion of the ABCP, which accounted for over 40 per cent of the problem ABCP that was outstanding. The Caisse moved quickly to make its difficulties a national issue by calling on a prominent Toronto lawyer, Purdy Crawford, to chair a committee consisting of other holders of paper and international banks.[33] All of the committee members signed what became known as the Montreal accord. J.P. Morgan served as the adviser to the committee.[34]

The problem arose when the sellers of the CDSs could not fulfil their obligations under the contracts used to insure the original purchases of ABCPs. The rationale for the CDSs was that they improved efficiency in capital markets, although critics saw them as avoiding regulation. In a 2004 Bank of Canada paper the author concluded, "CDSs contribute to financial stability by facilitating the ability to hedge credit risk and improve diversification, as well as by allowing credit risk to be held by those most willing to bear it."[35] Economist John Chant contended, however, that there were several problems with ABCP, including minimal regulation, lack of disclosure by conduits, unjustified credit ratings, and salespeople who were peddling a product they did not understand.[36]

Through what may be a uniquely Canadian approach, involving both the political and financial elites, a solution was found. "Globally it was the only private sector restructuring … unlike all other countries that faced ABCP problems, the Canadian solution involved no direct government intervention."[37] A restructuring was approved, which, in spite of the large number of players involved, was dominated by the Caisse and Deutsche Bank. The restructuring created a market for the paper, allowing owners who needed cash immediately to sell, though anyone who sold had to take a loss. Investors who bought the paper in the days after the restructuring have profited handsomely as the fear came out of the market.[38]

America's financial leaders, financiers, central bankers, and regulators had a great many more concerns. In retrospect, the Panic of 2008 is not so surprising considering how blind most "irrationally exuberant" financial leaders were to the build-up of risk. So many of the safeguards employed before and during the crisis, such as international banking capital standards and monetary policy, appeared hapless in the face of massive changes to American institutional and organizational financial architecture.[39] American banks performed relatively well under international norms. Three of the largest banks ranked by Tier One Capital in 2004 were American.[40] On a percentage basis, most of the American banks exceeded Basel II requirements.[41]

As U.S. property and other markets weakened in 2007 and 2008, banks and other financial institutions were faced with a bank panic, not with individuals forming lines in front of branches, but rather on a grand scale, invisible to the public, with many new causes and effects. Increasingly sophisticated investors no longer felt comfortable evaluating the counter-party risk of major institutions, whose holdings of large quantities of complicated securities and derivatives made them suspect. Financial reporting, whose rules for marking to market had been stretched beyond recognition, could not capture the bank's true balance sheet, in part because modelling assumptions used to calculate them, such as the price volatility of underlying assets, no longer seemed applicable. Unlike their counter-parties in 1907, financial leaders in the private and public sector could not in the space of a few weeks ascertain which banks[42] could be saved or allowed to perish, a necessary step in determining whether the banks were suffering from a liquidity shortage or were insolvent.[43]

Without this information, their decisions seemed random and added to the sense of panic. Consequently, efforts to provide increased liquidity appeared to be more like adding gasoline to the fire than striving to extinguish it. Many of the most dangerous organizations were not banks at all, such as AIG, the multinational insurance corporation. Some, such as Fannie Mae and Freddie Mac, were originally government creations, with implied federal ties even before their rescue in 2008. In retrospect, we can be thankful that emergency measures saved America from even worse, but we should also question how so many knowledgeable people were blind to so many important institutional developments and had so few plans to deal with what was substantially a liquidity, not a solvency, crisis. That the 2008 Crisis was indeed a bank run requiring confidence-building measures is borne out by the fact all of the US$800 million in Troubled Asset Release Program (TARP) money was repaid. The degree to which political and regulatory leaders have learned from these experiences and applied those lessons is questionable, to say the least.[44]

While eight years is a short time in a history that spans more than three centuries, it can be noted that Canada enjoyed better growth then did the United States – both population and GDP – as well as a strengthening currency and a reduction rather than an increase in federal government debt (see appendix 6).

Now, nearly a decade after the panic, financial markets have stabilized, but there is still much reason for concern. Central banks seemed trapped in low interest rate policies and purchases of banking assets for which there is no easy exit. Much derivative trading is done through exchanges or with clearing houses, but the overall size of the market has increased and much remains OTC, and therefore less transparent. Many of the reforms passed by the United States, Europe, and the G20 countries remain unenforced and rely on the same logic used before, and the reforms themselves are extremely complex, having been drafted by regulators whose complacency contributed to the recent breakdown. High-speed trading seems to defy control and may contribute to instability. Controls designed to protect from terrorism increase costs and a loss of privacy. Worse still, the counter-trade from low interest countries to emerging markets is once again adding to instability in the developing world. For good or ill, American capital markets and the dollar, as of this writing, remain relatively strong, but many of the issues that led to the 2008 Crisis remain part of the financial architecture. North America, particularly the United States, is still at the epicentre of what one economist dubbed the world financial "fault lines," but, paradoxically, America still serves as a safe haven.

Use and Abuse of Historical Lessons

Perhaps a better understanding of the building blocks of the financial system and contrasting paths, their development over a long time horizon in two countries, will contribute to finding a better mix of stability and innovation. This is our hope. One lesson of our narrative is that principles are adapted to particular national circumstances. But as we have often noted, from our introduction through to this chapter, and reflected in our title, from Alexander Hamilton to renowned commercial banker Walter Wriston, financial ideas, for good or ill, have travelled from south to north. Given the fragility of America's financial system, which has had many costs for much of its history and has had worldwide ramifications, as illustrated by the 2008 Crisis, perhaps a look north before the next crisis might be timely. Sadly, the evidence supporting our capacity to learn the right lessons from history is mixed, at best. Indeed, those most responsible for financial stability show relatively little recognition of the *collective* responsibility of private bankers, political leaders, their constituencies, the economics profession, and regulators to avoid a financial perfect storm. There seems a lack of regard for the weak, unstable economic environment that followed – a consequence of our financial system that should rival global warming as a source of social concern. The unwillingness to admit wide-ranging culpability may be part of the moral hazard that seems so rife in our current financial system and part of the political appeal of those who seem "untainted" or unaffected by the past.

As noted in the introduction, comparing the development of financial systems is useful, but it is also difficult. The systems are products of complex political and social configurations, themselves the results of a series of events, cultural preferences, foreign influences, and path dependencies. No two countries, no matter how close in culture or proximity, develop at the same pace or with the same priorities. The connection between finance and general national aspirations and capacities points to many insights but also poses many policy limitations, not the least of which is that historical differences make a simple transplant of one country's institutions and organizations to another difficult, to say the least.

We have built the organization of this book around important dates in North American history, but the choices are somewhat arbitrary. The periods covered by the dates do not often have the same significance for both countries, adding to the difficulty of telling a purely chronological story.

Several major differences in the structure of each country's political, social, and economic environment are striking. The American system is much larger, more complex, and older than the Canadian system. America, as a nation, was born largely in one revolutionary event from what was perceived as a tyrannical master; Canadian independence evolved over many decades from a nation it continued to loyally admire and emulate. Fearing centralized power associated with their colonial masters, Americans divided federal powers among executive, legislative, and later judicial branches of government. All powers not granted in the Constitution to the federal government devolved to individuals or states, which retained power over many aspects of finance. Perhaps most importantly, America's general history and financial system cannot be separated from its long experience as a slave-based economy, with many long-standing political, social, and economic consequences, just as Canada cannot be torn from the ramifications of its bilingual, bicultural heritage.

Both countries' developments were influenced by many foreign connections, however in unique ways. Each country's integration of foreign influences reflected its own unique cultural heritage. While Americans remained deeply ambivalent about British political and economic influences, Canadians essentially felt a strong attachment to the Crown and its institutions. Canada's political and economic system borrowed from both the United Kingdom and the United States. Its political system evolved gradually rather than springing fully formed into life like the goddess Athena of Greek mythology, as in the case of the United States. Like America, Canada adopted a federal system, but, unlike its southern neighbour, it did not separate the executive and legislative functions to the same degree. In addition, Canada adopted aspects of the early American financial system, as envisioned by Alexander Hamilton, including its division of currency into dollars and cents rather than pounds, shillings, and pence, but rejected what was left of the American system after Andrew Jackson's populist "reforms" of the 1830s.

Even when the timing of major milestones intersects, the nature and significance of events may be very different. The decade of the 1860s in particular is crucial to understanding the similarities and differences between the two systems. In that decade the North defeated the South in the Civil War and new legislation was enacted to regulate banking and currency. The acts were national in scope, but failed to change many basic dynamics of the fragmented American banking system. The Civil War increased Canadian anxieties as citizens of the northern country observed the size and strength of the Union Army and feared annexation to the United States. The United Kingdom was happy to pass the necessary legislation to establish a more independent Canada, in turn reducing U.K. financial commitments to the British North American colonies. In creating their country Canadians were determined to build a banking and currency system that would apply lessons learned from American errors. Its leaders decided that both banking and currency would be national rather than provincial/state functions.

During the period between 1870 and 1914, both Canada and the United States made the transition from emerging outposts of European culture to developed economies. The two countries experienced rapid growth in population, GDP, and territory, with regions becoming either states or provinces. A domestic insurance market and regulation took shape in both countries, but two very different banking systems emerged on the continent, both with national laws and few foreign financial organizations: the American system with its thousands of mostly state-confined joint-stock banks, no branches, and many private investment banks versus the Canadian system with a few large joint-stock banks with hundreds of branches and better protection for creditors.[45] Whereas the Canadian system evolved without major turmoil because of a legislated mandate for regular decennial reviews, American pressure for reform mounted as the country moved from one crisis to another. Instead of merely reacting to crises, Canadians tried to anticipate problems in the system. But no amount of anticipation could ward off the effects of the Great War.

Although the interwar period caused dramatic changes in both Canada and the United States, their experiences and outcomes differed greatly. The cataclysmic impact of the Great Depression, for example, resulted in very different government responses. With thousands of bank failures, the United States adopted "Keynesian" economic remedies much earlier than Canada did and made many more changes to its financial system, including many new national regulations for the securities sector and new initiatives to encourage home buying and small bank lending, initiatives that were rejected in Canada.

During the twenty-five years following the Second World War, the two countries' financial paths diverged even more, perhaps helping to explain their reactions to the reckless lending and international financial convergence of the 1970s and 1980s. The United States was the world's dominant military, political, and financial superpower. Its economy was at the centre of a new world order for fixed exchange rates and capital flows. But while most of the developed world lived with the Bretton Woods system, Canada took the lead in managing its economy with a flexible exchange rate regime. Politically, as a middle power, it joined NATO and later the G7. In comparison to American banks, whose prospects for growth inside the United States were limited by state banking laws well into the 1980s, Canadian banks were less aggressive internationally. But like American banks, they too got caught up in the LDC crisis and subsequently removed barriers to universal banking, but with new, enhanced, and concentrated regulation of the system.

A natural question that arises from this and other studies of the two systems is whether the citizens of the two countries were well served by their financial systems. At first blush, the answer must be an overwhelming yes. Both countries are prosperous. Although their currencies have witnessed great variations in value against each other and other currencies, for most of our period the currencies have been convertible and have kept their status as a store of value and means of exchange in their country of issuance, and in much of the world. Despite various setbacks, both countries have well-functioning credit systems and can borrow at low rates by world standards, attract foreign investment and immigration, and have avoided revolutionary activity that has accompanied financial meltdowns in some other countries. Having said this, their experiences are far from identical.

Canada has met more success by far than America in realizing the intentions of the creators of the country's financial system. Despite its proximity to the United States, Canada has avoided many of the sharp financial convulsions endured by its southern neighbour. It has avoided the corporate governance scandals that nearly destroyed investor faith in American equities in the nineteenth century, in the 1920s, and most recently during the first few years of the twenty-first. Its legal system has avoided the excesses of the American tort system, making insurance cheaper and easier to acquire. Its corporate governance system remained more elitist and is still more activist than the American, whose New Deal legislation in 1930s increased the obstacles and decreased the incentives for active shareholder governance, a shift that has only recently begun to be reversed. Perhaps most importantly, Canada's more concentrated, domestic banks have given it a large measure of financial independence from America and the rest of the world.

In contrast, neither Thomas Jefferson nor Alexander Hamilton would be satisfied with the American financial system today. It is larger, more centralized, and powerful, while being less responsive to the needs of the average citizen than the former would have wanted, and far less stable than the latter envisioned. Although Hamilton would have been pleased with the system's ability to raise capital for new ventures from all over the world, he would probably be aghast at its fragility, which requires massive government and central bank assistance. As with so many historical studies, though, this one raises the question of whether changes in a few critical decisions or events might have radically altered the outcomes in each country's financial system.

We leave such speculation to our readers. That said, a historical study provides some lessons about good and bad practice, but it also suggests limits on how the strengths of one system can be easily incorporated into another. Finance is tied to countries' histories and value systems. Gaining the advantages of one system or jettisoning disadvantages often entails major social-political changes, often associated with dramatic shifts in national fortunes, involving great passion rather than reasoned judgment. At critical junctures general economic outcomes can be affected by political and regulatory measures, but so many decisions end up having little effect or producing unintended consequences. Canada has a better track record in making dispassionate choices in this regard. It has learned more from both the strengths and weaknesses of its southern neighbour than vice versa, both in framing regulations and making transactions. Indeed, the very strengths of American finance today help mask some of the weaknesses of its northern neighbour. Canadian banks wanting to trade exotic derivatives, for example, can go to American banks. The Canadian economy in general has profited from American venture and other equity capital, either by bringing that investment into Canada or by accessing American market makers. Canada today needs less financing, precisely because of modern multinational cash management and the great number of foreign commercial entities active there, many of which are American. In addition, American states have provided Canadian financial companies with some of their most important growth opportunities.

Although we think that understanding the past helps avoid faddish, short-term thinking, it is no panacea for policy dilemmas. The unfolding of history is a complex mixture of old and new phenomena, with contradictory indications of what is appropriate for the here-and-now. How simple it would all be if "history would just repeat itself." Our very habit of trying to learn from history ensures that it will not repeat itself, as opinions about the past will affect policymakers' decisions in the present.

But this study can stimulate discussion and reflection on how financial systems develop and can be improved by providing examples of what has worked well and what has worked poorly. While Canadians have profited from the size and innovation of American finance, sadly one of the leitmotifs of this book is that Canadians have been more open to benefiting from cross-border exchanges about the structure of finance and innovation than Americans. To be sure, Canada's impact on American life is significant, but subtle and less recognized. Much comes through transplanted Canadians who become important parts of American intellectual life, such as John Kenneth Galbraith, Robert Mundell, and Myron Scholes, rather than wholesale export of Canadian models. In other fields, too, evidence of American cultural reach is apparent, but Canada's influence on America life is less evident but significant. In the entertainment and news fields, for example, individuals such as Leonard Cohen, Pamela Anderson, William Shatner, Peter Jennings, Morley Safer, Ashley Banfield, and even Justin Bieber have all made their mark on American life.

Although this book outlines many achievements of American finance, we hope that it will make some contribution to increasing American awareness of some of the long-standing fragilities in its financial system and, more interestingly, how Canada avoided them. Among those flows we have highlighted are America's extensive reliance on debt financing for social projects, off–balance sheet (private and public) financing, and consolidated rather than fragmented regulation. Some of the Canadian virtues we have emphasized are regular reviews of its banking system, with or without a crisis.

But a study of the past provides no blueprint for the future. Indeed, by the time this book is in print, the world may, sadly, find itself again in a new financial crisis, brought on by some combination of unique and commonplace causes. This examination of two financial systems in North America, north of the Rio Grande, both based on British traditions adapted to each nation's own sensibilities, raises more questions than answers. It also reveals more complexity about possible outcomes than can be found in simple patterns and policies. We see it as a necessary but still insufficient step in rethinking and remaking our financial future.

Appendices

Sources for Quantitative Appendices

Population

Maddison Project, http://www.ggdc.net/maddison/maddison-
    project/home.htm, 2013 version.
McEvedy and Jones, (1978), *Atlas of World Population History*, 285, 287.
Statistics Canada, historical statistics

GDP

Maddison-Project, http://www.ggdc.net/maddison/maddison-
    project/home.htm, 2013 version.

Currency

James Powell, *History of the Canadian Dollar*
Statistics Canada

Debt

Statistics Canada, "Table 385-0010: Federal Government Debt, for
  Fiscal Year Ending March 31, Annual (dollars) (in millions)."
Treasury Direct, https://www.treasurydirect.gov/govt/reports/pd/
  histdebt/histdebt.htm

Chapter 1: 1700–1860

Appendix 1.1 Canada U.S. Population (in '000s), 1700–1860

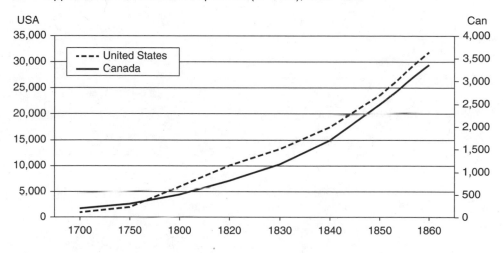

Appendix 1.2 Canada U.S. GDP (in millions 1990 Geary-Khamis dollars), 1700–1860

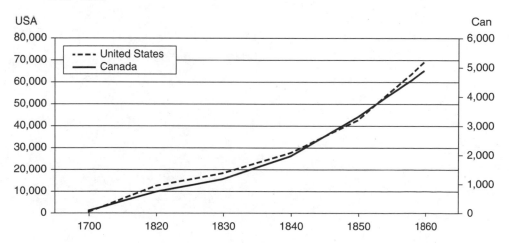

Appendix 1.3 Canada U.S. GDP per capita (1990 Geary-Khamis dollars), 1700–1860

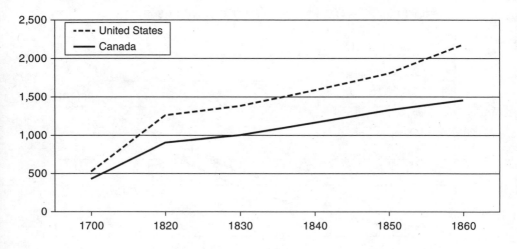

Chapter 2: 1860–1869

Appendix 2.1 Canada, U.S. population (in '000s),
1860–1869

	1860	1869	% increase
Canada	3,369	3,565	6
United States	31,839	39,385	24

Appendix 2.2 Canada, U.S. GDP (in millions 1990
Geary-Khamis dollars)

	1860	1870	% increase
Canada	4,887	6,407	31
United States	69,346	98,374	42

Appendix 2.3 Canada, U.S. GDP per Capita
(in 1990 Geary-Khamis dollars)

	1860	1870	% increase
Canada	1,451	1,695	17
United States	2,178	2,445	12

Appendix 2.4 Exchange Rate, Canadian Dollar as Compared to U.S dollar,
1861–1869

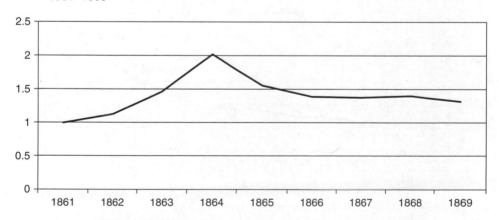

*Note: In July 1864 the Gold Room in Washington was closed and the U.S. dollar fell
to less than 40 cents Canadian.

Chapter 3: 1869–1914

Appendix 3.1 Canada, U.S. Population (in '000s), 1869–1914

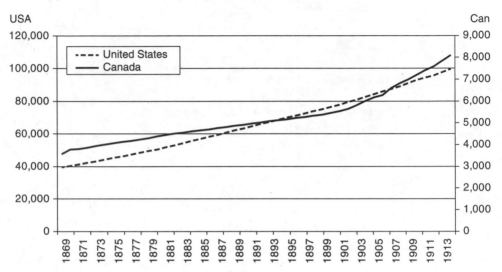

Appendix 3.2 Canada, U.S. GDP (in $millions 1990 Geary-Khamis dollars), 1870–1914

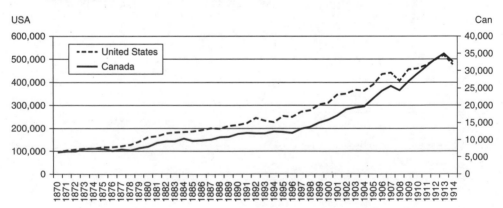

Appendix 3.3 Canada, U.S. GDP per Capita (in 1990 Geary-Khamis dollars), 1870–1914

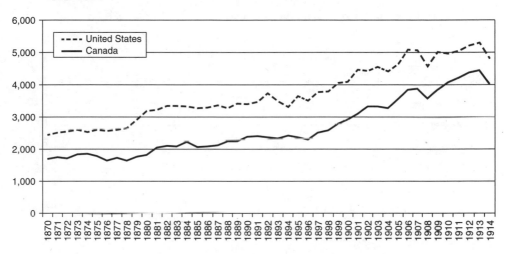

Appendix 3.4 Canada, U.S. Federal Debt (in $millions), 1869–1914

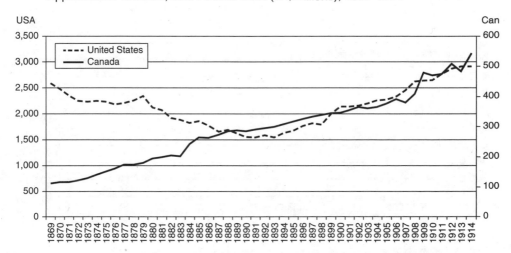

Chapter 4: 1914–1945

Appendix 4.1 Canada, U.S. population (in '000s), 1914–1945

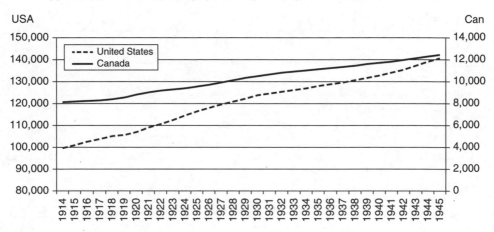

Appendix 4.2 Canada, U.S. GDP (in millions 1990 Geary-Khamis dollars), 1914–1945

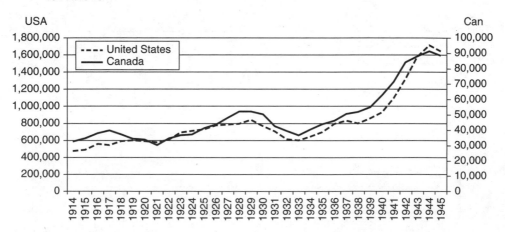

Appendix 4.3 Canada, U.S. GDP per Capita (in 1990 Geary-Khamis dollars), 1914–1945

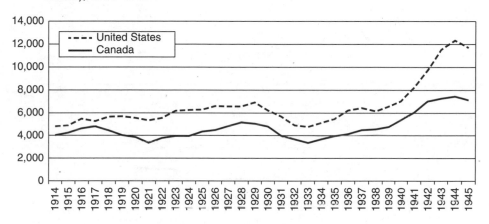

Appendix 4.4 Exchange Rate, Canadian dollar as compared to U.S. dollar, 1914–1945

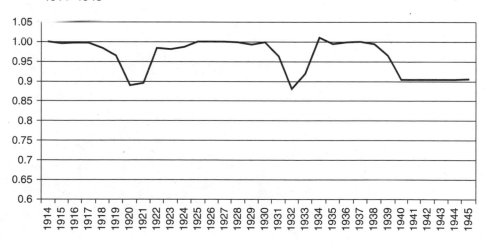

Appendix 4.5 Canada, U.S. Federal Debt (in $millions), 1914–1945

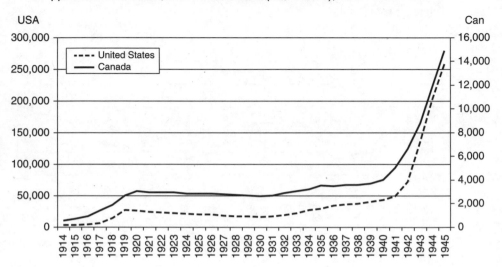

Chapter 5: 1945–2000

Appendix 5.1 Canada, U.S. population (in '000s), 1945–2000

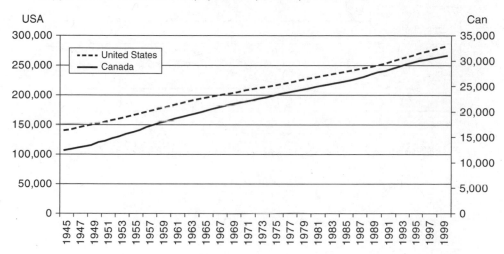

Appendix 5.2 Canada, U.S. GDP (in millions 1990 Geary-Khamis dollars), 1945–2000

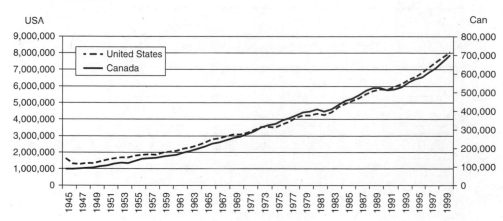

Appendix 5.3 Canada, U.S. GDP per Capita (in 1990 Geary-Khamis dollars), 1945–2000

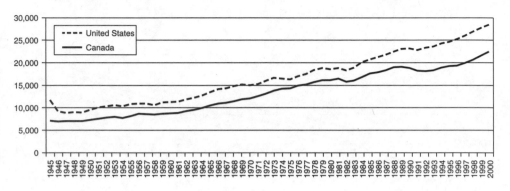

Appendix 5.4 Exchange Rate, Canadian Dollar as Compared to U.S. dollar, 1945–2000

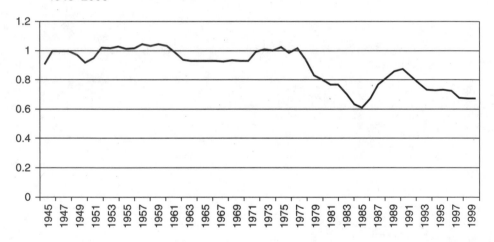

Appendix 5.5 Canada, U.S. Federal Debt (in $millions), 1945–2000

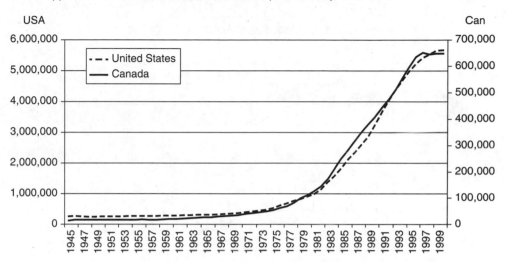

Chapter 6: 2000–2008

Appendix 6.1 Canada, U.S. Population, 2000–2008
(in '000s)

	2000	2008	% change
Canada	30,686	33,246	8.3
U.S.	282,158	304,228	7.8

Appendix 6.2 Canada, U.S. GDP (in millions 1990
Geary-Khamis dollars), 2000–2008

	2000	2008	% change
Canada	699,382	839,199	20.0
U.S.	8,032,209	9,485,136	18.1

Appendix 6.3 Canada, U.S. GDP per Capita (in 1990
Geary-Khamis dollars), 2000–2008

	2000	2008	% change
Canada	22,488	25,267	12.4
U.S.	28,467	31,178	9.5

Appendix 6.4 Exchange Rate, Canadian Dollar as Compared to U.S. Dollar,
2000–2008

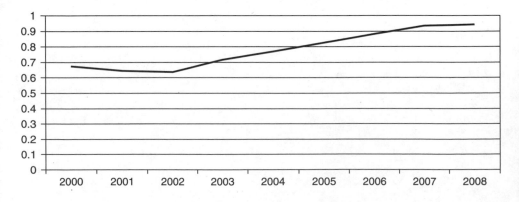

Appendix 6.5 Canada, U.S. federal debt (in $millions), 2000–2008

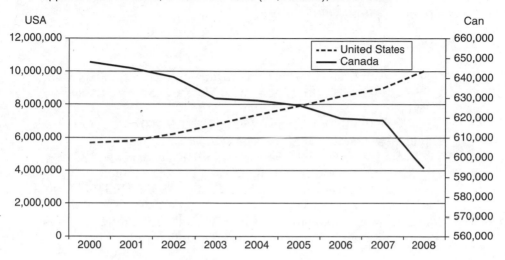

Appendix 7.1 Case Studies, Harvard Business School and Rotman School of Management

Harvard Business School

"Financing American Housing Construction in the Aftermath of War,"
  HBS-9-708-032, 2009, Professor David Moss and Research Associate
  Cole Bolton
"Fannie Mae: Public or Private?," HBS-9-709-025, 2009, Professor
  David Moss and Research Associate Cole Bolton
"The Pecora Hearings," HBS-9-711-046, 2010, Professor David Moss
  and Research Associates Cole Bolton and Eugene Kintgen
"The Federal Reserve and the Banking Crisis of 1931," HBS-9-709-040,
  2009, Professor David Moss and Research Associate Cole Bolton
"The Armstrong Investigation," HBS-9-708-034, 2009, Professor David
  Moss and Research Associate Eugene Kintgen

Rotman School of Management

"The Forgotten Credit Crisis of 1907," 2014, Professor Joe Martin and
  Research Associate Darren Karn
"How Toronto Became the Financial Capital of Canada: The Stock
  Market Crash of 1929," 2012, Professor Joe Martin and Research
  Associate Darren Karn
"Building a Legacy: Lessons from Cadillac Fairview's First Leader,"
  2013, Professor Joe Martin and Research Associate Madison
  Isaacman
"The Toronto-Dominion Bank and Canada's 'Little Bang' of 1987,"
  2012, Professor Joe Martin and Research Associate Ashwini
  Srikantiah
"The Commercial Real Estate Crisis of the Late 1980s and Early
  1990s," 2017, Professor Joe Martin and Research Associate Darren
  Karn
"The Creation of TMX Group: Dramatic Change on the Canadian
  Stock Exchange Scene, 1999 to 2008," 2014, Professor Joe Martin and
  Research Associate Amelia Young

Notes

Introduction

1 They focused on different issues, reflecting perceived weaknesses in each country's financial system. The Pecora investigation concentrated on the reasons for the stock market crash, the Macmillan on monetary policy.

2 Maddison Project, http://www.ggdc.net/maddison/maddison-project/home.htm.

3 Morningstar, http://www2.morningstar.ca/homepage/h_ca.aspx.

4 Joseph Sirois, *Royal Commission on Dominion-Provincial Relations: The Rowell Sirois Report* (Ottawa: King's Printer, 1940).

5 Ron Chernow, *The House of Morgan* (New York: Atlantic Monthly, 1990).

6 Around the same time, the Duff Royal Commission on Railways and Transportation was underway. It consisted of six commissioners, two of whom were foreign – one British and the other American. The American was L.F. Loree, president of the Delaware and Hudson Railway and chair of the Board of Rutgers University.

7 Two of the three Canadians voted against the creation of a central bank.

8 Bank of Canada, "The Bank's History," http://www.bankofcanada.ca/about/history/.

9 Volker R. Berghahn, *American Big Business in Britain and Germany: A Comparative History of Two "Special Relationships" in the 20th Century* (Princeton: Princeton University Press, 2014); Mary Nolan, *The Transatlantic Century: Europe and America 1890–2010* (Cambridge: Cambridge University Press, 2012); Daniel T. Rodgers, *Atlantic Crossings: Social Politics in a Progressive Age* (Cambridge, MA: Harvard University Press, 1998); Harm G. Schröter, *The Americanization of the European Economy: A Compact Survey of American Economic Influence in Europe since the 1880s* (Dordrecht: Springer, 2005).

10 Charles W. Calomiris and Stephen H. Harber, *Fragile by Design: The Political Origins of Banking Crises & Scarce Credit* (Princeton: Princeton University Press, 2014).

11 In a sense, our contribution might best be understood as a financial extension of Bothwell's *Your Country, My Country*, predicated on the principle that only a unified history can adequately account for the similarities and differences between the two systems. Robert Bothwell, *Your Country, My Country: A Unified History of the United States and Canada* (Oxford: Oxford University Press, 2015).

12 Stanley L. Engerman and Robert E. Gallman, eds., *The Cambridge Economic History of the United States*, vol. 2, *The Long Nineteenth Century* (Cambridge: Cambridge University Press, 2000).

13 More recently Douglas McCalla has contended that much of the staple use did not simply lead to the export of raw materials; much material remained in Canada and was used in the development of local manufacturing and industry. Harold A. Innis, *The Fur Trade in Canada: An Introduction to Canadian Economic History* (Toronto: University of Toronto Press, 1999).

14 Albert O. Hirschman, *Rival Views of Market Society and Other Recent Essays* (Cambridge, MA: Harvard University Press, 1992).

15 Charles H. Turner and Fons Trompenaars, *The Seven Cultures of Capitalism: Value Systems for Creating Wealth in the United States, Britain, Japan, Germany, France, Sweden and the Netherlands* (New York: Doubleday, 1993), 2.

16 Ibid., 4.

17 Ibid.; Peter A. Hall and David Soskice, eds., *Varieties of Capitalism: The Institutional Foundations of Comparative Advantage* (Oxford: Oxford University Press, 2001); Geert Hofsede, *Culture's Consequences: Comparing Values, Behaviours, Institutions and Organizations across Nations*, 2nd ed. (Thousand Oaks, CA: Sage, 2001).

18 Michael D. Bordo and Angela A. Redish, "Why Did the Bank of Canada Emerge in 1935?" *Journal of Economic History* 47, no. 2 (1987): 405–17; Lawrence D. Booth, "The Secret of Canadian Banking: Common Sense?" *World Economics* 10 (2009): 1–16; Andrew Smith, "Continental Divide: The Canadian Banking and Currency Laws of 1871 in the Mirror of the United States," *Enterprise & Society* 13, no. 3 (2012): 455–503; Donald J.S. Brean, Lawrence Kryzanowski, and Gordon S. Roberts, "Canada and the United States: Different Roots, Different Routes to Financial Sector Regulation," *Business History* 53, no. 2 (2011): 249–69.

19 Robert J. Shiller, *Finance and the Good Society* (Princeton: Princeton University Press, 2012).

20 Tom Wolfe, *The Bonfire of the Vanities* (New York: Farrar, Straus & Giroux, 1987).
21 Alexis de Tocqueville, *Democracy in America*, trans. Arthur Goldhammer (New York: Library of America, 2004); Max Lerner, *America as a Civilization* (New York: Simon and Schuster, 1957).
22 Douglass C. North and Robert Paul Thomas, *The Rise of the Western World: A New Economic History* (Cambridge: Cambridge University Press, 1995).
23 One interesting outcome of this project is the recognition of how much financial history has been impeded by lack of or closed archives, especially in Canada.
24 Although both countries span the continent, there are some geographic and timing dissimilarities even after the Civil War. Canada, for example, never had what was considered a Midwest because of the Canadian Shield or Laurentian Plateau and no real "West" until the twentieth century.
25 A notable exception was the Ford Motor Company of Canada, which was a public company long before its parent was.

1 Foreign and Domestic Beginnings: From Colonies to Civil War, Events, Individuals, and Ideologies

1 Charles A. Beard, *The Rise of American Civilization* (New York: MacMillan, 1937), 72.
2 Gordon S. Wood, *Empire of Liberty: A History of the Early Republic, 1789–1815* (Oxford: Oxford University Press, 2009).
3 The *Oxford Dictionary of Economics* gives as its second definition of capital "A stock of financial assets, which can be used to provide income," which clearly recognizes the distinction between capital and its close relation, money.
4 Bray Hammond, *Banks and Politics in America from the Revolution to the Civil War* (Princeton: Princeton University Press, 1957), 3–37.
5 Winston Churchill described the French and Indian War (or the Seven Years' War) as the First World War, because it was fought on a global scale.
6 Conrad Black, *Flight of the Eagle: A Strategic History of the United States* (Toronto: McClelland & Stewart, 2013), 21.
7 Theodore Draper, *A Struggle for Power: The American Revolution* (New York: Random House, 1996), 1–25.
8 Eric Williams, *Capitalism and Slavery* (New York: Russell & Russell, 1944).
9 John J. McCusker and Russell R. Menard, *The Economy of British North America, 1607–1789* (Chapel Hill: University of North Carolina Press, 1991), 40.

10 Nuala Zahedieh, *The Capital and the Colonies: London and the Atlantic Economy, 1600–1700* (Cambridge: Cambridge University Press, 2010), 280–92.

11 McCusker and Menard, *Economy of British North America*, 54.

12 Ibid., 103, 112. British and French policies contributed to this dramatic difference. The French government restricted non-Catholic emigration while the British government encouraged non-establishment emigration.

13 McCusker and Menard, *Economy of British North America*.

14 Draper, *Struggle for Power*.

15 Robert E. Wright, *One Nation under Debt: Hamilton, Jefferson, and the History of What We Owe* (New York: McGraw Hill, 2008).

16 Draper, *Struggle for Power*, 103–29.

17 Beard, *Rise of American Civilization*, 13; Niall Ferguson, *Empire: The Rise and Demise of the British World Order and the Lessons for Global Power* (New York: Basic Books, 2002).

18 Beard, *Rise of American Civilization*, 99, 201, 211.

19 Black, *Flight of the Eagle*.

20 Ibid.

21 Draper, *Struggle for Power*.

22 Beard, *Rise of American Civilization*, 73.

23 Draper, *Struggle for Power*.

24 Samuel E. Morrison, Henry S. Commager, and William E. Leuchtenburg, *The Growth of the American Republic*, vol. 1 (Oxford: Oxford University Press, 1980).

25 A century and a quarter later the British government asked the "white" dominions to contribute to the costs of the naval build-up prior to the First World War – Canada, led by a French-Canadian prime minister declined to contribute. Margaret MacMillan, *The War That Ended Peace: The Road to 1914* (Toronto: Penguin Group, 2013), 124.

26 G.M. Trevelyan, *History of England* (New York: Doubleday Anchor Books, 1954), 3:123.

27 Black, *Flight of the Eagle*, 40.

28 Wright, *One Nation under Debt*.

29 Edwin J. Perkins, *American Public Finance and Financial Services, 1700–1815* (Columbus: Ohio State University, 1994); Wright, *One Nation under Debt*.

30 Draper, *Struggle for Power*, 197–8.

31 R. Louis Gentilcore, ed., *Historical Atlas of Canada*, vol. 2, *The Land Transformed, 1800–1891* (Toronto: University of Toronto Press, 1993).

32 Ibid.

33 Beard, *Rise of American Civilization*, 241; Perkins, *American Public Finance and Financial Services*; Wright, *One Nation under Debt*.

34 Joseph J. Ellis, *American Creation: Triumphs and Tragedies at the Founding of the Republic* (New York: Knopf, 2007), 91–3.

35 Ibid., 107–11.

36 Perkins, *American Public Finance and Financial Services.*

37 United States, *Declaration of Independence*, 1776.

38 Ellis, *American Creation*, 170.

39 Ibid.; Wright, *One Nation under Debt.*

40 Ron Chernow, *Alexander Hamilton* (New York: Penguin Books, 2004).

41 Richard Sylla, "Reversing Financial Reversals: Government and the Financial System since 1789," in *Government and the American Economy: A New History*, ed. Price Fishback, 115–47 (Chicago: University of Chicago Press, 2007).

42 Hammond, *Banks and Politics in America*, 41.

43 Thomas K. McCraw, *The Founders and Finance: How Hamilton, Gallatin, and Other Immigrants Forged a New Economy* (Cambridge, MA: Harvard University Press, 2012), 100.

44 Wright, *One Nation under Debt.*

45 McCraw, *Founders and Finance*, 108.

46 Perkins, *American Public Finance and Financial Services*; Wright, *One Nation under Debt.*

47 Wright, *One Nation under Debt.*

48 The Bank of England was privately owned until 1946, when it was nationalized by the Labour government of the day.

49 Wright, *One Nation under Debt.*

50 Perkins, *American Public Finance and Financial Services.*

51 In 1784 Hamilton had established the Bank of New York.

52 Perkins, *American Public Finance and Financial Services*; Wright, *One Nation under Debt.*

53 Perkins, *American Public Finance and Financial Services*; Wright, *One Nation under Debt.*

54 Catherine R. Schenk and Emmanuel Mourlon-Druol, "Bank Regulation and Supervision." In *The Oxford Handbook of Banking and Financial Regulation*, ed. Youssef Cassis et al. 395–419 (Oxford: Oxford University Press, 2016).

55 Wright, *One Nation under Debt.*

56 Perkins, *American Public Finance and Financial Services.*

57 Ibid.

58 Gallatin was an early nineteenth-century Republican and would be a Democrat today.

59 McCraw, *Founders and Finance*, 296.

60 Perkins, *American Public Finance and Financial Services*.
61 *The Alien and Sedition Acts of 1798*, 5th Cong., General Records of the United States Government Record Group 11 (6 July 1798).
62 Black, *Flight of the Eagle*.
63 Hammond, *Banks and Politics in America from the Revolution to the Civil War*.
64 Ibid., 36.
65 Black, *Flight of the Eagle*.
66 Beard, *Rise of American Civilization*, 429.
67 Ibid., 429–30.
68 Arthur Schlesinger Jr, *The Age of Jackson* (New York: Book Find Club, 1945).
69 J.C. Furnas, *The Americans: A Social History* (New York: Capricorn, 1969).
70 Hammond, *Banks and Politics in America from the Revolution to the Civil War*.
71 Ibid.
72 Ibid., 320–1.
73 Ibid., 322; Howard Bodenhorn, *A History of Banking in Antebellum America: Financial Markets and Economic Development in an Era of Nation Building* (Cambridge: Cambridge University Press, 2000).
74 Glyndon G. Van Deusen, *The Jacksonian Era: 1828–1848* (New York: Harper & Row, 1959).
75 Naomi R. Lamoreaux, *Insider Lending: Banks, Personal Connections, and Economic Development in Industrial New England* (Cambridge: Cambridge University Press, 1994), 31.
76 Schlesinger Jr, *Age of Jackson*; Peter Temin, *The Jackson Economy* (New York: Norton, 1969); Van Deusen, *Jacksonian Era*.
77 Howard Bodenhorn, *State Banking in Early America: A New Economic History* (Oxford: Oxford University Press, 2003), 3.
78 Perkins, *American Public Finance and Financial Services*.
79 Charles W. Calomiris and Stephen H. Harber, *Fragile by Design: The Political Origins of Banking Crises & Scarce Credit* (Princeton: Princeton University Press, 2014.
80 Robert E. Wright, *The First Wall Street: Chestnut Street, Philadelphia, & the Birth of American Finance* (Chicago: University of Chicago Press, 2005).
81 Bodenhorn, *State Banking in Early America*, 50–1.
82 Ibid., 55.
83 Ibid..
84 Stephen Mihim, *A Nation of Counterfeiters: Capitalists, Con Men, and the Making of the United States* (Cambridge, MA: Harvard University Press, 2007).
85 Bodenhorn, *State Banking in Early America*.
86 Lamoreaux, *Insider Lending*, 1–9.

87 Robert E. Wright, "Bank Ownership and Lending Patterns in New York and Pennsylvania, 1781–1831," *Business History Review* 73, no. 1 (1999): 40–60.

88 Hammond, *Banks and Politics in America from the Revolution to the Civil War*, 144.

89 Bodenhorn, *State Banking in Early America*, 12.

90 Ibid., 13–15.

91 Ibid., 18–19.

92 Ibid., 23.

93 Ibid., 73–5.

94 Ibid., 5.

95 Stuart Bruchey, *The Roots of American Economic Growth, 1607–1861* (New York: Harper & Row, 1965),148.

96 Bodenhorn, *State Banking in Early America*.

97 Ibid., 3.

98 Ibid., 221.

99 Ibid., 222–3.

100 Ibid., 252.

101 Ibid., 3.

102 Ibid., 5.

103 Ibid., 183.

104 Ibid., 159.

105 Ibid., 183.

106 Wright, *One Nation under Debt*.

107 David B. Davis, *Slavery and Human Progress* (Oxford: Oxford University Press, 1984), xiii.

108 See Sharon A. Murray, *Investing in Life: Insurance in Antebellum America* (Baltimore, MD: Johns Hopkins University Press, 2010, as an exception.

109 Gavin Wright, *The Political Economy of the Cotton South: Households, Markets, and Wealth in the Nineteenth Century* (New York: Norton, 1978); William Fogel and Stanley L. Engerman, *Time on the Cross: The Economics of American Negro Slavery* (Boston: Little, Brown, 1974); Eugene D. Genovese, *The Political Economy of Slavery: Studies in the Economy and Society of the Slave South* (New York: Pantheon, 1965); Genovese, *The World the Slaveholders Made: Two Essays in Interpretation* (New York: Pantheon, 1969); Harold D. Woodman, *King Cotton and His Retainers: Financing and Marketing the Cotton Crop of the South, 1800–1925* (Lexington: University of Kentucky Press, 1968).

110 Seth Rockman, "The Future of Civil War Era Studies: Slavery and Capitalism," *Journal of the Civil War Era* 2, no. 1 (2012): 627–50.

111 Paul Johnson, *A History of the American People* (London: Weidenfeld & Nicolson, 1997), 97.
112 *U.S. Constitution*, art. 1, sec. 2.
113 In Canada, the majority of slaves were of Aboriginal origin. Canada's principal economic sectors required relatively little manual labour. In 1833, the official abolition of slavery in the British Empire simply confirmed the status that had prevailed for several years.
114 Lewellyn Woodward, *The Age of Reform, 1815–1870* (Oxford: Clarendon, 1997), 240–1.
115 Calvin Schermerhorn, *The Business of Slavery and the Rise of American Capitalism, 1815–1860* (New Haven, CT: Yale University Press, 2015).
116 Amanda Foreman, *A World on Fire: The Epic History of Two Nations Divided* (London: Allen Lane, 2010).
117 Beckert, *Empire of Cotton.*
118 Bruchey, *Roots of American Economic Growth*, 142.
119 Black, *Flight of the Eagle*, 194.
120 Henry Bamford Parkes, *The United States of America: A History* (New York: Alfred A. Knopf, 1956).
121 Black, *Flight of the Eagle*, 199.
122 Beard, *Rise of American Civilization*, 31.

2 Transitional Decade: The Birth and Rebirth of Nations

1 James M. McPherson, *The War That Forged a Nation: Why the Civil War Still Matters* (New York: Oxford University Press, 2015), 2.
2 Sumner J. La Croix, "Government and the People: Labor, Education, and Health," in *Government and the American Economy: A New History*, ed. Price Fishback, 323–63 (Chicago: Chicago University Press, 2007).
3 Robert E. Wright, *Fubarnomics: A Lighthearted, Serious Look at America's Economic Ills* (Amherst: Prometheus Books, 2010), 114.
4 McPherson, *War That Forged a Nation.*
5 Jeffrey Rogers Hummell, "The Civil War and Reconstruction," in *Government and the American Economy: A New History*, ed. Price Fishback (Chicago: University of Chicago Press, 2007), 197.
6 Ibid., 151.
7 Ibid., 171.
8 Sylla, "Reversing Financial Reversals, 134–5.
9 Woodward, *Age of Reform*, 312; Sven Beckert, *Empire of Cotton: A Global History* (New York: Knopf, 2014).
10 Woodward, *Age of Reform*, 313–14.

11 McPherson, *Battle Cry of Freedom*; and Woodward, *Age of Reform*, 307–15.

12 McPherson, *Battle Cry of Freedom*.

13 In 1864, a small contingent of Confederate troops robbed three American banks simultaneously. The thieves escaped to British North America, which declined to extradite the soldiers but did return the funds. The only surviving bank of this raid is fittingly enough a branch of TD bank. John Boyko, *Blood and Daring: How Canada Fought the American Civil War and Forged a Nation* (Toronto: Knopf Canada, 2013), 226.

14 Foreman, *World on Fire*.

15 Jeffery R. Hummel, "The Civil War and Reconstruction," in *Government and the American Economy: A New History*, ed. Price Fishback (Chicago: University of Chicago Press, 2007), 212–18.

16 Donald Creighton, *John A. Macdonald: The Young Politician* (Toronto, Macmillan Company of Canada, 1956), 469.

17 Andrew David Allan Smith, "British Businessmen and Canadian Confederation: Gentlemanly Capitalism at Work" (PhD diss., University of Western Ontario Faculty of Graduate Studies, 2005).

18 *New York Times*, "Dominion of Canada," 3 July 1867.

19 *New York Times*, "Inauguration of the New Regime," 7 July 1867.

20 Oscar D. Skelton, *The Day of Sir Wilfrid Laurier* (Toronto: Glasgow Brock, 1916), 412.

21 The number of imperial troops also jumped from fewer than 5,000 to nearly 20,000. Gentilcore, *Historical Atlas of Canada*.

22 Trevelyan, *History of England*, 3:109.

23 P.J. Cain and A.G. Hopkins, *British Imperialism: 1688–2000*, 2nd ed. (London: Longman, 2001).

24 The Fordney Mccumber Act was a protective tariff passed by the U.S. Congress in 1922.

25 B.W. Wilkinson. "Section G: The Balance of International Payments, International Investment Position and Foreign Trade," Statistics Canada, http://www.statcan.gc.ca/pub/11-516-x/sectiong/4147439-eng.htm#4.

26 Joseph Sirois, *Royal Commission on Dominion-Provincial Relations: The Rowell Sirois Report* (Ottawa: King's Printer, 1940), 19.

27 Thomas D. McGee, *Two Speeches on the Union of the Provinces: Minister of Agriculture* (Quebec: Hunter, Rose, 9 February 1865).

28 Robin B. Burns, "McGee, Thomas D'Arcy," *Dictionary of Canadian Biography*, vol. 9. 1976. http://www.biographi.ca/en/bio/mcgee_thomas_d_arcy_9E.html.

29 Winston Churchill, *A History of the English Speaking Peoples*, Vol. 4, *The Great Democracies* (Toronto: McClelland & Stewart, 1958), 103–4.

30 Smith, "British Businessmen and Canadian Confederation," 268.
31 Oscar D. Skelton, *The Life and Times of Sir Alexander Tilloch Galt* (Toronto: Oxford University Press, 1920), 410.
32 Sirois, *Royal Commission on Dominion-Provincial Relations*, 29.
33 John Boyd, *Sir George Etienne Cartier, His Life and Times: A Political History of Canada from 1814 until 1873* (Toronto: Macmillan of Canada, 1914), 222.
34 To be sure, America's "universal suffrage" was well ahead of other countries, but applied only to white males.
35 Richard Gwynn, *John A., the Man Who Made Us: The Life and Times of John A. Macdonald*, vol. 1, *1815–1867* (Toronto: Random House, Canada, 2007).
36 Conrad Black, *Rise to Greatness: The History of Canada from the Vikings to the Present* (Toronto: McClelland & Stewart, 2014), 290.
37 Gwynn, *John A.*
38 Charles P. Stacey, *Canada and the Age of Conflict*, Vol. 1, *1867–1921: A History of Canadian External Policies* (Toronto: University of Toronto Press, 1984); Gordon T. Stewart, *The Origins of Canadian Politics: A Comparative Approach* (Vancouver: University of British Columbia Press, 1986).
39 J.-C. Bonenfant, "Cartier, Sir George-Étienne," *Dictionary of Canadian Biography*, vol. 10, 1972, http://www.biographi.ca/en/bio/cartier_george_etienne_10E.html.
40 H.V. Nelles, *A Little History of Canada* (Toronto, Oxford University Press, 2004). Ironically Alexander Hamilton, who played such a crucial role in the development of the Canadian financial system, was strongly opposed to the Quebec Act. Chernow, *Alexander Hamilton*, 66.
41 Robert Bothwell, *Your Country, My Country: A Unified History of the United States and Canada* (Oxford: Oxford University Press, 2015).
42 Gentilcore, *Historical Atlas of Canada*.
43 Fernand Ouellet, "Papineau, Louis-Joseph." *Dictionary of Canadian Biography*, vol. 10, 1972, http://www.biographi.ca/en/bio/papineau_louis_joseph_10E.html.
44 Frederick H. Armstrong and Ronald J. Stagg, "Mackenzie, William Lyon," *Dictionary of Canadian Biography*, vol. 9, 1976, http://www.biographi.ca/en/bio/mackenzie_william_lyon_9E.html.
45 Nelles, *Little History of Canada*, 104.
46 In 1838 Canada also experienced the so-called Patriot Wars, a series of invasions from the United States by Canadian exiles and American volunteers including Irish Fenians: "To the colony's British governors – and apparently most of its residents – the raiders were not patriots but pirates, not liberators but invaders, not rescuers but rebel terrorists." Chris Raible, review of *The Patriot War along the Michigan-Canadian Borders:*

Raiders and Rebels, by Shaun J. McLaighlin, *Ontario History* 106, no. 1 (2014): 136.

47 Fernand Ouellet, "Lambton, John George, 1st Earl of Durham," *Dictionary of Canadian Biography*, vol. 7. http://www.biographi.ca/en/bio/lambton_john_george_7E.html.

48 Gwynn, *John A*.

49 Hammond, *Banks and Politics in America from the Revolution to the Civil War*.

50 From 1845 to 1852, with the failure of the potato crop, approximately two million people died in or emigrated from Ireland, reducing the island's population, which was highly dependent on the potato, by around 25 per cent. Cecil Woodham-Smith, *The Great Hunger: Ireland 1845–1849* (London: Penguin Books, 1991).

51 William L. Morton, *The Critical Years: The Union of British North America, 1857–1873* (Toronto: McClelland and Stewart, 1964), 220.

52 W.L. Morton, "Bruce, James, 8th Earl of Elgin and 12th Earl of Kincardine." *Dictionary of Canadian Biography*, vol. 9, 1976, http://www.biographi.ca/en/bio/bruce_james_9E.html.

53 Robert Bothwell, *The Penguin History of Canada* (Toronto: Penguin Group, 2006), 203.

54 A.G. Kenwood and A.L. Lougheed, *The Growth of the International Economy, 1820–1990: An Introductory Text*, 3rd ed. (London: Routledge, 1992); Ferguson, *Empire*.

55 Jean-Pierre Kesteman, "Galt, Sir Alexander Tilloch," *Dictionary of Canadian Biography*, vol. 12, 1990. http://www.biographi.ca/en/bio/galt_alexander_tilloch_12E.html.

56 Morton, *Critical Years*, 16.

57 Ibid., 65.

58 Joseph Pope, *Memoirs of the Right Honourable Sir John Alexander Macdonald, First Prime Minister of Canada* (Toronto: Musson Book, 1930), 691.

59 James Powell, *A History of the Canadian Dollar* (Ottawa: Bank of Canada, 2005), 16–17.

60 *Daily Globe*, "The Great Confederation," 4 October 1864.

61 Skelton, *Life and Times of Sir Alexander Tilloch Galt*, 372.

62 G.P. Browne, *Documents on the Confederation of British North America* (Toronto: McClelland and Stewart, 1969), 47.

63 Ibid., 76–7, 158, 221, 238, 259, 323.

64 Ibid., xi.

65 Desmond Morton, *A Short History of Canada* (Toronto: McClelland & Stewart, 2007), 161–2.

66 Christopher Moore, *Three Weeks in Quebec City: The Meeting That Made Canada* (Toronto: Penguin Canada Books, 2015), 186, 187. Although Moore is silent on the key question for this book, and that is the decision to make banking a federal responsibility.

67 Ibid., 144–5.

68 Sirois, *Royal Commission on Dominion-Provincial Relations*, 38.

69 Note that outside of the main cities, there was little municipal development in Nova Scotia and New Brunswick, which was not the case in the province of Canada.

70 In the case of excises, this applied only in Canada. Sirois, *Royal Commission on Dominion-Provincial Relations*, 40.

71 Christopher Moore, *1867: How the Fathers Made a Deal* (Toronto: McClelland & Stewart, 1997), 128–9.

72 Powell, *History of the Canadian Dollar*, 3.

73 Ibid., 4.

74 Adam Shortt, *History of Canadian Currency and Banking, 1660–1880* (Toronto: Canadian Bankers' Association, 1986), 50–1.

75 A number of people seem to think that a number of people seem to think the Canadian system was derived from the Scottish system, with free banking and light governmental regulation, because of the number of Scots in Canadian banking. But Shortt disputes this by pointing out that once the Scots came to Canada their trade was with New York, the New England states, and the Caribbean. Furthermore, in the period 1793 to 1815 the United Kingdom was at war with France and "both English and Scottish banking were in a most unstable condition and subject of frequent crises. In 1797 the Bank of England suspended cash payments, followed immediately by the Scottish banks and did not resume until 1821." Although Canadians adopted joint-stock banking, fractional creation of bank currencies, and some other aspects of banking in which Scotland was considered a leader, others, such as free banking, were a long time coming to Canada. Ibid., 11, 25.

76 Ibid., 15–16.

77 Neufeld contends that the bank was probably operating illegally. E.P. Neufeld, *The Financial System of Canada: Its Growth and Development* (Toronto: Macmillan Company of Canada, 1972), 39.

78 N.S.B. Gras *and Henrietta M. Larson, Casebook in American History (New York: F.S. Crofts*, 1939), 328.

79 Merill Denison, *Canada's First Bank: A History of the Bank of Montreal*, vol. 2 (Toronto: McClelland & Stewart, 1967).

80 Denison, *Canada's First Bank*, vol. 1, 53, 76; Roeliff M. Breckenridge, *The History of Banking in Canada* (Washington, DC: Government Printing Office, 1910).

81 Shortt, *History of Canadian Currency and Banking*, 73.
82 Breckenridge, *History of Banking in Canada*, 6.
83 Ibid., 6–7.
84 Hammond, *Banks and Politics in America from the Revolution to the Civil War*, 656–8.
85 Mira Wilkins, *The History of Foreign Investment in the United States to 1914* (Cambridge, MA: Harvard University Press, 1989).
86 Shortt, *History of Canadian Currency and Banking*, 325.
87 Geoffrey Jones, *British Multinational Banking: 1830–1990* (Oxford: Clarendon, 1993), 14.
88 Breckenridge, *History of Banking in Canada*, 41.
89 Ibid., 36.
90 Craig R. McIvor, *Canadian Monetary, Banking and Fiscal Development* (Toronto: Macmillan of Canada, 1958), 42–4.
91 Peter Baskerville, *The Bank of Upper Canada* (Ottawa: Carleton University Press, 1987), lxxxviii.
92 Wright, *One Nation under Debt*.
93 Powell, *History of the Canadian Dollar*, 7–8.
94 Breckenridge, *History of Banking in Canada*, 43, 72.
95 Powell, *History of the Canadian Dollar*, 10–11.
96 J.M.S. Careless, *Brown of the Globe* (Toronto: Dundurn, 1996), 2:263–4.
97 Breckenridge, *History of Banking in Canada*, 52.
98 Robert Macintosh, "Origins of Financial Stability in Canada: The Bank Act of 1871," in *Relentless Change: A Casebook for the Study of Canadian Business History*, ed. Joe Martin (Toronto, Rotman/UTP Publishing, 2010), 33.
99 Hammond, *Banks and Politics in America from the Revolution to the Civil War*, 668.
100 Shortt, *History of Canadian Currency and Banking*, 531.
101 Breckenridge, *History of Banking in Canada*, 79.
102 *Year-Book and Almanac of British North America for 1867: Being an Annual Register of Political, Vital, and Trade Statistics, Tariffs, Excise and Stamp Duties; and All Public Events of Interest in Upper and Lower Canada; New Brunswick; Nova Scotia; Newfoundland; Prince Edward Island; and The West India Islands* (Montreal: Lowe and Chamberlin, 1866).
103 Breckenridge, *History of Banking in Canada*, 86.
104 Ibid., 88.
105 *The Canada Year Book 1955: The Official Statistical Annual of the Resources, History, Institutions, and Social and Economic Conditions of Canada* (Ottawa: Queen's Printer and Controller of Stationery, 1955), 1198.

106 Kesteman, "Galt, Sir Alexander Tilloch."
107 David M.L. Farr, "Rose, Sir John," *Dictionary of Canadian Biography*, vol. 11. http://www.biographi.ca/en/bio/rose_john_11E.html.
108 Shortt, *History of Canadian Currency and Banking*, 576.
109 Ibid., 94–5.
110 Farr, "Rose, Sir John."
111 *Globe*, "The Banking Debate," 3 June 1869.
112 "McMaster, William," *Dictionary of Canadian Biography*, vol. 11, 1982, http://www.biographi.ca/en/bio/mcmaster_william_11E.html.
113 Farr, "Rose, Sir John."
114 R.E. Rudin, "King, Edwin Henry," *Dictionary of Canadian Biography*, vol. 12, 1990, http://www.biographi.ca/en/bio/king_edwin_henry_12E.html.
115 King was living in Monte Carlo when he died in 1895.

3 The Maturing: 1869–1914

1 Although the New York Stock Exchange had been in existence since 1817, the creation of DJIA coincided with the growth of modern exchanges. Samuel H. Williamson, "Daily Closing Value of the Dow Jones Average, 1885 to Present," Measuring Worth, https://www.measuringworth.com/DJA.
2 The opening of the Canadian West did not begin until the late 1890s.
3 Alfred D. Chandler Jr., *The Visible Hand: The Managerial Revolution in American Business* (Cambridge, MA: Belknap Press of Harvard University Press, 1977).
4 Ibid., 81–94.
5 Gary M. Walton and Hugh Rockoff, *History of the American Economy*, 8th ed. (New York: Dryden, 1998), 354–70.
6 Chandler Jr, *Visible Hand*, 503–13.
7 Philip Scranton, *Endless Novelty: Specialty Production and American Industrialization, 1865–1925* (Princeton: Princeton University Press, 1997); Lesile Hannah, "Pioneering Modern Corporate Governance: A View from London in 1900," *Enterprise and Society* 8, no. 3 (2007): 643–86.
8 Although Rupert's Land had much less arable land than the Louisiana purchase, it had far more oil and gas, pulp and paper, and nickel, gold, copper, and zinc.
9 A.E. Safarian, *The Canadian Economy in the Great Depression* (Toronto: McClelland & Stewart, 1970), 108.
10 Later some Canadian companies listed in New York, where for a while they enjoyed some special privileges as foreign securities.

Mira Wilkins, *The History of Foreign Investment in the United States: 1914 to 1945* (Cambridge, MA: Harvard University Press, 2004).

11 William J. Hausman, Peter Hertner, and Mira Wilkins, *Global Electrification: Multinational Enterprise and International Finance in the History of Light and Power, 1878–2007* (New York: Cambridge University Press, 2008).

12 Walton and Rockoff, *History of the American Economy*, 428.

13 Sidney Homer and Richard Sylla, *A History of Interest Rates* (New Brunswick, NJ: Rutgers University Press, 1996).

14 Ronald S. Longley, *Sir Francis Hincks: A Study of Canadian Politics, Railways, and Finance in the Nineteenth Century* (Toronto: University of Toronto Press, 1943), 354.

15 C.M. Wallace. "Tilley, Sir Samuel Leonard." *Dictionary of Canadian Biography, vol. 12.* http://www.biographi.ca/en/bio/tilley_samuel_leonard_12E.html.

16 Andrew Smith, "Continental Divide: The Canadian Banking and Currency Laws of 1871 in the Mirror of the United States," *Enterprise and Society* 13, no. 3 (2012): 489.

17 Canadian cabinet ministers have to be elected to the House of Commons.

18 Longley, *Sir Francis Hincks*, 367.

19 Shortt, *History of Canadian Currency and Banking*, 611.

20 *Canada Year Book, 1938: The Official Statistical Annual of the Resources, History, Institutions, and Social and Economic Conditions of the Dominion* (Ottawa: King's Printer, 1938), 903.

21 This arrangement "was cited in the United Kingdom as a well-working operational model" for its adaption of notes as the First World War began. Richard Roberts, *Saving the City: The Great Financial Crisis of 1914* (Oxford: Oxford University Press, 2013), 120.

22 Harold van B. Cleveland and Thomas F. Huertas, *Citibank: 1812–1970* (Cambridge, MA: Harvard University Press, 1985), 24.

23 MacIntosh, "Origins of Financial Stability in Canada," 36.

24 Longley, *Sir Francis Hincks*, 363.

25 William G. Ormsby, "Hinicks, Sir Francis," *Dictionary of Canadian Biography,* vol. 11. http://www.biographi.ca/en/bio/hincks_francis_11E.html.

26 Ibid.

27 *Canada Year Book, 1938: The Official Statistical Annual of the Resources, History, Institutions, and Social and Economic Conditions of the Dominion*, 904.

28 Neufeld, *Financial System of Canada*, 90.

29 Ibid., 92–3.

30 *The Canada Year Book, 1921* (Ottawa: King's Printer, 1922), 719.

31 Ormsby, "Hincks, Sir Francis."

32 Ironically the general manager, P.M. Stewart, had made a major address to the Empire Club of Canada a few years earlier pointing out the superiority of the Canadian banking system over the American system.

33 The disappearance of small, regional banks was due, in part, to their local specialization and customer base, which did not meet the needs of the growing industrial national businesses. This specialization increased their risk if their local markets faltered; local savers could not provide sufficient deposits to create the credit demanded by the growing industrial firms, so they turned to larger, national banks.

34 *The Statistical Year-Book of Canada for 1900* (Ottawa: Government Printing Bureau, 1901).

35 Neufeld, *Financial System of Canada*, 480.

36 Kenneth Buckley, *Capital Formation in Canada, 1896–1930* (Toronto: McClelland and Stewart, 1974), 96.

37 Ibid, 102.

38 Michael Bliss, *Northern Enterprise: Five Centuries of Canadian Business* (Toronto: McClelland & Stewart, 1987), 280–1.

39 Aitken had a highly successful career in the United Kingdom, where he served as a member of Parliament before being knighted and granted a peerage. He also owned a major newspaper chain, including the *Daily Express*, the largest selling newspaper in the world, and served as minister of aircraft production in the Second World War.

40 Milton Friedman and Anna J. Schwartz, *A Monetary History of the United States 1867–1960* (Princeton: Princeton University Press, 1963), 3.

41 Ibid., 7. With the return to the gold standard the two currencies once again traded at par and would until the outbreak of the First World War.

42 Ibid., 7.

43 Ibid., 7.

44 Hepburn v Griswold, 75 U.S. 603 (1870).

45 Hummel, "The Civil War and Reconstruction," 215.

46 Walton and Rockoff, *History of the American Economy*, 424–8.

47 Ibid., 424–8; Sylla, "Reversing Financial Reversals"; Naomi Lamoreaux, *The Great Merger Movement in American Business, 1895–1904* (New York: Cambridge University Press, 1985).

48 Walton and Rockoff, *History of the American Economy*, 425–9.

49 Wilkins, *History of Foreign Investment in the United States*, 454.

50 Cleveland and Huertas, *Citibank*, 24–5, 73–5.

51 Martin Konings, *The Development of American Finance* (New York: Cambridge University Press, 2011), 50.

52 Cleveland and Huertas, *Citibank*, 38–46.

53 BMO, Annual Reports, 1880s Archives.

54 Henry V. Poor, *Poor's Manual of the Railroads of the United States* (New York: H.V. & H.W., 1895), 46.

55 Cleveland and Huertas, *Citibank*.

56 Walton and Rockoff, *History of the American Economy*, 425–9.

57 Sylla, "Reversing Financial Reversals."

58 Jeffrey R. Fear and R.D. Wadhwani, "Populism and Political Entrepreneurship: The Universalization of German Savings Banks and the Decline of American Savings, 1907–1934," in *Business in the Age of Extremes: Essays in Modern German and Austrian Economic History Series*, ed. Juergen Kocka, Dieter Ziegler, and Hartmut Berghoff (Cambridge: Cambridge University Press, 2013), 101.

59 Ibid., 105.

60 Wilkins, *History of Foreign Investment in the United States*, 489.

61 Ibid., 455–6.

62 With significant investment from America.

63 Wilkins, *History of Foreign Investment in the United States*, 64–5.

64 Ibid., 99.

65 Ibid., 76–7.

66 Ibid., 82.

67 Ibid., 78.

68 Ibid., 457.

69 Ibid., 458–62.

70 B. Desjardins et al., *Le Credit Lyonnais: 1863–1996* (Geneva: Droz, 2003), 83, 487.

71 Christopher Kobrak, *Banking on Global Markets: Deutsche Bank in the United States, 1870 to the Present* (Cambridge: Cambridge University Press, 2007).

72 Wilkins, *History of Foreign Investment in the United States*, 501–11.

73 Canadian banks came under fire in 1907 for holding significant reserves with New York banks rather than lending money in Canada.

74 Wilkins, *History of Foreign Investment in the United States*, 486–7.

75 Susie Pak, *Gentleman Bankers: The World of J.P. Morgan* (Cambridge, MA: Harvard University Press, 2013).

76 Homer and Sylla, *History of Interest Rates*; Youssef Cassis, *Capitals of Capital* (Cambridge: Cambridge University Press, 2006); Stefano Battilossi, "Introduction: International Banking and the American Challenge in Historical Perspective." In *European Banks and the American Challenge: Competition and Cooperation in International Banking under Bretton Woods,*, ed. Stefano Battilossi and Youssef Cassis, 1–35 (Oxford: Oxford University Press, 2002).

77 Walton and Rockoff, *History of the American Economy*, 358–9.
78 Wilkins, *History of Foreign Investment in the United State*, 137.
79 Ibid., 145.
80 Ibid., 147.
81 Ibid., 159, 173.
82 Ibid., 194–9.
83 Poor, *Poor's Manual of the Railroads of the United States*, 128.
84 Wilkins, *History of Foreign Investment in the United States*, 122.
85 Kobrak, *Banking on Global Markets*, 65.
86 Poor, *Poor's Manual of the Railroads of the United States*, 668; Chandler Jr, *Visible Hand*; Paul J. Miranti Jr., *Accountancy Comes of Age: The Development of an American Profession, 1886–1940* (Chapel Hill: University of North Carolina Press, 1990).
87 Poor, *Poor's Manual of the Railroads of the United States*, 80–3.
88 Kobrak, *Banking on Global Markets*, 65.
89 Ibid.
90 Ibid.
91 Longley, *Sir Francis Hincks*, 190.
92 A.A. den Otter, *The Philosophy of Railways: The Transcontinental Railway Idea in British North America* (Toronto: University of Toronto Press, 1997), 19.
93 Baring Archive, "The Baring Timeline," http://www.baringarchive.org.uk/history/timeline/.
94 Ann M. Carlos and Frank Lewis, "The Profitability of Early Canadian Railroads: Evidence from the Grand Trunk and Great Western Railway Companies," in *Strategic Factors in Nineteenth Century American Economic History: A Volume to Honor Robert W. Fogel*, ed. Claudia Goldin and Hugh Rockoff (Chicago: University of Chicago Press, 1992), 421.
95 Joe Martin, *Relentless Change: A Casebook for the Study of Canadian Business History* (Toronto: University of Toronto Press, 2010), 111.
96 Financial Post Corporation Service; FP Corporate Service Card.
97 Pierre Berton, *The Last Spike: The Great Railway 1881–1885* (Toronto: McClelland and Stewart, 1971), 352.
98 Ibid., 320–1.
99 Hays died on the *Titanic*.
100 Martin, *Relentless Change*, 103.
101 Kobrak, *Banking on Global Markets*.
102 Ibid.
103 Wilkins, *History of Foreign Investment in the United States*, 531.
104 Kobrak, *Banking on Global Markets*.

105 Ibid.
106 Ibid.
107 Douglass North, "Capital Accumulation in Life Insurance between the Civil War and the Investigation of 1905," in *Men in Business: Essays in the History of Entrepreneurship*, ed. William Miller, 238–53 (Cambridge, MA: Harvard University Press, 1952).
108 Morton Keller, *The Life Insurance Enterprise, 1885–1910* (Cambridge, MA: Harvard University Press, 1963).
109 K.J. Meier, *The Political Economy of Regulation: The Case of Insurance* (Albany: State University of New York, 1988), 63.
110 Although there was one significant difference: Canadians bought much less property and casualty insurance than did Americans.
111 James Darroch and Matthias Kipping, "Canada: Taking Life Insurance Abroad." In *World Insurance: The Evolution of a Global Risk Network*, eds. Peter Borscheid and Niels V. Haueter (Oxford: Oxford University Press, 2012), 253.
112 Joseph E. Martin, "Opportunities in the Asia-Pacific Region for Canadian Life Insurance Companies in the Early 1990's," in *Studies in Banking and Financial History*, 512–52 (Warsaw: European Association for Banking and Financial History, 2013).
113 *The Year Book and Almanac of Canada for 1870; Being an Annual Statistical Abstract for the Dominion and a Record of Legislation and of Public Men in British North America* (Montreal: Montreal Printing and Publishing from Stereotyped Plates, 1869), 95–8.
114 No comparable position to that of the superintendent position was established to deal with banking for another half century.
115 Martin, "Opportunities in the Asia-Pacific Region."
116 *The Canada Year Book, 1914* (Ottawa: King's Printer, 1915), 613–14.
117 FP Corporation Service cards
118 Neufeld, *Financial System of Canada*, 247.
119 David Faure and Elisabeth Koll, "China: The Indigenization of Insurance." In *World Insurance: The Evolution of a Global Risk Network*, eds. Peter Borscheid and Niels V. Haueter (Oxford: Oxford University Press, 2012), 477.
120 Rod McQueen, *Manulife: How Dominic D'Alessandro Built a Global Giant and Fought to Save It* (Toronto: Viking Canada, 2009), 107.
121 Christopher Armstrong and H.V. Nelles, *Southern Exposure: Canadian Promoters in Latin America and the Caribbean, 1896–1930* (Toronto: University of Toronto Press, 1988), 120–1.
122 Martin, *Relentless Change*, 5.

123 The commission was named after its chairman, Duncan McTavish, a county court judge.

124 Michael Bliss, "George Albertus Cox," *Dictionary of Canadian Biography*, vol. 14. http://www.biographi.ca/en/bio/cox_george_albertus_14E.html.

125 Keith Jamieson,, Michelle A. Hamilton *Dr. Oronhyatekha, Security, Justice and Equality* (Toronto, Dundurn, 1916)

126 J. Castell Hopkins, ed., *The Canadian Annual Review, 1908* (Toronto: Canadian Review, 1908), 221–2.

127 Kobrak, *Banking on Global Markets*.

128 Melvin Zimet and Ronald G. Greenwood, eds., *The Evolving Science of Management: The Collected Papers of Harold Smiddy and Papers by Others in His Honor* (New York: AMACOM, 1979), 479.

129 Christopher McKenna, *The World's Newest Profession: Management Consulting in the Twentieth Century* (Cambridge: Cambridge University Press, 2006).

130 Chandler Jr, *Visible Hand*.

131 Wanda A. Wallace, "Commentary on Rowan A. Miranda," *Research in Governmental and Non-Profit Accounting* 8 (1994): 267–75.

132 Wilkins, *History of Foreign Investment in the United States*, 536–8.

133 Wallace, "Commentary on Rowan A. Miranda"; Gary J. Previs and Barbara D. Merino, *A History of Accountancy in the United States: The Cultural Significance of Accounting* (Columbus: Ohio State University Press, 1998).

134 Rowena Olegario, *A Culture of Credit: Embedding Trust and Transparency in American Business* (Cambridge, MA: Harvard University Press, 2006).

135 Deloitte Canada, *150 Years and Counting: Our Legacy and Our Future* (Toronto: Deloitte Canada, 2010), 9.

136 The original Ross firm merged in Canada with a British-based firm called George A. Touche, in the late 1950s, which in turn merged with another firm, the American company of Deloitte Haskins & Sells, in 1990.

137 Deloitte Canada, *150 Years and Counting*, 31.

138 Morris W. Chambers, "Who We Are and Our History," Canadian Institute of Actuaries, http://www.cia-ica.ca/about-us/the-institute/who-we-are-and-our-history.

139 Robert L. Heibroner, *The Worldly Philosophers: The Lives, Times, and Ideas of the Great Economic Thinkers* (New York: Simon and Schuster, 1953); Richard Hofstadter, *The Age of Reform: From Bryan to F.D.R.* (New York: Knopf, 1955); Thomas Piketty, *Capital in the Twenty-First Century* (Cambridge, MA: Belknap Press of Harvard University Press, 2014); Price Fishback et al., *Government and the American Economy: A New History* (Chicago: University of Chicago Press, 2007).

140 Lamoreaux, *Great Merger Movement in American Business*.

141 Lamoreaux, *Insider Lending*, 133–42.

142 *Best Insurance News*, various dates.

143 Adolf A. Berle and Gardiner C. Means, *The Modern Corporation and Private Property* (New York: Harcourt, Brace & World, 1932).

144 Alfred D. Chandler Jr, *Scale and Scope: The Dynamics of Industrial Capitalism* (Cambridge, MA: Belknap Press of Harvard University Press, 1990); Hannah, "Pioneering Modern Corporate Governance0."

145 Mark Guglielmo and and Werner Troesken, "The Gilded Age," in *Government and the American Economy: A New History*, ed. Price V. Fishback, 255–87 (Chicago: University of Chicago Press, 2007).

146 Fishback et al., *Government and the American Economy*.

147 Jeffrey Fear and Christopher Kobrak, "Diverging Paths: Accounting for Corporate Governance in America and Germany," *Business History Review* 80, no. 1 (2006): 1 46; Leslie Hannah, "J.P. Morgan in London and New York before 1914," *Business History Review* 85, no. 1 (2011): 113–50.

148 Miranti Jr, *Accountancy Comes of Age*.

149 Doris K. Goodwin, *Team of Rivals: The Political Genius of Abraham Lincoln* (New York: Simon and Schuster, 2005), 666.

150 Ron Chernow, *The House of Morgan: An American Banking Dynasty and the Rise of Modern Finance* (New York: Grove, 2001).

151 Friedman and Schwartz, *Monetary History of the United States*, 9.

152 Chernow, *House of Morgan*.

153 Canada, *House of Commons Debates* (Hansard), 17 March 1908, 10th Parl., 4th Sess., Vol. 3.

154 Roger Lowenstein, *America's Bank: The Epic Struggle to Create the Federal Reserve* (New York: Penguin, 2015).

155 Ibid., 257.

156 Ibid.

157 Ibid.

158 Ibid.

159 MacIntosh, "Origins of Financial Stability in Canada," 65–6.

160 D.M. Stewart, "The Banking Systems of Canada and the United States Speech" (Empire Club of Canada Addresses, Toronto, ON, 14 December 1905).

4 "The Great Disorder" and Growing Social Demands: 1914–1945

1 Gerald D. Feldman, *The Great Disorder: Politics, Economics and Society in the German Inflation, 1914–24* (New York: Oxford University Press, 1993), 3.

2 Ian M. Drummond. "Finance Act." *The Canadian Encyclopedia*. http://
www.thecanadianencyclopedia.ca/en/article/finance-act/.

3 Elections were normally every four years and required every five. The
imperial Parliament had to approve a span of six years without an
election.

4 Less than a week after war was declared, the Bank of England opened
an official facility in Ottawa for gold. "Britain especially needed it – and
the German navy keenly wanted Britain not to have it. A Federal Reserve
organized committee on which Benjamin Strong took a position of
leadership set about collecting the gold held in innumerable American
banks. A part of all this treasure would be pledged to pay British claims.
Sensibly, it would be shipped not to London but to the Canadian capital,
Ottawa. The committee's credible promise of $100 million in American
gold to a secure portion of the British Empire more than satisfied London's
gold craving." James Grant, *The Forgotten Depression 1921: The Crash That
Cured Itself* (New York: Simon & Schuster, 2014), 45.

5 Wilkins, *History of Foreign Investment in the United States*, 9; Roberts, *Saving
the City*, 27, 170.

6 In 1873 and 1907, also difficult years for banking, the closure numbers
were 100 and 80 respectively. Ben S. Bernanke, *The Federal Reserve and the
Financial Crisis* (Princeton: Princeton University Press, 2013), 10.

7 Stuart Chase, *Government in Business* (New York: Macmillan, 1935);
Kobrak, *Banking on Global Markets*); Wilkins, *History of Foreign Investment in
the United States*.

8 600,000 Canadians enlisted and 400,000 served overseas. Nearly half of
those were injured and more than 60,000 lost their lives.

9 Excessive monetary expansion led to a sharp drop in the value of the
Canadian dollar after the war – see appendix 4.4.

10 John H. Perry, *Taxes, Tariffs, & Subsidies: A History of Canadian Fiscal
Development*, vol. 2 (Toronto: University of Toronto Press, 1955), table 6.

11 Raghuram G. Rajan, *Banks and Markets: The Changing Character of European
Finance* (Cambridge: National Bureau of Economic Research, 2003); Julia
Ott, "The Free and Open People's Market: Political Ideology and Retail
Brokerage at the New York Stock Exchange, 1913-1933," *Journal of American
History* 96, no. 1 (2009): 44–71.

12 Neufeld, *The Financial System of Canada*, 505.

13 Geoffrey J. Matthews, *Historical Atlas of Canada* (Toronto: University of
Toronto Press, 1987), 3:33.

14 But, as a later royal commission noted, "The taxation measures adopted
by the Dominion to meet the obligations inherited from the War were a

revolutionary change from the simple system of pre-War days." Sirois, *Royal Commission on Dominion-Provincial Relations*, 104.

15 The individuals in the poster are Kaiser Wilhelm II, the German emperor and Queen Victoria's grandson; Field Marshal Paul von Hindenburg, the chief of the German General Staff; Crown Prince Wilhelm, the son of the emperor and heir to the throne; and Grand Admiral Alfred von Tirpitz, commander of the German Navy.

16 Wilkins, *History of Foreign Investment in the United States*.

17 Youssef Cassis, "Big Businesses." In *The Oxford Handbook of Business History*, ed. Geoffrey G. Jones and Jonathan Zeitlin, 171–93 (Oxford: Oxford University Press, 2007).

18 Mira Wilkins, *The Maturing of Multinational Enterprise: American Business Abroad from 1914 to 1970* (Cambridge: Harvard University Press, 1974), 30–1, 55, 182.

19 Ibid., 282.

20 Gary M. Walton and Hugh Rockoff, *History of the American Economy*, 8th ed. (New York: Dryden, 1998), 490–514.

21 Ibid.

22 Alfred D. Chandler Jr., *Strategy and Structure: Chapters in the History of the Industrial Enterprise* (Cambridge, MA: MIT Press, 1990).

23 Berle and Means, *Modern Corporation and Private Property*, 52, 56; Mary A. O'Sullivan, "The Expansion of the U.S. Stock Market, 1885–1930: Historical Facts and Theoretical Fashions," *Enterprise and Society* 8, no. 3 (2007): 489–532; O'Sullivan, *Dividends of Development: Securities Markets in the History of US Capitalism, 1866–1922* (Oxford: Oxford University Press, 2016).

24 The comparable U.S. figure was 4.1 per cent, 1921 was the second-worst year in the twentieth century, exceeded only by 1931.

25 In 1922 the United Farmers of Ontario government created a government-owned bank that survived for eight decades. In Alberta too the progressives' political parties were referred to as United Farmers.

26 In spite of Canada's transition from colony to nation, the role of governor general in Canada, the head of state, was still held by a series of British lords, dukes, earls, and viscounts until the appointment in 1952 of Vincent Massey, the first Canadian-born governor general.

27 *The Canada Year Book 1930: The Official Statistical Annual of the Resources, History, Institutions and Social and Economic Conditions of the Dominion* (Ottawa: King's Printer, 1930), 463.

28 Includes investments in CPR using Department of Commerce figures.

29 Neufeld, *Financial System of Canada*, 622–4.

30 During the First World War, its north-end branch handled more business than any branch of a chartered bank.

31 Of the eleven, one was the recently chartered Barclays Bank (Canada), which started in 1929 and was absorbed by the Imperial Bank in 1956. In 1931 the Imperial Bank of Canada absorbed the Weyburn Security Bank.

32 This is similar to the reasoning in the state of California during the same period. *The Canada Year Book 1938: The Official Statistical Annual of the Resources, History, Institutions and Social and Economic Conditions of the Dominion* (Ottawa: King's Printer, 1938).

33 *The Canada Year Book 1922–23: The Official Statistical Annual of the Resources, History, Institutions and Social and Economic Conditions of the Dominion* (Ottawa: King's Printer, 1924).

34 Only one-third of the $18 million of assets (one-quarter billion in 2015 dollars) were realizable. Robert MacIntosh, *Different Drummers, Banking and Politics in Canada* (Toronto: Macmillan Canada, 1991), 56–7.

35 23 and 24 June 1925 House of Commons and Senate debates.

36 This is in striking contrast to California, where, although inspection was reduced, the inspector still visited at least two branches every year.

37 Powell, *History of the Canadian Dollar*, 21.

38 In a footnote, Bryce cites a source that the departmental solicitor inserted the clause because of an understanding that the United Kingdom would be returning to the gold standard and this would help settlement of war debts.

39 Liaquat Ahamed, *Lords of Finance: The Bankers Who Broke the World* (New York: Penguin, 2009); Lowenstein, *America's Bank*.

40 Lowenstein, *America's Bank*.

41 Wilkins, *Maturing of Multinational Enterprise*.

42 Geoffrey Jones, *Multinationals and Global Capitalism: From the Nineteenth to the Twenty-First Century* (Oxford: Oxford University Press, 2005).

43 Cleveland and Huertas, *Citibank*.

44 Wilkins, *History of Foreign Investment in the United States*.

45 Ahamed, *Lords of Finance*.

46 Ibid.

47 Charles G. Dawes, *Dawes Plan*, 1924.

48 William C. McNeil, *American Money and the Weimer Republic: Economics and Politics on the Eve of the Great Depression* (New York: Columbia University Press, 1986); Adam Tooze, *The Deluge: The Great War, America, and the Remaking of the Global Order, 1916–1931* (New York: Viking, 2014).

49 Rick Watson and Jeremy Carter, *Asset Securitisation and Synthetic Structures: Innovations in the European Credit Market* (London: Euromoney Books, 2006).

50 Kobrak, *Banking on Global Markets*.

51 Cleveland and Huertas, *Citibank*.

52 Mira Wilkins, "Multinational Enterprise in Insurance: An Historical Overview," *Business History* 51, no. 3 (2009), 343.

53 Wilkins, *History of Foreign Investment in the United States to 1914*, 57, 270.

54 Christopher Kobrak, "USA: The International Attraction of the US Insurance Market." In *World Insurance: The Evolution of a Global Risk Network*, eds. Peter Borscheid and Niels V. Haueter, 274–310 (Oxford: Oxford University Press, 2012).

55 Wilkins, *History of Foreign Investment in the United States*; Kobrak, "USA: The International Attraction of the US Insurance Market."

56 Wilkins, *History of Foreign Investment in the United States*.

57 Kobrak, "USA: The International Attraction of the US Insurance Market."

58 Ibid.

59 John M. Barry, *The Great Influenza: The Epic Story of the Deadliest Plague in History* (New York: Viking, 2004); John Gudmundsen, *The Great Provider: The Dramatic Story of Life Insurance in America* (South Norwalk, CT: Industrial Production, 1959).

60 Kobrak, "USA: The International Attraction of the US Insurance Market."

61 Ibid.

62 Robert E. Wright and George D. Smith, *Mutually Beneficial: The Guardian and Life Insurance in America* (New York: New York University Press, 2004).

63 Ibid.

64 Kobrak, "USA: The International Attraction of the US Insurance Market."

65 R.D. Brock, "Insurance Regulation in the United States: A Regulator's Perspective," *Journal of Insurance Regulation* 8, no. 3 (1989): 277–89.

66 As discussed earlier, many states forbade insurance companies from issuing insurance for more than one type of risk, although the number of jurisdictions forbidding multi-line polices, such as fire and personal liability, was increasing.

67 Meier, *Political Economy of Regulation*.

68 Sun Life's fascinating performance is an unpublished story. The data found here are based largely on an interview with John Gardner, former president of the company.

69 *The Canada Year Book 1931: The Official Statistical Annual of the Resources, History, Institutions and Social and Economic Conditions of the Dominion* (Ottawa: King's Printer, 1931).

70 Neufeld, *Financial System of Canada*, 298.

71 The real bills doctrine asserts that the central bank should discount bills created only in connection with the sale of goods.

72 Peter Temin, "Transmission of the Great Depression," *Journal of Economic Perspectives* 7, no. 2 (1993): 87–102.

73 The effect of the tariff on the American economy was not great and may even have been positive, since the United States was not very dependent on trade, and some jobs may have been added by substituting domestic for foreign production. But the U.S. actions themselves stunted the economies of other countries and contributed to a round of tariff increases in other countries, whose impact was more important and widely perceived afterwards as devastating to the world economy. This contributed to a greater commitment to free trade after the First World War. For a more extensive discussion of the impact of tariffs, see Douglas A. Irwin, *Peddling Protectionism: Smoot-Hawley and the Great Depression* (Princeton: Princeton University Press, 2011).

74 Walton and Rockoff, *History of the American Economy*, 523–5.

75 Maddison Project, http://www.ggdc.net/maddison/maddison-project/home.htm.

76 Bernanke, *Federal Reserve and the Financial Crisis*, 17.

77 *The Canadian Annual Review of Public Affairs, 1935–1936* (Toronto: Canadian Review, 1937), 381, 382; Walton and Rockoff, *History of the American Economy*, 515; Bernanke, *Federal Reserve and the Financial Crisis*, 18–19.

78 Joe Martin, "Great Depression Hit One Country Hardest of All," Bloomberg (blog), 26 March 2013, https://www.bloomberg.com/view/articles/2013-03-26/great-depression-hit-one-country-hardest-of-all.

79 Sirois, *Royal Commission on Dominion-Provincial Relations*.

80 Bernanke, *Federal Reserve and the Financial Crisis*, 20; Walton and Rockoff, *History of the American Economy*, 522–38.

81 Walton and Rockoff, *History of the American Economy*, 534–59.

82 Ibid., 559.

83 Eugene N. White, "Banking and Finance in the Twentieth Century," in *Cambridge Economic History of the United States*, ed. Stanley L. Engerman and Robert E. Gallman (Cambridge: Cambridge University Press, 2000), 3:743–803.

84 "Facts & Figures: Interactive Viewer." *New York Stock Exchange Data*. http://www.nyxdata.com/nysedata/asp/factbook/viewer_edition.asp?mode=table&key=2169&category=4o.

85 Thomas K. McCraw, *Prophets of Regulation: Charles Francis Adams, Louis D. Brandeis, James M. Landis, Alfred E. Kahn* (Cambridge, MA: Belknap Press of Harvard University Press, 1984).

86 Miranti Jr, *Accountancy Comes of Age*.

87 McCraw, *Prophets of Regulation*.

88 Ibid.; Charles R. Geisst, *Wall Street: A History from Its Beginnings to the Fall of Enron* (Oxford: Oxford University Press, 2004); O'Sullivan, "Expansion of the U.S. Stock Market, 1885–1930."

89 Gregory P. Marchildon, "The Impact of the Great Depression on the Global Wheat Trade, Unpeaceable Exchange: Trade and Conflict in the Global Economy, 1000–2000." University of Lisbon, 16–17 July 2010.

90 Bennett's party won twenty-two seats in the Prairies. Previously Bennett had been the only Conservative on the Prairies, and increased the number of seats in rural Quebec from four to twenty-four. Judith McDonald, Anthony P. O'Brien, and Colleen M. Callahan, "Trade Wars: Canada's Reaction to the Smoot-Hawley Tariff," *Journal of Economic History* 57, no. 4 (1997): 802–26.

91 To complicate matters further, the assistant deputy minister was in the penitentiary.

92 Sirois, *Royal Commission on Dominion-Provincial Relations*, 160–2.

93 Perry, *Taxes, Tariffs, & Subsidies*, 2:292.

94 The greatest support for a central bank came from a group of left-wing farm and labour MPs who were called the "Ginger Group." The Ginger Group made the point that "many New York bankers refer to Canada as a 13th federal reserve district." Canada, *House of Commons Debates* (Hansard), 1932, 17th Parl., 2nd Sess., vol. 1, 1551, 3391; Canada, *House of Commons Debates* (Hansard), 1932, 17th Parl., 3rd Sess., vol. 3, 3391.

95 Lord Macmillan had chaired a similar commission in Great Britain. Sir Charles Addis was a former director of the Bank of England. George S. Watts, *The Bank of Canada: Origins and Early History* (Ottawa: Carleton University Press, 1993), 10. Three Canadians were appointed; Sir Thomas White, who had served as Canada's finance minister during the First World War; Beaudry Leman, general manager of the Banque Canadienne Nationale; and J.E. Brownlee, the United Farmers of Alberta premier. It was uncommon to have two Brits and no American commissioner. "It is unfortunate that no officer or competent person from a Federal Reserve Bank was on the Commission. Irrespective of the relative merits of the commercial banking systems of the United States and Canada, the experience of the Federal Reserve System is particularly apropos in Canada." C.A. Curtis, "The Canadian Macmillan Commission," *Economic Journal* 44, no. 173 (1934): 59.

96 "It is difficult to avoid the conclusion that the investigation was rather cursory." Watts, *Bank of Canada*, 10.

97 Two of the three Canadians dissented. Both were distinguished financial men who did not see how the bank could possibly achieve all that was expected of it and still be independent on monetary policy.

98 Prime Minister Bennett contended that world experience showed government ownership was bad, it was essential for the Bank to be free of government control, and profits would accrue to the people even under private ownership because of the way it was structured.

99 The original election was run by the Chamber of Commerce. Watts, *Bank of Canada*, 24.

100 Milton L. Stokes, *The Bank of Canada: The Development and Present Position of Central Banking in Canada* (Toronto: Macmillan, 1939), 23.

101 Watts, *Bank of Canaday*, 32.

102 Stokes, *Bank of Canada*, 253–69.

103 The collapse of the real estate market in New York hit Clark personally: he had purchased a home in Scarsdale, which then lost a great deal of its value. He was unable to pay off the mortgage and it was eventually foreclosed.

104 Robert A. Wardhaugh, *Behind the Scenes: The Life and Work of William Clifford Clark* (Toronto: University of Toronto Press, 2010).

105 H.P. Oberlander, and Arthur L. Fallick, *Housing a Nation: The Evolution of Canadian Housing Policy* (Vancouver: Centre for Human Settlements, University of British Columbia, for Canada Mortgage and Housing Corporation, 1992). Reformers were not impressed with this bill, which was described as "the most conservative housing legislation in the English-speaking world." David Hulchanski, "The 1935 Dominion Housing Act: Setting the Stage for a Permanent Federal Presence in Canada's Housing Sector" *Urban History Review* 15, no. 1 (1986): 20–1.

106 Darryl King, "Federal Policy and the Canadian Housing Market" (paper presented at Rotman School of Management, University of Toronto, 30 May 2014), 5–6.

107 Christopher Armstrong, *Blue Skies and Boiler Rooms: Buying and Selling Securities in Canada, 1870–1940* (Toronto: University of Toronto Press, 1997).

108 The first was in the period 1869–71, when Toronto doused an attempt to make the Bank of Montreal the national bank of Canada. The second was the shift of debt financing from Montreal to Toronto during the First World War.

109 In spite of the old saw that "when the United States economy catches cold, the Canadian one gets pneumonia," the Canadian economy grew that year, even though 1937/8 marked the year of the lowest grain yield on the Canadian Prairies. Marchildon, *Impact of the Great Depression on the Global Wheat Trade*.

110 Kobrak, "USA: The International Attraction of the US Insurance Market."

111 Wilkins, *History of Foreign Investment in the United States to 1914.*
112 Kobrak, "USA: The International Attraction of the US Insurance Market."
113 Michael Szalay, *New Deal Modernism: American Literature and the Invention of the Welfare State* (Durham, NC: Duke University Press, 2000), 1–23. The reference to "insurance for everything" comes from Wallace Stevens of the Hartford Fire and Indemnity Company.
114 Meier, *Political Economy of Regulation.*
115 Mark Roe, *Strong Managers, Weak Shareholders* (Princeton: Princeton University Press, 1992).
116 Only 2 per cent of California's commercial banks were suspended in 1933 when California represented nearly 6.5 per cent of all bank deposits of the Federal Reserve System. *Banking and Monetary Statistics, 1914–1941* (Washington, DC: Board of Governors of the Federal Reserve System, 1943).
117 Canadian financial companies are more illustrative of Chandlerian concepts of sophisticated management than are Canadian industrial companies, many of which are subsidiaries of American parents.
118 *The Canada Year Book 1938: The Official Statistical Annual of the Resources, History, Institutions and Social and Economic Conditions of the Dominion,* 920–21.
119 *Canada Year Book 1956: The Official Statistical Annual of the Resources, History, Institutions and Social and Economic Conditions of the Dominion* (Ottawa: Queen's Printer and Controller of Stationery, 1956).
120 Arnold Edinborough, *A History of Canadian Imperial Bank of Commerce,* vol. 4, *1931–1973* (Toronto: Canadian Imperial Bank of Commerce, 1995), 23, 25. This was true for all banks. The example of Noble Dagg, who joined the Solsgirth, Manitoba, branch of the Union Bank as a nineteen-year-old trainee in 1922 is illustrative. He made steady progress, even after the Union was acquired by the Royal. His peak earning year was 1930. In the next two years his compensation was cut 25 per cent before he decided to try his luck selling life insurance.
121 Ibid., 4:25–7; Denison, *Canada's First Bank.*
122 Joseph Schull and J. Douglas Gibson, *The Scotiabank Story: A History of the Bank of Nova Scotia, 1832–1982* (Toronto: Macmillan of Canada, 1982), 153.
123 Duncan McDowall, *Quick to the Frontier: Canada's Royal Bank* (Toronto: McClelland & Stewart, 1993), 252.
124 J.A. McLeod, "The Present Working of the Canadian Banking System," *Journal of the Canadian Bankers' Association,* 41 (1933–4): 33.
125 Prime Minister R.B. Bennett, minister of finance and receiver general, president of the Privy Council, secretary of state for external affairs in the House of Commons, 13 May 1931. Canada, *House of Commons Debates* (Hansard), 31 May 1931, 17th Parl., 2nd Sess., vol. 2.

126 Sun Life Assurance Company of Canada, Financial Post Corporation
     Service, 29 December 1945. Martin, "Opportunities in the Asia-Pacific
     Region for Canadian Life Insurance Companies."
127 The Hepburn administration in Ontario, the Duplessis administration in
     Quebec, and the Patullo administration in British Columbia.
128 McIvor, *Canadian Monetary, Banking and Fiscal Development*.
129 By December 1939 Canadian troops were in Great Britain, and by
     February 1940 the first squadron of the RCAF was also in Britain.
130 Perry, *Taxes, Tariffs, & Subsidies*, 2:341.
131 Ibid., 2:626.
132 McIvor, *Canadian Monetary, Banking and Fiscal Development*, 174.
133 Robert B. Bryce, *Canada and the Cost of World War II: The International
     Operations of Canada's Department of Finance, 1939–1947* (Montreal and
     Kingston: McGill-Queen's University Press, 2005), 41.
134 Toronto accounted for 95 per cent of the stocks traded on all Canadian
     exchanges and two-thirds of the value. G.R. Conway, *The Supply of, and
     Demand for Canadian Equities* (Toronto: Toronto Stock Exchange, 1970), 48.
135 *The Canada Year Book 1947: The Official Statistical Annual Resources, History,
     Institutions, and Social and Economic Conditions of the Dominion* (Ottawa:
     King's Printer, 1947).
136 Kobrak, "USA: The International Attraction of the US Insurance Market."
137 Wilkins, *History of Foreign Investment in the United States to 1914*.
138 Kobrak, "USA: The International Attraction of the US Insurance Market."
139 Ronald K. Shelp and Al Ehrbar, *Fallen Giant: The Amazing Story of Hank
     Greenberg and the History of AIG* (Hoboken, NJ: John Wiley & Sons, 2006).
140 Kobrak, "USA: The International Attraction of the US Insurance Market."
141 Lawrence Solomon, "Lawrence Solomon: Radical Republicans," *Financial
     Post*, 20 November 2015.

5 The Short Pax Americana: 1945–2000

1 World Trade Organization, "B. Trends in International Trade," https://
   www.wto.org/english/res_e/booksp_e/wtr13-2b_e.pdf.
2 Maddison Project, http://www.ggdc.net/maddison/maddison-project/
   home.htm.
3 Ibid.
4 From the end of the Korean War to 1971. Unemployment hovered between
   3 and 7 per cent; inflation from zero to 5 per cent. In the following twenty
   years, the ranges went from 6 to 11 per cent and 3 to 14 per cent. Walton and
   Rockoff, *History of the American Economy*, 642–3.

5 Benn Steil, *The Battle of Bretton Woods: John Maynard Keynes, Harry Dexter White, and the Making of the New World Order* (Princeton: Princeton University Press, 2013).

6 Essentially the system could work well if countries gave up one of three policies: permitting free flow of capital, using an independent fiscal policy to stimulate or deflate their economies, or maintaining a stable rate of exchange against other currencies.

7 Robert B. Bryce, *Maturing in Hard Times: Canada's Department of Finance through the Great Depression* (Montreal and Kingston: McGill-Queen's University Press, 1986); Bruce Muirhead, *Against the Odds: The Public Life and Times of Louis Rasminsky* (Toronto: University of Toronto Press, 1999).

8 Canada was in this regard a trailblazer in that it had a flexible exchange rate system in 1933–9, when most countries were still ostensibly fixing their rates, even though this meant that cross-border transfers were effectively blocked.

9 Lawrence Schembri, "Arbitrage in Foreign Policy in Canada: Lessons from the Past, Implications for the Future," in *Trends in Monetary Policy Issues*, ed. Albert V. Tavidze, 121–43 (New York: Nova Science Publishers, 2008).

10 Niall Ferguson, *High Financier: The Lives and Time of Siegmund Warburg* (London: Allen Lane, 2010), 170–1.

11 Schembri, "Arbitrage in Foreign Policy in Canada."

12 Barry Eichengreen, *Exorbitant Privilege: The Rise and Fall of the Dollar and the Future of the International Monetary System* (New York. Oxford University Press, 2011).

13 Walton and Rockoff, *History of the American Economy*, 597–8.

14 Bernanke, *The Federal Reserve and the Financial Crisis*, 34–5.

15 Ibid., 36–9.

16 Wilkins, *Maturing of Multinational Enterprise*, 311, 346–7.

17 Ibid., 330–1.

18 Janice M. Traflet, *A Nation of Small Shareholders* (Baltimore, MD: Johns Hopkins University Press, 2013).

19 Ibid., 172.

20 Richard Sylla, "United States Bank and Europe: Strategy and Attitudes," in *European Banks and the American Challenge: Competition and Cooperation in International Banking under Bretton Woods*, ed. Stefano Battilossi and Youssef Cassis, 53–73 (Oxford: Oxford University Press, 2002).

21 Catherine R. Schenk, "The Origins of the Eurodollar Market in London 1955–1963," *Explorations in Economic History* 2, no. 1 (1998): 221–38.

22 Harold James, "Central Banks and the Process of Financial Internationalization: A Secular View," in *European Banks and the American*

Challenge: Competition and Cooperation in International Banking under Bretton Woods, ed. Stefano Battilossi and Youssef Cassis, 200–18 (Oxford: Oxford University Press, 2002).

23 Battilossi, "Introduction."

24 Cassis, *Capitals of Capital*.

25 Jane E. Hughes and Scott B. MacDonald, *International Banking: Text and Cases* (Boston: Addison Wesley, 2002).

26 Battilossi, "Introduction: International Banking and the American Challenge in Historical Perspective."

27 Shelagh Heffernan, *Making Banking in Theory and Practice* (New York: Wiley, 1996).

28 Cleveland and Huertas, *Citibank*, 253–4.

29 When the bank was established in 1953 it was understood that it would specialize in financing foreign trade and would not be a significant factor in domestic banking. John Fayerweather, *The Mercantile Bank Affair: A Case Study of Canadian Nationalism and a Multinational Firm* (New York: New York University Press, 1974).

30 Stephen Azzi, *Walter Gordon and the Rise of Canadian Nationalism* (Montreal and Kingston: McGill-Queen's University Press, 1999).

31 Muirhead, *Against the Odds*.

32 Charles Freedman, *The Canadian Banking System* (Ottawa: Bank of Canada, 1998).

33 MacIntosh, *Different Drummers*; Cleveland and Huertas, *Citibank*.

34 Cleveland and Huertas, *Citibank*, 258–9.

35 *Crédit Lyonnais Annual Report*, 1973.

36 Kevin Ross, *Market Predictability of ECB Monetary Policy Decisions: A Comparative Examination* (Washington, DC: International Monetary Fund, European Department, 2002).

37 Heffernan, *Making Banking in Theory and Practice*.

38 Sylla, "Reversing Financial Reversals." It may seem paradoxical to the reader, but despite the recent financial crisis, confidence in the dynamism and efficiency of the American banking system remains relatively high. The actions of the U.S. federal government combined with the resilience of many banks have contributed to high demand for U.S. government and private securities, prima facie evidence that American markets are still seen as safe havens for investors.

39 Dean Kloner, "The Commodity Futures Modernization Act of 2000," *Securities Regulation Law Journal* 29, no. 1 (2001): 286–97.

40 Roe, *Strong Managers, Weak Shareholders*.

41 CIO from IDG, http://www.cio.com/.

42 Royal Bank of Canada, *2000 Annual Report: People to People Building Relationships in the New Economy*, http://www.rbc.com/investorrelations/pdf/ar_2000_e.pdf.

43 Harry Markowitz, "Portfolio Selection," *Journal of Finance* 7, no. 1 (1952): 77–91.

44 William F. Sharpe, "Capital Asset Prices: A Theory of Market Equilibrium under Conditions of Risk," *The Journal of Finance* 19, no. 3 (1964): 425–42; John Lintner, "The Valuation of Risk Assets and the Selection of Risky Investments in Stock Portfolios and Capital Budgets," *Review of Economics and Statistics* 47, no. 1 (1965): 222–4.

45 Eugene F. Fama, "Efficient Capital Markets: A Review of Theory and Empirical Work," *Journal of Finance* 25, no. 2 (1970): 383–417.

46 Fischer Black and Myron Scholes, "The Pricing of Options and Corporate Liabilities," *Journal of Political Economy* 81, no. 3 (1973): 637–54; Robert C. Merton, "Theory of Rational Option Pricing," *Bell Journal of Economics and Management Science* 4, no. 1 (1973): 141–83; J.C. Hull, *Futures, Options and Other Derivative Securities* (Englewood Cliffs, NJ: Prentice Hall, 1997).

47 Ismail Erturk, Julie Froud, Sukhev Johal, Adam Leaver, and Karel Williams, *Financialization at Work* (London: Routledge, 2008).

48 Raghuram G. Rajan and Luigi Zingales, "The Great Reversals: The Politics of Financial Development in the Twentieth Century," *Journal of Financial Economics* 69, no. 1 (2003): 5–50.

49 Niall Ferguson, *The Ascent of Money: A Financial History of the World* (New York: Penguin, 2008).

50 G.O. Bierwag and George G. Kaufman, "Duration Gap for Financial Institutions," *Financial Analysts* 41, no. 2 (1985): 68–71.

51 Erturk et al., *Financialization at Work*.

52 Ibid.

53 Christopher Kobrak and Michael Troege, "From Basel to Bailouts: Forty Years of International Attempts to Bolster Bank Safety," *Financial History Review* 22, no. 2 (2015): 133–56.

54 Ibid.

55 A royal commission was used only one other time in Canadian history as the vehicle to conduct the decennial review. That was the Macmillan Royal Commission in the Great Depression. The Porter Royal Commission provided a much more thorough analysis of the Canadian banking system than did the Macmillan Commission.

56 Katherine Macklem, "RBC Yesterday, Today, and Tomorrow." In *Relentless Change: A Casebook for the Study of Canadian Business History*, ed. Joe Martin, 000–303–18 (Toronto: University of Toronto Press, 2010).

57 Joe Martin, ed., *Relentless Change: A Casebook for the Study of Canadian Business History* (Toronto: University of Toronto Press, 2010).

58 Statistics Canada, "Table 378-0121 National Balance Sheet Accounts," http://www5.statcan.gc.ca/cansim/a26?lang=eng&id=3780121.

59 Claudio Verbeeten and David Eggert, "Canada's Big Banks at Home and Abroad in the New Millennium" (Research Paper, Rotman School of Management, 2014), 20–1.

60 McDowall, *Quick to the Frontier*, 334.

61 David A. Dodge, *Bank of Canada Annual Report: 2001* (Ottawa: Bank of Canada, 2002).

62 While there were comparable reviews in the United States and United Kingdom, there were Canadian-specific reasons for the appointment, i.e., the contretemps between the government and former governor Coyne. The American commissions (both private and public) called for more gradual changes than did Porter. Francis H. Schott, "The Report of the Canadian Royal Commission on Banking and Finance: A Review," *Federal Reserve Bank of New York* 46, no. 8 (1964): 156.

63 "The essential feature of banking regulation must be good and thorough supervision and inspections such as that which now takes place within the framework of the Bank Act.... It is essential to make this supervision as flexible and free of rigid rules and regulations as possible in order to avoid inducing an unnecessarily conservative approach by our financial institutions in the conduct of their business." Dana H. Porter, *Report of the Royal Commission on Banking and Finance* (Ottawa: Queen's Printer, 1964), 380.

64 It is also interesting to note that in a 1964 Dominion Securities research report, research analyst Tony Fell predicted that the changes produced by the Porter Commission "should enable the banks to achieve a significantly higher average rate of return on their loan portfolio." Anthony S. Fell, *The Canadian Chartered Banks: A Dominion Securities Corporation Limited Research Report* (Toronto: Dominion Securities Corporation, 1964), 1. While the Porter Commission did not recommend deposit insurance, the government introduced it the same year that it introduced the Porter Commission recommendations. MacIntosh, *Different Drummers*.

65 Andreas Busch, *Banking Regulation and Globalization* (Oxford: Oxford University Press, 2009).

66 James L. Darroch, *Canadian Banks and Global Competitiveness* (Montreal and Kingston: McGill-Queen's University Press, 1994), 261.

67 Regulation of life insurance companies was divided between the two levels of government.

68 Six months earlier the FRB allowed commercial banks to make a forays into underwriting.

69 The venerable Wood Gundy, the principal investment dealer for most of the twentieth century, was hurt the most, as it had many bought deals on its balance sheet. The BP privatization, which Gundy led in Canada, was the end for Wood Gundy. Wood Gundy had negotiated a sale of a minority position to First Chicago, but that deal fell through. Gundy had to be rescued by Brascan and was finally acquired for a minimal amount by CIBC. BMO acquired Nesbitt Burns, BNS acquired McLeod, Young, Weir; RBC acquired Dominion Securities; and National Bank acquired Levesque Beubien. Gordon F. Boreham, "Three Years after Canada's 'Little Bang,'" *Canadian Banker* 97, no. 5 (1990): 6–15.

70 Henry N.R. Jackman, ed., *The Letters and Diaries of Henry Rutherford Jackman*, vol. 15 (Toronto: Harmony Printing, 2013).

71 Freedman, *Canadian Banking System*.

72 The deal had been concluded just before Christmas 1997 in what became known as the "egg nog agreement" between the two CEOs.

73 Macklem, "RBC Yesterday, Today, and Tomorrow."

74 See note 73.

75 It is not clear that Finance Minister Martin, a future prime minister, opposed the mergers. However, Jean Chrétien, a former TD director and prime minister in the late 1990s, did object.

76 Eric Reguly, "Mergers Will Resurface: Bank Chairman," *Globe and Mail*, 4 December 1999.

77 Only one of the world's five largest banks, Bank of America, was also one of the top five in shareholder returns. Macklem, "RBC Yesterday, Today, and Tomorrow."

78 Neufeld, *Financial System of Canada*.

79 Francois Moreau, *Le Développement International des Banques Canadiennes: Croissance, Expansion and Concentration* (Montreal: Editions Saint-Martin, 1985), 89, 97.

80 Verbeeten and David Eggert, "Canada's Big Banks at Home and Abroad in the New Millennium."

81 Ibid.

82 In 1980, with government encouragement and assistance, HSBC (formerly the Hong Kong and Shanghai Banking Corporation) acquired the Bank of British Columbia.

83 The Financial Post 500, 2001.

84 Office of the Superintendent of Financial Institutions, "Guide to Foreign Bank Branching," 2002, http://www.osfi-bsif.gc.ca/eng/fi-if/app/aag-gad/pages/fbbguide.aspx.

85 Christine Hinchley. "Foreign Banks in the Canadian Market," Statistics Canada, 2009, http://www.statcan.gc.ca/pub/11-621-m/11-621-m2006041-eng.htm.

86 Stijn Claessens and Neeltje van Horen, "Foreign Banks: Trends, Impact and Financial Stability" (research paper, IMF, January 2012).

87 Donald Kerr and Deryck Holdsworth, *Historical Atlas of Canada*, vol. 3, *Addressing the Twentieth Century, 1891–1961* (Toronto: University of Toronto Press, 1990).

88 Black, *Rise to Greatness*, 867.

89 Charles P. Kindleberger, *Economic Response: Comparative Studies in Trade, Finance, and Growth* (Cambridge, MA: Harvard University Press, 1978), 109.

90 Within francophone Quebec, the void left by the anglo banks was filled. Their place would be taken by French-Canadian banks, caisses populaires (credit unions), and pension plans.

91 One sees this elsewhere, with Milan in Italy, Zurich in Switzerland, Mumbai in India, and Shanghai in China, each serving as a financial centre in its country, while the political capital is elsewhere.

92 Neufeld, *Financial System of Canada*, 383.

93 Department of Finance, "Information Canada's Financial Services Sector: Property and Casualty Insurance in Canada," 2003, http://www.fin.gc.ca/activty/factsheets/property_e.pdf.

94 World Council, "2012 Global Credit Union *Statistical Report* Now Available," news release, 12 July 2013, http://www.woccu.org/newsroom/releases/2012_Global_Credit_Union_iStatistical_Report_i_Now_Available.

95 Meir Kohn, *Financial Institutions and Markets* (New York: McGraw-Hill, 1994).

96 Individual stock market participation fell to 54 per cent, with the rest coming from life insurance companies and trusts, which were also profiting from greater sense of private funding as a protection against risk.

97 Kohn, *Financial Institutions and Markets*.

98 Ibid.

99 Martin N. Neil and Jacob F. Kirkegaard, *US Pension Reform: Lessons from Other Countries* (Washington, DC: Peterson Institute for International Economics, 2009).

100 Kohn, *Financial Institutions and Markets*.

101 Erturk et al., *Financialization at Work.*
102 *Investment trusts* is an older, general term for pooled investments and often used in the United Kingdom. Closed-end funds are the original type of U.S. mutual funds. There are a fixed number of shares, which are bought and sold on exchanges and heavily regulated by the SEC. Open-end funds are more prevailing. The funds are obligated to buy back shares at their net asset value. All funds may have different investment strategies and charge management fees. The advantage to shareholders is access to diversity and expert management. Even hedge funds might be viewed as mutual funds, but they are aimed at high-end investors with a large appetite for risk, despite their names.
103 White, "Banking and Finance in the Twentieth Century."
104 Neufeld, *Financial System of Canada*, 442.
105 Ibid., 444.
106 "Maple Revolutionaries," *Economist*, 3 March 2012, http://www.economist.com/node/21548970.
107 Bruce Little, *Fixing the Future: How Canada's Usually Fractious Governments Worked Together to Rescue the Canada Pension Plan* (Toronto: Rotman – University of Toronto Publishing, 2008).
108 The CIO of CALPERS did not think this would be politically feasible in the United States.
109 Neufeld, *Financial System of Canada*, 359.
110 Ibid., 361.
111 Porter, *Report of the Royal Commission on Banking and Finance*, 303.
112 Investors Group, 31 per cent; United Funds, 14 per cent; AGF, 10 per cent; Canadian Funds Management, 8 per cent; Calvin Bullock, 5 per cent; Capital Management, 5 per cent; Mutual Funds Management, 4 per cent; Canadian Security Management, 2 per cent; total, 79 per cent. Neufeld, *Financial System of Canada*, 377.
113 In 1956/7 Investors sold the Canadian subsidiary to a group of Canadian investors.
114 Statistics Canada, "Table 378-0121 National Balance Sheet Accounts."
115 AIM Funds Management, Mackenzie Financial, AGF Funds, and CI Mutual Funds.
116 Fidelity Investments, Franklin Templeton.
117 Financial Post, 500, 2001.
118 Price Fishback, Jonathan Rose, and Kenneth Snowden, *Well Worth Saving: How the New Deal Safeguarded Home Ownership* (Chicago: University of Chicago Press, 2013).
119 Ibid.

120 Samuel E. Morrison, Henry S. Commager, and William E. Leuchtenburg, *The Growth of the American Republic*, vol. 1 (Oxford: Oxford University Press, 1980).
121 Fishback, Rose, and Snowden, *Well Worth Saving*.
122 Bernanke, *The Federal Reserve and the Financial Crisis*, 42–7.
123 Ibid., 54–76.
124 Canada Mortgage and Housing Corporation and U.S. Census Bureau.
125 Wardhaugh, *Behind the Scenes*, 110.
126 Oberlander and Fallick, *Housing a Nation*.
127 Humphrey Carver, *Houses for Canadians: A Study of Housing Problems in the Toronto Area* (Toronto: University of Toronto Press, 1948), 107–8.
128 Oberlander and Fallick, *Housing a Nation*, 33.
129 Lawrence B. Smith, "Canadian Housing Policies in the Seventies," *Land Economics* 57, no. 3 (1981): 338–52.
130 MacIntosh, *Different Drummers, Banking and Politics in Canada*.
131 *Globe and Mail*, "Wants High-Rises, Board Told Builder Allowing House to Deteriorate, Homeowners Say," 25 April 1968.
132 Smith, "Canadian Housing Policies in the Seventies."
133 Virginie Traclet, "An Overview of the Canadian Housing Finance System," *Housing Finance International* 25, no. 1 (2010): 6.
134 Kristopher Gerardi, Harvey S. Rosen, and Paul Willen, *Do Households Benefit from Financial Deregulation and Innovation? The Case of the Mortgage Market* (Cambridge: National Bureau of Economic Research, 2007).
135 Scott Reynolds Nelson, *A Nation of Deadbeats: An Uncommon History of America's Financial Disasters* (New York: Vintage Books, 2012), 217.
136 Louis Hyman, *Debtor Nation: The History of American Red Ink* (Princeton: Princeton University Press, 2011).
137 Raghuram G. Rajan, *Fault Lines: How Hidden Fractures Still Threaten the World Economy* (Princeton: Princeton University Press, 2010).
138 Erturk et al., *Financialization at Work*.
139 Christopher Kobrak, "USA: The International Attraction of the US Insurance Market."
140 Ibid.
141 Wilkins, *Maturing of Multinational Enterprise*.
142 Kobrak, "USA: The International Attraction of the US Insurance Market."
143 Wilkins, "History of the Multinational Enterprise."
144 Kobrak, "USA: The International Attraction of the US Insurance Market."
145 Ibid.
146 Ibid.
147 McKenna, *World's Newest Profession*; Miranti Jr, "Associationism, Statism, and Professionalization Regulation."

148 J.A. Yates, *Structuring the Information Age: Life Insurance and Technology in the Twentieth Century* (Baltimore: Johns Hopkins University Press, 2005).

149 Peter Bernstein, *Against the Gods: The Remarkable Story of Risk* (New York: John Wiley & Sons, 1996).

150 Kobrak, "USA: The International Attraction of the US Insurance Market."

151 Ibid.

152 Ibid.

153 Robert J. Shiller, *The New Financial Order: Risk in the 21st Century* (Princeton: Princeton University Press, 2003); Tom Baker and Jonathan Simon, eds., *Embracing Risk: The Changing Culture of Insurance and Responsibility* (Chicago: University of Chicago Press, 2002).

154 Kohn, *Financial Institutions and Markets.*

155 Kobrak, "USA: The International Attraction of the US Insurance Market."

156 Ibid.

157 Ibid.

158 Jeffrey Norman, *The Path of the Sun: An Informal History of Sun Life Assurance Company of Canada* (Toronto: Arthur Jones, 1996).

159 Neufeld, *Financial System of Canada.*

160 Martin, "Opportunities in the Asia-Pacific Region."

161 Office of the Superintendent of Financial Institutions. "About Us." 2016. http://www.osfi-bsif.gc.ca/eng/osfi-bsif/pages/hst.aspx.

162 Martin, "Opportunities in the Asia-Pacific Region."

163 Financial Post, 500, 2001.

164 Although not in the top seven, three foreign-owned companies – Scottish-based Standard Life, which claimed to be the oldest insurer in Canada, and two US-based firms, mutually owned Metropolitan and investor-owned Prudential, joined the ranks of major Canadian Life Insurance companies.

165 In 2004 Manufacturer's acquired John Hancock of Boston in the largest cross border transaction in Canadian history, which made Manufacturers the second largest insurer in North America and fifth in the world.

166 Financial Post Corporation Service cards.

167 Before the Second World War Sun Life was the largest foreign insurer in Japan. After the war, Sun Life decided not to return there.

168 Department of Finance, "Information Canada's Financial Services Sector."

169 The Independent Order of Foresters (IOF) began in Britain but came to North America in the late nineteenth century, originally to the United States and then to Canada. One of its longest serving supreme chief rangers was Oronhyatekha, a member of the Mohawk tribe.

170 Geisst, *Wall Street*.

171 Robert E. Wright, *The First Wall Street: Chestnut Street, Philadelphia, & the Birth of American Finance* (Chicago: University of Chicago Press, 2005).

172 Geisst, *Wall Street*.

173 Ibid.

174 The end of Bretton Woods saw back-to-back years of decline of the Dow Jones Average, followed by two more in 1977/8.

175 Geisst, *Wall Street*.

176 Ibid.

177 Ibid.

178 Ibid.

179 Merton H. Miller and Franco Modigliani, "Dividend Policy, Growth, and the Valuation of Shares," *Journal of Business* 34, no. 4 (1961): 411–33.

180 Patrick A. Gaughan, *Mergers, Acquisitions, and Corporate Restructuring*, 2nd ed. (New York: John Wiley, 1999).

181 Kohn, *Financial Institutions and Markets*.

182 Geisst, *Wall Street*.

183 Richard A. Brealey and Stewart C. Myers, *Principles of Corporate Finance*, 6th ed. (Boston: Irwin McGraw-Hill, 2000).

184 Geisst, *Wall Street*.

185 Ibid.; Richard Sylla, personal interview, 2007.

186 Christopher Armstrong, *Moose Pastures and Mergers: The Ontario Securities Commission and the Regulation of Share Markets in Canada, 1940–1980* (Toronto: University of Toronto Press, 2001).

187 Ibid.

188 Ibid.

189 Wilkins, *History of Foreign Investment in the United States*.

190 Armstrong, *Moose Pastures and Mergers*.

191 Ibid.

192 Ibid.

193 Elvis Picardo, "History of the Toronto Stock Exchange," Investopedia, http://www.investopedia.com/articles/stocks/08/history-of-toronto-stock-exchange.asp.

194 http://www.tmx.com/en/pdf/TMXHistory.pdf, Aug. 9, 2013.

195 Amy Young, "The Creation of TMX Group: Dramatic Change on the Canadian Stock Exchange Scene – 1999 to 2008." Case study, Rotman – University of Toronto, 2014.

196 The most egregious example in Canada was Bre-X, a Calgary-based mining company that was involved in a gold mining scandal in Indonesia in 1997, one of the biggest stock scandals in Canadian history.

6 Conclusion: Continuities and Discontinuities in North American Finance Leading to 2008

1 Fukuyama, *The End of History*.
2 The political and economic characteristics of the period were by no means uniform in their nature or impact. Rising oil prices were good for Canada, but not for most other OECD countries, and the United States actually made travel and trade between America and Canada more difficult after 9/11.
3 Jacob Soll, *The Reckoning: Financial Accountability and the Rise and Fall of Nations* (New York: Basic Books, 2014).
4 Organization for Economic Co-operation and Development, "Social Expenditure: Aggregated Data," http://stats.oecd.org/Index. aspx?datasetcode=SOCX_AGG.
5 Department of Finance Canada, "Archived – Fiscal Reference Tables – 2013: Part 10 of 10," 2013, http://www.fin.gc.ca/frt-trf/2013/frt-trf-1309-eng.asp.
6 White, "Banking and Finance in the Twentieth Century."
7 Alan Greenspan, *The Age of Turbulence: Adventures in a New World* (New York: Penguin, 2007).
8 Robert E. Wright and Richard Sylla, *Genealogy of American Finance* (New York: Columbia University Business School, 2015); White, "Banking and Finance in the Twentieth Century."
9 Greenspan, *Age of Turbulence*.
10 MacIntosh, *Different Drummers*.
11 Ibid.
12 Ibid.
13 It was misguided because it penalized producers but not consumers.
14 Maddison Project.
15 The most egregious example was Dome Petroleum, whose CEO boasted of having a larger navy than the government of Canada, which had $6.6 billion of debt spread among Canadian, American, European, and Japanese banks before being taken over by Amoco.
16 Mercantile Bank, the Bank of British Columbia, and the Continental Bank were the seventh-, ninth-, and tenth-largest Canadian banks. Martin, *Relentless Change*.
17 Former Canadian deputy minister of finance Stanley Hartt, personal interview, 2 November 2016.
18 MacIntosh, *Different Drummers*.
19 Now part of Ernst & Young.

20 MacIntosh, *Different Drummers*.
21 This process was completed by Bank Act amendments in 1992 that permitted banks, insurance companies, and trust companies to buy each other. Since banks were the largest institutions, they became dominant in the resulting consolidation.
22 Soll, *Reckoning*.
23 Ibid.
24 Ben S. Bernanke, *The Courage to Act* (New York: Norton, 2015).
25 Rajan, *Fault Lines*.
26 Christopher Kobrak and Mira Wilkins, "The '2008 Crisis' in an Economic History Perspective," *Business History* 53, no. 2 (2011): 175–92.
27 Etienne Bordeleau and Walter Engert, "Procylicality and Compensation," in *Financial System Review*, 45–50 (Ottawa: Bank of Canada, 2009).
28 In January 2008 the IMF judged Canada's financial system to be mature, sophisticated, and well managed and their stress tests showed that the major banks could withstand sizable shocks, which proved accurate. Jamie Caruana and Anoop Singh, *Canada: International System Stability Assessment – Update* (Washington, DC: International Monetary Fund, 2008).
29 Laurence Booth, "Structured Finance; Subprime, Market Meltdown and Learning from the Past," in *The Finance Crisis and Rescue: What Went Wrong? Why? What Lessons Can Be Learned? Expert Views from the Rotman School of Management*, ed. Roger Martin, 33–52 (Toronto: University of Toronto Press, 2008).
30 Tony Fell, "Remarks at Toronto Board of Trade Annual Dinner," Board of Trade, Toronto, 26 January 2009).
31 Donald J.S. Brean, Lawrence Kryzanowski, and Gordon S. Roberts, "Canada and the United States: Different Roots, Different Routes to Financial Sector Regulation," *Business History* 53, no. 2 (2011): 249–69; Calomiris and Haber, *Fragile by Design*; Michael D. Bordo, Angela A. Redish, and Hugh Rockoff, "Why Didn't Canada Have a Banking Crisis in 2008 (or in 1930, or 1907, or 1893)?" *Economic History Review* 68, no. 1 (2015): 218–43.
32 The Home Bank, the biggest failure up to that date.
33 ABN, AMBRO, Barclay's Capital, Deutsche Bank, Merrill Lynch, and UBS.
34 The committee looked at both J.P. Morgan and Lehman Brothers and fortunately chose Morgan.
35 Christopher Reid, "Credit Default Swaps and the Canadian Context," in *Financial System Review* (Ottawa: Bank of Canada, 2004), 51.
36 Quebec, National Assembly, Standing Committee on Public Finance, *Journal des debats (Hansard)*, 1st sess., 38th Legislature, meeting no. 20, 2007,

http://www.assnat.qc.ca/en/travaux-parlementaires/commissions/
cfp-38-1/journal-debats/CFP-071128.html.

37 "It was a private sector problem that needed a private sector solution."
Paul Halpern, *Back From the Brink* (Toronto: University of Toronto Press,
2016), 202.

38 Eric Reguly, "Germany Moves Fast to Help Ease ECB Tension," *Globe and
Mail*, 12 September 2011.

39 Kobrak and Troege, "From Basel to Bailouts"; Bernanke, *Courage to Act*.

40 The Banker, July 2005. Shortly before the 2008 Financial Crisis, American
and British banks were ranked high in terms of Tier One Capital, the
preferred Basel I measurement for determining bank safety. Within a few
years, several of these banks were in receivership or required state aid to
avoid collapse. Although no Canadian bank was among the top thirty,
Canadian banks fared very well during the crisis.

41 Christopher Kobrak and Donald Brean, "Financial Crises and Global
Financial Regulations," in *Risk and EU Law*, ed. Hans-Wolfgang Micklitz
and Takis Tridimas, 220–48 (Cheltenham, UK: Edward Elgar, 2015).

42 For example, the reason the government did not buy Lehman Brothers
bonds was because no one could figure out who legally owned the bonds.
David Dayen, *Chain of Title: How Three Ordinary Americans Uncovered Wall
Street's Great Foreclosure Fraud* (New York: New Press, 2016).

43 Bernanke, *Courage to Act*.

44 Kobrak and Brean, "Financial Crises and Global Financial Regulations."

45 There were some American exceptions. The California system was not
dissimilar to the Canadian system.

Bibliography

Ackrill, Margaret, and Leslie Hannah. *Barclays: The Business of Banking, 1690–1996*. Cambridge: Cambridge University Press, 2001.

Aggarwal, Reena. "Demutualization and Corporate Governance of Stock Exchanges." *Journal of Applied Corporate Finance* 15, no. 1 (2002): 105–13.

Ahamed, Liaquat. *Lords of Finance: The Bankers Who Broke the World*. New York: Penguin, 2009.

Aizenstat, Janet, Ian Gentles, and Paul Romney. *Canada's Founding Debates*. Toronto: Stoddart Publishing, 1999.

Alain, Robert. "Sir Thomas White and Canadian Wartime Financial Policy." Master's thesis, Queen's University, 1975.

Anastakis, Dimitry. *Autonomous State: The Struggle for a Canadian Car Industry from OPEC to Free Trade*. Toronto: University of Toronto Press, 2013.

Armstrong, Christopher. *Blue Skies and Boiler Rooms: Buying and Selling Securities in Canada, 1870–1940*. Toronto: University of Toronto Press, 1997.

– *Moose Pastures and Mergers: The Ontario Securities Commission and the Regulation of Share Markets in Canada, 1940–1980*. Toronto: University of Toronto Press, 2001.

Armstrong, Christopher, and H.V. Nelles. *Southern Exposure: Canadian Promoters in Latin America and the Caribbean, 1896–1930*. Toronto: University of Toronto Press, 1988.

Armstrong, Frederick H., and Ronald J. Stagg. "Mackenzie, William Lyon." *Dictionary of Canadian Biography*, vol. 9, 1976. http://www.biographi.ca/en/bio/mackenzie_william_lyon_9E.html.

Ascah, Robert L. *Politics and Public Debt, the Dominion, the Banks and Alberta's Social Credit*. Edmonton: University of Alberta Press, 1999.

Azzi, Stephen. *Walter Gordon and the Rise of Canadian Nationalism*. Montreal and Kingston: McGill-Queen's University Press, 1999.

Baker, Tom, and Jonathan Simon, eds. *Embracing Risk: The Changing Culture of Insurance and Responsibility*. Chicago: University of Chicago Press, 2002.

Bank of Canada. "The Bank's History." http://www.bankofcanada.ca/about/history/.

Baring Archive. "Baring Timeline." http://www.baringarchive.org.uk/history/timeline/.

Barry, John M. *The Great Influenza: The Epic Story of the Deadliest Plague in History*. New York: Viking, 2004.

Baskerville, Peter. *The Bank of Upper Canada*. Ottawa: Carleton University Press, 1987.

Bates, Stewart. *Financial History of Canadian Governments: A Study Prepared for the Royal Commission on Dominion-Provincial Relations*. Ottawa: J.O. Patenaude, ISO, Printer to the King's Most Excellent Majesty, 1939.

Battilossi, Stefano. "Introduction: International Banking and the American Challenge in Historical Perspective." In *European Banks and the American Challenge: Competition and Cooperation in International Banking under Bretton Woods*, ed. Stefano Battilossi and Youssef Cassis, 1–35. Oxford: Oxford University Press, 2002.

Beard, Charles A. *An Economic Interpretation of the Constitution of the United States*. New York: Free Press, 1986.

– *The Rise of American Civilization*. New York: MacMillan, 1937.

Beckert, Sven. *Empire of Cotton: A Global History*. New York: Knopf, 2014.

– *The Monied Metropolis: New York City and the Consolidation of the American Bourgeoisie, 1850–1896*. Cambridge: Cambridge University Press, 2001.

Bender, Thomas. *A Nation among Nations: America's Place in World History*. New York: Hill and Wang, 2006.

Bennett, Richard E. *History of the Great-West Life Assurance Company*. Winnipeg: Great-West Life Assurance Company, 1992.

Berghahan, Volker R. *American Big Business in Britain and Germany: A Comparative History of Two "Special Relationships" in the 20th Century*. Princeton: Princeton University Press, 2014.

– *Industriegesellschaft und Kulturtransfer: Die deutsch-amerikanischen Beziehungen im 20. Jahrhundert*. Göttingen: Vandenhoeck & Ruprecht, 2010.

Berle, Adolf A., and Gardiner C. Means. *The Modern Corporation and Private Property*. New York: Harcourt, Brace & World, 1932.

Bernanke, Ben S. *The Courage to Act*. New York: Norton, 2015.

– *The Federal Reserve and the Financial Crisis*. Princeton: Princeton University Press, 2013.

Bernstein, Peter. *Against the Gods: The Remarkable Story of Risk*. New York: John Wiley & Sons, 1996.

Berton, Pierre. *The Great Depression: 1929–1939*. Toronto: McClelland and Stewart, 1990.

– *The Last Spike: The Great Railway 1881–1885*. Toronto: McClelland and Stewart, 1971.

Best, Alfred M. "*Best's Review* Speech Given to the Association of Insurance Agents." Association of Insurance Agents, Cleveland, OH, 18 September 1918.

Bierwag, G.O., and George G. Kaufman. "Duration Gap for Financial Institutions." *Financial Analysts* 41, no. 2 (1985): 68–71.

Black, Conrad. *Flight of the Eagle: A Strategic History of the United States*. Toronto: McClelland & Stewart, 2013.

– *Rise to Greatness: The History of Canada from the Vikings to the Present*. Toronto: McClelland & Stewart, 2014.

Black, John. *A Dictionary of Economics*. 2nd ed. Oxford: Oxford University Press, 2002.

Black, Fischer, and Myron Scholes. "The Pricing of Options and Corporate Liabilities." *Journal of Political Economy* 81, no. 3 (1973): 637–54.

Blinder, Alan S. *After the Music Stopped: The Financial Crisis, the Response, and the Work Ahead*. New York: Penguin, 2013.

Bliss, Michael. *Northern Enterprise: Five Centuries of Canadian Business*. Toronto: McClelland & Stewart, 1987.

"Cox, George Albertus." *Dictionary of Canadian Biography*, Vol 14. http://www.biographi.ca/en/bio/cox_george_albertus_14E.html.

Bodenhorn, Howard. *A History of Banking in Antebellum America: Financial Markets and Economic Development in an Era of Nation Building*. Cambridge: Cambridge University Press, 2000.

– *State Banking in Early America: A New Economic History*. Oxford: Oxford University Press, 2003.

Bonenfant, J.-C. "Cartier, Sir George-Étienne." *Dictionary of Canadian Biography*, vol. 10. 1972. http://www.biographi.ca/en/bio/cartier_george_etienne_10E.html.

Booth, Laurence. "Structured Finance: Subprime, Market Meltdown and Learning from the Past." In *The Finance Crisis and Rescue: What Went Wrong? Why? What Lessons Can Be Learned? Expert Views from the Rotman School of Management*, ed. Roger Martin, 33–52. Toronto: University of Toronto Press, 2008.

Booth, Laurence, and Sean Cleary. *Introduction to Corporate Finance: Managing Canadian Firms in a Global Environment*. Toronto: Wiley, 2008.

Booth, Laurence D. "The Secret of Canadian Banking: Common Sense?" *World Economics* 10 (2009): 1–16.

Bordeleau, Etienne, and Walter Engert. "Procylicality and Compensation." In *Financial System Review*, 45–50. Ottawa: Bank of Canada, 2009.

Borden, Henry, ed. *Robert Laird Borden: His Memoirs*. Vols 1 and 2. Toronto: Macmillan Company of Canada, 1938.

Bordo, Michael D., and Angela A. Redish. "Why Did the Bank of Canada Emerge in 1935?" *Journal of Economic History* 47 (1987): 405–17.

Bordo, Michael D., Angela A. Redish, and Hugh Rockoff. "Why Didn't Canada Have a Banking Crisis in 2008 (or in 1930, or 1907, or 1893)?" *Economic History Review* 68, no. 1 (2015): 218–43.

Boreham, G.F. "Three Years after Canada's 'Little Bang.'" *Canadian Banker* 97, no. 5 (1990): 6–15.

Borschied, Peter, and Niels Viggo Haueter, eds. *World Insurance: The Evolution of a Global Risk Network*. Oxford: Oxford University Press, 2012.

Bothwell, Robert. *The Penguin History of Canada*. Toronto: Penguin Group, 2006.

– *Your Country, My Country: A Unified History of the United States and Canada*. Oxford: Oxford University Press, 2015.

Boyd, John. *Sir George Etienne Cartier, His Life and Times: A Political History of Canada from 1814 until 1873*. Toronto: Macmillan Company of Canada, 1914.

Boyko, John. *Blood and Daring: How Canada Fought the American Civil War and Forged a Nation*. Toronto: Knopf Canada, 2013.

Brealey, Richard A., and Stewart C. Myers. *Principles of Corporate Finance*, 6th ed. Boston: Irwin McGraw-Hill, 2000.

Brean, Donald J.S., Lawrence Kryzanowski, and Gordon S. Roberts. "Canada and the United States: Different Roots, Different Routes to Financial Sector Regulation." *Business History* 53, no. 2 (2011): 249–69.

Breckenridge, Roeliff Morton. *The History of Banking in Canada*. Washington, DC: Government Printing Office, 1910.

Brock, R.D. "Insurance Regulation in the United States: A Regulator's Perspective." *Journal of Insurance Regulation* 8, no. 3 (1989): 277–89.

Brown, Robert Craig. *Robert Laird Borden: A Biography*. Vol. 2, *1914–1937*. Toronto: Macmillan of Canada, 1980.

Browne, G.P. *Documents on the Confederation of British North America*. Toronto: McClelland and Stewart, 1969.

Bruchey, Stuart. *The Roots of American Economic Growth, 1607–1861*. New York: Harper & Row, 1965.

Bruner, Robert F., and Sean D. Carr. *The Panic of 1907: Lessons Learned from the Market's Perfect Storm*. Hoboken, NJ: John Wiley & Sons, 2007.

Bryce, Robert. *Canada and the Cost of World War II: The International Operations of Canada's Department of Finance, 1939–1947*. Montreal and Kingston: McGill-Queen's University Press, 2005.

– *Maturing in Hard Times: Canada's Department of Finance through the Great Depression.* Montreal and Kingston: McGill-Queen's University Press, 1986.

Buckley, Kenneth. *Capital Formation in Canada, 1896–1930.* Toronto: McClelland and Stewart, 1974.

Burns, Robin B. "McGee, Thomas D'Arcy." *Dictionary of Canadian Biography,* vol. 9. 1976. http://www.biographi.ca/en/bio/mcgee_thomas_d_arcy_9E.html.

Busch, Andreas. *Banking Regulation and Globalization.* Oxford: Oxford University Press, 2009.

Cain, P.J., and A.G. Hopkins. *British Imperialism: 1688–2000.* 2nd ed. London: Longman, 2001.

Calomiris, Charles W., and Stephen H. Haber. *Fragile by Design: The Political Origins of Banking Crises & Scarce Credit.* Princeton: Princeton University Press, 2014.

Cameron, Rondo, and V.I. Bovykin, eds. *International Banking 1877–1914.* Oxford: Oxford University Press, 1991.

Canadian Foundation for Economic Education. *Money and Monetary Policy in Canada.* Toronto, 1994.

Capie, Forrest, and Geoffrey E. Wood, eds. *Financial Crises and the World Banking System.* London: Macmillan, in Association with Centre for Banking and International Finance, City University, 1986.

Careless, J.M.S. *Brown of the Globe.* Vol. 2. Toronto: Dundurn, 1996.

Carlos, Ann M., and Frank Lewis. "The Profitability of Early Canadian Railroads: Evidence from the Grand Trunk and Great Western Railway Companies." In *Strategic Factors in Nineteenth-Century American Economic History: A Volume to Honor Robert W. Fogel,* ed. Claudia Goldin and Hugh Rockoff, 401–26. Chicago: University of Chicago Press, 1992.

Carosso, Vincent P. *The Morgans: Private International Bankers, 1854–1913.* Cambridge, MA: Harvard University Press, 1987.

Caruana, Jamie, and Anoop Singh. *Canada: International System Stability Assessment – Update.* Washington, DC: International Monetary Fund, 2008.

Carver, Humphrey. *Houses for Canadians: A Study of Housing Problems in the Toronto Area.* Toronto: University of Toronto Press, 1948.

Cassis, Youssef. "Big Businesses." In *The Oxford Handbook of Business History,* ed. Geoffrey G. Jones and Jonathan Zeitlin, 171–93. Oxford: Oxford University Press, 2007.

– *Capitals of Capital.* Cambridge: Cambridge University Press, 2006.

– *Crisis and Opportunities: The Shaping of Modern Finance.* Oxford: Oxford University Press, 2012.

Chambers, Morris W. "Who We Are and Our History." Canadian Institute of
    Actuaries. http://www.cia-ica.ca/about-us/the-institute/who-we-are-and-
    our-history.
Chandler Jr, Alfred D. *Scale and Scope: The Dynamics of Industrial Capitalism*.
    Cambridge, MA: Belknap Press of Harvard University Press, 1990.
– *Strategy and Structure: Chapters in the History of the Industrial Enterprise*.
    Cambridge, MA: MIT Press, 1990.
– *The Visible Hand: The Managerial Revolution in American Business*. Cambridge,
    MA: Belknap Press of Harvard University Press, 1977.
Chant, John. *The ABCP Crisis in Canada: The Implications for the Regulation of
    Financial Markets; A Research Study Prepared for the Expert Panel on Security
    Regulations*. Ottawa: Expert Panel on Securities Regulation, 2008.
Chase, Stuart. *Government in Business*. New York: Macmillan, 1935.
Chernow, Ron. *Alexander Hamilton*. New York: Penguin Books, 2004.
– *The House of Morgan: An American Banking Dynasty and the Rise of Modern
    Finance*. New York: Grace, 1990.
Churchill, Winston. *A History of the English-Speaking Peoples*. Vol. 4, *The Great
    Democracies*. Toronto: McClelland & Stewart, 1958.
CIO from IDG. http://www.cio.com/.
Claessens, Stijn, and Neeltje van Horen. "Foreign Banks: Trends, Impact and
    Financial Stability." Research Paper, IMF, January 2012.
Cleveland, Harold van B., and Thomas F. Huertas. *Citibank: 1812–1970*.
    Cambridge, MA: Harvard University Press, 1985.
Conrad, Margaret. *A Concise History of Canada*. New York: Cambridge
    University Press, 2012.
Conway, G.R. *The Supply of, and Demand for Canadian Equities*. Toronto: Toronto
    Stock Exchange, 1970.
Cook, Tim. *War Lords, Borden, Mackenzie King, and Canada's World Wars*.
    Toronto: Allen Lane, 2012.
Creighton, Donald. *The Forked Road: Canada 1939–1957*. Toronto: McClelland
    and Stewart, 1976.
– *John A. Macdonald: The Young Politician*. Toronto: Macmillan Company of
    Canada, 1956.
– *The Old Chieftain*. Toronto: Macmillan Company of Canada Limited, 1955.
Curtis, C.A. "The Canadian Macmillan Commission." *Economic Journal* 44,
    no. 173 (1934): 48–59.
Darroch, James. *Canadian Banks and Global Competitiveness*. Montreal and
    Kingston: McGill-Queen's University Press, 1994.
Darroch, James, and Matthias Kipping. "Canada: Taking Life Insurance
    Abroad." In *World Insurance: The Evolution of a Global Risk Network*, ed.

Peter Borscheid and Niels V. Haueter, 252–73. Oxford: Oxford University Press, 2012.

Davis, David Brion. *Slavery and Human Progress*. Oxford: Oxford University Press, 1984.

Dayen, David. *Chain of Title: How Three Ordinary Americans Uncovered Wall Street's Great Foreclosure Fraud*. New York: New Press, 2016.

Deloitte Canada. *150 Years and Counting: Our Legacy and Our Future*. Toronto: Deloitte Canada, 2010.

Denison, Merrill. *Canada's First Bank: A History of the Bank of Montreal*. Vols 1 and 2. Toronto: McClelland & Stewart, 1966–7.

Den Otter, A.A. *The Philosophy of Railways: The Transcontinental Railway Idea in British North America*. Toronto: University of Toronto Press, 1997.

Department of Finance. "Archived – Fiscal Reference Tables – 2013: Part 10 of 10.". http://www.fin.gc.ca/frt-trf/2013/frt-trf-1309-eng.asp.

– "Information Canada's Financial Services Sector: Property and Casualty Insurance in Canada." 2003. http://www.fin.gc.ca/activty/factsheets/property_e.pdf.

Desjardins, B., M. Lescure, R. Nougaret, A. Plessis, and A. Straus. *Le Credit Lyonnais: 1863–1996*. Geneva: Droz, 2003.

Dodge, David A. *Bank of Canada Annual Report: 2001*. Ottawa: Bank of Canada, 2002.

Draper, Theodore. *A Struggle for Power: The American Revolution*. New York: Random House, 1996.

Drummond, Ian M. "Finance Act." *The Canadian Encyclopedia*. http://www.thecanadianencyclopedia.ca/en/article/finance-act/.

– "Why Canadian Banks Did Not Collapse in the 1930s." In *The Role of Banks in the Interwar Economy*, ed. Harold James, Hekan Lindgren, and Alice Teichova, 232–50. Cambridge: Cambridge University Press, 1991.

Duffy, Catherine R. *Held Captive: A History of International Insurance in Bermuda*. Toronto: Oakwell Boulton, 2004.

Edinborough, Arnold. *A History of Canadian Imperial Bank of Commerce*. Vol. 4, *1931–1973*. Toronto: Canadian Imperial Bank of Commerce, 1995.

Eichengreen, Barry. *Exorbitant Privilege: The Rise and Fall of the Dollar and the Future of the International Monetary System*. New York: Oxford University Press, 2011.

Ellis, Joseph J. *American Creation: Triumphs and Tragedies at the Founding of the Republic*. New York: Knopf, 2007.

Emerson, Ralph W. "Essay II: Self-Reliance." Essays First Series, 1841.

Engerman, Stanley L., and Robert E. Gallman, eds. *The Cambridge Economic History of the United States*. Vol. 2, *The Long Nineteenth Century*. Cambridge: Cambridge University Press, 2000.

– *The Cambridge Economic History of the United States*. Vol. 3, *The Twentieth Century*. Cambridge: Cambridge University Press, 2000.

Erturk, Ismail, Julie Froud, Sukhev Johal, Adam Leaver, and Karel Williams. *Financialization at Work*. London: Routledge, 2008.

Estey, Willard Z. *Report of the Inquiry into the Collapse of the CCB and Northland Bank*. Ottawa: Privy Council Office, 1986.

Euler, William D. *Canada Year Book, 1938: The Official Statistical Annual of the Resources, History, Institutions, and Social and Economic Conditions of the Dominion*. Ottawa: King's Printer, 1938.

Fama, Eugene F. "Efficient Capital Markets: A Review of Theory and Empirical Work." *Journal of Finance* 25, no. 2 (1970): 383–417.

Farr, David M.L. "Rose, Sir John." *Dictionary of Canadian Biography*, vol. 11. 1982.http://www.biographi.ca/en/bio/rose_john_11E.html.

Faure, David, and Elisabeth Koll. "China: The Indigenization of Insurance." In *World Insurance: The Evolution of a Global Risk Network*, ed. Peter Borschied and Niels V. Haueter, 472–94. Oxford: Oxford University Press, 2012.

Fayerweather, John. *The Mercantile Bank Affair: A Case Study of Canadian Nationalism and a Multinational Firm*. New York: New York University Press, 1974.

Fear, Jeffrey, and Christopher Kobrak. "Diverging Paths: Accounting for Corporate Governance in America and Germany." *Business History Review* 80, no. 1 (2006): 1–48.

Fear, Jeffrey R., and R.D. Wadhwani. "Populism and Political Entrepreneurship: The Universalization of German Savings Banks and the Decline of American Savings, 1907–1934." In *Business in the Age of Extremes: Essays in Modern German and Austrian Economic History Series*, ed. Juergen Kocka, Dieter Ziegler, and Hartmut Berghoff, 94–118. Cambridge: Cambridge University Press, 2013.

Feldman, Gerald D. *The Great Disorder: Politics, Economics and Society in the German Inflation, 1914–24*. New York: Oxford University Press, 1993.

Fell, Anthony S. *The Canadian Chartered Banks: A Dominion Securities Corporation Limited Research Report*. Toronto: Dominion Securities Corporation, 1964.

Fell, Tony. "Remarks at Toronto Board of Trade Annual Dinner." Board of Trade, Toronto, 26 January 2009.

Ferguson, Niall. *The Ascent of Money: A Financial History of the World*. New York: Penguin, 2008.

– *Empire: The Rise and Demise of the British World Order and the Lessons for Global Power*. New York: Basic Books, 2002.

– *High Financier: The Lives and Time of Siegmund Warburg*. London: Allen Lane, 2010.

Fergusson, Bruce. *Hon. W.S. Fielding*. Vol. 2. Windsor, NS: Lancelot, 1970.

Ferrabee, James, and Michael St B. Harrison. *Staying Connected: How MacDougall Family Traditions Built a Business over 160 Years*. Montreal and Kingston: McGill-Queen's University Press, 2009.

Fetherling, George. *Gold Diggers of 1929: Canada and the Great Stock Market Crash*. Toronto: Macmillan, 2004.

Fink, P. *The Rise of Mutual Funds: An Insider's View*. New York: Oxford University Press, 2008.

Fishback, Price, et al. *Government and the American Economy: A New History*. Chicago: University of Chicago Press, 2007.

Fishback, Price, Jonathan Rose, and Kenneth Snowden. *Well Worth Saving: How the New Deal Safeguarded Home Ownership*. Chicago: University of Chicago Press, 2013.

Fogel, William, and Stanley L. Engerman. *Time on the Cross: The Economics of American Negro Slavery*. Boston: Little, Brown, 1974.

Foreman, Amanda. *A World on Fire: The Epic History of Two Nations Divided*. London: Allen Lane, 2010.

Fox, Justin. *The Myth of the Rational Market: A History of Risk, Reward, and the Delusion of Wall Street*. New York: HarperCollins, 2009.

Foster, George E. *The Canada Year Book, 1914*. Ottawa: King's Printer, 1915.

Franklin, Benjamin. "Papers vol. 4." Franklin Papers, 25 March 1752.

Freedman, Charles. *The Canadian Banking System*. Ottawa: Bank of Canada, 1998.

– "The Canadian Banking System." Paper presented to the Conference on Developments in the Financial System: National and International Perspectives, Jerome Levy Economics Institute of Bard College Annandale-on-Hudson, 10–11 April 1997.

Frieden, Jeffry A. *Global Capitalism: Its Fall and Rise in the 20th Century*. New York: Norton, 2006.

Friedman, Milton, and Anna J. Schwartz. *A Monetary History of the United States 1867–1960*. Princeton: Princeton University Press, 1963.

Fukuyama, Francis. *The End of History and the Last Man*. Toronto: Maxwell Macmillan Canada, 1992.

Fullerton, Douglas H. *The Bond Market in Canada*. Toronto: Carswell, 1962.

Furnas, J.C. *The Americans: A Social History*. New York: Capricorn, 1969.

Galt, Alexander T. *Speech on the Proposed Union of the British North American Provinces*. Montreal: M. Longmore, 1864.

Garraty, John A. *Woodrow Wilson: A Great Life in Brief*. New York: Knopf, 1966.

Gaughan, Patrick A. *Mergers, Acquisitions, and Corporate Restructuring*. 2nd ed. New York: John Wiley, 1999.

Geisst, Charles R. *Wall Street: A History from Its Beginnings to the Fall of Enron.* Oxford: Oxford University Press, 2004.

Genovese, Eugene D. *The Political Economy of Slavery: Studies in the Economy and Society of the Slave South.* New York: Pantheon, 1965.

– *The World the Slaveholders Made: Two Essays in Interpretation.* New York: Pantheon, 1969.

Gentilcore, R. Louis, ed. *Historical Atlas of Canada.* Vol. 2, *The Land Transformed, 1800–1891.* Toronto, University of Toronto Press, 1993.

Gerardi, Kristopher, Harvey S. Rosen, and Paul Willen. *Do Households Benefit from Financial Deregulation and Innovation? The Case of the Mortgage Market.* Cambridge: National Bureau of Economic Research, 2007.

Globe and Mail. "Wants High-Rises, Board Told Builder Allowing House to Deteriorate, Homeowners say." *Globe and Mail,* 25 April 1968, 5.

Goodwin, Doris K. *Team of Rivals: The Political Genius of Abraham Lincoln.* New York: Simon & Schuster, 2005.

Gorton, Gary B. *Misunderstanding Financial Crises: Why We Don't See Them Coming.* Oxford: Oxford University Press, 2013.

Graham, Roger. *Arthur Meighen.* Vol. 3, *No Surrender.* Toronto: Clarke, Irwin, 1965.

Grant, James. *The Forgotten Depression; 1921: The Crash That Cured Itself.* New York: Simon & Schuster, 2014.

Gras, N.S.B., and Henrietta M. Larson. *Casebook in American History.* New York: F.S. Crofts, 1939.

Gray, James. *The Winter Years.* Markham, ON: Fifth House Publishers, 2003.

Green, Howard. *Banking on America: How TD Bank Rose to the Top and Took on the U.S.A.* Toronto: Harper Collins Publishing, 2013.

Greenspan, Alan. *The Age of Turbulence: Adventures in a New World.* New York: Penguin, 2007.

Gudmundsen, John. *The Great Provider: The Dramatic Story of Life Insurance in America.* South Norwalk, CT: Industrial Production, 1959.

Gugliemo, Mark, and Werner Troesken. "The Gilded Age." In *Government and the American Economy: A New History,* ed. Price V. Fishback, 255–87. Chicago: University of Chicago Press, 2007.

Gwynn, Richard. *John A., the Man Who Made Us: The Life and Times of John A. Macdonald.* Vol. 1, *1815–1867.* Toronto: Random House, Canada, 2007.

– *Nation Maker: Sir John A. Macdonald, His Life, Our Times.* Vol. 2, *1867–1891.* Toronto: Random House, Canada, 2011.

Hall, Peter A., and David Soskice, eds. *Varieties of Capitalism: The Institutional Foundations of Comparative Advantage.* Oxford: Oxford University Press, 2001.

Halpern, Paul, Caroline Cakebread, Christopher C. Nicholls, and Poonam
    Puri. *Back from The Brink: Lessons from the Canadian Asset-Backed Commercial
    Paper Crisis*. Toronto: University of Toronto Press, 2016.
Hamilton, Alexander. *Federalist Paper, no. 30*. New York: New York Packet, 1787.
Hammond, Bray. *Banks and Politics in America from the Revolution to the Civil
    War*. Princeton: Princeton University Press, 1957.
– "Long and Short Term Credit in Early American Banking." *Quarterly Journal
    of Economics* 49, no. 1 (1935): 79–103.
Hampden-Turner, Charles, and Fons Trompenaars. *The Seven Cultures of
    Capitalism: Value Systems for Creating Wealth in the United States, Britain,
    Japan, Germany, France, Sweden and the Netherlands*. New York: Doubleday,
    1993.
Hannah, Leslie. "J.P. Morgan in London and New York before 1914." *Business
    History Review* 85, no. 1 (2011): 113–50.
– "Pioneering Modern Corporate Governance: A View from London in 1900."
    Enterprise and Society 8, no. 3 (2007): 642–86.
Hart, Michael. *A Trading Nation: Canadian Trade Policy from Colonialism to
    Globalization*. Vancouver: UBC Press, 2002.
Harvey, Arthur, ed. *The Year Book and Almanac of Canada for 1870; Being an
    Annual Statistical Abstract for the Dominion and a Record of Legislation and
    of Public Men in British North America*. Montreal: Montreal Printing and
    Publishing, from Stereotyped Plates, 1869.
Hausman, William J., Peter Hertner, and Mira Wilkins. *Global Electrification:
    Multinational Enterprise and International Finance in the History of Light and
    Power, 1878–2007*. New York: Cambridge University Press, 2008.
Heaman, E.A. *Tax, Order, and Good Government: A New Political History of
    Canada, 1867–1917*. Montreal and Kingston: McGill-Queen's University
    Press, 2017.
Heffernan, Shelagh. *Making Banking in Theory and Practice*. New York: Wiley,
    1996.
Heguly, Eric. "Mergers Will Resurface: Bank Chairman." *Globe and Mail*,
    4 December 1999.
Heibroner, Robert L. *The Worldly Philosophers: The Lives, Times, and Ideas of the
    Great Economic Thinkers*. New York: Simon and Schuster, 1953.
Hinchley, Christine. "Foreign Banks in the Canadian Market." Statistics
    Canada. 2009. http://www.statcan.gc.ca/pub/11-621-m/11-621-m2006041-
    eng.htm.
Hirschman, Albert O. *Rival Views of Market Society and Other Recent Essays*.
    Cambridge, MA: Harvard University Press, 1992.

Hofsede, Geert. *Culture's Consequences: Comparing Values, Behaviours, Institutions and Organizations across Nations*. 2nd ed. Thousand Oaks, CA: Sage, 2001.

Hofstadter, Richard. *The Age of Reform: From Bryan to F.D.R.* New York: Knopf, 1955.

Homer, Sidney, and Richard Sylla. *A History of Interest Rates*. New Brunswick, NJ: Rutgers University Press, 1996.

Hou, Charles, and Cynthia Hou. *Great Political Cartoons, 1946 to 1982*. Vancouver: Moody's Lookout, 2011.

Howe, C.D. *Canada Year Book 1956: The Official Statistical Annual of the Resources, History, Institutions and Social and Economic Conditions of the Dominion*. Ottawa: Queen's Printer and Comptroller of Stationery, 1956.

Hughes, Jane E., and Scott B. MacDonald. *International Banking: Text and Cases*. Boston: Addison Wesley, 2002.

Hulchanski, David. "The 1935 Dominion Housing Act: Setting the Stage for a Permanent Federal Presence in Canada's Housing Sector." *Urban History Review* 15, no. 1 (1986): 20–1.

Hull, J.C. *Futures, Options and Other Derivative Securities*. Englewood Cliffs, NJ: Prentice Hall, 1997.

Hummel, Jeffery Rogers. "The Civil War and Reconstruction." In *Government and the American Economy: A New History*, ed. Price Fishback, 188–231. Chicago: University of Chicago Press, 2007.

Hürlimann, E. Bericht über Amerikanreise, Sept. bis Dez. 1920, Swiss Re Americas Corporation (SRAC).

Hyman, Louis. *Debtor Nation: The History of American Red Ink*. Princeton: Princeton University Press, 2011.

Ilsley, J.L. "Speaking of Money and War." Seigneury Club, Montebello, Quebec, 18 September 1941.

Innis, Harold A. *The Fur Trade in Canada: An Introduction to Canadian Economic History*. Toronto: University of Toronto Press, 1999.

– *Problems of Staple Production in Canada*. Toronto: Ryerson, 1933.

Investment Bankers' Association of America. Proceedings of the 1918 Annual Convention.

Irwin, Douglas A. *Peddling Protectionism: Smoot-Hawley and the Great Depression*. Princeton: Princeton University Press, 2011.

Jackman, Henry N.R., ed. *The Letters and Diaries of Henry Rutherford Jackman*. Vol. 15. Toronto: Harmony Printing, 2013.

James, Harold. "Central Banks and the Process of Financial Internationalization: A Secular View." In *European Banks and the American Challenge: Competition and Cooperation in International Banking under Bretton*

Woods, ed. Stefano Battilossi and Youssef Cassis, 200–18. Oxford: Oxford University Press, 2002.

James, John A. *Money and Capital in Postbellum America*. Princeton: Princeton University Press, 1978.

Jamieson, Keith, and Michelle A. Hamilton. *Dr Oronhyatekha, Security, Justice and Equality*. Toronto: Dundurn, 2016.

Johnson, Paul. *A History of the American People*. London: Weidenfeld & Nicolson, 1997.

Jones, Geoffrey. *British Multinational Banking: 1830–1990*. Oxford: Clarendon, 1993.

– *Multinationals and Global Capitalism: From the Nineteenth to the Twenty-First Century*. Oxford: Oxford University Press, 2005.

Jones, Robert H. *Building Futures: A History of Investors Group*. Winnipeg: Investors Group, 1993.

Kaplan, Ari N. *Pension Law*. Toronto: Irwin, Law, 2006.

Kaplan, Edward S. *American Trade Policy, 1923–1995: Contributions in Economics and Economic History*. Westport, CT: Greenwood, 1996.

Keegan, John. *The First World War*. Toronto: Key Porter, 1998.

Keller, Morton. *The Life Insurance Enterprise, 1885–1910*. Cambridge, MA: Harvard University Press, 1963.

Kenwood, A.G., and A.L. Lougheed. *The Growth of the International Economy, 1820–1990: An Introductory Text*. 3rd ed. London: Routledge, 1992.

Kerr, Donald. "Some Aspects of the Geography of Finance in Canada." *Canadian Geographer* 9, no. 4 (1965): 175–92.

Kerr, Donald, and Deryck Holdsworth. *Historical Atlas of Canada*. Vol. 3, *Addressing the Twentieth Century, 1891–1961*. Toronto: University of Toronto Press, 1990.

Kesteman, Jean-Pierre. "Galt, Sir Alexander Tilloch." *Dictionary of Canadian Biography*, vol. 12. 1990. http://www.biographi.ca/en/bio/galt_alexander_tilloch_12E.html.

Kindleberger, Charles P. *Economic Response: Comparative Studies in Trade, Finance, and Growth*. Cambridge, MA: Harvard University Press, 1978.

– *Manias, Panics, and Crashes: A History of Financial Crises*. New York: John Wiley & Sons, 2005.

King, Darryl. "Federal Policy and the Canadian Housing Market." Research paper, Rotman School of Management, 30 May 2014.

Kloner, Dean. "The Commodity Futures Modernization Act of 2000." *Securities Regulation Law Journal* 29, no. 1 (2001): 286–97.

Knaplund, Paul. "James Stephen on Canadian Banking Laws, 1821–1846." *Canadian Historical Review* 31, no. 2 (1950): 177–87.

Kobrak, Christopher. *Banking on Global Markets: Deutsche Bank in the United States, 1870 to the Present*. Cambridge: Cambridge University Press, 2007.
– "Banking on Governance: U.K. and U.S. Financial Markets and Management in the 20th Century." *Bankhistorisches Archiv* 37, no. 2 (2011): 137–63.
– "USA: The International Attraction of the US Insurance Market." In *World Insurance: The Evolution of a Global Risk Network*, ed. Peter Borscheid and Niels V. Haueter, 274–310. Oxford: Oxford University Press, 2012.
Kobrak, Christopher, and Donald Brean. "Financial Crises and Global Financial Regulations." In *Risk and EU Law*, ed. Hans-Wolfgang Micklitz and Takis Tridimas, 220–48. Cheltenham, UK: Edward Elgar, 2015.
Kobrak, Christopher, and Michael Troege. "From Basel to Bailouts: Forty Years of International Attempts to Bolster Bank Safety." *Financial History Review* 22, no. 2 (2015): 133–56.
Kobrak, Christopher, and Mira Wilkins. "The '2008 Crisis' in an Economic History Perspective." *Business History* 53, no. 2 (2011): 175–92.
Kohn, Meir. *Financial Institutions and Markets*. New York: McGraw-Hill, 1994.
Kolko, Gabriel. *The Triumph of Conservatism: A Reinterpretation of American History, 1900–1913*. New York: Free Press, 1993.
Konings, Martin. *The Development of American Finance*. New York: Cambridge University Press, 2011.
Kyer, Ian C. *From Next Best to World Class: The People and Events That Have Shaped the Canada Deposit Insurance Corporation, 1867–2017*. Toronto: Canada Deposit Insurance Corporation, 2017.
Kynston, David. *City of London: The History*. London: Chatto & Windos, 2011.
La Croix, Sumner J. "Government and the People: Labor, Education, and Health." In *Government and the American Economy: A New History*, ed. Price Fishback, 323–63. Chicago: Chicago University Press, 2007.
Lamoreaux, Naomi R. *The Great Merger Movement in American Business, 1895–1904*. Cambridge: Cambridge University Press, 1985.
– *Insider Lending: Banks, Personal Connections, and Economic Development in Industrial New England*. Cambridge: Cambridge University Press, 1994.
Landes, David. *The Unbound Prometheus*. Cambridge: Cambridge University Press, 1969.
Lash, Z.A. "The United States Federal Reserve Act and the Canadian Banking System with Some Contrasts." *Journal of the Canadian Bankers Association* 26, no. 3 (1919): 224–44.
Leacock, Stephen. *Literary Lapses*. Toronto: McClelland and Stewart, 2008.
Lerner, Max. *America as a Civilization*. New York: Simon and Schuster, 1957.
Lincoln, Abraham. "Acceptance Speech for the Senate Nomination." 16 June 1858.

Lintner, John. "The Valuation of Risk Assets and the Selection of Risky Investments in Stock Portfolios and Capital Budgets." *Review of Economics and Statistics* 47, no. 1 (1965): 222–4.

Lipset, Seymour Martin. *Continental Divide: Values and Institutions of Canada and America*. New York: Routledge, 1990.

Little, Bruce. *Fixing the Future: How Canada's Usually Fractious Governments Worked Together to Rescue the Canada Pension Plan*. Toronto: Rotman – University of Toronto Publishing, 2008.

Livingston, James. *Origins of the Federal Reserve System: Money, Class, and Corporate Capitalism, 1890–1913*. Ithaca, NY: Cornell University Press, 1986.

Lockwood, Brent. "O' Canada." Blog. https://ocanadablog.com/2015/10/30/early-u-s-canada-political-cartoons/.

Longley, Ronald Stewart. *Sir Francis Hincks: A Study of Canadian Politics, Railways, and Finance in the Nineteenth Century*. Toronto: University of Toronto Press, 1943.

Low, Thomas A. *The Canada Year Book 1922–23: The Official Statistical Annual of the Resources, History, Institutions and Social and Economic Conditions of the Dominion*. Ottawa: F.A. Acland, 1924.

Lowenstein, Roger. *America's Bank: The Epic Struggle to Create the Federal Reserve*. New York: Penguin, 2015.

MacIntosh, Robert. *Different Drummers: Banking and Politics in Canada*. Toronto: Macmillan Canada, 1991.

– "Origins of Financial Stability in Canada: The Bank Act of 1871." In *Relentless Change: A Casebook for the Study of Canadian Business History*, ed. Joe Martin, 21–38. Toronto: Rotman – University of Toronto Publishing, 2010.

Macklem, Katherine. "RBC Yesterday, Today, and Tomorrow." In *Relentless Change: A Casebook for the Study of Canadian Business History*, ed. Joe Martin, 303–18. Toronto: University of Toronto Press, 2010.

Macmillan, Hugh P. *Report of the Royal Commission on Banking and Currency in Canada*. Ottawa: J.O. Patenaude, 1933.

MacMillan, Margaret. *The War That Ended Peace: The Road to 1914*. Toronto: Penguin Group, 2013.

Maddison Project. http://www.ggdc.net/maddison/maddison-project/home.htm.

Malcolm, James. *The Canada Year Book 1930: The Official Statistical Annual of the Resources, History, Institutions and Social and Economic Conditions of the Dominion*. Ottawa: F.A. Acland, 1930.

"Maple Revolutionaries." *Economist*, 3 March 2012. http://www.economist.com/node/21548970.

Marchildon, Gregory P. "The Impact of the Great Depression on the Global Wheat Trade, Unpeaceable Exchange: Trade and Conflict in the Global Economy, 1000–2000." University of Lisbon, 16–17 July 2010.

Markowitz, Harry. "Portfolio Theory." PhD diss., University of Chicago, 1962.

Markowitz, Mark. "Portfolio Selection." *Journal of Finance* 7, no. 1 (1952): 77–91.

Marshall, Herbert, Frank A. Southard, and Kenneth W. Taylor. *Canadian-American Industry: A Study in International Investment*. New Haven, CT: Yale University Press, 1936.

Martin, Joe. "Great Depression Hit One Country Hardest of All." Bloomberg (blog), 26 March 2013. https://www.bloomberg.com/view/articles/2013-03-26/great-depression-hit-one-country-hardest-of-all.

– "Opportunities in the Asia-Pacific Region for Canadian Life Insurance Companies in the Early 1990's." In *Studies in Banking and Financial History*, 517–52. Warsaw: European Association for Banking and Financial History, 2013.

–, ed.   *Relentless Change: A Casebook for the Study of Canadian Business History*. Toronto: University of Toronto Press, 2010.

Martin, Roger. *The Finance Crisis and Rescue: What Went Wrong? Why? What Lessons Can Be Learned? Expert Views from the Rotman School of Management*. Toronto: University of Toronto Press, 2008.

Masters, D.C. *The Rise of Toronto*. Toronto: University of Toronto Press, 1947.

Matthews, Geoffrey J. *Historical Atlas of Canada*. Vol. 3, *Addressing the Twentieth Century*. Toronto: University of Toronto Press, 1987.

McCallum, Bennett T. *International Monetary Economics*. New York: Oxford University Press, 1996.

McCraw, Thomas K., ed. *Creating Modern Capitalism: How Entrepreneurs. Companies, and Countries Triumphed in Three Industrial Revolutions*. Cambridge, MA: Harvard University Press, 1997.

– *The Founders and Finance: How Hamilton, Gallatin, and Other Immigrants Forged a New Economy*. Cambridge, MA: Harvard University Press, 2012.

– *Prophet of Innovation: Joseph Schumpeter and Creative Destruction*. Cambridge, MA: Harvard University Press, 2007.

– *Prophets of Regulation: Charles Francis Adams, Louis D. Brandeis, James M. Landis, Alfred E. Kahn*. Cambridge, MA: Belknap Press of Harvard University Press, 1984.

McCusker, John J., and Russell R. Menard. *The Economy of British America, 1607–1789*. Chapel Hill: University of North Carolina Press, 1991.

McDonald, Judith, Anthony P. O'Brien, and Colleen M. Callahan. "Trade Wars: Canada's Reaction to the Smoot-Hawley Tariff." *Journal of Economic History* 57, no. 4 (1997): 802–26.

McDowall, Duncan. *Quick to the Frontier: Canada's Royal Bank*. Toronto: McClelland & Stewart, 1993.

McGee, Thomas D. *Two Speeches on the Union of the Provinces: Minister of Agriculture*. Quebec: Hunter, Rose, 9 February 1865.

McInnis, Edgar. *Canada: A Political and Social History*. New York. Rinehart, 1957.

McIvor, R. Craig. *Canadian Monetary, Banking and Fiscal Development*. Toronto: Macmillan Company of Canada, 1958.

McKenna, Christopher. *The World's Newest Profession: Management Consulting in the Twentieth Century*. Cambridge: Cambridge University Press, 2006.

McLeod, J.A. "The Present Working of the Canadian Banking System." *Journal of the Canadian Bankers' Association* 41 (1933): 31–47.

McMullough, David. *John Adams*. New York: Simon and Schuster, 2001.

McNeil, William C. *American Money and the Weimer Republic: Economics and Politics on the Eve of the Great Depression*. New York: Columbia University Press, 1986.

McPherson, James. *Battle Cry of Freedom*. New York: Oxford University Press, 1988.

– *The War That Forged a Nation: Why the Civil War Still Matters*. New York: Oxford University Press, 2015.

McQueen, Rod. "The Collapse of Confederation Life." In *Relentless Change: A Casebook for the Study of Canadian Business History*, ed. Joe Martin, 286–302. Toronto: University of Toronto Press, 2010.

– *Manulife: How Dominic D'Alessandro Built a Global Giant and Fought to Save It*. Toronto: Viking Canada, 2009.

– *The Money-Spinners: An Intimate Portrait of the Men Who Run Canada's Banks*. Toronto: Macmillan of Canada, 1983.

Meier, K.J. *The Political Economy of Regulation: The Case of Insurance*. Albany: State University of New York, 1988.

Merton, Robert C. "Theory of Rational Option Pricing." *Bell Journal of Economics and Management Science* 4, no. 1 (1973): 141–83.

Mihm, Stephen. *A Nation of Counterfeiters: Capitalists, Con Men, and the Making of the United States*. Cambridge, MA: Harvard University Press, 2007.

Miller, Ian H.M. *Our Glory and Our Grief: Torontonians and the Great War*. Toronto: University of Toronto Press, 2002.

Miller, Merton H., and Franco Modigliani. "Dividend Policy, Growth, and the Valuation of Shares." *Journal of Business* 34, no. 4 (1961): 411–33.

Miranti Jr, Paul J. *Accountancy Comes of Age: The Development of an American Profession, 1886–1940*. Chapel Hill: University of North Carolina Press, 1990.

Moore, Christopher. *1867: How the Fathers Made a Deal*. Toronto: McClelland & Stewart, 1997.

– *Three Weeks in Quebec City: The Meeting That Made Canada.* Toronto: Penguin Canada Books, 2015.

Moreau, Francois. *Le Développement International des Banques Canadiennes: Croissance, Expansion and Concentration.* Montreal: Editions Saint-Martin, 1985.

Morningstar. http://www2.morningstar.ca/homepage/h_ca.aspx? culture=en-CA.

Morrison, Samuel E., Henry S. Commager, and William E. Leuchtenburg. *The Growth of the American Republic.* Vol. 1. Oxford: Oxford University Press, 1980.

Morton, Desmond. *A Short History of Canada.* Toronto: McClelland & Stewart, 2007.

Morton, Desmond, and J.L. Granatstein. *Marching to Armageddon: Canadians and the Great War, 1914–1919.* Toronto: Lester & Orpen, 1989.

Morton, W.L. "Bruce, James, 8th Earl of Elgin and 12th Earl of Kincardine." *Dictionary of Canadian Biography*, vol. 9. 1976. http://www.biographi.ca/en/ bio/bruce_james_9E.html.

– *The Critical Years: The Union of British North America, 1857–1873.* Toronto: McClelland and Stewart, 1964.

– *The Kingdom of Canada.* Toronto: McClelland & Stewart, 1963.

Mowery, David, and Nathan Rosenberg. "Twentieth-Century Technological Change." In *The Cambridge Economic History of the United States*, Vol. 3, ed. Stanley L. Engerman and Rogert E. Gallman, 803–927. Cambridge: Cambridge University Press, 2000.

Muirhead, Bruce. *Against the Odds: The Public Life and Times of Louis Rasminsky.* Toronto: University of Toronto Press, 1999.

Munro, William B. *American Influences on Canadian Government.* Toronto: Macmillan, 1929.

Murray, Sharon Ann. *Investing in Life: Insurance in Antebellum America.* Baltimore, MD: Johns Hopkins University Press, 2010.

Mussio, Laurence B. *A Vision Greater Than Themselves: The Making of the Bank of Montreal, 1817–2017.* Montreal: McGill-Queen's University Press, 2016.

Neil, Martin N., and Jacob F. Kirkegaard. *US Pension Reform: Lessons from Other Countries.* Washington, DC: Peterson Institute for International Economics, 2009.

Nelles, H.V. *A Little History of Canada.* Toronto: Oxford University Press Canada, 2004.

Nelles, H.V., and Christopher Armstrong. *Monopoly's Moment: The Organization and Regulation of Canadian Utilities, 1830–1930.* Toronto: University of Toronto Press, 1988.

Nelson, Scott Reynolds. *A Nation of Deadbeats: An Uncommon History of America's Financial Disasters.* New York: Vintage Books, 2012.

Neufeld, E.P. *The Financial System of Canada: Its Growth and Development*. Toronto: Macmillan Company of Canada, 1972.

The New York Times Current History: The European War. Vol. 16. New York: New York Times, 1918.

Noiseux, Marie-Helene. "Canadian Bank Mergers, Rescues and Failures." PhD diss., John Molson School of Business, Concordia University, 2002.

Nolan, Mary. *The Transatlantic Century: Europe and America 1890–2010*. Cambridge: Cambridge University Press, 2012.

– *Visions of Modernity: American Business and the Modernization of Germany*. Oxford: Oxford University Press, 1995.

Norman, Jeffrey. *The Path of the Sun: An Informal History of Sun Life Assurance Company of Canada*. Toronto: Arthur Jones, 1996.

Norrie, Kenneth, Douglas Owram, and J.C. Herbert Emery. *A History of the Canadian Economy*. 4th ed. Toronto: Thomson, Nelson, 2008.

North, Douglass. "Capital Accumulation in Life Insurance between the Civil War and the Investigation of 1905." In *Men in Business: Essays in the History of Entrepreneurship*, ed. William Miller, 238–53. Cambridge, MA: Harvard University Press, 1952.

– *Institutions, Institutional Change and Economic Performance*. St Louis: Washington University Press, 1990.

North, Douglass C., and Robert Paul Thomas. *The Rise of the Western World: A New Economic History*. Cambridge: Cambridge University Press, 1995.

Oakes, James. *The Ruling Race: A History of American Slaveholders*. New York: Knopf, 1982.

Oberlander, H. Peter, and Arthur L. Fallick. *Housing a Nation: The Evolution of Canadian Housing Policy*. Vancouver: Centre for Human Settlements, University of British Columbia for Canada Mortgage and Housing, 1992.

Office of the Superintendent of Financial Institutions. "Guide to Foreign Bank Branching." 2002. http://www.osfi-bsif.gc.ca/eng/fi-if/app/aag-gad/pages/fbbguide.aspx.

Olegario, Rowena. *A Culture of Credit: Embedding Trust and Transparency in American Business*. Cambridge, MA: Harvard University Press, 2006.

Organization for Economic Co-operation and Development. "Social Expenditure: Aggregated Data." 2017. http://stats.oecd.org/Index.aspx?datasetcode=SOCX_AGG.

Ormsby, William G. "Hincks, Sir Francis." *Dictionary of Canadian Biography*. Vol. 11. http://www.biographi.ca/en/bio/hincks_francis_11E.html.

O'Sullivan, Mary A. *Dividends of Development: Securities Markets in the History of US Capitalism, 1866–1922*. Oxford: Oxford University Press, 2016.

– "The Expansion of the U.S. Stock Market, 1885–1930: Historical Facts and Theoretical Fashions." *Enterprise and Society* 8, no. 3 (2007): 489–532.

Ott, Julia. "The Free and Open People's Market: Political Ideology and Retail Brokerage at the New York Stock Exchange, 1913–1933." *Journal of American History* 96, no. 1 (2009): 44–71.

– *When Wall Street Met Main Street: The Quest for an Investors' Democracy.* Cambridge, MA: Harvard University Press, 2011.

Ouellet, Fernand. "Lambton, John George, 1st Earl of Durham." *Dictionary of Canadian Biography*, vol. 7, 1988, http://www.biographi.ca/en/bio/lambton_john_george_7E.html.

– "Papineau, Louis-Joseph." *Dictionary of Canadian Biography*, vol. 10, 1972. http://www.biographi.ca/en/bio/papineau_louis_joseph_10E.html.

Pak, Susie. *Gentleman Bankers: The World of J.P. Morgan.* Cambridge, MA: Harvard University Press, 2013.

Parker, Beth. *Unstoppable: The Story of Asset-Based Finance and Leasing in Canada.* Toronto: Barlow Book Publishing, 2014.

Parkes, Henry Bamford. *The United States of America: A History.* New York: Alfred A. Knopf, 1956.

Perkins, Edwin J. *American Public Finance and Financial Services, 1700–1815.* Columbus: Ohio State University Press, 1994.

Perry, J. Harvey. *Taxes, Tariffs, & Subsidies: A History of Canadian Fiscal Development.* Vols 1 and 2. Toronto: University of Toronto Press, 1955.

Picardo, Elvis. "History of the Toronto Stock Exchange." Investopedia. http://www.investopedia.com/articles/stocks/08/history-of-toronto-stock-exchange.asp.

Piketty, Thomas. *Capital in the Twenty-First Century.* Cambridge, MA: Belknap Press of Harvard University Press, 2014.

Pitts, Gordon. *Fire in the Belly: How Purdy Crawford Rescued Canada and Changed the Way We Do Business.* Halifax: Nimbus Publishing, 2014.

Poor, Henry V. *Poor's Manual of the Railroads of the United States.* New York: H.V. & H.W., 1895.

Pope, Joseph. *Memoirs of the Right Honourable Sir John Alexander Macdonald, First Prime Minister of Canada.* Toronto: Musson Book, 1930.

Porter, Dana H. *Report of the Royal Commission on Banking and Finance.* Ottawa: Queen's Printer, 1964.

Powell, James. *A History of the Canadian Dollar.* Ottawa: Bank of Canada, 2005.

Previs, Gary J., and Barbara D. Merino. *A History of Accountancy in the United States: The Cultural Significance of Accounting.* Columbus: Ohio State University Press, 1998.

Puri, Poonam. "Canada: 'Bank Bashing' Is a Popular Sport." In *Banking Systems in the Crisis: The Faces of Liberal Capitalism*, ed. Suzanne J. Konzelmann and Marc Fovargue-Davies, 155–85. New York: Routledge, 2012.

Quebec. National Assembly. Standing Committee on Public Finance. *Journal des débats (Hansard)*. 1st Session, 38th Legislature. Meeting No. 20, 2007. http://www.assnat.qc.ca/en/travaux-parlementaires/commissions/cfp-38-1/journal-debats/CFP-071128.html.

Raible, Chris. Review of *The Patriot War along the Michigan-Canadian Borders: Raiders and Rebels*. *Ontario History* 106, no. 1 (2014): 136–37.

Rajan, Raghuram G. *Banks and Markets: The Changing Character of European Finance*. Cambridge: National Bureau of Economic Research, 2003.

– *Fault Lines: How Hidden Fractures Still Threaten the World Economy*. Princeton: Princeton University Press, 2010.

Rajan, Raghuram G., and Luigi Zingales. "The Great Reversals: The Politics of Financial Development in the Twentieth Century." *Journal of Financial Economics* 69, no. 1 (2003): 5–50.

Rea, J.E., *T.A. Crerar: A Political Life*. Montreal and Kingston: McGill-Queen's University Press, 1997.

Redlich, Fritz. *The Molding of American Banking*. New York: Johnson Reprint, 1968.

Reguly, Eric. "Germany Moves Fast to Help Ease ECB Tension." *Globe and Mail*, 12 September 2011.

Reid, Christopher. "Credit Default Swaps and the Canadian Context." In *Financial System Review*, 1–45. Ottawa: Bank of Canada, June 2004.

Reinhart, Carmen M., and Kenneth S. Rogoff. *This Time Is Different: Eight Centuries of Financial Folly*. Princeton: Princeton University Press, 2009.

Rich, George. "Canadian Banks, Gold and the Crisis of 1907." *Explorations in Economic History* 26, no. 1 (1989): 135–60.

Robb, J.A. *The Canada Year Book, 1921*. Ottawa: King's Printer, 1922.

Roberts, Andrew. *A History of the English-Speaking Peoples since 1900*. London: Weidenfeld & Nicolson, 2006.

Roberts, Richard. *Saving the City: The Great Financial Crisis of 1914*. Oxford: Oxford University Press, 2013.

Rockman, Seth. "The Future of Civil War Era Studies: Slavery and Capitalism. *Journal of the Civil War Era* 2, no. 1 (2012): 627–50.

Rodgers, Daniel T. *Atlantic Crossings: Social Politics in a Progressive Age*. Cambridge, MA: Harvard University Press, 1998.

Roe, Mark. *Strong Managers, Weak Shareholders*. Princeton: Princeton University Press, 1992.

Ross, Kevin. *Market Predictability of ECB Monetary Policy Decisions: A Comparative Examination*. Washington, DC: International Monetary Fund, European Department, 2002.

Ross, Victor. *A History of the Canadian Bank of Commerce*. Vol. 2. Toronto: University of Toronto Press, 1922.

Royal Bank of Canada. *2000 Annual Report: People to People Building Relationships in the New Economy.* 2000. http://www.rbc.com/ investorrelations/pdf/ar_2000_e.pdf.

Rudin, R.E. "King, Edwin Henry," *Dictionary of Canadian Biography*, vol. 12, 1990, http://www.biographi.ca/en/bio/king_edwin_henry_12E.html

Safarian, A.E. *The Canadian Economy in the Great Depression.* Toronto: McClelland & Stewart, 1970.

– *Foreign Ownership of Canadian Industry.* Toronto: University of Toronto Press, 2011.

Schenk, Catherine R. "Origins of the Eurodollar Market in London, 1955– 1963." *Explorations in Economic History* 35, no. 2 (1998): 221–38.

Schembri, Lawrence. "Arbitrage in Foreign Policy in Canada: Lessons from the Past, Implications for the Future." In *Trends in Monetary Policy Issues*, ed. Albert V. Tavidze, 121–43. New York: Nova Science Publishers, 2008.

Schenk, Catherine R., and Emmanuel Mourlon-Druol. "Bank Regulation and Supervision." In *The Oxford Handbook of Banking and Financial Regulation*, ed. Youssef Cassis et al., 395–419. Oxford: Oxford University Press, 2016.

Schermerhorn, Calvin. *The Business of Slavery and the Rise of American Capitalism, 1815–1860.* New Haven, CT: Yale University Press, 2015.

Schlesinger, Arthur M., Jr. *The Age of Jackson.* New York: Book Find Club, 1945.

Schott, Francis H. "The Report of the Canadian Royal Commission on Banking and Finance: A Review." *Federal Reserve Bank of New York* 46, no. 8 (1964): 151–6.

Schröter, Harm G. *The Americanization of the European Economy: A Compact Survey of American Economic Influence in Europe since the 1880s.* Dordrecht: Springer, 2005.

Schull, Joseph, *100 Years of Banking in Canada: A History of the Toronto-Dominion Bank.* Toronto: Copp Clark Publishing, 1958.

Schull, Joesph, and J. Douglas Gibson. *The Scotiabank Story: A History of the Bank of Nova Scotia, 1832–1982.* Toronto: Macmillan of Canada, 1982.

Schweikart, Larry. *Banking in the American South from the Age of Jackson to Reconstruction.* Baton Rouge: Louisiana University Press, 1987.

– "Entrepreneurial Aspects of Antebellum Banking." In *American Business History: Case Studies*, ed. Henry C. Dethloff and C. Joseph Pusateri, 122–39. Arlington Heights, IL: Harlan Davidson, 1987.

Scranton, Philip. *Endless Novelty: Specialty Production and American Industrialization, 1865–1925.* Princeton: Princeton University Press, 1997.

Sharpe, William F. "Capital Asset Prices: A Theory of Market Equilibrium under Conditions of Risk." *Journal of Finance* 19, no. 3 (1964): 425–42.

Shelp, Ronald K., and Al Ehrbar. *Fallen Giant: The Amazing Story of Hank Greenberg and the History of AIG.* Hoboken, NJ: John Wiley & Sons, 2006.

Shiller, Robert J. *Finance and the Good Society*. Princeton: Princeton University Press, 2012.
– *The New Financial Order: Risk in the 21st Century*. Princeton: Princeton University Press, 2003.
Shortt, Adam. *History of Canadian Currency and Banking, 1600–1880*. Toronto: Canadian Bankers' Association, 1986.
Sirois, Joseph. *Royal Commission on Dominion-Provincial Relations: The Rowell-Sirois Report*. Ottawa: King's Printer, 1940.
Skelton, Oscar D. *The Day of Sir Wilfrid Laurier*. Toronto: Glasgow Brock, 1916.
– *The Life and Times of Sir Alexander Tilloch Galt*. Toronto: Oxford University Press, 1920.
Smith, Andrew. "Continental Divide: The Canadian Banking and Currency Laws of 1871 in the Mirror of the United States." *Enterprise & Society* 13, no. 3 (2012): 455–503.
Smith, Andrew David Allan. "British Businessmen and Canadian Confederation: Gentlemanly Capitalism at Work." PhD diss., University of Western Ontario, 2005.
Smith, Andrew, and Laurence Mussio. *"Canadian Entrepreneurs and the Preservation of the Capitalist Peace in the North Atlantic Triangle in the Civil War Era, 1861–1871." Enterprise & Society* 17, no. 3 (2015): 515–45.
Smith, Lawrence B. "Canadian Housing Policies in the Seventies." *Land Economics* 57, no. 3 (1981): 338–52.
Soll, Jacob. *The Reckoning: Financial Accountability and the Rise and Fall of Nations*. New York: Basic Books, 2014.
Solomon, Lawrence. "Lawrence Solomon: Radical Republicans." *Financial Post*, 20 November 2015.
Sorkin, Andrew Ross. *Too Big to Fail*. New York: Viking, 2009.
Stacey, Charles P. *Canada and the Age of Conflict*. Vol. 1, *1867–1921: A History of Canadian External Policies*. Toronto: University of Toronto Press, 1984.
Statistics Canada. "Table 378-0121 National Balance Sheet Accounts." http://www5.statcan.gc.ca/cansim/a26?lang=eng&id=3780121.
Steil, Benn. *The Battle of Bretton Woods: John Maynard Keynes, Harry Dexter White, and the Making of a New World Order*. Princeton: Princeton University Press, 2013.
Stewart, D.M. "The Banking Systems of Canada and the United States." Empire Club of Canada Addresses, Toronto, ON, 14 December 1905.
Stewart, Gordon. *The American Response to Canada since 1776*. East Lansing: Michigan State University Press, 1992.
– *The Origins of Canadian Politics: A Comparative Approach*. Vancouver: University of British Columbia Press, 1986.

Stokes, Milton L. *The Bank of Canada: The Development and Present Position of Central Banking in Canada*. Toronto: Macmillan, 1939.

Sylla, Richard. *The American Capital Market, 1846–1914: A Study of the Effects of Public Policy on Economic Development*. New York: Arno, 1975.

– "Reversing Financial Reversals: Government and the Financial System since 1789." In *Government and the American Economy: A New History*, ed. Price Fishback, 115–47. Chicago: University of Chicago Press, 2007.

– "United States Bank and Europe: Strategy and Attitudes." In *European Banks and the American Challenge: Competition and Cooperation in International Banking under Bretton Woods*, ed. Stefano Battilossi and Youssef Cassis, 53–73. Oxford: Oxford University Press, 2002.

Szalay, Michael. *New Deal Modernism: American Literature and the Invention of the Welfare State*. Durham, NC: Duke University Press, 2000.

Talbot, Robert J. *Negotiating the Numbered Treaties: An Intellectual & Political Biography of Alexander Morris*. Saskatoon: Purich Publishing, 2009.

Taylor, Graham D. *The Rise of Canadian Business*. Oxford: Oxford University Press, 2009.

Telfer, Thomas G.W. *Ruin and Redemption: The Struggle for a Canadian Bankruptcy Law, 1867–1919*. Toronto: University of Toronto Press, 2014.

Temin, Peter. *The Jackson Economy*. New York: Norton, 1969.

– "Transmission of the Great Depression." *Journal of Economic Perspectives* 7, no. 2 (1993): 87–102.

Thelen, Kathleen. "Varieties of Capitalism and Business History." *Business History Review* 84, no. 4 (2010): 646–8.

Tocqueville, Alexis de. *Democracy in America*. Translated by Arthur Goldhammer. New York: Library of America, 2004.

Tooze, Adam. *The Deluge: The Great War, America, and the Remaking of the Global Order, 1916–1931*. New York: Viking, 2014.

Traclet, Virginie. "An Overview of the Canadian Housing Finance System." *Housing Finance International* 25, no. 1 (2010): 6–13.

Traflet, Janice M. *A Nation of Small Shareholders*. Baltimore, MD: Johns Hopkins University Press, 2013.

Trevelyan, G.M. *History of England*. Vol. 3. New York: Doubleday Anchor Books, 1954.

Trigge, A. St L. *A History of the Canadian Bank of Commerce; With an Account of Other Banks Which Now Form Part of Its Story*. Vol. 3, *1919–30*. Toronto: Canadian Bank of Commerce, 1934.

Turner, Charles H., and Fons Trompenaars. *The Seven Cultures of Capitalism: Value Systems for Creating Wealth in the United States, Britain, Japan, Germany, France, Sweden and the Netherlands*. New York: Doubleday, 1993.

Van Buren, Martin. *The Autobiography of Martin Van Buren*. Washington, DC: Government Printing Office, 1920.

Van Deusen, Glyndon G. *The Jacksonian Era: 1828–1848*. New York: Harper & Row, 1959.

Verbeeten, Claudio, and David Eggert. "Canada's Big Banks at Home and Abroad in the New Millennium." Research Paper, Rotman School of Management, 2014.

Wallace, C.M. "Tilley, Sir Samuel Leonard." *Dictionary of Canadian Biography*. Vol. 12. http://www.biographi.ca/en/bio/tilley_samuel_leonard_12E.html.

Wallace, Wanda A. "Commentary on Rowan A. Miranda." *Research in Governmental and Non-Profit Accounting* 8 (1994): 267–75.

Wallis, John Joseph. "The National Era." In *Government and the American Economy: A New History*, ed. Price Fishback, 148–87. Chicago: University of Chicago Press, 2007.

Walton, Gary M., and Hugh Rockoff. *History of the American Economy*. 8th ed. New York: Dryden, 1998.

Wardhaugh, Robert A. *Behind the Scenes: The Life and Work of William Clifford Clark*. Toronto: University of Toronto Press, 2010.

Watson, Rick, and Jeremy Carter. *Asset Securitisation and Synthetic Structures: Innovations in the European Credit Market*. London: Euromoney Books, 2006.

Watts, George S. *The Bank of Canada: Origins and Early History*. Ottawa: Carleton University Press, 1993.

White, Eugene N. "Banking and Finance in the Twentieth Century." In *The Cambridge Economic History of the United States*. Vol. 3, ed. Stanley L. Engerman and Robert E. Gallman, 743–803. Cambridge: Cambridge University Press, 2000.

White, William Thomas. *The Story of Canada's War Finance*. Montreal, 1921.

Whittington, Les. *The Banks: The Ongoing Battle for Control of Canada's Richest Business*, Toronto: Stoddart Publishing, 1999.

Wilkins, Mira. *The Emergence of Multinational Enterprise: American Business Abroad from the Colonial Era to 1914*. Cambridge, MA: Harvard University Press, 1970.

– *The History of Foreign Investment in the United States: 1914 to 1945*. Cambridge, MA: Harvard University Press, 2004.

– *The History of Foreign Investment in the United States to 1914*. Cambridge, MA: Harvard University Press, 1989.

– *The Maturing of Multinational Enterprise: American Business Abroad from 1914 to 1970*. Cambridge, MA: Harvard University Press, 1974.

– "Multinational Enterprise in Insurance: An Historical Overview." *Business History* 51, no. 3 (2009): 334–63.

Wilkinson, B.W. "Section G: The Balance of International Payments, International Investment Position and Foreign Trade." Statistics Canada. 2014. http://www.statcan.gc.ca/pub/11-516-x/sectiong/4147439-eng. htm#4.

Williams, Eric. *Capitalism and Slavery*. New York: Russell & Russell, 1944.

Williamson, Samuel H. "Daily Closing Value of the Dow Jones Average, May 2, 1885 to Present." Measuring Worth. https://measuringworth.com/DJA/.

Wolfe, Martin. *Fixing Global Finance*. Baltimore, MD: Johns Hopkins University Press, 2008.

Wolfe, Tom. *The Bonfire of the Vanities*. New York: Farrar, Straus & Giroux, 1987.

Wood, Gordon S. *Empire of Liberty: A History of the Early Republic, 1789–1815*. Oxford: Oxford University Press, 2009.

Woodham-Smith, Cecil. *The Great Hunger: Ireland 1845–1849*. London: Penguin Books, 1991.

Woodman, Harold D. *King Cotton and His Retainers: Financing and Marketing the Cotton Crop of the South, 1800–1925*. Lexington: University of Kentucky Press, 1968.

Woodward, Lewellyn. *The Age of Reform, 1815–1870*. Oxford: Clarendon, 1997.

World Council. "2012 Global Credit Union *Statistical Report* Now Available." News release, 12 July 2013. http://www.woccu.org/newsroom/ releases/2012_Global_Credit_Union_iStatistical_Report_i_Now_Available.

World Digital Library. 1917. "4 Reasons for Buying Victory Bonds." https:// www.wdl.org/en/item/4532/.

World Trade Organization. "B. Trends in International Trade." World Trade Organization. https://www.wto.org/english/res_e/booksp_e/wtr13-2b_e. pdf.

Wright, Gavin. *The Political Economy of the Cotton South: Households, Markets, and Wealth in the Nineteenth Century*. New York: Norton, 1978.

Wright, Robert E. "Bank Ownership and Lending Patterns in New York and Pennsylvania, 1781–1831." *Business History Review* 73, no. 1 (1999): 40–60.

– *The First Wall Street: Chestnut Street, Philadelphia, & the Birth of American Finance*. Chicago: University of Chicago Press, 2005.

– *Fubarnomics: A Lighthearted, Serious Look at America's Economic Ills*. Amherst: Prometheus Books, 2010.

– *One Nation under Debt: Hamilton, Jefferson, and the History of What We Owe*. New York: McGraw Hill, 2008.

Wright, Robert E., and George D. Smith. *Mutually Beneficial: The Guardian and Life Insurance in America*. New York: New York University Press, 2004.

Wright, Robert E., and Richard Sylla. *Genealogy of American Finance*. New York: Columbia University Business School, 2015.

Yates, J.A. *Structuring the Information Age: Life Insurance and Technology in the Twentieth Century.* Baltimore: Johns Hopkins University Press, 2005.

Year-Book and Almanac of British North America for 1867: Being an Annual Register of Political, Vital, and Trade Statistics, Tariffs, Excise and Stamp Duties; and All Public Events of Interest in Upper and Lower Canada; New Brunswick; Nova Scotia; Newfoundland; Prince Edward Island; and the West India Islands. Montreal: Lowe and Chamberlin, 1866.

Young, Amy. "The Creation of TMX Group: Dramatic Change on the Canadian Stock Exchange Scene – 1999 to 2008." Case Study, Rotman – University of Toronto, 2004.

Zahedieh, Nuala. *The Capital and the Colonies: London and the Atlantic Economy, 1660–1700.* Cambridge: Cambridge University Press, 2010.

Zimet, Melvin, and Ronald G. Greenwood, eds. *The Evolving Science of Management: The Collected Papers of Harold Smiddy and Papers by Others in His Honor.* New York: AMACOM, 1979.

Zingales, Luigi and Raghuram G. Rajan. *Banks and Markets: The Changing Character of European Finance.* Cambridge: National Bureau of Economic Research, 2003.

Other Sources: Archives, Journals, Online Resources

The Alien and Sedition Acts of 1798, 5th Cong., General Records of the United States Government Record Group 11 (6 July 1798).

Best Insurance News, various dates.

BMO, annual reports, 1880s archives.

Canada, House of Commons Debates (Hansard): 1908, 1931, 1932.

Canada Year Books: 1867, 1870, 1900, 1914, 1921, 1922–3, 1930, 1931, 1938, 1947, 1955, 1956.

Canadian Annual Review, 1908, 1935, 1936.

Canadian Encyclopedia.

Daily Globe.

Dictionary of Canadian Biography. Vols 7–15.

Financial Post

Financial Post Corporation Service; FP Corporate Service Card.

Globe / Globe and Mail.

Hepburn v Griswold, 75 US 603 (1870).

U.S. Declaration of Independence, 1776.

Index